CRITICAL PERSPECTIVES ON WORK AND EMPLOYMENT

Series editors
Irena Grugulis, Durham University Business School, UK
Caroline Lloyd, School of Social Sciences, Cardiff University, UK
Chris Smith, Royal Holloway University of London School of Management, UK
Chris Warhurst, University of Warwick, UK

Critical Perspectives on Work and Employment combine the best empirical research with leading edge, critical debate on key issues and developments in the field of work and employment. Extremely well regarded and popular, the series has links to the highly successful International Labour Process Conference.

Formerly edited by David Knights, Hugh Willmott, Chris Smith and Paul Thompson, each edited volume in the series includes contributions from a range of disciplines, including the sociology of work and employment, business and management studies, human resources management, industrial relations and organizational analysis.

Further details of the International Labour Process Conference can be found at www.ilpc.org.uk.

Published:

Kirsty Newsome, Phil Taylor, Jennifer Bair and Al Rainnie
PUTTING LABOUR IN ITS PLACE

Marco Hauptmeier and Matt Vidal
COMPARATIVE POLITICAL ECONOMY OF WORK

Carol Wolkowitz, Rachel Lara Cohen, Teela Sanders and Kate Hardy
BODY/SEX/WORK

Chris Warhurst, Françoise Carré, Patricia Findlay and Chris Tilly
ARE BAD JOBS INEVITABLE?

Irena Grugulis and Ödül Bozkurt
RETAIL WORK

Paul Thompson and Chris Smith
WORKING LIFE

Alan McKinlay and Chris Smith
CREATIVE LABOUR

Maeve Houlihan and Sharon Bolton
WORK MATTERS

Chris Warhurst, Doris Ruth Eikhof and Axel Haunschild
WORK LESS, LIVE MORE?

Bill Harley, Jeff Hyman and Paul Thompson
PARTICIPATION AND DEMOCRACY AT WORK

Chris Warhurst, Irena Grugulis and Ewart Keep
THE SKILLS THAT MATTER

Andrew Sturdy, Irena Grugulis and Hugh Willmott
CUSTOMER SERVICE

Craig Prichard, Richard Hull, Mike Chumer and Hugh Willmott
MANAGING KNOWLEDGE

Alan Felstead and Nick Jewson
GLOBAL TRENDS IN FLEXIBLE LABOUR

Paul Thompson and Chris Warhurst
WORKPLACES OF THE FUTURE

More details of the publications in this series can be found at www.palgrave.com/business/cpwe

---

Critical Perspectives on Work and Employment Series
Series Standing Order ISBN 978–0–230–23017–0 (pb); 978–0–230–23016–3 (hb)

You can receive future titles in this series as they are published by placing a standing order. Please contact your bookseller or, in the case of difficulty, write to us at the address below with your name and address, the title of the series and one of the ISBNs quoted above.

Customer Services Department, Macmillan Distribution Ltd, Houndmills, Basingstoke, Hampshire, RG21 6XS, UK

Putting Labour in its Place

Labour Process Analysis and Global Value Chains

Edited by
Kirsty Newsome
Reader, University of Sheffield, UK

Phil Taylor
Professor, University of Strathclyde, UK

Jennifer Bair
Associate Professor, University of Colorado, USA

and

Al Rainnie
Honorary Senior Research Fellow, Business School, University of Western Australia, Australia

Selection and editorial matter © Kirsty Newsome, Phil Taylor, Jennifer Bair
and Al Rainnie 2015
Individual chapters © Contributors 2015

All rights reserved. No reproduction, copy or transmission of this publication may be made without written permission.

No portion of this publication may be reproduced, copied or transmitted save with written permission or in accordance with the provisions of the Copyright, Designs and Patents Act 1988, or under the terms of any licence permitting limited copying issued by the Copyright Licensing Agency, Saffron House, 6–10 Kirby Street, London EC1N 8TS.

Any person who does any unauthorized act in relation to this publication may be liable to criminal prosecution and civil claims for damages.

The authors have asserted their rights to be identified as the authors of this work in accordance with the Copyright, Designs and Patents Act 1988.

First published 2015 by
PALGRAVE

Palgrave in the UK is an imprint of Macmillan Publishers Limited, registered in England, company number 785998, of 4 Crinan Street, London, N1 9XW.

Palgrave Macmillan in the US is a division of St Martin's Press LLC,
175 Fifth Avenue, New York, NY 10010.

Palgrave is a global imprint of the above companies and is represented throughout the world.

Palgrave® and Macmillan® are registered trademarks in the United States, the United Kingdom, Europe and other countries.

ISBN 978–1–137–41038–2   hardback
ISBN 978–1–137–41035–1   paperback

This book is printed on paper suitable for recycling and made from fully managed and sustained forest sources. Logging, pulping and manufacturing processes are expected to conform to the environmental regulations of the country of origin.

A catalogue record for this book is available from the British Library.

A catalog record for this book is available from the Library of Congress.

Typeset by MPS Limited, Chennai, India.
Printed and bound by CPI Group (UK) Ltd, Croydon, CR0 4YY

Contents

List of Illustrations vii
Acknowledgements viii
Notes on Contributors ix

1 **Putting Labour in its Place: Labour Process Analysis and Global Value Chains** 1
   Phil Taylor, Kirsty Newsome, Jennifer Bair and Al Rainnie

Part I Integrating Labour Process and Global Value Chains

2 **Value in Motion: Labour and Logistics in the Contemporary Political Economy** 29
   Kirsty Newsome

3 **Labour and Asymmetric Power Relations in Global Value Chains: The Digital Entertainment Industries and Beyond** 45
   Paul Thompson, Rachel Parker and Stephen Cox

4 **Positioning Labour in Service Value Chains and Networks: The Case of Parcel Delivery** 64
   Bettina Haidinger and Jörg Flecker

5 **Labour and Segmentation in Value Chains** 83
   Nikolaus Hammer and Lone Riisgaard

6   Articulation of Informal Labour: Interrogating the E-waste Value
    Chain in Singapore and Malaysia   100
    Aidan M. Wong

Part II   Unpacking Labour: Power, Agency and Standards

7   Global Production and Uneven Development: When Bringing
    Labour in isn't Enough   119
    Jennifer Bair and Marion Werner

8   Understanding Labour's Agency under Globalization: Embedding
    GPNs within an Open Political Economy   135
    Andrew Cumbers

9   Social Downgrading and Worker Resistance in Apparel Global
    Value Chains   152
    Mark Anner

10 Labour and Global Production Networks: Mapping Variegated
    Landscapes of Agency   171
    Neil M. Coe

Part III   Sector Studies

11 The Significance of Grass-Roots Organizing in the Garment and
    Electrical Value Chains of Southern India   195
    Jean Jenkins

12 Human Security in Evolving Global Value Chains: Reconsidering
    Labour Agency in a Livelihoods Context   213
    Lee Pegler

13 The Apple Ecosystem and App Developers: A GPN Analysis   231
    Birgitta Bergvall-Kåreborn and Debra Howcroft

14 Wasted Commodities, Wasted Labour? Global Production
    and Destruction Networks and the Nature of Contemporary
    Capitalism   249
    Al Rainnie, Andrew Herod, Susan McGrath-Champ and
    Graham Pickren

15 Labour and the Changing Landscapes of the Call Centre   266
    Phil Taylor

Author Index   287
Subject Index   291

List of Illustrations

Tables

2.1	Case-study organizations	35
9.1	GDP, apparel and remittances (USD millions)	159
10.1	Types of transnational labour regulation	183
10.2	Intersections of transnational and 'local' labour regulatory contexts	184
13.1	Number and type of interviews	236
15.1	Call centre growth in Scotland (1997–2011)	275

Figures

3.1	A post-GVC framework	51
6.1	E-waste circuit of capital	104
9.1	Apparel, value added	158
15.1	Call centre employment (2002–2013)	273

Acknowledgements

The editors are greatly indebted to the editors of the *Critical Perspectives on Work and Employment* series for the opportunity to compile this book and for their constructive support throughout the publication process. Additional thanks are extended to Paul Thompson for his encouragement throughout the long preparatory period and to the organizers of the International Labour Process Conference at Rutgers University in 2013, who permitted us to organize the stream on global value chains, labour and the labour process from which the chapters derived. The blindingly obvious debt of gratitude must go the authors of the chapters, without whom there would have been no book! We hope that we have undertaken our editorial duties effectively in relation to your excellent contributions. The editors would also like to extend a sincere thank you to Jessica Bair for her work in compiling the index.

Finally, our appreciation must be extended to the many, many millions of workers who perform surplus generating labour at various nodes of the global value chains. We hope that we have been able to analyse the conditions of their working lives, revealing the hidden abode of labour. After all, behind the shirts we wear is a chain that may link to a Rana Plaza in Bangladesh and behind our shiny mobile devices might lie a Foxconn suicide in Shenzhen. The editors hope that this volume can contribute, however modestly, to improving our understanding of the world in order to change it.

The editors and publishers would like to thank the following for their permission to use copyright material: Escarpment Press for Table 10.1 reprinted from Pries, L. and Seeliger, M. (2013) 'Work and employment relations in a globalized world: the emerging texture of transnational labour regulation', *Global Labor Journal*, 4(1): 26–47.

Notes on Contributors

Mark Anner is Associate Professor of Labour and Employment Relations, and Political Science, and he is Director of the Center for Global Workers' Rights at the Pennsylvania State University. He holds a PhD in Government from Cornell University and a Master's Degree in Latin American Studies from Stanford University. His research examines freedom of association and corporate social responsibility, labour law reform and enforcement, and workers' rights in apparel global value chains with a focus on Central America and Vietnam. He lived in El Salvador for eight years where he worked with labour unions and a labour research centre, and studied economics at the Universidad Centroamérica (UCA).

Jennifer Bair is Associate Professor of Sociology at the University of Colorado at Boulder. Her research interests lie at the intersection of political economy and development studies, with a regional focus on Latin America and the Caribbean. She is the editor of *Frontiers of Commodity Chains Research* (2009) and co-editor of *Free Trade and Uneven Development: The North American Apparel Industry after NAFTA* (2002) and *Workers' Rights and Labor Compliance in Global Supply Chains: Is a Social Label the Answer?* (2013). Her publications include articles in the journals *Social Problems, World Development, Global Networks, Economy and Society, Signs* and *Environment and Planning A*. Together with Marion Werner, she is currently working on a project examining the emergence, development and diffusion of the Global Value Chain Framework as a new development paradigm. She is also studying issues of labour regulation in supply chains, with a particular focus on the concept of joint liability in subcontracting networks.

Notes on Contributors

Birgitta Bergvall-Kåreborn is Professor of Social Informatics at Lulea University of Technology. Her current research interests concern participatory design in distributed and open environments; human-centric and appreciative methodologies for design and learning; as well as the relationship between IT use and IT design.

Neil M. Coe is Professor of Economic Geography at the National University of Singapore. His research interests are in the areas of global production networks and local economic development; the geographies of local and transnational labour markets; the geographies of innovation; and institutional and network approaches to economic development. These concerns have been explored through research into computer services, temporary staffing and logistics in the UK, Europe and Asia Pacific, the film and television industry in the UK and Canada, and retailing in the UK, East Asia and Eastern Europe. He has published over 75 articles and book chapters on these topics, and is a co-author of *Spaces of Work: Global Capitalism and the Geographies of Labour* (2003) and *Economic Geography: A Contemporary Introduction* (2013, second edition).

Stephen Cox is Director of Higher Degree Research Studies at Queensland University of Technology Business School. He undertakes research examining the development and consequences of power imbalances within global value chains. He has published in leading journals including *Regional Studies* and *Environment and Planning A*.

Andrew Cumbers is Professor of Urban and Regional Political Economy in the Adam Smith Business School at the University of Glasgow. He has published widely on urban and regional economic development, employment relations and economic democracy. He is the author of *Reclaiming Public Ownership: Making Space for Economic Democracy* (2012). He is also editor in chief of the international journal *Urban Studies*.

Jörg Flecker is Professor of Sociology at the University of Vienna and Chair of the Board of the Working Life Research Centre (FORBA). His main research interests focus on economic internationalization and restructuring, labour process analysis, industrial relations, and work and employment in the public services. Most recent publications include *Privatization of Public Services* (2012, together with Christoph Hermann) and *Im Dienste öffentlicher Güter* (2014, together with Franz Schultheis and Berthold Vogel).

Bettina Haidinger is a senior researcher at the Working Life Research Centre (FORBA) in Vienna and an external lecturer for economic policy and sociology of work and migration at the Universities of Vienna and

Linz. Her research includes migration, work and gender relations, industrial relations and employment policy. Recently, she published together with Käthe Knittler the book *Feministische Ökonomie* (2014).

Nikolaus Hammer is Lecturer in Employment Studies, School of Management and a member of the Centre for Sustainable Work and Employment Futures, University of Leicester. His research interests centre on work and employment in global value chains, labour process and labour market analysis in emerging economies. He has published in leading journals such as the *British Journal of Industrial Relations, European Journal of Industrial Relations* and *Transfer* and is currently the co-editor of *Work, Employment and Society* as part of a team based at the University of Leicester. His current research investigates supply chain relations and working conditions in UK garment manufacturing.

Andrew Herod is Distinguished Research Professor of Geography and Adjunct Professor of International Affairs and of Anthropology at the University of Georgia, Athens, GA, USA. He writes frequently on the topic of labour and globalization. He is the author of *Scale* (2010) for the Routledge 'Key Ideas in Geography' Series, *Geographies of Globalization: A Critical Introduction* (2009), and *Labor Geographies: Workers and the Landscapes of Capitalism* (2001). He has edited or co-edited the *Handbook of Employment and Society: Working Space* (2010), *The Dirty Work of Neoliberalism: Cleaners in the Global Economy* (2006), *Geographies of Power: Placing Scale* (2002), *Organizing the Landscape: Geographical Perspectives on Labor Unionism* (1998), and *An Unruly World? Globalization, Governance and Geography* (1998). He is also an elected official, serving as a member of the Unified Government of Athens-Clarke County, Georgia.

Debra Howcroft is Professor of Technology and Organization at Manchester Business School and is a member of FairWRC (Fairness at Work Research Centre). She is the co-editor of *New Technology, Work and Employment* and also serves on a number of editorial boards. Her research interests are centred on how technology is influencing and shaping working practices, changing skills and reframing occupational identities. This includes a particular focus on IT workers and their response to workplace change and sectoral trends and developments.

Jean Jenkins is Senior Lecturer in Employment Relations at Cardiff Business School, Cardiff University. Her research interests originated in employment relations in manufacturing industry, and she has published on aspects of union strategy. She has a longstanding interest in the British garment sector, and among her publications (with her co-author on that project, Paul Blyton) are several on the Burberry workers' campaign against factory closure in the UK. In addition to her interests in mobilization theory and the effects of involuntary part-time working in mature economies, that grew out of the Burberry study, her recent research has adopted a wider, international perspective, to reflect the dynamics of the global value chain in garment production. She currently focuses in the main on labour conditions and worker organizing in the Indian garment sector.

Susan McGrath-Champ is Associate Professor in the Work and Organisational Studies Discipline at the University of Sydney Business School. Her research interests include the geographical aspects of the world of work, employment relations and international human resource management. Recent research projects include organizations' emergency evacuation policies for international assignees in the not-for-profit and corporate sectors and gender pay equity. Susan was awarded jointly a Swedish-funded International Collaboration Grant (2014–2018) for research concerning the effects of competition and privatization on school teachers' work and working conditions. She is first editor of the *Handbook of Employment and Society: Working Space* (with Andrew Herod and Al Rainnie, 2010). Her work has been published in *Work, Employment and Society*, *Journal of Economic Geography* and *Construction Management and Economics*.

Kirsty Newsome is Reader in Employment Relations at the University of Sheffield and Visiting Fellow at the Centre for Sustainable Work and Employment Futures at the University of Leicester. Her research interests are focused around three interconnected themes: the changing character of employment regulation; the shifts and transformations in the politics of production; and the dynamic interplay of global value chains and the labour process. The empirical focus of her research has been concerned with exploring labour process change in the UK supermarket supply chain. Most recently her research has examined the interplay of internal and external forces in the restructuring of the labour process and value chains in retail distribution and logistics. She is a member the research network 'The Changing Nature of Employment in Europe', an international comparative European FP7 Marie Curie Initial Training Network (ITN) coordinated by the University of Strathclyde.

Rachel Parker is Professor in the Business School at the Queensland University of Technology, Australia. Her research focuses on the institutional foundations of innovation and industrial competitiveness and power relations in global production networks. Her work has contributed to understandings of the way in which political-institutional environments affect firm and industry behaviour and therefore industrial development and transformation. Recent projects focus on power relations in global value chains and how they affect the ability of firms to negotiate value for their products and services and to compete in global markets.

Lee Pegler is a lecturer (Work, Organisation and Labour Rights) within the Social Policy for Development (SPD) Major at the ISS, The Hague. He spent a large proportion of his early career working as an economic advisor to the Australian Labour Movement. He has a keen interest in labour and developing countries, and more recent times have seen him researching and publishing on the labour implications of 'new' management strategies of Trans National Companies (TNCs) in Latin America. This interest has expanded to a broader focus on the implications of value chain insertion on labour/industrial relations, both for formal and informal workers, in countries such as Brazil, Colombia and Vietnam. He was joint convenor of a national, CERES, cross-institution network on 'Value Chains, Local Economic Development and Social Inclusion'. Most recently he has developed and coordinates an international project (GOLLS) concerning sustainable value chains – one which links ports, logistics and advanced services (in the Netherlands) with production, employment, livelihoods and development questions in Brazil.

Graham Pickren is currently Postdoctoral Teaching and Learning Fellow with Vantage College and the Department of Geography at the University of British Columbia. His past research included work on the development of labelling schemes in the electronics recycling industry. He is currently working on a new project examining the labour processes and organization of 'makerspaces', which are technology sharing- and skill-building hubs.

Al Rainnie is Honorary Senior Research Fellow, Business School, University of Western Australia, Australia. He has worked at the University of Hertfordshire, Monash University, the University of Leicester and Curtin University. He has written and researched on small firms, industrial relations, regional development, labour process analysis and state restructuring. More recently he has been working on spatiality, work and employment, Global Production Networks, Global Destruction Networks and the role of labour. This work is a joint project with Andrew Herod and Graham Pickren (University of Georgia, US) and Susan McGrath-Champ (Sydney University, Australia).

Lone Riisgaard is Assistant Professor in International Development Studies at the Department of Society and Globalisation, Roskilde University. She has researched on sustainability standards, labour rights issues and global value chain analysis with focus on the cut flower value chain originating in Kenya and Tanzania and published in prominent journals such as *World Development, Journal of Agrarian Change* and *Industrial Relations*. She has led research projects for the Fairtrade Labelling Organisation, UNIDO, IFAD, the Danish Foreign Ministry and Traidcraft. Current research interests focus on labour management systems in large-scale agriculture.

Phil Taylor is Professor of Work and Employment Studies in the Department of Human Resource Management and also Vice Dean International in Strathclyde Business School at the University of Strathclyde. He has researched and published extensively on employment relations and work organization in call centres for two decades. Other research areas include the globalization of business services, offshoring to India, occupational health and safety, lean working, performance management, trade union organizing and industrial conflict and privatization. He was editor of *Work, Employment and Society* between 2008 and 2011 and is currently co-editor of *New Technology, Work and Employment*. He was a lead member of the groundbreaking project 'The Meaning of Work in the New Economy' in the Economic Research Council's Future of Work Programme.

Paul Thompson is Professor of Organisational Analysis at the University of Strathclyde. Informed by labour process theory, his research interests focus on skill and work organization; creative industries and labour; control, resistance and organizational misbehaviour; financialization, value chains and the changing political economy of capitalism. He has published 11 books and over 50 refereed journal articles, and is currently convenor of the International Labour Process Conference and co-editor of the Palgrave Series 'Management, Work and Organization'.

Marion Werner is Assistant Professor in the Department of Geography at the University at Buffalo, SUNY. Her research is located at the nexus of critical development studies, feminist theory and political economy with a focus on Latin America and the Caribbean. She brings these theoretical perspectives to her work on the economic restructuring of export industries, the gender and racial politics of labour value, and, more recently, development policy and politics. Her book, *Global Displacements: The Making of Uneven Development in the Caribbean* (2015), unpacks processes of restructuring in the export garment industry to reveal how uneven geographies of capitalist development shape – and are shaped by – the aspirations and everyday struggles of people in the Global South. Her work has appeared in several academic journals including *Gender, Place and Culture*, *Antipode: A Journal of Radical Geography*, *Economic Geography*, *Environment and Planning A* and *New West Indian Guide*. Marion's current research explores development policy interventions into global supply chains, together with Jennifer Bair, and contemporary food politics and policy in the Dominican Republic.

Aidan M. Wong is a post-doctoral fellow at the Department of Geography, National University of Singapore. He recently obtained his PhD from the School of Geography and the School of Business and Management at Queen Mary University of London, and is interested in global value chains, global production networks, the geographies of waste, labour geographies and radical political economy.

Putting Labour in its Place: Labour Process Analysis and Global Value Chains

CHAPTER 1

Phil Taylor, Kirsty Newsome,
Jennifer Bair and Al Rainnie

The objective of this edited volume in the *Critical Perspectives on Work and Employment* series is to explore the interrelationships – theoretically and empirically – between the labour process and labour process theory (LPT), on the one hand, and global value chains (GVC) and related frameworks, such as global commodity chains (GCC) and global production networks (GPN), on the other. Until relatively recently the extent of convergence between these two bodies of work had been quite undeveloped. In summary, GCC, GVC and GPN theorizing and research, notwithstanding significant distinctions between them (Bair, 2008), neglected or *generally* understated labour as an analytical category (Smith *et al.*, 2002; Cumbers *et al.*, 2008), while conversely LPT *generally* eschewed the significance of these various global frameworks.

It is no longer legitimate to claim the categorical omission of labour in studies of global production networks. This objection remained largely valid in terms of GVC research, which, following Gereffi *et al.*'s (2005) influential theory of GVC governance, has tended to concentrate on inter-sectoral and firm linkages in ways that minimize the concerns of labour (Gibbon *et al.*, 2008). Yet with the emergence of the 'Manchester school' and the development of an alternative GPN more attention was given to the importance of labour within the matrix of factors that help to explain global geographies of production and exchange (Henderson *et al.*, 2002; Coe *et al.*, 2004). When Henderson *et al.* (2002: 448) stated that GPNs should acknowledge the 'conditions under which labour power is converted into actual labour through the labour process', they hinted not merely at the general inclusion of labour as a factor of production affecting firms' locational decisions and resultant production geographies, but also at the potential integration of labour process analysis with chain or network theorizing.

However, this specific promise went largely unfulfilled thereafter. For although some saw workers and collective organizations as integral to the GPN project (Coe et al., 2008), much of the burgeoning literature rather tended to consider labour as the object of the restructuring process, reflecting and reproducing an orthodox 'factor of production' approach. For Cumbers et al. (2008) the urgent task was to 'bring labour back in' by, initially, theorizing its *agency* in GPNs as an active constituent of the global economy, and then exploring the 'positionality' of unions within this framework.

In recent years, a growing responsiveness to this critique and a proliferation of attempts to redress the 'labour deficit' from within economic geography and its labour geography sub-field (e.g. Cumbers et al., 2008, 2010; Coe and Jordhus-Lier, 2011; Rainnie et al., 2011; Coe and Hess, 2013 and special edition of *Geoforum*), have occurred. In a parallel trend, scholars working within the GVC tradition have become increasingly sceptical of the 'upgrading' hypothesis in the literature on global chains. Simply put, there is now widespread criticism of the idea that participating in GVCs necessarily leads to economic upgrading for workers in terms of improved labour standards (e.g. Barrientos et al., 2011; Werner 2012; Barrientos, 2013; and the 2013 special issues of *Competition and Change* edited by Taylor et al.).

Just as scholars of global production networks were acknowledging the importance of integrating labour into their analytical frameworks, LPT influenced studies were seeking to utilize the explanatory purchase of the global chain and network perspectives to grapple with the nature of employment and the experience of work in contemporary capitalism (e.g. Flecker and Meil, 2010; Newsome, 2010; Newsome et al., 2013; Taylor, 2010; Riisgaard and Hammer, 2011). Nevertheless, these engagements constituted only the beginnings of an integration between hitherto discrete domains. An *explicit* focus on the labour process and LPT, as opposed to labour in its manifold dimensions, has remained underdeveloped.

Having indicated the limited and selective convergence between LPT and the GCC/GVC/GPN frameworks to date, in the remainder of this introduction we lay out the broad conceptual territory that underpins and informs this volume. It is appropriate to begin with a consideration of LPT, identifying what have been regarded as its core characteristics and articulating some recently acknowledged problematics, including that of 'connectivity' (Thompson, 2010). How the mechanisms of control and workplace transformation are related to the broader political economy clearly has significance for understanding the power, asymmetry and coordination within and across global value chains and production networks.

This preface then reflects on the loosely connected frameworks (Bair, 2008) of chains and frameworks, but hones in on some essential differences between them in their diverse attempts to map, describe, analyse and understand geographically dispersed systems of production and the position of labour within them. Subsequently, the introduction appraises the recent debates in economic and labour geography, assessing the strengths and limitations of the attempts made to overcome the 'labour deficit'. This discussion includes a critical evaluation of the salience of labour process analysis. Finally, we provide brief summaries of the volume's chapters before concluding with some observations regarding directions for future research and conceptual development.

Labour Process Theory and Analysis

With its origins in a Marxist understanding of the nature of work under capitalism, a focus on the labour process has provided a fertile arena for scholars wishing to develop a critical sociology of work and employment. Triggered by the publication of Braverman's *Labour and Monopoly Capital* in 1974, Labour Process Theory (LPT) has remained at the forefront of analysis exploring the changing dynamics of work and employment. Over four decades, LPT has demonstrated its analytical purchase and contemporary relevance, as evidenced in the annual International Labour Process Conference (ILPC) and the publication of numerous edited volumes and countless articles which embrace LPT as the key theoretical resource. In simple terms, labour process analysis has recognized the indeterminacy of labour as a 'particular' commodity through uncovering the mechanisms that transform the capacity to work into actual work (Smith and Thompson, 2009; Thompson and Newsome, 2004).

Attempts to provide a coherent framework and a degree of analytical integrity to labour process analysis have been facilitated by the construction of a 'core theory', based essentially on ideas rooted in Marx's *Capital*. Most keenly developed by Thompson (1989; 1990), the core principles include, firstly, the fundamental idea that the labour process involves the generation of a surplus as the capacity for work (labour power) is transformed into concrete or actual work. It follows that the role of labour and the capital-labour relationship are analytically privileged. Secondly, there is a logic of accumulation which arises from competition between capitalists – and between capital and labour – which compels capital to revolutionize the production of goods and services. Thirdly, a key proposition is that market mechanisms alone are insufficient to regulate the labour process and to ensure that a surplus is generated. An endemic control imperative within capitalist production compels management to limit or overcome labour's indeterminacy. Fourthly, the structured antagonism at the heart of the capitalist employment relationship is concerned not only with closing down indeterminacy but also with securing the co-operation of labour. The outcome is a continuum of situationally-driven and overlapping worker responses that ranges from resistance to accommodation, compliance and consent.

In essence, core labour process theory has been concerned with exploring the dynamics of control, consent and resistance at the point of production. Privileging developments at the point of production as a distinct site of analysis has been theorized predominantly by Edwards (1990; see also Hammer and Riisgaard in this volume). Edwards' argument rests on the understanding that the labour process is 'relatively autonomous', in the sense that forces external to it are simultaneously mediated by internal forces. The implication is that similar external situations can produce different internal labour process outcomes because of the distinctiveness and peculiarities of particular workplaces. Thus, the patterns of control that emerge within the labour process depend in part on the activities of managers and workers in the immediate 'effort-bargain' (Edwards, 1990). The focus of so-called 'second wave' labour process theory (e.g. Burawoy, 1979; Edwards, 1979; Friedman, 1977) is particularly important, not least in the understanding of factory and workplace dynamics.

This emphasis on developments at the 'point of production' has been utilized as a framing device to demarcate the focus of labour process enquiry and subsequent research agendas. As Thompson (2010) has highlighted, the narrow version of core theory successfully prioritizes the labour process only to answer questions relevant to that sphere. Yet, this seemingly narrow dimension and the reach of labour process analysis remain 'contested' (Edwards, 2010). Aspects of contestation have revolved around the limitations of LPT in its ability to explain developments within points of production, most notably in relation to gender and race, as well as issues lying outside the workplace, such as non-wage labour, familial ideology and informality (see also chapters by Wong and Pegler in this volume). Attempts to position an understanding of the dynamics of the labour process within a wider framework of changes at the level of political economy have recently intensified.

The disjuncture between the dynamics of the labour process at the point of production with the broader political economy shaping the nature of contemporary production has been termed the 'connectivity problem'. Recognition of this problem and attempts to redress it by engaging with complementarily theoretical and explanatory resources has become increasingly common for theorists of the labour process (Smith and Thompson, 2009). The renewed case for LPT to work at multiple levels of analysis, thereby rendering more explicit the connections between the dynamics of workplace transformation, political economy and shifting regimes of accumulation, is compelling. In this respect, then, the attempt to engage with the comparatively recent (in relation to the longer history of LPT) theoretical resources and projects of GCCs, GVCs and GPNs is consistent and apposite.

GCC, GVC and GPN

An extended review of Global Commodity Chain (GCCs), global value chains (GVCs) and global production networks (GPNs) is not needed, given the widespread dissemination of knowledge of these frameworks from their respective heartlands in the world systems tradition, development studies and economic and labour geography. Moreover, Bair provides a lucid account of the genealogy of commodity chains and value chains (2008; 2009), while a number of key articles, which heralded the distinctive variant of the GPN, are quite accessible to non-specialists (e.g. Dicken *et al.*, 2001; Henderson *et al.*, 2002; Coe *et al.*, 2004). Nevertheless, comment is required in order to foreground our critical discussion of labour, its agency and the labour process within what is, by now, an extensive literature on global chains and networks of production.

Even though GCCs, GVCs and GPNs may be regarded as loosely integrated traditions (Gibbon *et al.*, 2008), using them interchangeably might be problematic. Terminological variation (the chain or network metaphor) does signify contrasting intellectual orientations, methods, approaches and objects of study (Bair, 2005). Even when comparing GCCs and GVCs, the contrasting acronyms signify distinctions in theoretical and disciplinary affinity, and in substantive emphases and empirical concerns, to describe 'the sequence of processes by which goods and services are conceived, produced and brought to market' (Bair, 2009: 2). In sum, then, notwithstanding similarities and overlap, the 'acronym soup', to use Coe's phrase, is meant to portend analytical difference, even if, in reality, variation among these frameworks is not nearly as clear at the level of empirical research.

Whatever their differences, it is instructive to recall briefly that each of the chain/network frameworks was striving to solve real-world problems, lest the bigger picture gets lost in the forensic examination of the difference between them. In essence, they share the common objective of describing and analysing the expanding and increasingly interconnected transnational systems of production (Dicken, 2011). As developing countries became important sites for basic manufacturing, GCC research was a way to map and analyse the changing geographies of different economic activities between and within the global North and South. Gereffi and colleagues' original objective (see Gereffi et al., 1994)[1] was to describe these functionally integrated and geographically dispersed systems of production, and the GCC approach had the great strength of permitting the highly abstract idea of globalization to be apprehended concretely in terms of relations organized around tangible commodities. In addition, because they focused on connections between particular territories and world markets, commodity chains proved attractive to development scholars, especially in light of the shift to export-oriented industrialization strategies in the South.

In early GCC formulations, Gereffi and colleagues focused on the unequal returns that accrued to chain participants, and the link between these outcomes and the different forms of control – or governance – exercised by the powerful firms that 'drive' commodity chains. Governance was understood to be a function of the type of lead firm found in a chain, with Gereffi proposing a central distinction between Producer Driven Commodity Chains (PDCC) and Buyer Driven Commodity Chains (BDCC). BDCCs, in particular, provoked considerable interest as they betokened novel forms of inter-firm linkages in the light manufacturing industries, associated with the internationalization and externalization of production to independent contractors and suppliers. Several early contributions to the expanding field of GCC research investigated the utility and applicability of Gereffi's governance typology, with some scholars suggesting that the PDCC and BDCC categories failed to capture the range of governance forms in actual chains (Gereffi et al., 2005).

These assessments of the governance forms proposed in Gereffi's GCC framework, and the growing interest in global production networks beyond Gereffi's own discipline of sociology, gave rise to a second iteration – the theory of global value chains – in which questions of inter-firm or transactional (as opposed to 'whole chain') governance assumed greater importance (cf. Ponte and Sturgeon, 2014). GVCs were conceived as 'the set of inter-sectoral linkages between firms and other actors through which ... geographical and organisational reconfiguration has taken place' (Gibbon et al., 2008: 318). If globalization was causing increased geographical dispersion and differentiation between places and actors, then GVCs were to be conceived of as the integrative counterpart to these processes. However, there is no doubting that the signal episode in the trajectory from GCC to a distinctive GVC approach was Gereffi et al.'s (2005) seminal article in Review of International Political Economy, in which they elaborate a theory that specifies the determinants of inter-firm governance types. Using three independent variables – knowledge and information complexity, the degree to which this information can be codified and thus transmitted more easily between parties, and the existing capacities or capabilities in the supply base – produces a typology of five possible governance forms: market, modular, relational, captive and hierarchy. In this typology, as value chains move from hierarchy to market, the level of explicit coordination and power asymmetry between exchange partners increases. As Bair has observed, governance as coordination (GVC) signified a disjuncture from governance as 'driving' (GCC), narrowing the focus to the immediate dyadic links in a value chain (Bair, 2008). Gereffi et al. (2005) scaled down the concept of governance from a characteristic of an entire chain to a description of the mode of coordination prevailing at a particular link.

In response to the more constricted GVC, the GPN approach of the 'Manchester school' went in the other direction, claiming to restore a larger analytic picture. Global production activities should be conceived, not as vertical and linear sequences, but as highly complex networks, in which intricate horizontal, diagonal and vertical links formed multi-dimensional, multi-layered lattices of economic activity (Henderson et al., 2002). As is well known, GPN theory emphasized 'the dialectics of global-local' relations, for the principal reason that firm-centred production networks are deeply influenced by the concrete socio-political contexts in which they are embedded. GPN sought to restore the 'territorial' dimension of the specific locations comprising the nodes of global networks, emphasizing that institutional and regulatory contexts, and non-firm actors – especially the state – also shape the dynamics of production systems. In particular, they developed the notion of 'strategic coupling' (Coe et al., 2004) of global production networks with regional assets as a way to 'tie down' productive activities in a particular place. Three conceptual categories were identified as central to GPN analysis: value (how it is created, enhanced and captured);

power (how it is created and maintained within production networks); and how agents and structures are embedded in particular territories (Henderson *et al.*, 2002).

As editors of this collection, and convenors of the conference stream that gave rise to it, we have consciously avoided advocating a particular approach. Instead, we encouraged contributing authors to work with what framework has most appropriately suited their analytical purposes, particularly in respect of the scalar level being addressed. We have not privileged one framework to the exclusion of another.

Nevertheless, certain limitations and strengths of the respective constructs must be recognized in the context of integrating LPT into studies of global production. GVC governance, at least as conceived by Gereffi *et al.* (2005), excessively narrows the analysis of chain dynamics to dyadic linkages in a value chain (Bair, 2008), obscuring or neglecting, in the interests of parsimony and intellectual rigour, how these linkages are embedded within the logics of and shifts in global capitalist political economy (Palpacuer, 2008; Werner and Bair, 2011; also Bair and Werner in this volume). Further, its flatter ontology hinders the development of an understanding of power asymmetries across chains. Indeed, the slicing-up of value chains has significant governance implications profoundly affecting the power relations between increasing numbers of actors in distant locales. However, the greatest weakness of the GVC remains its relative neglect of labour,[2] both as a source of value or even as an object of chain dynamics (Taylor *et al.*, 2013).

Conversely, the strengths of the GPN approach lie precisely in its broader scope, its multi-level scalarity, its greater spatial sensitivity, and its attempt to understand the dynamics and complexities of power relations between and among firm and non-firm actors. Further, the GPN framework has, despite qualifications, explicitly acknowledged the importance of labour among the territorial factors that give GPNs their structure, and shape their consequences for both global and local actors. Yet, the inclusivity of the GPN concept also proves to be a weakness, since it lacks a discrete research question of the sort that motivates the GVC governance theory, and, perhaps not surprisingly given the framework's ambition, empirical analyses of GPNs do not necessarily deliver on the claims made by proponents of this approach. In this sense, it runs the risk of being too expansive, a totalizing theory lacking explanatory bite (Taylor, 2010), or 'a theory of everything', as Thompson *et al.* put it in their contribution to this volume. In the next section, we turn to a consideration of how each of these frameworks can more satisfactorily address questions about the labour process in the context of globalized production.

Addressing the Labour Deficit – Strengths, Limitations and Uncompleted Tasks

Smith *et al.* (2002) critiqued the literature on global chains for disregarding the social relations of production in favour of an over-prioritization of economic governance. While the flourishing literature on GPNs did then produce a growing awareness of the different forms of labour 'enrolled into them', to use Coe and Hess's (2013: 5) phrase, it remained largely independent of a parallel literature on the impacts of global production systems on workers and their potential responses. For some, this neglect could be remedied only by making labour integral to an understanding of GPNs (Cumbers *et al.*, 2008) in two senses: first, as 'abstract labour', that lies at the heart of all systems of commodity production (whether local or global) within capitalism and; second, as labour in specific collective organizational forms (trade unions) representing workers within systems of production. Relatedly, other economic geographers have highlighted the difference between labour's structural power and its associational power (e.g. Coe and Jordhus-Lier, 2011; Selwyn, 2011; 2013), concepts first formulated by Wright (2000).[3] Structural power, derived from workers' position in the production process, can be distinguished from their associational power, based on their collective organization to extract meaningful concessions from the state and/or capital. In a similar vein, Thompson *et al.* (this volume) neatly contrasts labour power with labour's power.[4] Nevertheless, the idea of associational power has benefited from labour geography's growing acknowledgement of labour *agency* – of workers, their organizations and activity within GPNs.[5]

Unpacking Labour Agency

A brief retrospective helps explain the recent attention paid to labour agency. The Marxist economic geography of the 1980s, which emphasized capital-labour relations (Harvey, 1982; Massey, 1984; Storper and Walker, 1989), generally characterized workers as an oppressed class, incapable of shaping the geographies of the capitalist system through their collective action (Coe and Jordus-Lier, 2011).[6] The reaction was to privilege workers' capacity to create their own economic geographies (Herod, 2001), in which labour adopted multi-scalar strategies to challenge the growing power of global capital (Castree *et al.*, 2004).[7] While an important corrective to treating labour in purely objective terms, the championing of labour agency, in turn, stimulated a critique, still ongoing, of the limitations of this approach. Several strands stood out initially: the tendency to amplify (if not exaggerate) the highpoints of workers' triumphs (Coe, 2013; see Cumbers in this volume), disabling a more sober but realistic assessment of labour's weaknesses; an emphasis on groups of strong workers with the capacity to leverage concessions from capital; and a conflation of trade union activity with labour agency in general (Lier, 2007). Along these lines, it is difficult to ignore the irony that that this efflorescence of a labour geography avowing worker action and labour capacity has occurred in a period of working class retreat and the erosion of international trade unionism.

It is widely acknowledged that 'labour agency' as a concept has been under-theorized (Castree, 2010) and that its usage had simply come to mean any meaningful manifestation of collective worker *activity*. Certainly, efforts to deconstruct agency have been welcome. Cumbers *et al.* (2010) and others have utilized Katz's (2004) distinction between resilience (everyday coping practices), reworking (efforts to materially improve conditions), the principal sense in which agency has been used within labour geography, and resistance (direct challenges to capitalist social relations). While helpful heuristically, this categorization is not so robust analytically, failing to capture the multi-layered nature of 'labour's power' and exercise, and the nature of collective organization.

Reworking, for instance, may be tightly entwined with quotidian resilience,[8] their combined 'agential' impact on global capital being greater than the sum of their constituent elements. In short, diminishing the significance of resilience may be misplaced.[9]

An ancillary criticism of these attempts to deconstruct agency is that, existing at a level of abstraction, they fall short of the rigour needed for concrete explanation of collective *agency* within GPNs. In this regard, knowledge might be required of important contexts and factors including the type, nature and structure of union(s) involved[10] in one or more geographies, multiple institutional characteristics including the organizational mechanisms for generating international action and solidarity, union membership densities, the degree of managerial acceptance/opposition, employers' strategies and orientations, the processes and outcomes of bargaining and so on. In short what needs to be included is a more finely grained scalar and organizational analysis of employment relations that is not reducible to the beguiling but vague categorizations of resilience, reworking or resistance. This is not to reject the utility of these categories *in toto*, but to suggest that they are work in progress, requiring further elaboration. For example, the interconnections between resilience, reworking and resistance as labour agency 'strategies' may benefit from the application of mobilization theory (e.g. Kelly, 1998) and its key stages (grievance, attribution, mobilization, organization), helping us to understand the dynamics of transnational (across GPNs) as well as local or nationally based labour action.

Further qualification has been made of the tendency to champion worker agency for its own sake, not least the need to create an 'analytical space' for individual, as well as collective, action. Parenthetically, LPT has engaged with similar themes through its exploration of identity and interests (Marks and Thompson, 2010). Reflecting on other 'subject positions', beyond those of the worker and union member, leads to a consideration of the intersections between forms of social difference, including class, gender, race and ethnicity, to wider labour agencies (e.g. migration, community unionism) and even to the realm of social reproduction.Bezuidenhout and Buhlungu (2011: 257) stretch the definitional boundaries of worker agency to the 'informal or formal, individual or collective, spontaneous or goal oriented, sporadic or sustained [which] can operate on different scales'. Nevertheless, the danger of such definitional promiscuity is that it can lead to analytical relativism, blunting our ability to distinguish the inconsequential from the meaningful. We do need to have a sense of what matters most, what worker actions and organizations have the ability to alter the shape and dynamic of chains by impacting the decision-making of lead firms, their suppliers, the state (at local and national levels) and regulatory bodies.

Hence, the most significant qualification to the unrestrained celebration of worker agency lies in understanding how 'labour's power' and, as argued below, labour power, are embedded within transnational, national and local spheres of production. If labour needed to be 'written in' to the script and have its agency restored, it does not follow that capital and its agency, the transnational firm and the state, should be written out. The fragmented, but tightly coordinated, organization of global capital structurally constrains and conditions labour agency in multiple ways. The spatial and functional reconfigurations of value-added activities may inhibit associational power and pose major challenges for labour (Mosley, 2011). Indeed, outsourcing and offshoring invariably deliver a double whammy of disintermediation that can undermine organized labour in the global North and exacerbate difficulties for building collective worker organization in the global South (see Taylor and Bain, 2008 for the example of call centres). One does not have to accept that subcontracting is a universal paradigm (Wills, 2009) to acknowledge its deleterious impacts on labour's terms and conditions and the exercise of effective agency.

Social Upgrading

Parallel to the discussion of labour agency in the GPN literature, labour has been brought into GVCs and GPNs via the vis-à-vis the problematic of upgrading. Scholars from the field of Development Studies challenged earlier GCC and GVC formulations for either neglecting to consider the position of workers, or for depicting them merely as an endogenous factor of production at the bottom of value chains. The broader problem is that when attention is focused on dyadic relations between, say, buyers and suppliers, and the degree to which these facilitate firm-level upgrading, the experience and interests of labour tend to be subsumed within a consideration of the position of suppliers. The work of Barrientos and colleagues and others (e.g. Palpacuer, 2008) has been influential in analytically distinguishing between economic and social upgrading, and diagnosing why the former does not automatically produce the latter (Barrientos *et al.*, 2011; Milberg and Winkler, 2011). There is no shortage of examples of failed social upgrading. An appalling case is that of the Taiwanese Foxconn factories in China, where an oppressive dormitory employment regime, inhumane working conditions and oppressive managerial practices led to enormous worker discontent, culminating in a spate of attempted and successful suicides in factories producing for Apple, Nokia and other leading electronics brands (Chan, 2013; Chan *et al.*, 2013).

Barrientos *et al.* (2011) argue that it is necessary to capture the different dimensions of labour within value chains analysis. It should include labour as a productive factor (where the commercial driver is quality standards and not only cost pressures) and labour as socially embedded, in which labour standards, rights, ILO conventions and human rights can and should play a role. The emergence of this social upgrading concept constitutes a promising development in that it raises the issue of how to achieve improved conditions. However, its principal analytical weakness lies in the fact that the capitalist imperatives of cost-minimization and profit-maximization in fiercely competitive global markets operating at the level of the firm level and beyond (e.g. local labour regime) may thwart, neutralize or trump interventions ostensibly designed to improve conditions, such as codes of practice, multilateral initiatives (ILO and OECD guidelines) or government legislation (see Mayer and Pickles, 2010; Barrientos *et al.*, 2011: 337; Anner *et al.*, 2013). The framing of value chain participation and firm-level upgrading as a 'win-win' scenario that emphasizes mutual gains for TNCs and workers may well be illusory, especially when the responsibility, ultimately, for reforming practices lies with the voluntary actions of firms themselves. Social upgrading and how it can be achieved are important questions and are addressed in this volume by Anner and Pegler.

Labour Power and the Labour Process

We now turn to consider structural power, labour power and the labour process more fully. There is justification for this conceptual linkage. Structural power, to reprise, focuses on workers' position in the productive process. Labour power is the capacity to labour, which only becomes real as concrete labour when set in motion by the owners (or controllers) of the means of production, through the labour process (Marx, 1976: chapters 6–7). Thus, both structural power and labour power can be distinguished from associational power, which is concerned principally with workers', particularly unions', activity and their ability to exploit their 'positionality'. The labour process can be seen to involve a dual agency, by capital in its assembling, organizing and controlling of workers in order to ensure that surplus labour can be extracted and, by labour itself, as it acts to create that surplus (value). Thus, LPT recognizes and is centrally focused on the indeterminacy of labour – labour as the peculiar commodity – and seeks to reveal and analyse the mechanisms that convert the potential to work into actual work. The purpose of this exegesis is to call attention to the fact that labour agency in these related senses has been (relative to associational power) underexplored.

Some have highlighted the need to overcome this deficit even though it remains a challenge to execute empirically. For Rainnie *et al.* (2011), GPNs are as much systems of embodied labour as they are interlinked systems of firms and, consequently, 'labour, as the ultimate source of value ... must lie at [GPNs'] heart' (161). For Cumbers *et al.* (2008), as indicated, abstract labour is the key to all systems of commodity production.[11] For Riisgaard and Hammer (2011: 186), 'labour needs to be conceptualised *a priori* as a value producer in GVCs and thus as a social actor with its own interests regarding the organisational, spatial and political structure of a value chain'.

Coe and colleagues (see this volume) and others have undoubtedly taken significant steps towards formulating 'an expanded GPN' that has workers and their collective organizations centre stage and not merely as an add-on. Nevertheless, a labour process deficit remains. To be sure, workers are 'not simply a production input' (Coe *et al.*, 2008), but if the 'production input' of conventional economics is re-theorized through the lens of labour process analysis, then it assumes a far greater salience for the sphere of production in GPN analysis. Some questions suggest themselves. To what extent are differing control mechanisms appropriate for, and used by, lead firms and/or suppliers at the different stages of a value chain/production network? What contrasting mechanisms for leveraging surplus and for ensuring the creation of value, ironically missing from *value chain* theory (Gibbon et al., 2008; Taylor, 2010), are utilized in the different places? Beyond the transactions costs and inter-firm governance, in what ways is concrete labour in the multiple locations and worksites connected – a question that invokes Marx's concept of the collective worker, or Glucksmann's (2005) total social organization of labour.

For all its many strengths, the expanded, labour-integrated version of the GPN understates the importance of the workplace as a key site for the extraction of surplus. Given the catholic nature of recent labour geography, its intellectual openness to diverse disciplines and research agendas, this general oversight is perhaps surprising. One would have expected more to have been written on management control strategies, labour indeterminacy, the immediate wage-effort bargain and worker responses at the workplace level, all core concerns of LPT as indicated in Part II. To provide an illustration of what is missing, it may be helpful to draw the contrast between the notions of the *local labour regime* and that of the *workplace regime*. While the local labour regime, and its role in mediating inter-firm governance, is extensively explored in the labour geography and GPN literature, the *workplace regime* is notable for its absence.

The intention here is not to narrow the labour process to the workplace alone but to maintain that an emphasis on the point(s) of production or service delivery – or at least their inclusion in a broader theorizing of structural and associational power and agency – has analytical validity. Driven by firms' incessant restructuring and relocation strategies,[12] GPNs are constantly evolving, spatially variable divisions of labour that involve the creation of new or the transformation of existing *places* of work. As Smith and Meiskins (1995: 261) have argued, within the broader cross-national variation of management style, industrial relations, technological capability and so on, 'factory regimes and the labour process [are] particularly dynamic and variegated'. In fact, the slicing-up – or stretching – of chains or networks across space may throw into sharper relief the inescapable problematic for capital of overcoming labour indeterminacy. What mechanisms of control are adopted by lead firms to ensure the transformation of labour power in and across the geographically distant workplaces?

Recent research, first presented at the International Labour Process Conference,[13] provides examples of how LPT can be utilized to conceptualize such differences. Feuerstein (2013) identifies contrasting strategies of management control, respectively responsible autonomy and direct control (Friedman, 1977), in two variants of the offshored Indian IT industry. The evidence challenges the notion of industry-wide uniformity and the dominance of a single type of workplace regime, while emphasizing the contingency of work organization and the variability of workplace control. Pawlicki (2013) demonstrates how a German software engineering firm in its Global Design Network (GDN) intermingled autonomy and control strategies at its nearshore site in Bucharest, Romania.

Then, there is the 'connectivity' problem (Smith and Thompson, 2009; Thompson and Smith, 2010), of how the dynamics of core labour process theory are embedded within or, related to, a wider framework of change at the scale of the global political economy. In the edited collection on labour process theory, Taylor (2010) analysed how the *macro* and the *micro* might be articulated through the *meso* level of GVC coordination and GPN networks in his study of globalized call centres. Similarly and subsequently, Rainnie *et al.* (2011) urged labour process analysis 'to engage with a more sophisticated form of analysis of inter-firm relationships, value creating and capture', advice reflected in a number of chapters in this volume, which analyse the causal connections between *macro* level political economy and the labour process at the *micro* level of the workplace.

While certain LPT theorists favour financialization as a designation for, and as a means of, understanding, the contemporary *macro* political economy (e.g. Thompson, 2003; Thompson *et al.* in this volume), others, although acknowledging the significance of financialization and its effects, have preferred to integrate it with the broader concept of global neoliberal capitalism. Some labour geographers have even drawn labour process implications from their interpretation of the *macro* to *micro* mechanisms of neoliberalism. Kelly (2010: 171), for example, sees the global capitalist system as containing 'internal logics that require the constant intensification of labour and production processes, an ever-decreasing turnover time for capital to generate profit and an incessant restructuring that finds new technological, regulatory and spatial arrangements for production'. Nevertheless, it is perhaps surprising, given these critical understandings of the 'connectivities' of neoliberal capitalism that, despite exceptions (Taylor *et al.*, 2014), little work still has directly engaged with the labour process, work organization and workplace consequences of the 2007–2008 crisis and subsequent global recession.[14]

This introductory essay has argued that the focus on labour agency should not eclipse the broader conditions that shape labour's 'positionality', to use the currently fashionable term. Associational power should not automatically be privileged at the expense of the structural, for weakness in labour's structural power may well undermine its capacity to generate associational power, particularly in geographically stretched, sliced-up and outsourced value chains. Equally, labour's structural position may confer certain potential advantages, such as the so-called 'choke points' within the highly integrated, just-in-time systems of production and service delivery (Bonacich and Wilson, 2008). As labour geography has emphasized in its unpacking of labour agency, there is a need to reconnect worker agency with the variable, spatialized dynamics of capital accumulation that condition labour's structural power. Such generalized insight is invaluable, but analytical leverage will most likely follow a rigorous, highly concrete and geographically sensitive examination of structural power, associational power, labour agency and the labour process.

The terrain has changed greatly from the time when a general injunction to researchers in the fields of work and employment studies to adopt spatiality and make the geographical turn was pertinent (Herod *et al.*, 2007; Rainnie *et al.*, 2007). The theoretical landscape has widened as many working in the tradition of labour process analysis have adopted the diverse frameworks of global value chains (GVCs) and global production networks (GPNs). It is heartening that, rather than fighting framework wars, many researchers have appropriately drawn on the expanded conceptual toolkits provided both by GVCs, such as the specification of governance as related to complexity, codification and capabilities (Gereffi *et al.*, 2005), and by GPNs, such as the emphasis on embeddedness and strategic coupling, when 'putting labour in' to space, scale and place. The chapters in this book exemplify the ways in which work at the frontier of labour and global production adopts and adapts the diverse formulations of global chains and networks.

The great majority of the chapters collected here originated as papers presented at the 31st International Labour Process Conference, which was held in March 2013 at Rutgers University in New Brunswick, New Jersey. We recognize that this conference stream and the resulting volume represent only the beginnings of a theoretical and empirical engagement between labour process theory and analysis and global value chains and networks. In the light of this observation, and because it is customary in the edited collections resulting from the labour process conference to comment on what kind of future research agenda might proceed from the volume's theme, we offer a few (by no means definitive or exhaustive) thoughts on possible directions that this emergent engagement might take. Theoretically, much still needs to be done regarding the fundamental questions of value and labour power. Mainstream GVC theory frequently operates with an orthodox formulation of value as valued-added, and while GPN has been concerned with value capture and creation, its position vis-à-vis labour as the source of value in global production remains undeveloped. Arguably, the intellectual challenge of the GCC/GVC/GPN project has stimulated renewed interest in essential questions that at one time dominated LPT, notably the labour theory of value.

The question of 'connectivity' has arisen in a number of the chapters, including Thompson, Cox and Parker's notable attempt to construct a post-GVC framework. The articulations between the broader global political economy, capital accumulation, markets, firm-level strategies, labour process, labour power, the workplace and labour's power are self-evidently important. Such articulation involves much more than the capital-labour duality, including particularly the role of the state at all levels. The editors willingly acknowledge that this volume is deficient in this important respect and emphasize that the state should be prominent in future labour process–inspired global chain or network research.

Of course, a single volume will be unable to encompass all of the pertinent conceptual questions and research areas, especially given the supply-side nature of the conference paper and publication process. Although constrained by the fact of submission, a collective *mea culpa* may not be entirely inappropriate when it comes to issues of gender, race, ethnicity and migration. We might have done more to solicit contributions in these inescapably important areas of global production and labour. This is a critical lacuna which we hope future scholarship will fill.

Structure of the Book

The book is divided into three parts. The first part, 'Integrating Labour Process and Value Chains', includes chapters that combine theoretical development and conceptual insight with empirical research that elucidates the interrelationships between the labour process, labour process theory and value chain analysis. The chapters develop and render more transparent the interrelationships between core labour process theory and global value chains/production networks. The chapter by Newsome draws on the notion of 'value in motion' to explore the critical role retail logistics plays in contributing to the value creation within overall production networks. It explores how the struggle between logistics companies and retailers impacts on the labour process. The theoretical insights that can be gained from re-integrating labour and labour power with the articulated relations between production, distribution and exchange are explored.

Extending the concern to integrate labour process analysis with GVC perspectives, the chapter by Thompson, Parker and Cox explores issues of control and value capture faced by small and medium-sized producers of digital entertainment products. A model of value capture is developed that goes beyond complexity of information exchange, codifiability of the production process and competence of the supplier base, in part by incorporating labour power – value inputs, agency and impacts – fully into the framework.

The following chapter by Haidinger and Flecker also explores the capacity of LPT to deliver insight, in this case into parcel delivery services as part of a global logistics sector. It explores labour's structural power resulting from the sector's position in the supply chain. The case for extending the territory of prevailing labour process analysis to reflect how the social relations of production are integrated into the global economy along different trajectories is advanced in the chapter by Hammer and Riisgaard. They argue this process is based on new dynamics of segmentation and variegated relations between the formal and informal sectors. The final chapter in this part, by Wong, also reflects on the concern to incorporate informality into labour process analysis. By interrogating the articulation of informal labour in the e-waste value chain, this chapter highlights the distinctive and irreducible significance of informal labour to the functioning of value chains. It also underscores the relative lacuna on informal labour in labour process and value chain analysis.

The second part, 'Unpacking Labour: Power, Agency and Standards', complements the first in that it deconstructs and re-appraises the category of labour. Chapters consider labour as agency, labour as a source of power and labour as central to the capacity for social upgrading. The chapter by Bair and Werner maps the literature on GPN and labour by identifying two main streams and the key questions motivating each. The first perspective includes a voluminous literature on labour as object, documenting how global production arrangements affect the conditions of employment and other labour outcomes of particular groups of workers. The second stream centres labour as agent, asking what role, collectively and individually, workers play in shaping GPNs. They criticize both of these approaches for a 'network essentialism' which delimits the analysis of labour to those processes illuminated by the chain construct, and potentially confuses the 'trees' of global value chains with the 'forest' of a capitalist world economy that cannot be reduced to the network configurations traced in the GVC and GPN literatures.

The role of workers in shaping global production networks (GPN) is explored in the chapter by Cumbers. He develops a conceptualization of the complex geographies of trade union action by using and extending the GPN framework, arguing for the importance of developing the, as yet unrealized, potential of a GPN framework for understanding labour's predicament. The following chapter by Anner draws on evidence from the global value chain for apparel to explore domestic and transnational sources of worker power. He argues that the international restructuring of employment relations dynamics through global value chains (GVCs) necessitates a reconceptualization of worker power that is sensitive to the difference between *micro* (firm) level sources of worker power and *macro* level (national and international) sources of worker power in GVCs. The final chapter in this part by Coe also seeks to advance the theorization of labour agency within global production networks (GPNs), specifically via a focus on the uneven geographies and temporalities of labour agency within GPNs.

The third part, 'Sectoral Studies', provides cutting-edge, theoretically informed empirical studies of specific industrial sectors. Jenkins explores the grass-roots organizing activities taking place at the bottom of garment and electrical value chains in India. This chapter raises issues of community and gender and the associated challenges involved in mobilizing new and vulnerable constituencies of labour to resist exploitation at the local level. The following chapter by Pegler aims to expand our understanding of the impacts of value chain inclusion on labour from a social sustainability perspective. It focuses on the tasks and subjectivities of Amazonian flood plain peasants (*ribeirinhos*) who collect a new 'wonder fruit', açaí, for sale to an expanding market.

Shifting gears to a high-tech sector, Bergvall-Kåreborn and Howcroft examine the highly complex network structure of Apple's GPN, directing particular attention to issues of value, power and embeddedness. Reporting on fieldwork with software developers in Sweden, the UK and the US, their chapter explains how the applications offered to Apple's consumers are developed via a crowdsourcing model that has proved integral to the success of the company's business model and ongoing expansion.

The next chapter by Rainnie, Herod, Pickren and McGrath-Champ introduces the concept of 'wasted labour' as a way to integrate issues of waste, particularly e-waste, into our understanding of work and employment in GPNs. The authors propose Global Destruction Network (GDN) framework, which highlights the centrality of the labour process in the form and function of these circuits. The final chapter by Taylor draws on longitudinal evidence, over two decades, from the global call/contact centre sector. He argues that the call/contact centre can only be understood through the analytical integration of the dynamics of political economy, technological innovation, spatial and locational dimensions and, crucially, the qualities of labour. Theoretically, the chapter contributes by focusing on the indeterminacy of labour and the labour process in the contradiction between labour mobility and fixity at national and transnational scale.

In short, this collection inaugurates what we hope will be a sustained engagement between labour process analysis, labour geography and the study of global value chains/global production networks. In assessing the field of labour geography, Coe and Jordhus-Lier (2011: 216) declare their commitment to developing strategies capable of shifting the *status quo* in favour of workers, an objective shared by the editors and by contributors. Recalling the anti-capitalist, labour emancipatory outlook of early labour process theory and Labour Process Conferences reaffirms our conviction that the collective project this book represents is not solely theory-building for its own sake, important though this undoubtedly is. Rather, as a scholarly community we are fundamentally concerned with producing greater knowledge of the workings of global capitalism in order to deepen our ability to articulate alternative futures and mechanisms of change. Therefore, further research on labour agency is vital, particularly that which addresses, in concrete ways and not as empty rhetoric, the ways in which the structural power of workers can be made manifest in associational power.

Notes

1 Gereffi and Korzeniewicz's (1994) volume is commonly held to be the founding document of the GCC tradition yet, as Bair (2005) has demonstrated, a 'disjuncture' between the earlier World Systems tradition of commodity chain research and the GCC framework was in evidence.
2 Bair (2009) has observed that World Systems Theory did place an emphasis on labour but that although based in this theory GCC tended to deal only indirectly with the impact on labour from BDCCs.
3 These terms have been widely cited. However, it should be noted *en passant* that Wright (2000) had very little to say about structural power – a mere three references in but one paragraph, and his employment of associational power is at a high level of abstraction.

4 However beguiling the structural power/associational power binary, its utility is more metaphorical than analytical. Both terms/concepts still require conceptual refinement and elaboration.
5 Coe and Hess (2013) emphasize the growing overlap between GPN scholarship and research areas that prioritize labour agency – particularly labour geography – and cite the edited collections of Bergene et al. (2010) and McGrath-Champ et al. (2010). This latter excellent collection, in common with a broader literature, certainly does entwine labour, work GCC, CVC and GPN, but contains only a few references to key GVC or GPN scholars, including Bair, Coe, Gereffi or Dicken, and explicitly to these frameworks.
6 An interesting intellectual parallel is that Braverman's (1974) seminal work on the capitalist labour process similarly treats workers as object.
7 It might be suggested again, in parallel to the trajectory of LPT, that 'second wave' LPT (e.g. Friedman, 1977; Burawoy, 1979) attempted to correct the missing object although the worker subject was not as emphatically re-inserted as in much of labour geography.
8 To be fair, Coe and Jordhus-Lier (2011: 216) concede that it is necessary to be sensitive to the possible connections between the different strategies.
9 Many illustrations could be advanced, but the following has particular salience for labour process analysis and because it involved spatially imaginative labour activity across the GPN of a transnational corporation. In the prolonged British Airways dispute (2009–2011), cabin crew and their union BASSA (British Airways Stewards and Stewardesses Association) undertook collective action (including 21 strike days) to defend terms and conditions in an archetypal reworking strategy, according to Katz's typology. However, research reveals deep roots of collective action as embedded in workers' coping 'strategies' and the daily union defence of their workplace (in-flight) 'frontiers of control' against managerial incursions (Taylor and Moore, 2015).
10 The simple counter-position of business unionism with community unionism, common in labour geography, fails to capture the complex typologies of unions, extent of member activity and politics.
11 See Thompson et al. (this volume) for a critique of Cumbers et al.'s (2008) and of Selwyn's (2011) tendency to define GVCs or GPNs principally as labour control regimes.
12 The use of the term 'strategies' may attribute to firms' decision-making a sense of long-range planning and purpose that its tactical and reactive nature does not merit. Capital's 'spatial fix' (Harvey, 1982) in the abstract cannot be seamlessly translated into corporate decisions to reconfigure and relocate.

13 The articles by Feuerstein (2013) and Pawlicki (2013) were first presented as papers to a special stream similarly entitled 'Putting Labour in its Place: Global Value Chains and Labour Process Analysis' at the 30th International Labour Process Conference in Stockholm (27–29 March 2012) and were selected for publication in a special issue of *Competition and Change*, volume 17, issue 1.

14 Some attempts have been made to consider the impacts on value chains from a development perspective (e.g. Cattaneo *et al.*, 2010).

REFERENCES

Anner, M., Bair, J. and Blasi, J. (2013) 'Towards joint liability in global supply chains: addressing the root causes of labour violations in international subcontracting networks', *Comparative Labour Law and Policy Journal*, 35(1): 1–43.

Bair, J. (2005) 'Global capitalism and commodity chains: looking back, going forward', *Competition and Change*, 9(2): 153–180.

Bair, J. (2008) 'Analysing global economic organisation: embedded networks and global chains compared', *Economy and Society*, 37(3): 339–364.

Bair, J. (2009) 'Global commodity chains: genealogy and review', in J. Bair (ed.) *Frontiers of Commodity Chain Research*, Stanford: Stanford University Press, pp. 1–34.

Barrientos, S. (2013) 'Corporate purchasing practices in global production networks: a socially contested terrain', *Geoforum*, 44(1): 44–51.

Barrientos, S., Gereffi, G. and Rossi, A. (2011) 'Economic and social upgrading in global production networks: a new paradigm for a changing world', *International Labour Review*, 150(3–4): 320–340.

Bergene, A. C., Endresen, S. B. and Knutsen, H. M. (eds) (2010) *Missing Links in Labour Geography*, Aldershot: Ashgate.

Bezuidenhout, A. and Buhlungu, S. (2011) 'From compounded to fragmented labour: mineworkers and the demise of compounds in South Africa', *Antipode*, 43(2): 237–263.

Bonacich, E. and Wilson, J.B. (2008) *Getting the Goods: Ports, Labour and the Logistics Revolution*, Ithaca: Cornell University Press.

Braverman, H. (1974) *Labour and Monopoly Capital*, New York: Monthly Review Press.

Burawoy, M. (1979) *Manufacturing Consent*, Chicago: Chicago University Press.

Castree, N. (2010) 'Workers, economies, geographies', In S. McGrath-Champ, A. Herod and A. Rainnie (eds) *Working Space: Handbook of Employment and Society*, Cheltenham: Edward Elgar, pp. 457–476.

Castree, N., Coe, N. M., Ward, K. and Samers, M. (2004) *Spaces of Work: Global Capitalism and Geographies of Labour*, Sage: London.

Cattaneo, O., Gereffi, G. and Staritz, C. (2010) *Global Value Chains in a Postcrisis World: A Development Perspective*, Washington: World Bank.

Chan, J. (2013) 'A suicide survivor – the life of a Chinese worker', *New Technology, Work and Employment*, 28(2): 84–99.

Chan, J., Pun, N. and Selden, J. (2013) 'The politics of global production: Apple, Foxconn and China's new working class', *New Technology, Work and Employment*, 28(2): 100–115.

Coe, N. M. (2013) 'Geographies of production III: making space for labour', *Progress in Human Geography*, 37(2): 271–284.

Coe, N. M. and Hess, M. (2013) 'Global production networks, labour and development', *Geoforum*, 44(1): 4–9.

Coe, N. M. and Jordhus-Lier, D. C. (2011) 'Constrained agency? Re-evaluating the geographies of labour', *Progress in Human Geography*, 35(2): 211–233.

Coe, N. M., Dicken, P. and Hess, M. (2008) 'Global production networks: realising the potential', *Journal of Economic Geography*, 8(3): 271–295.

Coe, N., Hess, M., Wai-cheung, H., Dicken, P. and Henderson, J. (2004) 'Globalising regional development', *Transactions of Institute of British Geographers*, 29: 464–484.

Cumbers, A., Nativel, C. and Routledge, P. (2008) 'Labour agency and union potentialities in global production networks', *Journal of Economic Geography*, 8(3): 369–387.

Cumbers, A., Helms, G. and Swanson, K. (2010) 'Class, agency and resistance in the old industrial city', *Antipode*, 12(1), 46–73

Dicken, P. (2011) *Global Shift: Mapping the Changing Contours of the World Economy* (6th edition), London: Sage.

Dicken, P., Kelley, P. F., Olds, K. and Yeung, H. (2001) 'Chains and networks, territories and scales: towards a relational framework for analysing the global economy', *Global Networks*, 1(2): 89–112.

Edwards, P. K. (1990) 'Understanding conflict in the labour process: the logic and autonomy of struggle', in D. Knights and H. Willmott (eds) *Labour Process Theory*, Basingstoke: Macmillan, pp. 125–152.

Edwards, P. K. (2010) 'Developing labour process analysis: themes from industrial sociology and future directions', in P. Thompson and C. Smith (eds) *Working Life – Renewing Labour Process Analysis*, Basingstoke: Palgrave Macmillan, pp. 47–69.

Edwards, R. (1979) *Contested Terrain: The Transformation of the Workplace in the Twentieth Century*, London: Heinemann.

Feuerstein, P. (2013) 'Patterns of work reorganization in the course of the IT industry's internationalization', *Competition and Change* 17(1): 24–40.

Flecker, J. and Meil, P. (2010) 'Organisational restructuring and emerging service value chains – implications for work and employment', *Work, Employment and Society*, 24(1): 1–19.

Friedman, A. (1977) *Industry and Labour: Class Struggle at Work Monopoly Capitalism*, London: Macmillan.

Gereffi, G. and Korzeniewicz, M. (1994) (eds) *Commodity Chains and Global Capitalism*, Westport CT: Praeger.

Gereffi, G., Humphrey, J. and Sturgeon, T. (2005) 'The governance of global value chains', *Review of International Political Economy*, 12(1): 78–104.

Gereffi, G., Korzeniewicz, M. and Korzeniewicz, R. (1994) 'Introduction: global commodity chains', in G. Gereffi and M. Korzeniewicz (eds) *Commodity Chains and Global Capitalism*, Westport, CT: Praeger, pp. 1–14.

Gibbon, P., Bair, J. and Ponte, S. (2008) 'Governing global value chains: an introduction', *Economy and Society*, 37(3): 315–338.

Glucksmann, M. (2005) 'Shifting boundaries and interconnections: extending the "total social organisation of labour"', *The Sociological Review*, 53(2): 19–36.

Harvey, D. (1982) *The Limits to Capital*, Oxford: Blackwell.

Henderson, J., Dicken, P., Hess, M., Coe, N. and Yeung, H. W-C. (2002) 'Global production networks and the analysis of economic development', *Review of International Political Economy*, 9(3): 436–464.

Herod, A. (2001) *Labour Geographies*, New York: Guildford Press.

Herod, A., McGrath-Champ, S. and Rainnie, A. (2007) 'Working space: why incorporating the geographical is central to theorizing work and employment practices', *Work, Employment and Society*, 21(2): 47–64.

Katz, C. (2004) *Growing up Global: Economic Restructuring and Children's Everyday Lives*, Minneapolis: University of Minnesota Press.

Kelly, J. (1998) *Rethinking Industrial Relations*, London: Routledge.

Kelly, P. F. (2010) 'Filipino migration and the spatialities of labour market segmentation', in S. McGrath-Champ, A. Herod and A. Rainnie (eds) *Handbook of Employment and Society – Working Space*, Cheltenham: Edward Elgar, pp. 159–178.

Lier, D. C. (2007) 'Places of work, scales of organising: a review of labour geography', *Geography Compass*, 1(4): 814–833.

Marks, A. and Thompson, P. (2010) 'The globalisation of service work: analysing the transnational call centre value chain', in P. Thompson and C. Smith (eds) *Working Life – Renewing Labour Process Analysis*, Basingstoke: Palgrave Macmillan, pp. 316–339.

Marx, K. (1976) *Capital Volume 1*, Harmondsworth: Penguin.

Massey, D. (1984) *Spatial Divisions of Labour*, London: Macmillan.

Mayer, F. W. and Pickles, J. (2010) *Re-Embedding Governance: Global Apparel Value Chains and Decent Work*, Capturing the Gains Working Paper No. 2010/1, http://www.capturingthegains.org/pdf/ctg-wp-2010-01.pdf (accessed 22 August 2014).

McGrath-Champ, S., Herod, A. and Rainnie, A. (eds) (2010) *Working Space – Handbook of Employment and Society*, Cheltenham: Edward Elgar.

Milberg, W. and Winkler, D. (2011) *Economic and Social Upgrading in Global Production Networks: Problems of Theory and Measurement*, Capturing the Gains Working Paper No. 4, University of Manchester.

Mosley, L. (2011) *Labour Rights and Multinational Production*, Cambridge: Cambridge University Press.

Newsome, K. (2010) 'Work and employment in distribution and exchange: moments in the circuits of capital', *Industrial Relations Journal*, 41(3): 190–205.

Newsome, K., Thompson, P. and Commander, J. (2013) '"You monitor performance every hour": labour and the management of performance in the supermarket supply chain', *New Technology, Work and Employment*, 28(1): 1–15.

Palpacuer, F. (2008) 'Bringing the social back in: governance and wealth distribution in global commodity chains', *Economy and Society*, 37(3): 393–419.

Pawlicki, P. (2013) 'Control in an internationalized labour process: engineering work in global design', *Competition and Change*, 17(1): 41–56.

Ponte, S. and Sturgeon. T (2014) 'Explaining governance in global value chains: a modular theory-building effort', *Review of International Political Economy*, 21(1): 195–223.

Rainnie, A., Herod, A. and McGrath, S. (2007) 'Spatialising industrial relations', *Industrial Relations Journal*, 38(2): 102–118.

Rainnie, A., Herod, A. and McGrath, S. (2011) 'Review and positions: global production networks and labour', *Competition and Change*, 15(2), 155–168.

Riisgaard, L. and Hammer, N. (2011) 'Prospects for labour in global value chains: labour standards in the cut flower and banana industries', *British Journal of Industrial Relations*, 49(1): 168–190.

Selwyn, B. (2011) 'The political economy of class compromise: trade unions, capital-labour relations and development in north east Brazil', *Antipode*, 43(4): 1305–1329.

Selwyn, B. (2013) 'Social upgrading and labour in global production networks: a critique and an alternative conception', *Competition and Change*, 17(1): 75–90.

Smith, C. and Meiskins, P. (1995) 'System, society and dominance effects in cross-national organizational analysis', *Work, Employment and Society*, 9(2): 241–267.

Smith, C. and Thompson, P. (2009) 'Labour power and labour process – contesting the marginality of the sociology of work', *Sociology*, 43(5): 913–930.

Smith, N., Rainnie, A., Dunford, M., Hardy, J., Hudson, R. and Sadler, D. (2002) 'Networks of value, commodities and regions: reworking divisions of labour in macro-regional economies', *Progress in Human Geography*, 26(1): 41–63.

Storper, M. and Walker, R. (1989) *The Capitalist Imperative: Territory, Technology and Industrial Growth*, Oxford: Blackwell.

Taylor, P. (2010) 'The globalisation of service work: analysing the transnational call centre value chain', in P. Thompson and C. Smith (eds) *Working Life: Renewing Labour Process Analysis*, Basingstoke: Palgrave Macmillan, pp. 244–268.

Taylor, P. and Bain, P. (2008) 'United by a common language? Trade union responses in the UK and India to call centre offshoring', *Antipode*, 40(1), 132–154.

Taylor, P. and Moore, S. (2015 *forthcoming*) 'Cabin crew collectivism: labour process and the roots of mobilisation', *Work, Employment and Society*, 28.

Taylor, P., D'Cruz, P., Noronha, E. and Scholarios, D. (2014) '"From boom to where?" the impact of crisis on work and employment in Indian BPO', *New Technology, Work and Employment*, 29(2), 105–123.

Taylor. P., Newsome, K. and Rainnie, A. (2013) 'Putting labour in its place: global value chains and labour process analysis', *Competition and Change*, 17(1): 1–5.

Thompson, P. (1989) *The Nature of Work* (2nd edition), Basingstoke: Palgrave Macmillan.

Thompson, P. (1990) 'Crawling from the wreckage: the labour process and the politics of production', in D. Knights and H. Willmott (eds) *Labour Process Theory*, Basingstoke: Macmillan, pp. 95–124.

Thompson, P. (2003) 'Disconnected capitalism: or why employers can't keep their side of the bargain', *Work, Employment and Society*, 17(2): 359–378.

Thompson, P. (2010) 'The capitalist labour process – concepts and connections', *Capital and Class*, 34(1): 7–14.

Thompson, P. and Newsome, K. (2004) 'Labour process theory, work and the employment relation', in B. E. Kaufman (ed.) *Theoretical Perspectives on Work and the Employment Relationship*, Cornell, NY: Cornell University Press, pp. 133–162.

Thompson, P. and Smith, C. (2010) *Working Life – Renewing Labour Process Analysis*. Basingstoke: Palgrave Macmillan.

Werner, M. (2012) 'Beyond upgrading: gendered labour and the restructuring of firms in the Dominican Republic', *Economic Geography*, 88(4): 403–422.

Werner, M. and Bair, J. (2011) 'Commodity chains and the uneven geographies of global capitalism: a disarticulations perspective', *Environment and Planning A*, 43(5): 988–997.

Wills, J. (2009) 'Subcontracted employment and its challenge to labour', *Labour Studies Journal*, 34(4): 441–460.

Wright, E. O. (2000) 'Working class power, capitalist class interests and class compromise', *American Journal of Sociology*, 105(4): 957–1002.

Integrating Labour Process and Global Value Chains

PART I

CHAPTER 2

Value in Motion: Labour and Logistics in the Contemporary Political Economy

Kirsty Newsome

This chapter will provide a conceptual arena for understanding the dynamics and drivers of labour process change in the logistics sector, focusing specifically on retail distribution and warehousing in the UK. Distribution, according to the classical Marxist perspective, was deemed unproductive labour, providing the necessary movement in the circuit of capital. Recent debates have, however, recognized that increasingly complex global value chains are predicated upon a concomitant logistics network. Responding to the call to 'bring labour in', this chapter will highlight the position of labour and the labour process within the logistics function. Utilizing the analytical currency of the circuit of capital and adopting the notion of 'value in motion', this chapter will reveal at a concrete level how the battle over 'value capture' (between logistics and retailers) shapes the labour process within distribution companies. It explores the theoretical insights gained from re-integrating labour and the labour process within the articulated relations between production, distribution and exchange. The chapter will contribute to growing debates which seek to rectify the absence of labour in debates on Global Value Chains (GVC)/Global Production Networks (GPN[1]).

The chapter is divided into two main sections: section one explores the role of logistics and distribution in the contemporary political economy and introduces the notion of 'value in motion'. Section two provides research evidence from the retail logistics companies in the UK. It explores how retailers' concern to 'preserve value in motion' and the battle over 'value capture' impacts upon the labour process. The research data is presented in two main sections. 'Preserving value' refers to the relationship between retailers and third-party logistics companies to protect value in motion within the circuit of capital. 'Capturing value' unpacks the impact of the relations between capitals on the labour process. This section highlights the degradation of work and employment as a key outcome of the battle for value capture, between the logistics companies and the retailers.

Retail Logistics: Value in Motion – Preserving and Capturing Value?

A much-cited quote from Wal-Mart's leadership to Wall Street analysts states, 'The misconception is that we're in the retail business, we're in the distribution business'.[2]

The increasing demands of 24/7 consumption within the grocery retail sector have been much documented in recent academic debates. The desire for the 'instant gratification' of consumer demands, coupled with the capacity of retailers to respond to these demands, has necessarily involved the transformation of the once relatively hidden domain of logistics, distribution and warehousing. To satisfy these changing patterns of consumption the 'logistics mix' of storage and warehousing facilities, inventory and transportation has inescapably been reconfigured, sending reverberations into the supply chain.

Within the mainstream management literature this transformation of relations between retailers, producers and logistics companies is predicated upon two main drivers: cost and service delivery. The logistics apparatus of stock holding, warehousing and distribution centres, as well as transport and haulage, is recognized as being essential but nevertheless a costly element within the retail supply chain. Immobile goods, remote from the point of consumption, are acknowledged as having considerable associated costs. The movement of goods within grocery distribution is time-critical. The necessity for retailers to implement IT systems across the supply chain which track and respond to demand with corresponding product movement is increasingly paramount (Fernie et al., 2010). These cost and service pressures have transformed retailers' strategies with regard to 'goods in motion' and the logistics function. This transformation has effectively facilitated the shift from retailers as the passive recipients of goods, to retailers actively (re)shaping relations with distribution and logistics companies. As a result, retailers have increased control over the logistics function, facilitated by their IT systems which track demand and replenish stock levels. In addition, retailers have made considerable investments into regional distribution centres (RDCs) to consolidate deliveries to their exacting requirements. In turn this reconfiguration has not only fashioned a burgeoning logistics infrastructure, but has created an increasingly competitive market for third party distribution companies (Fernie et al., 2010).

More critical debates have attempted to secure greater analytical purchase on the drivers and the dimensions of the 'logistics transformation'. In an attempt to illuminate the changing dynamics of relations between production, distribution and consumption these debates are increasingly turning to the GPN literature. Logistics, Hess and Rodrigue (2004) argue, supports, shapes and provides coherence to GPN with its scope and remit operating beyond the simple storage of goods. With the increasing geographical fragmentation of production from points of consumption, logistics provides the necessary capacity to integrate the movement of goods under the supremacy of the retailers (Coe et al., 2008). Distribution, orthodoxly regarded as a 'necessary evil' providing a link between production and consumption, is thus increasingly recognized as presenting the possibility for adding value (Bonacich and Wilson, 2008). This critical debate has recognized that the 'logistic revolution', intimately tied to the domination of the major retailers, has the capacity to play a more important 'value-adding' and 'value capture' role within global production networks (Harvey et al., 2002; Bonacich and Wilson, 2008; Coe, 2013).

The rise in retailer supremacy, based upon their ability to harness production, distribution and consumption, is predicated upon a number of key developments (Bonacich and Wilson, 2008; Lichtenstein, 2009; Hamilton and Petrovic, 2011). Firstly, retailers have monopolized access to the consumer, thereby shifting power within the retail value chain away from manufacturing to consumption (Fine and Leopold, 1993). This shift in power relations, coupled with the highly competitive nature of the sector in the UK, which remains dominated by a small number of powerful players, has enabled retailers to search for and secure additional cost savings within the supply chain. As a result of the inexorable pressures emanating from the retailers, suppliers are constantly searching for ways to deliver cost savings (Abernathy et al., 1999; Lichenstein, 2009). As Bonacich and Wilson (2008) note, given the capacity to mobilize these power resources, retailers have systematically closed down the capacity of suppliers to pass costs onto consumers directly. In addition, significant investment in IT systems by the retailers has facilitated the ability to integrate the management, monitoring and movement of information and goods within the overall supply chain. These technological advances have not only enabled retailers to monitor consumption patterns within stores, but also legitimized the extension of control and surveillance within the supply chain. In essence these developments have enabled retailers to recast and reshape the supply chain according to their rigorous requirements. As Jaffe (2010) highlights, 'goods moving', as opposed to the production of goods per se, must increasingly be regarded as an arena for securing cost savings and competitive advantage within supply chains. Locating an understanding of the position of logistics (and logistics labour) within the circuit of capital, he argues that savings in the sphere of distribution are increasingly 'based upon speed imperative and time based competition' (Jaffe, 2010).

Harvey et al. (2002) extend this argument with the suggestion that retailers not only reconfigure relations under their exacting patronage, they also simultaneously 'orchestrate competition' amongst third party providers (3PLs) as a mechanism to maximize efficiency and drive down costs. Retailers are also able to protect themselves from vulnerability to disruption by spreading risk across a number of competing logistics providers both in-house and third party. Contracts between retailers and logistics providers are thus short-term, contingent and transparent – creating a quasi-market – controlled by the retailers. This also highlights the possibility of 'new conflicts over who captures the added values along the routes' (Harvey et al., 2002). The battle over value capture in distribution thus becomes 'contested terrain' between retailers and the logistics providers (Hesse, 2002; Hesse and Rodrigue, 2006). Coe (2013) highlights this contested territory between logistics organizations as contributors to 'value creation and capture' in their client organizations and the protection and mobilization of their own interests of value capture. This argument provides a valuable vehicle to 'put labour back' and more fully integrate the labour process into value chain analysis.

To date there is a growing body of research evidence which focuses on the implications for labour of this 'contested terrain' between retailers and logistics companies. Logistics workers find themselves within a 'perfect storm' of globalization, fragmentation of production, new logistics technologies, de-regulated labour markets and eroding collective regulation (Newsome, 2010; Coe, 2013, see also Haidinger and Flecker, this volume). A recent report in the US, for example, entitled 'Chains of Greed', reveals how Wal-Mart's domestic outsourcing strategy produces low wages, poor working conditions and labour abuses for logistics workers. These violations of workers' rights 'are largely the product of Wal-Mart's signature and aggressive practice of outsourcing elements of its warehousing and goods-delivery systems to companies that, in turn, often further subcontract the work to other entities or individuals' (Cho et al., 2012). Wal-Mart sets the parameters for the working conditions in these facilities, either by employing their own managers on site and/or indirectly through setting challenging price demands coupled with the stringent monitoring of operating costs on their third party providers. The report highlights that when retailers, such as Wal-Mart, demand tighter margins and lower costs, 'suppliers may feel they have little choice but to replicate low-wage, largely part-time, highly contingent employment practices' (Cho *et al.*, 2012: 9). The next section outlines the theoretical argument adopted to explore the impact on labour and the labour process of this 'perfect storm' between retailers and logistics companies.

As this volume demonstrates, efforts to integrate labour generally and the labour process more specifically with prevailing GPN analysis have been gaining momentum in recent years (Taylor, 2010; Flecker and Meil, 2010; Rainnie *et al.*, 2011; Riisgaard and Hammer, 2011; Taylor *et al.*, 2013). There is, however, more than a small measure of ambiguity about the sites and sources of 'value' within GPN (Cumbers *et al.*, 2008; Taylor *et al.*, 2013). Writers have highlighted the importance of addressing the labour deficit in GPN with an inclusion of labour power and the labour process as the source and creator of value. Labour process analysis and wider production networks issues have the capacity to be combined, by positioning labour and the labour process as the ultimate source of value at the heart of GPN analysis (Cumbers 2008; Taylor 2010; Rainnie *et al.*, 2011; Selwyn, 2012). In more concrete terms, by focusing on the labour process within logistics and distribution, insights can be gained as to how value capture is fought for in an overall production network (circuit of capital). This wider embrace has the capacity to embed an understanding of the labour process within the full circuit of capital which recognizes the creation, movement and flow of value across the spheres of production, distribution and exchange. Distribution is thus positioned as central to the process of realizing value generated through the exercise of labour power in production. In this sense, 'value in motion' explores the critical role of distribution in the 'preservation of value' already within the circuit of capital.

The role of distribution work, and specifically the emergence of the logistics companies that intervene between production companies and retailers, is central to the process of realizing surplus value generated through the exercise of labour power and the performance of unpaid labour time in production. The movement of commodities in the sphere of circulation involves the expenditure of labour power that is productive of surplus value (e.g. transport), and labour that is necessary to ensure that products ultimately realize a surplus value in exchange but has traditionally been regarded as not directly productive of value. The latter includes storage and marketing and is ultimately a cost against or deduction from surplus value (Fine and Leopold, 1993; Harvey, 2007). The drive to contain these costs in order to 'preserve value' in motion is critical to understanding the competitive relations between monopoly retailers which, in this, embraces logistics companies and the direct producers. Moreover, the concern to preserve value in motion is also critical to understanding the context and the dynamics of changes in the labour process within these 3PLs. The subsequent focus on the battle for value capture between logistics companies and the retailers provides evidence at a more concrete level of how this battle impacts upon the labour process.

Research Method

The chapter draws on research evidence from three third party distribution companies operating from regional distribution centres (RDCs) which are located in the UK. Each of the logistics organizations are part of multi-national companies (MNCs) and provide dedicated third party logistics for one of the UK major supermarkets. All the sites were unionized with varying degrees of union density and levels of organizing. To ensure and protect anonymity the case study organizations are referred to as Mirror, Signal and Manoeuvre. Mirror enjoyed strong levels of unionization and closely guarded collective agreements. Signal had a union presence on site but, with relatively low levels of density as a result, union activity tended to revolve around more individual matters. Finally, Manoeuvre was also unionized with collective agreements on site; however, these were proving to be increasingly difficult to police in the face of growing pressures within the sector.

Qualitative research data was secured using semi-structured interviews with a number of respondents in each of the case-study organizations. Approximately eight to 12 interviews with management respondents took place in each case study, along with interviews with first-line managers, team-leaders and/or supervisors. Each interview took between one and two hours and was recorded. Between four and six focus groups of warehouse pickers also took place in each organization with a typical number of five employees in each group. Warehouse pickers in all of the organizations were predominantly male. Picking, a physically demanding job, involves the unloading, storage and reassembling of products in the required amounts for delivery to store. The data was coded and analysed using Nvivo, a software package that is used to analyse qualitative research data (see Table 2.1).

Table 2.1 Case-study organizations

	Mirror	Signal	Manoeuvre
Size	Large	Medium	Large
Ownership	MNC	MNC	MNC
	Third party logistics	Third party logistics	Third party logistics
Type of customer	Single multiple	Single multiple	Single multiple
Unionized	Yes	Yes	Yes

Preserving Value in Motion: Relations between Retailers and Distribution

This section explores the attempts by retailers to construct relations with 3PLs that preserve value in motion. All of the case-study organizations, themselves part of large MNCs, were in single supply agreement with one of the major grocery retailers in the UK. The retailers badge the RDC under their name and own the infrastructure and stock but the site is operated by the 3PL. In essence the 3PLs provide and manage the labour to run the site. The resulting contractual status between all of these organizations and their dominant customers was predicated upon 'open book contracts'. All costs associated with running the site were covered by the retailer and in return the 3PL received a negotiated management fee. The retailers set rigorous and tightly monitored key performance indicators (KPIs) for the companies to run the site and ensure delivery to store. These KPIs related to overall costs, as well as service and delivery levels. To ensure that these KPIs were adhered to, all of the organizations were subject to tight monitoring and review. Failure to meet with the required standards would be subject to a series of penalties and fines. These penalties would be deduced from the management fee. Many of the KPIs related to direct labour costs – these included productivity levels and absence levels, as well as overall staffing levels. All of the organizations were accountable for delivering on these KPIs and were subject to at least weekly updates of progress. If KPIs were not met, action plans were put in place to rectify the problem.

The IT systems which integrated the supply chain and monitored the movement of goods also had the capacity to provide detailed analysis on the performance of labour and on labour costs. The facility for these IT systems to 'quantify' or further 'commodify' labour was evident. This capacity becomes a key mechanism through which retailers are able to drive down costs and preserve value in motion. All of these 3PL organizations referred to constant daily statistics that were scrutinized by the retailers. A manager in Manoeuvre argued,

> We have a key page of stats for each area. At the beginning there will be the actual cases delivered or picked so that tells them how much the volume was. Then there will be the cases per warehouse hour or cases per driver hour because that is the key stat. Then there will be the cases per direct hour. In warehouses there will be other stats such as the pick rates and the loading rates and the unloading rates. And then there will be the absence stats, the percentage of absence because obviously that's another thing that we have to control because that incurs costs. It will show the percentage of overtime that we've used because they don't like us to use too much overtime because that's more expensive than using our own staff and managing our own staff by giving holidays etc. It's also more expensive than agency so they'll look at the percentage of agency of that we've used. So all that will be in the stats.
> (Manager, Manoeuvre)

In addition to the stringent and the fiercely monitored KPIs, all of the organizations were under considerable pressure to deliver on-going cost savings. Given the short-term nature of the contracts the pressure to not only reduce costs but deliver future cost savings and thus renew contracts in the future was paramount. The site manager in Mirror highlighted, 'they want us to be not just achieving budget but beating it and therefore saving their money, so costing them less to do the job'. The quid pro quo, it seemed, was some reassurance that contract renewal was a more distinct possibility. The site manager in Mirror, remarking on this constant pressure argued,

> 'I think we're proactive because I've got one objective and that's contract renewal. My whole existence is contract renewal. In behind that, there's just loads and loads and loads of things that we need to do to ensure that [supermarket X] get a good deal for the site and that they say yeah we'll just renew the contract'.

This 'orchestrated competition' (Harvey et al., 2002) amongst providers for contracts gave retailers the capacity to preserve 'value in motion' by imposing cost saving pressures on their logistics suppliers. In turn this could be used by the retailers to drive down costs in their own in-house RDC. Senior managers in Manoeuvre also highlighted that, as dedicated logistics experts, retailers expected that they would be better placed to deliver cost savings. He argued, 'the big retailers, particularly the grocery retailers, see the core business as retailing. Distribution, it's a necessary evil if you like because it facilitates what they now retail'. The argument was that retailers expected 3PLs to contribute their expertise, which in turn would 'develop' the overall network. A manager in Manoeuvre remarked,

> You can see that our added value, our willingness to contribute or our willingness to get involved, it will bring them along as well. You can see that we're always on the front foot. We're always willing. We're always eager and probably their own core people, at times, are not as eager as us because they're in-house.
> (Manager, Manoeuvre)

The impact of these inexorable cost pressures, coupled with the precarious nature of the contractual relationship, resulted in all of these 3PLs turning inward to secure further savings through cutting labour costs. Full-time trade union officials in the sector highlighted the downward impact the cost pressures were having on terms and conditions of employment within the sector. HR managers in all of the 3PL organizations indicated that they were attempting to revise existing terms and conditions of employment not only to ensure they meet existing KPIs but also to deliver further costs savings. The robustness of collective agreements and the capacity for the unions to protect existing terms and conditions was put to the test. For example, the stringent KPIs, coupled with sometimes fluctuating and unpredictable forecasting of volume levels, meant that labour in all of these organizations was required to be highly flexible and responsive to ensure that their organizations were able not only to meet the stringent service delivery requirements but also to keep costs down. HR managers in all of the organizations were reviewing existing shift patterns and prevailing patterns of workplace attendance. Attempts were made to facilitate this organizational flexibility with growing levels of temporary workers and/or agency workers. The influx of temporary workers was, however, fiercely rejected by strong union presence in Mirror and adherence to the collective agreement was maintained. Managers on site, however, recognized the delicate balancing act of ensuring cost pressures were managed but that the union was consulted and did not react unfavourably. It was clear that any industrial dispute which could escalate was to be avoided at all costs. One manager argued, 'I'm always conscious at the back of my mind if we do something on site here and a collective grievance is raised and then it could potentially be industrial action, if people threatened to like walk off site that's huge, that's massive press for [supermarket x]'.

The unremitting pressure to cut the costs was also manifest in all of the 3PLs systematically reviewing all of their HR policies and practices. As a result, policies such as shift patterns and working-time, bonus payments and sickness pay were all under scrutiny. Within Manoeuvre, for example, growing levels of sickness absence resulted in the company serving notice on the company's prevailing sick pay scheme under pressure from the customer. One manager recounted, 'that resulted in the unions saying, "Well, we're going to consult for industrial action". So at the final hour it was decided, "hold on, let's step back from the brink here and let's see if we can come up with a way of trying to reduce absence"'. Additional attempts were also made in Manoeuvre to further strip out what were regarded as additional 'unproductive' elements to the working day. Comfort breaks had been removed, which had resulted in the possibility of a collective grievance being raised.

The Battle over Value Capture: The Degradation of Work

This section explores how the concern to preserve value in motion extends to a battle over value capture between the retailers and the 3PL providers. The impact of this battle over value capture in concrete terms manifested in a greater degree of worker subordination and work degradation. This degradation took two forms. First, the implementation of time-and-motion studies which identified required levels of work effort and thus the removal of worker-autonomy and discretion. Second, and correspondingly, performance management techniques were implemented to render more visible and more accountable the commodity status of labour (see also Taylor, 2013).

It was acknowledged in all of the 3PLs that the capacity to focus on the performance of labour was predicated upon establishing required standards of workers' output and effort and measuring them more closely. As a result, all of the organizations employed external consultants to undertake time-and-motion studies to establish required 'norms' in levels of performance. From a management point of view this effectively eliminated the capacity of workers to shape and dictate the speed and intensity of their own work effort. Managers in both Mirror and Manoeuvre highlighted that warehouse work with its strong levels of union organization had traditionally been managed with high levels of informality, custom and practice and worker discretion. The physical size of these workplaces also enables workers to 'hide' and escape the management gaze. A warehouse manager in Mirror argued, 'basically we had some guys who would pick faster than others, and other guys we believe were just skiving and not really playing the game'. Supervisors in Mirror reinforced this view; one argued, 'it's a culture thing definitely, with those not wanting to work just going at their own pace'. Whilst piece rates and bonus payments may have managed (however crudely) the wage-effort bargain with a degree of consent, this approach was regarded as no longer feasible for the lean-retailing environment. A manager reported:

> [W]e've had all the functions measured by an outside company, time and motion people. They've told us based at walking pace, a 10 per cent rest and time to go to the toilet and that sort of idea and the time it takes them to put that case in the cage and then come back and get another case. They took all that into consideration, and obviously during the course of their eight hour shift they get more tired as the day goes on, they've come up with a rate per day. We then had to consult with the union and colleagues and say, look, we're going to bring guys in, this is what we're going to use.
>
> (Mirror Manager)

In addition, pickers working in the chilled warehouse (where products had limited shelf life and therefore had to be moved swiftly to dispatch) were required to wear watch scanners on their arms. These scanners allocated the work required, monitored activity and stored levels of effort. Supervisors reported that pickers found these scanners alienating and dehumanising; the suggestion was that pickers felt it was like 'Big Brother' watching you. One picker stated, '99 times out of 100 these are on our wrists, other people don't do it so often and when they say to Joe Bloggs "you've got to put a watch on" ... You feel as if somebody has just strangled their mother, the shock and horror on their faces that they've got to put a watch on'. A full-time union official representing workers in the sector highlighted that the cost pressures in the sector manifested in the removal of worker choice and decision-making. He argued,

> There is an indignity for the individual in that they no longer control their working day or the environment to any degree. They had choices to make, choices are all taken away. That is a big issue for us in terms of raising the profile on that. We saw that almost as an Americanization, if you like, of distribution and particularly warehouse picking coming insidiously into the UK.
>
> (Union FTO)

The limiting of opportunities for job rotation and multi-skilling to relieve the monotony of the working day was also attributed to a concern with achieving the required performance rates. In Mirror, particularly, pickers were concerned at the removal of this opportunity and reported on the negative impact this was having on the experience of work. Managers, however, acknowledged the contradictory pressures they faced in considering requests for job rotation. From a management point of view, greater performance levels could be achieved through familiarity and consistency with the role and its requirements. A manager argued, 'Job rotation sometimes means that people that aren't necessarily as good at one function or another. You need to have a fair crack at it, you can't just do a bit here and a bit there. If you're going to get good performance out of it you need guys to get continuity, get an understanding of how best to build a pallet'. Pickers similarly highlighted: 'At the end of the day all they see is figures, they can't get figures out the guys that rotate. It's common sense that you know the guys don't do the job very often, won't push the same amount of stuff than they guys doing it regular'.

Further attempts to reduce worker self-activity and invade any remaining pores in the working day were particularly evident in both Signal and Manoeuvre. Within Manoeuvre, the removal of the paid comfort breaks was causing levels of consternation and resentment. A warehouse manager revealed the level of discontent:

> We used to have people maybe go for their cigarette break or coffee break or whatever, it wasn't just really for smokers. But we took that away last May. The only time that they could have a cigarette or a coffee break was during their lunch break. We felt that, it's like everything else, it gets abused. We started off in saying right, so many people that had not hit certain targets they weren't allowed to go because the way we looked at it was if someone could go out there and have a quick cigarette or a quick cup of tea and it didn't affect their performance, we were happy for them to do that. But then you know people weren't achieving their targets. Obviously the client felt that having that paid break was enough because what was happening was it was maybe ten, 15 minutes in the morning and then one in the afternoon plus having their paid break as well.
>
> (Manager, Manoeuvre)

Performance management regimes were also implemented to ensure compliance to the required codes of performance and worker effort. In the absence of any additional payment and/or remuneration, increased levels of effort were 'delivered' by what could be regarded as forms of informal intimidation. As a result, all of the companies turned to the IT systems to monitor worker effort on a daily basis, resorting to direct supervision in the form of morning briefings as well as more implicit forms of coercion to deliver the required efforts. Signal and Manoeuvre introduced morning team briefing sessions, with hourly monitoring to ensure required levels were reached. The suggestion here was clear: if pickers could not be incentivized to work harder, they would have to be 'managed' to work to the required levels. As a result, first-line managers and supervisors were clearly responsible for delivering these results. Pickers in Signal highlighted that these meetings could be rather hostile, with supervisors often adopting a belligerent attitude. The rationale for the focus on results was recognized by the pickers in all of the organizations. One picker from Mirror argued, 'It's all down to figures and it's an arse-kicking thing right all the way down to us you know, from the top down; if they don't make their figures at the end of the day it's a domino effect isn't it and it happens and they're frightened for their job'. Supervisors in Signal were aware of the pressurized working environment but acknowledged the limited choice the organization faced given the demands placed upon them.

> It does feel as if you're constantly on these guys' back, constantly on their back, but we have to be, to make sure that we can get the work done. And to start with as well, kind of going down the lines of disciplinary action against a lot of these guys but as I said they've been given every opportunity. Obviously if the guys aren't hitting it then we're not hitting it, we're judged by what they do. Everybody is judged on, they say in here 'the pick is king in here', everything, as long as we pick the cases then everything else we can kind of let go slightly. We've got to make sure that we pick these cases.
>
> (Supervisor, Signal)

Within Signal and Manoeuvre, failure to meet the required standard would be met with an immediate 'informal' conversation with a supervisor. In Signal, this prompted a formal letter which would be sent to the picker's home outlining where and how their performance had been deficient. Only three formal letters would be tolerated in a six-month period. A fourth letter within the period would be escalated to formal disciplinary action. Within Manoeuvre a similar procedure was in place, whereby failure to meet the required standards was met with a warning procedure and further disciplinary action. Pickers acknowledged that Signal was, 'Disciplinary crazy. It is, it's like for the silliest little things'. Within Mirror, the levels of strong union organization meant that the introduction of the 'managed' performance was subject to on-going consultation and negotiation. The union was anxious to ensure that failure to meet the required levels of performance on a daily basis was not instantly met with disciplinary action.

Closing Comments

This chapter has explored how, theoretically and empirically, labour and the labour process can be situated at the centre of the articulated relations between production, distribution and exchange. It has been concerned with helping to overcome the missing link between labour process change at the point of production and wider global value chain analysis. The role of logistics within the contemporary political economy provides an insightful arena within which to explore more abstract theoretical concerns regarding the movement of value, referred to here as 'value in motion' within the circuit of capital, and how this impacts on the labour process at a more concrete level.

The evidence presented has explored the attempts by the dominant retailers to preserve value in motion (i.e. value created in production) by recasting relations with the 3PLs to their exacting requirements. As noted above, Harvey *et al.* (2002) have argued that retailers not only reconfigure relations under their exacting patronage, they also simultaneously 'orchestrate competition' amongst 3PLs as a mechanism to maximize profitability and drive down costs. Coe (2013), taking the argument forward, has emphasized the contested territory that logistics providers occupy. At one and the same time, these organizations contribute to value creation and capture for their clients, while simultaneously protecting and mobilizing their own interests. To preserve value in motion and essentially cut the costs associated with distribution, the retailers have adopted an array of techniques to drive down costs and reshape relations with the logistics providers. These mechanisms include orchestrated competition, the nature of the contract and stringent KPIs, all focused towards the required cost reductions. Indeed, for the logistics companies the continued survival of their contract is dependent not only on delivering the required KPIs but also searching for and securing further cost savings. Labour within these organizations is faced by pressures from both the retailers and their direct employer. As such the battle for value – either its capture or preservation – within these organizations is apparent; though as the evidence indicates, the sides of the battle are increasingly uneven.

The research also examined the impact of value in motion in more concrete terms on the labour process of these 3PLs. Referring to the dynamics of value capture, the evidence highlighted greater subordination of labour and work degradation. Employer attempts to remover worker self-activity, invade porosity and intensify the work process were all in evidence. The once necessary consent-making apparatus, regarded as a vital and valuable component in previous workplace regimes, had been ruthlessly abandoned (Burawoy, 1979; 1985). The structural dynamics, the recasting of relations between retailers and distribution, legitimized the particular direction to these labour process changes. However, where labour is organized and mindful of its unique position within the circuit of capital there remains some opportunity and some capacity to challenge the dynamics of 'value in motion'.

Notes

1 The concern of this chapter is not to repeat debates taking place elsewhere as to the relative merits of adopting the Global Value Chain or Global Production Network analysis. The term GPN is adopted in this chapter to reflect the wider embrace of this approach for integrating the labour process into wider production network (see Haidinger and Flecker (this volume).
2 Quoted in Nelson Lichtenstein's (2009) *The Retail Revolution: How Wal-Mart created a Brave New World of Business.*

REFERENCES

Abernathy, F. H., Dunlop, J., Hammond, J. H. and Weil, D. (1999) *A Stitch in Time: Lean Retailing and the Transformation of Manufacturing*, New York: Oxford University Press.

Bonacich, E. and Wilson, J. (2008) *Getting the Goods: Ports, Labor and the Logistics Revolution*, Ithaca and London: Cornell University Press.

Burawoy, M. (1979) *Manufacturing Consent: Changes in the Labor Process Under Monopoly Capitalism*, Chicago: University of Chicago Press.

Burawoy, M. (1985) *The Politics of Production: Factory Regimes under Capitalism and Socialism*, London: Verso.

Cho, E., Christman, A., Emsellem, M., Ruckelshaus, C. and Smith, R. (2012) *Chain of Greed: How Walmart's Domestic Outsourcing Produces Everyday Low Wages and Poor Working Conditions for Warehouse Workers*, New York: National Employment Law Project.

Coe, N. (2013) 'Missing links: logistics, governance and upgrading in a shifting global economy', *Review of International Political Economy*, 21(1), 224–256.

Coe, N., Dicken, P. and Hess, M. (2008) 'Global production networks: realizing the potential', *Journal of Economic Geography*, 8(3): 271–295.

Cumbers, A., Nativel, C. and Routledge, P. (2008) 'Labour agency and union positionalities in global production networks', *Journal of Economic Geography*, 8(3): 369–387.

Fernie, J., Sparks, L. and McKinnon, A. C. (2010) 'Retail logistics in the UK: past, present and future', *International Journal of Retail & Distribution Management*, 38(11/12), 894–914.

Fine, B. and Leopold, E. (1993) *The World of Consumption*, London: Routledge.
Flecker, J. and Meil, P. (2010) 'Organisational restructuring and emerging value chains: implications for work and employment', *Work, Employment and Society*, 24(4): 680–698.
Hamilton, G. and Petrovic, M. (2011) 'Retailers as market makers', in G. Hamilton, M. Petrovic and B. Senauer (eds) *The Market Makers: How Retailers are Reshaping the Global Economy*, Oxford: Oxford University Press.
Harvey, D. (2007) *The Limits to Capital*, London: Verso.
Harvey, M., Quilley, S. and Beynon, H. (2002) *Exploring the Tomato: Transformations of Nature, Society and Economy*, Cheltenham: Edward Elgar Publishing.
Hess, M. (2002) *Missing links: geographies of distribution*. Paper to AAG-Conference, Los Angeles/California.
Hess, M. and Rodrigue, J. P. (2004) 'The transport geography of logistics and freight distribution', *Journal of Transport Geography*, 12(3).
Hess, M. and Rodrigue, J. P. (2006) 'Global production networks and the role of logistics and transportation', *Growth and Change*, 37: 499–509.
Jaffe, D. (2010) 'Labor and the geographic reorganization of container shipping in the U.S.', *Growth and Change* (December 2010), 41(4): 520–539.
Lichtenstein, N. (2009) *The Retail Revolution: How Wal-Mart Created a Brave New World of Business*, New York: Henry Holt and Company.
Newsome, K. (2010) 'Employment in distribution and exchange: moments in the circuit of capital', *Industrial Relations Journal*, 41(3): 190–205.
Rainnie, A., Herod, A. and McGrath-Champ, S. (2011) 'Review and positions: global production networks and labour', *Competition and Change*, 15(20): 155–169.
Riisgaard, L. and Hammer, N. (2011) 'Prospects for labour in global value chains: labour standards in the cut flower and banana industries', *British Journal of Industrial Relations*, 49(1): 168–190.
Selwyn, B. (2012) 'Beyond firm-centrism: re-integrating labour and capitalism into global commodity chain analysis', *Journal of Economic Geography*, 12(2): 205–226.
Taylor, P. (2010) 'The globalization of service work: analysing the transnational call centre value chain', in P. Thompson and C. Smith (eds) *Working Life: Renewing Labour Process Analysis*, Basingstoke: Palgrave Macmillan, pp. 244–268.
Taylor, P. (2013) *Performance Management and the New Workplace Tyranny: A Report for the Scottish Trades Union Congress*, Glasgow: Strathclyde University.
Taylor, P., Newsome, K. and Rainnie, A. (2013) 'Putting labour in its place: global value chains and labour process analysis introduction', *Competition and Change*, 17(1): 1–5.

CHAPTER 3

Labour and Asymmetric Power Relations in Global Value Chains: The Digital Entertainment Industries and Beyond

Paul Thompson, Rachel Parker and Stephen Cox

The chapter draws on research that situates development studios – games and visual effects (VFX) – in the global value chain, concerned with issues of control and value capture faced by small and medium-sized producers of digital entertainment products. In the context of the relevant industries, it shows how mainstream global value chain (GVC) perspectives are unable to deal with asymmetric power relations between capitals and between capital and labour. A preliminary model of value and power dynamics is developed that goes beyond complexity of information exchange, codifiability and competence of the supplier base (cf. Gereffi et al., 2005), in part by incorporating labour power – value inputs, agency and impacts – more fully into the framework. The chapter is, therefore, a contribution both to developing less workplace-centric versions of labour process theory and exploring its compatibility with value chain models that have a more radical intent.

Problems and Problematics

Locating and explaining the dynamics of work relations at workplace level has become progressively more challenging as intra- and inter-organizational relations have become more complex, employment systems more fragmented and business environments subject to continual restructuring within national and global contexts. The need for revised conceptual frameworks has also been driven by recognition of the limits of single, workplace or company case studies and the need for multi-case, multi-levelled approaches. It is within such a problematic that the particular challenge for labour process theory (LPT) can be situated. Though mainstream LPT has always been framed in terms of the causal pathways between capitalist political economy (CPE) and work/employment relations, it has often lacked the meso-level research tools needed to bridge the gap. Despite favouring industry-level analysis, the links have tended to be made in terms of generic features of capitalism, national varieties or modes of accumulation such as Fordism and post-Fordism.

As this volume reflects, there are a number of options available for making such connections along a GVC-global production network (GPN) spectrum. Building on a small amount of existing research following a similar path (e.g. Flecker and Meil, 2010; Flecker et al., 2013), this chapter opts to explore the extent to which a modified GVC framework is the most appropriate direction. The growing prominence and popularity of GVC analysis has led to some critiques, friendly and otherwise. Some, particularly those influenced by radical economic geography, have focused on the development of an alternative GPN perspective (Coe et al., 2008; Cumbers et al., 2008). Objections to GVC focus on the preference of that perspective for the linear governance structures of lead firms. In contrast, GPN approaches have a much broader scope, with multi-level analyses that examine more fluid networks of power, complex interactions between actors in the creation of value and intra-firm and non-firm actors such as functional groups, labour, consumers and non-governmental organizations. Many of these points are accurate and pertinent. The point with respect to labour is of particular importance for this book. Though there is some recognition that the availability of types of labour (cheaper, more mobile, more skilled) might affect contractual or other aspects of exchange, it is now widely acknowledged that the GVC mainstream neglects labour as a source and/or target of GVC dynamics (see for example, Newsome et al., 2013).

Despite all these criticisms, the essential rationale for exploring the potential for GVC frameworks is precisely their more parsimonious character. LPT needs expanded tools to address more complex industry structures, particularly within globalizing contexts. GPN critiques of GVC frameworks have focused particularly on that parsimony. Yet, Selwyn (2011: 2) is, in our view, rightly sceptical of attempts to 'incorporate all the relevant actors, relationships and network configurations' in a meaningful way in a single framework. For all its imperfections, GVC has offered a theory-building project that can, in principle, link issues of power and value capture to inter-firm dynamics and industry restructuring. There is a danger that LPT would swap a workplace-centric focus for a 'theory of everything'.

Having set out our general intent, the rest of this chapter unfolds as follows. We begin by exploring the expanding emergent commentaries and critiques of the dominant governance model, with the objective of developing a post-GVC model that can address some of the main concerns. The question of labour – the main concern of this volume – is a wider one than governance. We review existing attempts to insert and integrate labour, largely from a GPN perspective, before again setting out some alternatives. Finally, we seek to apply that new approach to labour to the digital entertainment industries. We show that while Australian games development firms are participating to a greater extent in global markets, the power asymmetries along the value chain have resulted in a situation in which they are at a severe disadvantage, with largely negative consequences for labour.

What GVC Doesn't Explain or Explain Well Enough

The governance structure taxonomy developed by Gereffi *et al.* (2005) has facilitated a significant growth in research and theory building. As is well known, their theory of GVC governance rests on the 'three Cs': complexity of information exchange, codifiability of that information/knowledge and competence/capacity of the suppliers. Whilst all these questions are legitimate, particularly with respect to issues of upgrading (of companies and countries), they lead to a focus on particular linear and dyadic transactions. Power and value are then filtered through a narrow(er) lens. As Gibbon *et al.* (2008: 323) note, 'the theory of GVC governance suggests that power is a contingent property of only certain types of inter-firm coordination'. A firm-level dyadic focus is thus unable or less likely to 'see' and explain broader changes in the political economy, for example concentration of capital or financialization (Milberg, 2008; Palpacuer, 2008).

Recent papers from scholars with at least one foot inside the GVC tent have identified some of the underlying reasons for a 'progressive narrowing' of governance and chain constructs from their inception in World Systems and Global Commodity Chain (GCC) frameworks (Gibbon *et al.* 2008; Bair, 2009). The latter focuses on the influence of 'network epistemologies', particularly those deriving from embeddedness arguments, originally associated with Granovetter (1985). Without sketching the detail or trajectory, it can be observed that this was premised more on interpersonal relations between actors and on trust as a mechanism of coordination. This kind of analysis was transferred or transposed to inter-firm coordination and networks were presented as a governance form in their own right, distinct from markets and hierarchies. Such analyses tended to 'privilege the local':

> ... because these are the contexts in which we can see at work the social structure that is at the explanatory core of the embeddedness paradigm – that is, networks of interpersonal relations. This micro-sociological conception of how social structure shapes economic outcomes produces what Hess (2004) calls an over-territorialized conception of embeddedness that neglects the multi-scalar dynamics of the global economy and the international dimension of contemporary economic organization.
> (Bair, 2008: 347)

However, a narrowing of the GVC frame is, arguably, more directly influenced by the importing of transaction cost economics than the embeddedness paradigm. In what Gibbon *et al.* (2008) dub the 'coordination turn', the focus of GVC is narrowed to inter-firm coordination and bilateral dependencies focusing on asset specificity – the core idea underlying the 3Cs. In previous frameworks such as global commodity chain (GCC), transaction costs had been only one factor affecting the organizational and spatial configuration of chains (Bair, 2008: 347). The 3Cs are important, but taken in isolation, or more precisely only or primarily in terms of dyadic interactions, they can be limited or misleading. Taken together, network epistemologies and the 3Cs narrow the frame, 'at the cost of a broader conceptualization of governance dynamics across the chain' (Bair, 2008: 353). Power becomes reduced to coordinative capacity, and key dimensions of the political economy are sidelined.

What of value?

> The trend toward a re-configuration of GVC analysis in terms of mainstream economics or some version of economic sociology has had the apparent side effect of moving practitioners' interest away from discussions of 'value' (a topic that an innocent observer might assume should lie at the heart of theories of global value chains).
> (Gibbon *et al.*, 2008: 331)

These authors argue that the question of value has two components: how value is created and how it is distributed. The first has been increasingly ignored, while the latter is largely untheorized, but implicitly or explicitly focuses on shares of final prices captured by actors at different links in particular chains. We can argue about how value is created and calculated, but again the main need is surely to move to a broader understanding of the conditions under which value *capture* takes place. This requires an emphasis on putting capital back in the picture. In the recent period this has tended to fall to researchers focusing on the significance of financialization. A metaphor used by Gibbon *et al.* (2008) is governance as driving, but who or what is doing it? In the past, lead-firm type has distinguished between buyer- (commercial capital) and producer-driven (industrial capital) chains. Whilst a focus on circuits of capital is useful, capital markets have become more important to the picture in the contemporary political economy (Thompson, 2013).

In an overview of macro-economic conditions leading to financialization in global chains, Milberg observes that 'externalization has developed from the logic of vertically integrated markets, with continued competition among suppliers, offloading of risk and increased focus on core competence; all aimed at raising shareholder value' (2008: 434). Palpacuer reinforces that view, arguing that pressures on suppliers from global buyers are no longer stemming only from competitive dynamics in product markets, but from the financialization of lead firms, and that 'intensification in corporate reporting to financial markets induced a more stringent monitoring of suppliers' performance based on formal systems of supplier relation management' (2008: 399). Financialization is only one, albeit significant, dimension of the need to focus on how actually existing capital shapes and constrains inter-firm relations at points in the chain. This process will be explored further with respect to digital entertainment industries later in the chapter.

Beyond (More) Missing Links – a Post-GVC Framework?

We began this chapter by referring to the omission or marginalization of labour in GVC and related frameworks. Bair (2008: 347) argues that it is necessary to go back to World Systems Theory to find a focus on labour in and beyond transaction costs. The immediate predecessor of the GVC theory, GCC analysis, was framed in terms of upgrading within the international division of labour and studies tended to deal only indirectly with the impact on labour from buyer-driven commodity chains. The problem is that in a focus on upgrading or dyadic inter-firm relations, the experiences and interests of labour tend to be subsumed within consideration of the supplier position (Palpacuer, 2008: 402).

As we shall see in the following section, the neglect of labour has been partly rectified, at least in broader GPN literatures. Picking up on this point, however, Smith (2014: 1) argues that 'the same cannot be said for analyses of the state'. He accepts that there has been some recognition of institutional and regulatory frameworks that add the state as an actor, particularly in promoting or constraining upgrading. However, Smith persuasively argues that it is not enough to consider the state as part of the context, for this 'has not provided a framework for understanding the articulation between state regulation, production networks and the wider accumulation strategies of which they are a part' (2014: 2).

Where do all these missing links and misconceptualizations leave us? In the two papers from Gibbon et al. (2008) and Bair (2008) that we have drawn from, the answer sometimes seems to be a preference for returning to some kind of GCC analysis, or scaling down the by now ubiquitous governance categories/typology of Gereffi et al. (2005) to a 'methodology' that can be enacted within different theoretical perspectives. However, it is not entirely clear what GVC as methodology option entails, and a danger would be that it evades questions about what would enable GVC categories to support better explanation. The diagram below sketches the outlines of an alternative. It seeks to elaborate a bigger 'chain' picture without falling into a multi-factor 'theory of everything'. Furthermore, it is broadly consistent with Gibbon et al.'s (2008: 333) call for moving away from viewing governance simply as a combination of specific 'coordination' issues between firms, and towards viewing governance more in the context of other factors such as firm size, market share and external regulatory environments.

In identifying issues concerning capital, labour and the state, the aim is to focus on prior 'driving' questions that help to locate or frame inter-firm relations across the whole chain, irrespective of what the concrete empirical focus is within particular parts. So, for example, what is the extent and character of market concentration; how financialized are the lead firms; and is there identifiable strategic coupling between lead firms and state actors? In particular, it is important to restore some of the earlier emphasis on lead firms and their 'external' relations, given that the 'lead firms have continued to dictate the terms and conditions of participation in networks and chains through different types of governance that act upon participants "at a distance"' (Neilson et al., 2014: 2). Five further points need to be made concerning this mapping. First, there is no intent to present or develop a totalizing model along the lines of regulation theory, in which integrated structures all function to reproduce capitalism. Domains should be treated as distinctive entities with various degrees of connection and disconnection (see Thompson, 2013). Second, though these entities have their own trajectories, they are overlapping and part of the challenge is to provide, for example, 'a framework for

A post-GVC framework?

International political economy / architecture of global economic organization

Capital	Labour	State
Accumulation regime	Managerial regime	Regulatory regime
Market concentration	Labour power	State strategies at
Conditions of competition	Labour's power	different scales
Circuits and fractions of capital		Institutional norms

◄──────────────── intermediaries ────────────────►

value ◄──────────────────────────────────► power

Network governance – dynamics

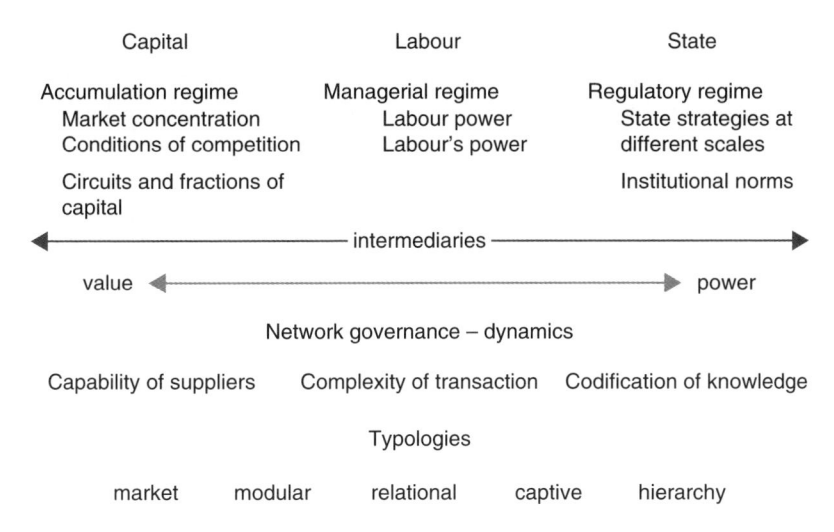

Capability of suppliers   Complexity of transaction   Codification of knowledge

Typologies

market   modular   relational   captive   hierarchy

Figure 3.1 A post-GVC framework

understanding the articulation between state regulation, production networks and the wider accumulation strategies of which they are a part' (Smith, 2014: 2). Third, the value–power line is there simply to indicate that the interplay of material and symbolic power resources and value capture takes place in the spheres between and within the macro regime and 'localized' network governance dynamics.

Part of the process that links domains together is the enhanced role of intermediaries such as consultants, labour market agencies and standard-setters (Coe and Jordhus-Lier, 2011; Neilson et al., 2014). As the latter note, 'These firm and non-firm intermediaries not only bridge and connect different value chains and production networks, but also offer other unique inputs, mostly intangible in nature, to make those networks work' (2014: 2). Fourth, capital, labour and the state are neither simply context nor background noise that can be bracketed out or only considered if the 'first cut' does not find the predicted governance patterns (Sturgeon in Bair, 2009: 357). These domains are *always* implicated in chain dynamics, though in different ways and to different extents. Fifth, what we are presenting here is to be understood as a two-way street rather than a set of top-down influences. To quote Neilson et al. (2014: 3) again, 'GVCs/GPNs impact recursively within the arenas in which they are connected' and this might include anything from pressure on the state to liberalize wage policies or to enhance research and training infrastructures. In sum, if these five points are taken into consideration when considering second-order questions about governance and asset specificity within dyads, or any other interactions within a chain segment, better explanations of chain dynamics are possible. That is not to say that the '3Cs' are simply left intact. Conceptualizations of power and value need to be strengthened, and, pertinent to this chapter, a stronger sense of labour characteristics needs to be folded into categories such as supplier capability and codification. Whether the existing five-governance typology is sustainable or will need modification is a question that can be left open to further research and theory building.

In this short explanation of the diagram, little mention has been made of labour because the rest of the chapter explores that dimension.

The Labour Problem(atic)

We have already noted the omission or marginalization of labour in GVC analysis. The partial and more recent exception focuses on upgrading, particularly in the context of the 'Capturing the Gains project' (http://www.capturingthegains.org/). Any attention paid to labour issues is welcome and such interventions are normatively linked to a decent work agenda associated with the International Labour Organization and other global bodies. However, these tend to be questions framed by an economic development agenda that is not necessarily coextensive with a labour focus per se. Furthermore, there is a naivety in some of the assumptions that 'moving along the value chain' and ensuring greater value capture is necessarily or predominantly associated with favourable outcomes for labour through various types of upgrading and higher skill content of jobs.

Whatever the merits or otherwise of this approach, it is in GPN debates that one finds a more appropriate starting point for a more detailed examination of the labour problematic. As Coe and Jordhus-Lier (2011) note in their excellent overview, much of that debate has been initiated and sustained by labour geographers, with many, especially in the first phase, determined to 'celebrate the agency of labour' and identify forms of 'heydays' and collective resistance. Two papers in the GPN and labour debate (Cumbers *et al.*, 2008; Selwyn, 2011) are particularly pertinent as they have some engagement with labour process themes. Cumbers *et al.* (2008: 371) argue that traditional (GVC/GPN) approaches are capital- and state-centric. Both papers want to go further than inserting labour as an additional actor. Selwyn argues for seeing labour as having a co-constitutive role in capitalist development. Drawing on autonomist Marxism, Cumbers *et al.* go further, placing labour agency, exploitation and class conflict at the centre of GPN dynamics. Though formulating their positions on agency in slightly different ways, both papers suggest that there are two dimensions to the way that the labour problem inserts itself into the logic of accumulation. On the one hand, there is the way in which abstract labour or labour power is mobilized, controlled and organized to produce the surplus. On the other are attempts by labour to leverage its positionality within relevant chains/networks to increase its share of the surplus. Setting aside the assumption – deriving from the labour theory of value – that abstract labour is the sole source of the surplus, this leads to a useful distinction between labour power and labour's power.

What is more contentious are the imputed connections between the processes. Labour power, agency and resistance are placed at the centre of capital accumulation. This is expressed in different ways in the two papers. For Selwyn (2011), labour regimes are the defining feature of GPNs and stretch from the workplace to commodity specialism and the whole sphere of social reproduction. Cumbers *et al.* (2008) meanwhile argue that 'capital is viewed as responding to the problem of labour control' (372) and is always 'in flight from labour', responding to the problem of value extraction from labour in production. It might seem odd for us to argue that LPT puts or should put less emphasis on labour or at least labour control, but a brief re-cap of some theoretical context might help. Second wave LPT was built around control and resistance models, so such emphases have clear echoes. However, mainstream LPT tends not to make such expansive claims about labour regimes. Following the notion of the relative autonomy of the labour process (Edwards, 1990), most researchers focus on the role of labour agency and capital-labour dynamics as a key driver of *workplace* social relations, avoiding any necessary connection to issues concerning the reproduction of capitalism as a whole. To make our critique of the positions in the two papers clear, focusing on exploitation and control of labour as *the* defining feature of capitalist development repeats a mistake made in earlier debates concerning the need to understand the role of the full circuit of capital in regimes of accumulation. In other words, whilst labour control is an integral feature of the transformation of labour power into profitable labour, it would be a mistake to define GPNs or GVCs solely or primarily as labour control regimes. One danger is that analyses move from being firm-centric to firms (and capital) being largely absent. As Coe and Jordhus-Lier (2011: 221) note, 'A fundamental starting point for a reassessment of labour agency has to be the changing nature and scale of the organisation of capital'.

There is a second problem concerning labour agency. Despite complaining that such agency is often conflated with trade unions as collective actors (Cumbers et al., 2008: 371), union strategies in the global economy is the empirical focus of that paper. Selwyn (2011: 18), similarly, utilizes a broader frame that is concerned with the 'experiences of working class formation in zones of commodity production'. There is nothing wrong with focusing empirically on such matters, but it may not be relevant to issues of labour agency in many workplaces. Researchers within a labour process and radical political economy tradition need to allow for the fact that 'positionality in relation to processes of value capture' (Cumbers et al., 2008: 373) may give little or no leverage to labour as a collective, organized actor, or that workers may choose not to exercise leverage collectively. Or to put it in Selwyn's favoured terminology, structural power at work may be associated with weak associational power.

In the absence of collective mobilization, that may mean that a local story in parts of a chain/network may be about impacts *on* labour. That does not mean that labour agency is irrelevant or marginal in struggles over value. LPT is premised on the indeterminacy of labour. Labour power is always both acted on and active in that struggle In general, however, there is a need to be clearer about what explanatory problem inserting labour is seeking to solve. We would distinguish between three categories: inputs, impact and agency. Labour may not often co-determine GVC/GPN dynamics, but labour power (cost and characteristics) is a significant input in decisions on sourcing and location, and issues of skill utilization, control and work intensity are central to value capture and distribution. Such processes overlap into the sphere of impacts. GVC analyses in particular need to do more to show how the division of labour along value chains and changes in work flows impact on employment relations and work practices' (Flecker et al., 2013). Contrary to the largely optimistic upgrading narrative, work externalization, subcontracting and other processes frequently lead to deteriorating work conditions at the base of the chain (Palpacuer, 2008: 401–405). Nor is it confined to that end. Flecker and Meil (2010: 694–695) demonstrate how even in industries such as software development, upgrading in service providers may lead to restructuring and job insecurity in the core firm.

With respect to agency, it is important that discussion does not simply become another territory to re-run mobilization and/or resistance debates. Whilst there is of course scope to apply concepts such as resistance, reworking and resilience to agency in chains and networks (see Coe and Jordhus-Lier, 2011: 216–218; Coe, 2013), a more concrete approach would draw on the relations between structural and associational power adapted by Selwyn (2011) from Erik Olin Wright. A framework of this sort has been recently outlined by Lakhani *et al.* (2013). Extending the 'configurational' approach embodied in Gereffi *et al.*'s governance typology, the authors 'argue that employment relations systems in GVCs need to be assessed on the basis of their specific configurations of firm interdependencies, task complexities and supplier capabilities' (2013: 7). They go on to develop employment system propositions allied to the five governance types. Such an approach has the definite advantage of integrating labour issues more closely into the 3Cs – complexity, codifiability and competence. However, it also suffers from the limitations of its 'parent'. Despite some reference to employment relations across chains, the focus remains on 'coordination between two links (or firms) in a chain' (2013: 8). The proposed micro-level configurations therefore suffer from the same problem – the bigger picture is bracketed off. As a result employment relations outcomes tend to be read-off from the dyadic relationship – for example, the assumption that (relational) chains that involve complex tasks performed by skilled workers are likely to offer stable employment. The problem with this assumption is that employment stability is not primarily a property of the dyadic relationship, as we shall see in the next section. The larger contexts of industry and political economy matter, and with this in mind, the final substantive section below returns to the two industries – VFX and games – to make some first and second order observations about labour.

Making the Link in High-Tech Creative Industries

We examine these issues further in the context of research into two digital content-based entertainment industries – visual effects for films, and games for both consoles and mobile devices. In both industries, data was gathered primarily through over 80 semi-structured interviews in two stages. In the first stage, interviews with firm owners were wide ranging and covered the range of issues necessary to identify key dynamics of the industry associated with financing, design, production and distribution and how these dynamics were affected by the structure of the global industry and international market developments. The interviews with employees/developers were also wide ranging and focused on the nature of work and employment within the industry as well as the nature of the labour process, covering hours of work, conditions of employment, levels of autonomy and how these were affected by the nature of the industry context as described in the first round of interviews.

Visual effects and games are now massive global industries. Digital entertainment is a particularly appropriate sector for GVC analysis. The task components of such 'immaterial' commodities can be allocated on a truly global basis, even to the margins. For example, with spiralling game development costs, increased competition and pressure to speed up the development cycle, publishers are taking advantage of digitalized technologies to (out)source work to an increasingly spatially dispersed 'network' of developers. As a consequence we can observe not only vertical but virtual integration of ownership and activities. Within these processes, conglomerate corporations form part of a shared ecology with 'SMEs, connected through a myriad of horizontal relationships in specific locations' (Fitzgerald, 2015: 1).

Gereffi *et al.* (2005) argue that the concept of a 'relational value chain' best describes the governance models of global value chains in industries in which (1) there is an exchange of complex information that cannot be codified and therefore relies on factors such as reputation and trust-building; (2) transactions are complex; and (3) supplier capabilities are high. On the surface this mirrors the characteristics of the VFX industry, which involves the provision of a service which is difficult to specify in advance, depends on ongoing communication and negotiation between the service provider and customer throughout the process of service provision, and in which the creative and technical capabilities of service providers and their employees are high. Furthermore, these capabilities are difficult to replicate in that they depend on prior experience in completing projects within the very limited Hollywood market and the time-consuming development of relationships with Hollywood producers. As with the VFX industry, the console games industry is characterized by repeated information exchange between developers and publishers/console manufacturers throughout the development process, and repeat business (rather than arms-length transactions) is the norm (Johns, 2006; Kerr, 2006).

Despite the appearance of a relational value chain with implied horizontal networks and dispersed power and opportunities for value capture, both industries demonstrate features of concentration and bottleneck (Jacobides *et al.*, 2006; Parker *et al.*, 2014). For example, the power of Hollywood studios is extensive at all points of the value chain from writing to distribution. Within the global film value chain, the production sector, of which VFX is a part, remains relatively independent from these media conglomerates in the sense that there are a large number of semi-independent production companies, although these companies remain dependent on the media conglomerates for finance and distribution (Coe and Johns, 2004). Australian VFX firms operating in the Hollywood global film production network are required to form close relations with Hollywood VFX supervisors and producers in order to facilitate complex information exchange regarding the nature of the VFX images and services. However, their relational interactions are moderated by the bottleneck position of Hollywood media conglomerates and therefore characterized by unequal power relations. As such, VFX firms struggle to capture value in these negotiations.

In the games industry, the console manufacturers and games publishers are positioned in the central regional locations of the USA, Japan and Europe and clearly dominate the industry. There is a trend towards industry concentration who play an important role in connecting games developers to global markets (Johns, 2006; Kerr, 2006; Martin and Deuze, 2009). Games developers create software titles that are played on specific console platforms. There is a complex competition for value capture between console manufacturers, publishers, development studios and retailers. Development studios are both the creative core and the weakest link in the chain, relatively isolated in terms of network connectivity and largely dependent on publishers for finance. Publishers, sometimes collaborating or overlapping in ownership with console manufacturers, are the fulcrum of power. This power is focused on market concentration, control of intellectual property rights, access to finance, transfer of risk and greater mobility/switching capacity. Industry concentration increased from the 1990s as game production costs escalated and firms sought economies of scale through acquisitions of successful independent developers. The dominant business model for Australian firms has traditionally been as second-party developers and working on licensed products.

After a period of significant expansion and maturation, the industry restructured and underwent a shake-out in the context of the global financial crash (GFC). This led to many closures and further concentration, with a smaller number of mid-sized firms servicing the console market and a new array of micro firms entering the casual gaming segment. This segment in principle offered up possibilities of different governance dynamics in the value chain, given lowered barriers to entry, formal independence during the development process and a move towards transactional, arms-length relations. However, a different basis for unequal bargaining power has emerged. The gatekeeper role of publishers has shifted but remains as quality controller. Lead firms (notably Apple and Google) are setting standards designed to make it hard for developers to switch between platforms, maintaining their bottleneck position that lock developers in to particular devices. Lead firms benefit from a combination of limited competition within the segment and intense competition amongst suppliers (Parker et al., 2014).

In digital entertainment, there are value capture options available. Upgrading might involve 'moving into content' through various means of capturing intellectual property rights, for example in a film project. This would normally involve some version of 'going global'. Successful Australian VFX firms such as Animal Logic have committed significant resources to developing and maintaining relationships with critical Hollywood decision-makers, including establishing offices in Los Angeles. This would be consistent with relational value chains in which reputational networks depend, in part, on close, face-to-face, repeated interactions between the key players. However, this path is a distinctly minority one, only available to the 'big boys' who have close networks with the studios and a track record delivering on large VFX projects. For the vast majority of development studios reputation is established primarily through market considerations associated with quality and cost and this is a very unequal struggle. These are professional service firms whose costing structure normally involves a fixed fee, whereby the risk lies with them rather than the buyer if work is unable to be completed within budget. A major issue for the service firm is how to cost variations which the director or producer often request when they are not happy with the product as projects unfold. 'Intangible service delivery' may be relational, but those relations are sufficiently hierarchical to place major constraints on capturing the value they create in films and games.

Labour in Digital Entertainment

Development studios in both industries are the creative core, but they are also the weak link in the struggle for value capture between the major actors. A fundamental issue is one of risk and its transfer. Though referring to a broader set of cultural commodities in audio-visual industries, Fitzgerald (2015) confirms the point in the observation that the majority of the costs and risks of production are borne by a myriad of relatively smaller, flexible and therefore often expendable firms. The core of this dynamic arises from the fact that supplier firms are constantly pitching for new work and trying to build reputation and trust with buyers. Yet VFX and games are characterized by a high degree of uncertainty regarding how the potential product will evolve during the course of development and therefore on the process of managing contract variation. This puts a premium on processes such as budgeting and time scheduling. Yet, what has often been neglected is the ways in which those issues of costs and risks are reflected and reproduced in the management of work and employment relations in the supplier firms. So, for example, where development studios are paid a fixed sum in a negotiated production contract with periodic advances throughout the development process, under-pricing and over-promising are persistent problems that shape contract variation. As a result, a portion of that risk is transferred to labour, given that creative labour power – high quality work at lower and controlled costs – is predominantly what the firm is selling to the corporate buyer. In other words, we have to recognize the links between winning work and constraints on labour *at* work.

Interviews with employees in development studios reveal that the uneven power struggle between firms in the value chain and the subsequent cost pressures have significant effects on and in the workflow (see Thompson *et al.*, 2015 for a more detailed analysis). These take three main forms. First, there are tightened controls. Complex tasks cannot be cannot be micro-managed, but within the delivery of projects oversight and direction can be strengthened. Respondents in both industries referred to what might be termed a system of dual control, whereby the firm manages relations with the client or its agent (for example an independent VFX supervisor acting on behalf of a Hollywood major) and exerts greater control over quality and costs within the project teams. This is typically expressed in the form of mini-hierarchies within functional groups (e.g. compositors, coders, artists) led by directors or overall supervisors. Employees made frequent reference to greater accountability to and interference by external agents, with the pipeline or workflow increasingly structured according to 'milestones' and organized through what one employee described as a 'strictly hierarchical structure'. Such trends are confirmed in other studies; Deuze *et al.* (2007: 350) refer to 'tighter supervisory procedures' and 'multiple milestones'.

Second, there is enhanced specialization. Within firms, there are still generalists as well as specialists, but with added complexity and the need for speed and reliability comes pressures to divide tasks and streamline the sequencing:

> It's definitely got more specialized. In the past you needed to have a broader skill set ... But now there is literally a person for everything ... and you can just focus on your niche and just improve your skill set in that area, just to be more productive.
>
> (VFX employee)

Third, there is the squeezing of additional effort from the collective creative process. Work intensity has traditionally been temporally uneven with that squeeze focused on extra hours and effort during 'crunch time' at the end of projects. This still continues in some companies and projects, but many respondents also reported faster work pace and pressure to 'do more with less' (games employee) and accomplish 'a lot more work in the same, if not less time' (VFX employee). The link to power asymmetry and contract variation is made clear in this observation from a VFX employee in a different firm: 'So there's a constant battle going on when companies just try to get jobs for less pay in total, which again forces them to deliver more work in less period of time and with less people'.

What do these trends mean for categories outlined in the previous session? Labour power issues are connected to the input and impact dimensions. The latter has been outlined through the triple trends just discussed. In terms of input, we have not dealt with the availability of qualified labour and its relationship with locational and sourcing issues. Our focus has been the centrality of labour power characteristics to 'supplier competence', to managerial intervention in the labour process and to the ability of development studios to deliver on their 'relational' exchanges with lead firms that occupy a dominant or bottleneck position in the chain. One of the outcomes of this particular dynamic is a certain degree of standardization and specialization, or what Flecker *et al.* (2013: 14) refer to as a tension between the 'circulation and codification of knowledge'.

As for labour's power and agency issues, games and VFX workers have traditionally occupied a relatively advantageous structural position so that associational power was largely unnecessary. In the early growth stages of both industries, a mainly young, internationally mobile and male talent pool was able to leverage expertise and mobility to access high-tech, high-status employment. Traditionally that mobile labour force was able to utilize exit to other firms and technology-intensive sectors rather than voice. However, a combination of the global financial crisis and the concentration of power in the two chains has led to greater instability and insecurity. We undertook our interviews in games firms after the financial crisis, which led to a significant shake-out in the industry, involving tighter budgets, shrunken workforces and disappearing or downsized firms. Our interviews revealed a clear trend of weakening work and industry attachments, if not organized opposition. Our interviews with VFX workers were undertaken prior to the equivalent restructuring and shake-out, so industry attachments were still relatively strong. Yet there have been subsequent rumblings of discontent and collective action as conditions worsen (for example see http://vfxtippingpoint.blogspot.co.uk/).

Conclusions

Whilst we agree with Bair (2008) and Taylor (2010) that there is value in GCC, GPN and GVC frameworks, and that their usefulness will depend on which scalar level or theoretical issue is being addressed, we have chosen to explore relations between modified GPN categories and LPT. The main reason is that in moving away from workplace-centric orientations, LPT has needed conceptual and methodological tools at a meso-level more than it has needed to become part of an all-encompassing theory-building project (that GPN has a tendency towards). In our review of the GVC framework and its application to digital entertainment, we have been very critical of the limitations of its conceptual categories. As we indicated earlier, using the Gereffi *et al.* framework, these industries should resemble relational governance, but they don't. In our view, this is a conceptual rather than a category error and one that cannot be rectified by reclassifying the governance dynamics found in these chains as modular or captive. However, we remain open to further exploration of whether a revised, multi-level approach offers a way forward. Our contribution to that offers a preliminary heuristic that adds an explanatory layer focusing on a 'higher' level of 'governance' that would compel investigations of chain dynamics (dyadic or otherwise) to consider core questions on capital, state and labour influences and interactions.

Implicit in the above is a contribution to the development of LPT and its capacity to engage in industry-level analysis at a global(izing) level. Part of that reorientation is situating LPT more clearly as part of the 'family' of radical political economy approaches, as well as a mainstay of the sociology of work. Part of what LPT brings to the political economy table is an extensive track record of research and concept development on labour issues. Bringing insights from that tradition to bear on the burgeoning debate on labour and GVC/GPN is a further contribution, in this case utilizing more careful distinctions between what labour issues are being inserted – inputs, impacts and agency. Again, it remains to be seen the extent to which labour can be successfully integrated into GVC governance categories.

Finally, drawing from more detailed examinations elsewhere (Parker *et al.*, 2014), we have sought to make a contribution to understanding particular value chains in digital entertainment industries. VFX and games are particularly useful in offsetting the developmental/upgrading bias in much of the historical and contemporary literatures. The production of these digitalized commodities can be sourced anywhere that capabilities exist, and the buyer-supplier relations are almost wholly in 'advanced' post-industrial economies. In particular it is valuable to have accounts of value capture and (sometimes worsening) conditions of labour 'up the chain'. The picture is necessarily partial given that the focus is on specific chain segments. For example, we concentrated here mainly on console games rather than casual games for smartphones (see Parker et al., 2014). If the value chain of, say, the iPhone is the focus, a quite different picture of value and labour emerges. As Clelland (2014) shows, whilst the monopolistic bottleneck position of Apple and its ability to capture the majority of the surplus is similar to its equivalent in games, the underpaid or unpaid labour of workers in Asia would be the focal point of labour analysis. This reinforces the general lesson: that meso-level frameworks privilege grounded industry-level analysis that can more effectively link macro (CPE) and micro (workplace) relations.

REFERENCES

Bair, J. (2008) 'Analysing global economic organization: embedded networks and global chains compared', *Economy and Society*, 37(3): 315–338.

Bair, J. (2009) 'Global commodity chains: genealogy and review', in J. Bair (ed.) *Frontiers of Commodity Chain Research*, Palo Alto, CA: Stanford University Press, pp. 1–34.

Clelland, D. A. (2014) 'The core of the apple: dark value and the degree of monopoly in global commodity chains', *Journal of World-Systems Research*, 20(1): 82–111.

Coe, N. (2013) 'Geographies of production III: making space for labour', *Progress in Human Geography*, 37(2): 271–284.

Coe, N. M. and Johns, J. L. (2004) 'Beyond production clusters: towards a critical political economy of networks in the film and television industries', in D. Power and A. J. Scott (eds) *The Cultural Industries and the Production of Culture*, London: Routledge, pp. 188–204.

Coe, N. M. and Jordhus-Lier, D. (2011) 'Constrained agency? re-evaluating the geographies of labour', *Progress in Human Geography*, 35(2): 211–223.

Coe, N. M., Dicken, P. and Hess, M. (2008) 'Global production networks: debates and challenges', *Journal of Economic Geography*, 8(3): 271–295.

Cumbers, A., Nativel, C. and Routledge, P. (2008) 'Labour agency and union positionalities in global production networks', *Journal of Economic Geography*, 8: 369–387.

Deuze, M., Bowen Martin, C. and Allen, C. (2007) 'The professional identity of gameworkers', *Convergence: The International Journal of Research into New Media Technologies*, 13(4): 335–353.

Edwards, P. (1990) 'Understanding conflict in the labour process: the logic and autonomy of struggle', in D. Knights and H. Willmott (eds) *Labour Process Theory*, Basingstoke: Macmillan, pp. 125–152.

Fitzgerald, S. (2015) 'Structure of the cultural industries: global corporations to SMEs', in K. Oakley and J. O'Connor (eds) *The Routledge Companion to the Cultural Industries*, London: Routledge.

Flecker, J. and Meil, P. (2010) 'Organisational restructuring and emerging service value chains: Implications for work and employment', *Work, Employment and Society*, 24(4): 680–698.

Flecker, J., Haidinger, B. and Schönauer, A. (2013) 'Divide and serve: the labour process in service value chains and networks', *Competition and Change*, 17(1): 6–23.

Gereffi, G., Humphrey, J. and Sturgeon, T. (2005) 'The governance of global value chains', *Review of International Political Economy*, 12(1): 78–104.

Gibbon, P., Bair, J. and Ponte, S. (2008) Governing global value chains: an introduction', *Economy and Society*, 37(3): 15–38.

Granovetter, M. (1985) 'Economic action and social structure: the problem of embeddedness', *The American Journal of Sociology*, 9(3): 481–510.

Jacobides, M. G., Knudsen, T. and Augier, M. (2006) 'Benefiting from innovation: value creation, value appropriation and the role of industry architectures', *Research Policy*, 35: 1200–1221.

Johns, J. (2006) 'Video games production networks: value capture, power relations and embeddedness', *Journal of Economic Geography*, 6: 151–180.

Kerr, A. (2006) *The Business and Culture of Digital Games*, London: Sage.

Lakhani, T., Kuruvilla, S. and Avgar, A. (2013) 'From the firm to the network: global value chains and employment relations theory', *British Journal of Industrial Relations*, 51(3): 440–472.

Martin, C. B. and Deuze, M. (2009) 'The independent production of culture: a digital games case study', *Games and Culture*, 4(3): 276–295.

Milberg, W. (2008) 'Shifting sources and uses of profits: sustaining US financialization with global value chains', *Economy and Society*, 37(3): 420–451.

Neilson, J., Pritchard, B. and Wai-Chung, H. (2014) 'Global value chains and global production networks in the changing international political economy: an introduction', *Review of International Political Economy*, 21(1): 1–8.

Newsome, K., Taylor, P. and Rainnie, A. (2013) 'Putting labour in its place: global value chains and labour process analysis', *Special Issue of Competition and Change*, 17(1): 1–5.

Palpacuer, F. (2008) 'Bringing the social context in: governance and wealth distribution in global commodity chains', *Economy and Society*, 37(3): 393–419.

Parker, R., Cox, S. and Thompson, P. (2014) 'How technological change affects power relations in global markets: remote developers in the console and mobile games industry', *Environment and Planning A*, 46(1): 168–185.

Selwyn, B. (2011) 'Beyond firm-centrism: re-integrating labour and capitalism into global commodity chains', *Journal of Economic Geography*, 12(1): 205–226.

Smith, A. (2014) 'The state, institutional frameworks and the dynamics of capital in global production networks', *Progress in Human Geography*, Published on-Line 7 February 2014, doi:10.1177/0309132513518292.

Taylor, P. (2010) 'The globalization of service work: analysing the call centre value chain', in P. Thompson and C. Smith (eds) *Working Life: Renewing Labour Process Analysis*, Basingstoke: Palgrave Macmillan, pp. 244–268.

Thompson, P. (2013) 'Financialization and the workplace: extending and applying the disconnected capitalism thesis', *Work, Employment and Society*, 27(3): 472–488.

Thompson, P., Parker, R. and Cox, C. (2015) 'Interrogating creative theory and creative work: inside the games studio', *Sociology*. In press.

CHAPTER 4

Positioning Labour in Service Value Chains and Networks: The Case of Parcel Delivery

Bettina Haidinger and Jörg Flecker

Introduction

In the research on Global Value Chains and Global Production Networks, issues related to work and employment have recently gained increasing currency. The quality of work and employment is directly related to the restructuring of value chains and production networks: wage differentials between countries are the main driver of work relocation in labour-intensive sectors, the position of companies within value chains impacts on the quality of work and there are big differences in working hours and health and safety regulations along such chains (Barrientos *et al.*, 2011; Flecker, 2012). In addition, many organizations and companies tend to shift risks and demands for flexibility down or across the value chain to less protected labour market segments or employee groups (Frade and Darmon, 2005) while cross-border networks and value chains allow 'regime shopping' and 'institutional arbitrage' (Hall and Soskice, 2001). In the analyses of these and related issues, labour mainly appears as an exchangeable factor of production. This raises the question of how conceptually to take better account of labour as both a productive factor and of workers as social agents (Cumbers *et al.*, 2008; Barrientos *et al.*, 2011; Selwyn, 2012).

This chapter discusses value chains in a particular sector of the service economy, namely the logistics sector, from a labour process and labour agency perspective. The logistics industry as such is not only of increasing systemic importance for ensuring the smooth functioning of contemporary global production networks. The sector itself has evolved into a globally organized industry of its own constituted by complex inter-firm networks and offering core business functions to other parts of the global economy (Coe, 2014: 225–226). These two essential features of the logistics sector – namely becoming a more and more independent, sophisticated and strategically important industry and being itself comprised of a tangled web of inter-firm networks tapping highly fragmented labour markets – will be the starting point of looking at labour processes and the dynamics of employment relations. Highly integrated delivery processes contrast with fragmented layers of subcontracting. While the vulnerability of integrated, time-sensitive logistics potentially provides workers with positional power, the fragmentation of employment and the casualization of labour prevent the formation of associational power (Wright, 2000). The question then is how the contradictory nature of industry structures and labour processes triggers workers' resistance and fosters the dynamic of changes in managerial control (Edwards, 1979).

The chapter will give insights into the parcel delivery sector as part of this globally operating and substantially deregulated logistics sector. First, we will lay down how the debates within labour process theory can give fruitful insights into the explanation of the functioning of global value chains in general and how labour agency can be integrated into the analytical framework of global production networks and value chains.

Second, the parcel delivery sector will be taken as an example for describing the fragmentation of work and the changes in labour processes stemming from a restructuring of highly integrated value chains and networks.

Third, the chapter discusses labour's potential and structural power resulting from the logistics and parcel delivery sector's particular position in the supply chain, as well as examples of workers' ability and constraints to disrupt the smooth functioning of the circulation process.

Global Service Value Chains and the Position of Labour

The contemporary world economy is characterized by entangled supply chains composed of organizationally or spatially separated stages (Dicken, 2011). This means that intermediate goods and services are traded to fuel fragmented and internationally dispersed production processes and are finally composed and distributed within so-called global value chains (GVC) (Gereffi *et al.*, 2005) or global production networks (GPN) (Coe *et al.*, 2008; Cumbers *et al.*, 2008). These are two concepts theorizing the increasing externalization and outsourcing of business functions across borders. GVC analysis examines the processes of value creation and value capture within and between firms engaged in global value chains of a specific sector including processes of up- and downgrading of their positions within the value chain. Its analyses attempt to understand and explain access to and mobility of firms within global value chains, their distinct modes of inter-firm coordination and their strategies to capture and retain profit, power and information advantages. Hence, it rather narrowly focuses on the analysis of capital-capital relations. Labour is herewithin merely understood as an input factor of production in terms of quantity (number of workers, wage level) and quality (skills). The GPN approach highlights more strongly the relational embeddedness of global value chain processes acknowledging not only the role of societal actors and systems but also stressing the firm itself as a relational network. This point of view can pave the way for taking a closer look at the role of labour processes and workers' agency shaping labour-capital relations, as will be done below.

Recently, the concepts of value chains and networks have been applied to the offshoring and/or the outsourcing also of services (next to manufacturing), these having become widespread in both the private and public sectors (Flecker and Meil, 2010; Flecker, 2012; Hermann and Flecker, 2012; Thompson et al., 2013). Complete generic business functions such as specialized accounting, research and development, human resource management and IT service provision and suppliers of business-process outsourcing, including call centres (Huws et al., 2004; Taylor, 2010) have been reshaped into value chains and networks of service provision that cross organizational and national boundaries.

One increasingly important externalized business function is logistics comprehending 'the process of planning, implementing and managing the movement and storage of raw materials, components, finished goods and associated knowledge from the point of origin to the point of consumption' (Coe, 2014: 225). The industry meanwhile does not only encompass transportation and warehousing, but also the management of an entire supply chain as a single integrated unit. In an overview of research on the logistics sector in the US, Bonacich and Wilson (2008: 3) refer to this development as a 'logistics revolution' entailing a power shift within value chains from producers to retailers, changes in the character of production towards flexible, outsourced and offshore production, logistics innovations, such as uniform containers, and the non-disrupted movement of goods across ship, rail and truck. Besides the technical business developments in the logistics industry, the general tendency towards outsourcing and the relocation of production to other countries has created a boom in demand for cross-border transport and logistics (Coe, 2014: 225). These trends fuel the growth of an independent logistics industry comprised of transnational third party logistics providers who are playing a strategic role in the circulation of goods and services within a global economy (Newsome, 2010). Many of them have developed from postal, courier and express parcel companies or from asset-based transport companies. According to Coe (2014: 236) 'a key mechanism for both functional upgrading and geographical expansion has been merger and acquisition activity, resulting in consolidation among the higher echelons of the global industry'.

As such, the logistics industry is an increasingly important systemic part not only to connect but also even to govern global production networks. The sector itself is constituted of complex inter-firm networks, while value chains in parts of the logistics industry may be composed of multiple layers of subcontracting as demonstrated below. Frade and Darmon (2005) describe such relations, characterized by short-term contracts and increased competition, as 'risk-and-flexibility-chains' in which the main reason for externalization is cost cutting and risk spreading. Here, also, the distinction between market transactions and employment relationships becomes blurred; 'extended hierarchies' in inter-firm networks (Thompson, 1993) impact on labour processes and hence working conditions under the control of both the employer and the employer's client organization (Marchington et al., 2005; Rubery, 2006). Inter-organizational contracting leads to a segmentation of production processes with wide-reaching consequences for the organization of industrial relations (Doellgast and Greer, 2007). Jobs may be moved from a well-organized core to a more poorly organized periphery of firms that have no collective agreements, or work may be shifted so that it is covered by new sectoral agreements, negotiated by different unions (Batt et al., 2009; Meil et al., 2009). The bypassing of employment protection by outsourcing, or by utilizing labour not covered by the 'original' sectoral employment regulations, contributes to increased variation and uneven distribution of wages and working conditions within a sector.

Recently, the GVC and GPN literatures have attempted to integrate the concepts of labour as a productive factor and workers as social agents into the analysis of the changing dynamics of global production networks (e.g. Cumbers et al., 2008; Barrientos et al., 2011: 322). Labour as a productive factor is addressed not only as a cost factor but also by taking into account labour intensity and skill levels required for different stages within global production processes. Understanding workers as socially embedded agents highlights the importance of workers' access to workplace-based rights and entitlements and to formal and informal social protection networks. Barrientos *et al.* (2011) connect these two dimensions for analysing the use and embeddedness of labour within value chains with the dynamics of economic and social upgrading along value chains. Economic upgrading implies a process in which economic actors – firms and workers – move from low-value to higher-value activities in global production networks by improving technology, knowledge and skill or by increasing benefits. Social upgrading implies the enhancement of the quality of employment and the improvement of the access to rights and entitlements of workers as social actors (Barrientos *et al.*: 324).

Referring to our example of the logistics sector, Coe (2014: 235) identifies trajectories of product or functional upgrading as forms of economic upgrading by offering either highly specialized and tailored logistics services to particular customers or by offering a bundle of integrated logistics services that have usually been carried out by the producers themselves. Another upgrading option involves process upgrading by optimizing transport and labour processes with technological innovations such as GPS (global positioning) and RFID (radio-frequency identification) systems. These three modes of economic upgrading enable third party logistics providers to retain a higher share of the added value of the entire logistics production process. When it comes to assessing the social dimension of upgrading in the logistics industry, Coe (2014), Bonacich and Wilson (2008), as well as Haidinger (2012), rather point towards downgrading of labour conditions both in terms of measurable standards (wages, benefits) as well as enabling rights (freedom of association, collective bargaining). Bonacich and Wilson (2008: 15–22) summarize the consequences of the logistics revolution on workers in all parts of the industry including maritime, landside, warehouse and distribution centre workers as including increased contingency, weakened unions, racialization and lowered labour standards. While workers' situation in the parcel delivery industry as part of the entire logistics industry is seemingly over-determined, in this contribution we are still looking for labour agency in the sense of resistance and struggles for the improvement of employment and working conditions.

Global Value Chains and Labour Process Theory

So far, the research on restructuring of value chains and production networks by and large has considered labour as a (passive) victim in multiple senses. *First*, the lengthening of value chains by the hollowing-out of large companies or outsourcing from the public sector has not only created a flexible service economy using segmented labour markets and increasingly fragmented employment (Rubery, 2006; Flecker, 2010), but has also considerably extended secondary labour markets and low-wage areas of employment. *Second*, competition between service providers and the pressures exerted by client organizations have continuously worsened employment conditions at subcontractor companies (Weil, 2009). *Third*, the fragmentation of employment and the concession bargaining on the basis of threats of further outsourcing have also lowered the standards in primary labour markets and for core workers of core companies (Huws *et al.*, 2009). *Fourth*, fragmentation is an effective divide-and-rule strategy, weakening labour by inhibiting solidarity and rendering obsolete some parts of the institutional arrangements of industrial relations (Doellgast and Greer, 2007).

While research often confirms these effects of outsourcing and the lengthening of value chains, we should not assume it is 'all quiet on the workplace front' (Thompson and Ackroyd, 1995). When analysing tendencies that structurally weaken labour, it is still necessary to identify labour agency both in restructuring and in the labour process itself (Selwyn, 2012). There is no denying that restructuring is in fact usually a management, if not capital representatives', prerogative, to define outsourcing strategies and to shape inter-firm relations, while union responses are often limited to dealing with the employment consequences of restructuring (Meil *et al.*, 2009: 65). To be able to analyse the position and the agency of labour we need to have a closer conceptual look at the intersection between value chain analysis and labour process theory.

For our purposes here, there are three aspects that deserve attention. *First*, value chain analysis makes it possible to connect the immediate labour process with the broader political economy (Thompson and Vincent, 2010). Here, we are particularly concerned with the position of labour processes in the wider global production and circulation processes and with the role of global logistics multinationals within them. In addition, it is important to look at the structure of the sector, the conditions for market access and the forms of competition between the various big and small companies. *Second*, the focus on value chains and production networks highlights capital-capital relations, e.g. in the sense of supply or subcontracting relations, that shape or influence work organization, managerial control strategies or the bargaining position of labour. Particularly instructive examples are service level agreements (SLAs) in the call centre industry that regulate details of the labour process as a kind of operational governance of subcontractors (Taylor, 2010). SLAs may also be interpreted as being part of hegemonic control structures, in that workers view them as externally imposed and a common challenge for management and workers (D'Cruz and Noronha, 2009). In relation to bargaining power, Selwyn (2012: 220) argues that more research should be invested into the interconnection between commodity production within functionally integrated economic networks and the 'nature and extent of workers' marketplace and workplace bargaining power as well as associational power'. *Third*, within value chains and networks, the immediate labour process is often not limited to one establishment under the control of one employer but spreads over several organizationally and spatially separated entities. This not only implies multiple employer constellations (Marchington *et al.*, 2005) in which the dynamics of management-labour relations take shape in particular ways; it may also mean that different managerial functions or aspects of management control are exerted in fact by representatives of legally and organizationally distinct companies. The parcel delivery sector provides extensive evidence of that.

To elaborate on the second point: with respect to many value chain and network settings, there is a striking contrast between the vulnerability of complex, dispersed production or service provision processes, on the one hand, as Neilson notes for the logistics sector (2012: 330–331), and scholars' and activists' portrayal of labour's weak and increasingly weakened bargaining power in such contexts, on the other hand (Bonacich and Wilson, 2008). While in principle unions gain positional power through their disruptive potential in closely integrated value chains and networks (Wallace *et al.*, 1989; Taylor and Bain, 2008), their actual influence is diminishing. Conceptually, this means that the existing 'positional' or 'primary' (Jürgens and Naschold, 1983) power resources cannot be transformed into actual power. Obviously, one reason is the lack of 'associational' power (Wright, 2000) due to the divide-and-rule strategies inherent in value chains and networks. Institutions of workers' representation are usually formed along organizational and industrial demarcations that are notoriously transgressed by outsourcing and other forms of external restructuring. Such divisions are exacerbated by national borders or ethnic differences within a country and further deepened by competition between groups of workers belonging to different establishments or firms along the value chain and network (see Bonacich and Wilson, 2008 for an assessment of labour power within logistics chains). Yet, as we learned from Edwards' (1979) historical analysis, each system of control brings forth inner contradictions that strengthen resistance, which in turn is answered by new forms of managerial control. The question then is what opportunities fragmented systems of service provision create for labour agency at both individual and collective levels. In other words, how does labour influence the shaping and the consequences of value chain restructuring and, second, how does individual and collective labour agency occur under conditions of organizationally and spatially separated stages of supply chains and fragmented employment structures?

Global Delivery Chains: Workers' Positional and Associational Power

Labour agency in logistics of which parcel delivery is an essential part provides a compelling case. Firstly, we will describe the highly fragmented labour markets, inter-firm relations and sector structure in general, characterizing the multi-level and cross-border operations of the parcel delivery sector and considering their impact on relations between capital and labour at the workplace. Secondly, the sector's strategic position, its streamlined and therefore vulnerable business processes within the entire global value chain are crucial points of entry for the positional power of labour. In other words, the social relations between capital and labour at this particular workplace are not only determined by structural constraints and 'by dynamics of exploitation and control' but also provoke 'worker responses – from resistance to accommodation, compliance, and consent' (Thompson and Vincent, 2010: 49). Therefore, workers' attempts to make use of this strategic position, to gain ground and leverage and hence to achieve social upgrading will be delineated and discussed.

The empirical foundation of this chapter rests on a sectoral study of parcel delivery as part of the logistics sector. The sector study was carried out as part of the joint project SODIPER[1] between researchers and trade union representatives, on global delivery chains in Austria, Germany, the Czech Republic and Hungary. Various kinds of empirical sources were approached, collected and used: all in all, 31 semi-structured interviews with couriers – including self-employed drivers and workers employed by subcontractors – were conducted. Additionally, the Austrian team used field notes from informal conversations with more than 30 drivers during two union organizing activities. Furthermore, 27 interviews with union activists, human resource managers of parcel delivery firms and other relevant experts and stakeholders from labour interest organizations, employers' associations, consultancy firms and public administration were carried out in all four countries involved in the project. Finally, findings and points of discussion compiled within country-specific and international workshops were also part of the empirical material used for the project reports (Haidinger, 2012).

Workers' Bargaining Power in Global Value Chains of the Parcel Delivery Sector

The parcel delivery sector is characterized by a scattered and multilayered structure involving several actors, encompassing diverse activities, including haulage, postal service providers and light lorry transport of different enterprise sizes. A variety of business types are to be found in the sector, such as transnational third party logistics service providers (e.g. Deutsche Post DHL or UPS), subcontracting firms and self-employed drivers, while temporary employment agencies also operate global transport and local delivery chains. In each of the countries covered by the SODIPER research, a dozen global competitors including former state-run incumbents of postal services are competing for market shares in the parcel delivery sector. They are the ones coordinating the supply chain and providing the international transport backbone and logistics; only some of them are still employing couriers at their company headquarters to carry out the actual operational business as such – the collection and delivery of parcels to and from customers as well as sorting processes. Instead, they award contracts to 'service partners': medium- and small-sized enterprises, that directly negotiate contracts stipulating areas, prices, fines, appearance of vehicles and drivers for delivery and collection. Whilst they are formally independent actors, they in fact remain heavily dependent on the original service provider and hardly enter negotiations on an equal footing with transnational corporations. The next link in the delivery chain is either the self-employed driver, the employed driver or again a smaller subcontracting entity hiring a few (self-employed) drivers for the delivery of the parcels. This means that the entire delivery chain can include up to four chain links – the last link in the chain being the courier himself.

The subcontracting entities have little substantial organizational relationship with the third party logistics service providers, and are characterized by individualized and insecure work arrangements. Workers in each of the layers are integrated into the institutions of work regulation to differing extents (Haidinger et al., 2014). According to Gallie (2007: 12), this segmentation of formerly internal labour markets is 'driven by ever greater international competition and more volatile product markets' and launched by employers seeking to maximize their flexibility.

The peripheral workforce down the delivery chain bears the main burden of adjustment to highly flexible employment relations; often it is recruited from vulnerable labour-market groups, such as migrants or the long-term unemployed, as evidence from the SODIPER project suggests (Holst and Singe, 2011; Haidinger, 2012).

Structural constraints and the 'dynamics of exploitation and control' (Thompson and Vincent, 2010: 49) characteristic of the labour and business relations in the parcel delivery sector seemingly point towards a lack of labour agency in this sector. However, within the SODIPER project we found examples of how workers were able to counter this structural powerlessness and to disrupt processes that are at the core for the smooth functioning of the entire supply chain (Haidinger, 2012). Along three domains of confinement – (1) the captive form of value chain governance characterizing the parcel delivery value chain; (2) the dispersed workplace settings of couriers hindering collective agency and the narrow scope for economic and social upgrading; and (3) the reluctance of unions to organize couriers – workers' potential, nevertheless, to realize positional and/or associational power at their workplaces will be traced.

First, the inter-firm relationship and, in particular, the contractual and power relations between the core firm and its suppliers, or so-called service partners, assume great significance for the workplace labour process. A small number of third party logistics companies dominate not only the market but also directly and indirectly control the labour processes in their subcontracting chains. This can be interpreted as a captive form of value chain governance (Gereffi *et al.*, 2005) including tight specifications for the provision of the service and technological surveillance. ICT devices directly monitor the performance and pace of the delivery process. The use of tracking devices implies full control over the courier's working schedule. On the basis of evaluating this tracking information, strict guidelines for how long a certain step may take are imposed to optimize labour processes from the employer's point of view. The use of scanning equipment also increases the transparency of a courier's work. Each step or stop can be traced and electronic control allows employers/contractors to closely monitor their employees' work and compels employees to provide explanations of delivery problems.

At the same time, the extremely high flexibility demands, in terms both of working time and work load placed on workers at the bottom end of the chains, are paradigmatic cases of risk-and-flexibility-transfer chains (Frade and Darmon, 2005). Drivers feel incapable and powerless to change the tight impositions they have to put up with in their daily delivery routine, as one driver from Austria summarizes:

> The scope of manoeuvre is determined and you have to adjust to it. You have some kind of flexibility when arranging your route as long as the customers are satisfied. But the rules are given – the parcels you get in the morning just MUST be delivered at the end of the day.

In the face of the limited and individualized scope for action described by the drivers, the occurrence of collective action is rare. Some were prepared to infer individual consequences from their discontentment with working situations: many reported intending to quit soon; only a few drivers reported industrial action and wildcat strikes, using the couriers' particular strategic position in the circulation process to avert deteriorations in working or payment conditions or to enforce entitlements. One illustration from Austria reveals that after weeks of delay in paying Christmas remuneration, employees of a service partner for a global third party logistics company gathered and jointly announced to refuse delivery if the employer was still reluctant to deliver the missing pay. Literally at the last second of this ultimatum, the payments were authorized. Bonacich and Wilson (2008: 245) refer to the 'unavoidable vulnerability' of the logistics sector. On the one hand, just-in-time production principles require a smooth and steady flow of goods linking production to demand as closely as possible. On the other hand, peak seasons of delivery to customers' businesses (such as before Christmas), and the requirement for goods having to pass through certain nodal points such as airports or distribution centres, pose a considerable potential threat for disrupting the supply chain: '[i]f it is possible to gum up the supply chain ... a great deal of damage can be done to the company' (Bonacich and Wilson, 2008: 245). Hence, couriers, though at the bottom end of a captive value chain, can make use of their strategically important position – resulting from the makings of organizationally and spatially separated stages of global supply chains – for social upgrading and for improving their working conditions.

Second, collective labour agency is also limited by individualized contracting relations and divisions of the workers in – in both geographical and organizational terms – dispersed settings. These factors impact on their potential for economic and social upgrading. Though workers' location in a strategically important sector for the production and circulation process (i.e. logistics) strengthens their marketplace bargaining power, workers' associational power across space, sectors, different employment relations and chain links is usually difficult to achieve (Selwyn, 2012: 220). Thus, the geographical and organizational separation can keep labour divided and not only allows capital to benefit from differentials in terms and conditions but also to find favourable preconditions for divide-and-rule strategies. General contractors are interested in high levels of competition among poorly resourced – in terms not only of financial capital but also of social capital – subcontractors. The allocation of contracts for certain geographical delivery areas to the subcontractors is subject to fierce cost competition. What is more, as is shown in the German case study of the SODIPER research (Holst and Singe, 2011), this actively fuels competition by 'promoting' employed couriers to the ranks of subcontractors. New start-ups in the sector are frequently founded by former drivers: to enter the sector as a business person you have to at least own one light lorry. In order to buy such a vehicle, drivers have to borrow money. This structural indebtedness serves as a crucial function for controlling market development and for undercutting prices.

'Upgrading' both in terms of functional upgrading to capture higher-value work and in terms of social upgrading to negotiate better working conditions with the logistics service providers is difficult and rare. It is contingent on overcoming (structural) constraints, such as access to loans and capital for financing a car fleet or compliance with the country-specific regulations of the trade. Switching from being an employee to a self-employed contractor does not necessarily imply the capture of higher-value work, i.e. economic upgrading, let alone the improvement of working conditions, i.e. social upgrading. One important factor for succeeding in upgrading is the level of (self-organized) cooperation among self-employed couriers. A success story of organizing the self-employed and, as a result, stepping up the chain ladder, was given by one Austrian driver. The drivers managed to build a coalition in order to improve their terms and conditions from a service partner's subcontractor who failed to pay them in time. As a result, this third link in the supply chain was abolished, with the drivers themselves taking over the geographical delivery area the subcontractor had covered beforehand and negotiating directly with the service partner, a contracting partner of the transnational logistics company.

Third, despite the structural imbalances of power among the different stakeholders within the specific chain links, employees, subcontractors or self-employed couriers did use their marketplace bargaining power combined with (temporary) associational power to contest unsatisfactory working conditions. This collective conflict resolution was done in all cases on a self-organized basis, without the help of any kind of representative body. In Hungary for instance, an employer intended to switch from a flat-rate salary to performance-based pay. The employees took this as a decrease in their salaries and planned to hold a wildcat strike on the day the measure was to be implemented. When the employer learned of this, he abandoned the plan to modify the salary system. In the example from Austria mentioned above, again without the organizational support of a union or a works council, the employees of a subcontractor jointly announced to refuse delivery if the employer failed to pay the missing remuneration.

When drivers were asked if they would appreciate a union's or another organization's active role in approaching and backing them, most of them were interested but sceptical. This scepticism was, on the one hand, due to the unions' absence from the field so far in all countries; drivers were doubtful of the unions' interest in supporting them. On the other hand, many saw themselves trapped in the sector's logic and were sceptical about strategies which could effectively pave the way to decent working conditions. In particular, drivers from Germany and Austria were conscious of their exploited situation. This outspoken discontent might be explained by the very low status and social protection, and high insecurity of this kind of work compared to labour standards in most other sectors. Drivers from the Czech Republic and Hungary, conversely, did have other benchmarks for comparing their work situation and were more critical, principally, of institutionalized representation.

In general, trade unions have not yet adjusted to the new workplace realities that have followed the 'logistics revolution' and the chain logic that dominates the parcel delivery industry. They adhere to the old principles of vertical representation of their constituencies and membership policies. At local level, they find it hard to gain access to workers and to organize them even in one place because of the combination of a flexible, integrated and centrally controlled delivery process and the markedly decentralized and often informal employment relations. Traditional forms of representation embedded in the national industrial relations system lack efficacy in this sector (Haidinger et al., 2014). A diversity of collective agreements with different labour regulations (as in Austria), the employers' unwillingness to engage in collective bargaining (as in Germany, the Czech Republic and Hungary) or the circumvention of collective agreements by contracting out the delivery process to self-employed drivers (all countries) make it impossible for unions to keep uniform wage levels and working conditions for the entire sector. Therefore, trade unions are losing their power to influence policymaking and decision-making in employment relations in the sector. As a result, many couriers remain without trade-union representation, so that social and working conditions are deteriorating. The sector is a paradigmatic example of unions' need to adopt alternatives to traditional ways of approaching, organizing and supporting workers and to open up union policies to a wider constituency, including the self-employed.

Conclusions

Research on restructuring, lengthening of value chains and dynamics of production networks often shows that labour is weakened in various ways (Frade and Darmon, 2005; Marchington et al., 2005; Meil et al., 2009; Weil, 2009): employment is being fragmented by the lengthening of value chains and the creation of networks; the supremacy of core companies or client organizations, as well as the competition between suppliers and service providers, continuously worsen employment conditions at subcontractor companies; concession bargaining on the basis of threats of further outsourcing also lowers the standards for core workers of core companies; and fragmentation supports effective divide-and-rule strategies that further weaken labour. While there is no denying these empirical trends, it seems necessary to better take into account workers' agency to get a more nuanced picture and to understand to what extent workers' resistance and compliance shape labour processes and influence value chain dynamics, but also how labour can utilize the inner contradictions of these new control structures.

Logistics and, in particular, parcel delivery is a very informative case in this context, one characteristic being that the delivery process is highly integrated both in an organizational and a technological sense, while employment and employment relations are extremely fragmented. Another is the vulnerability of logistics processes and wider production and circulation structures in which logistics play a crucial part. In principle, this results in a striking combination of high positional and very low associational power of labour. The latter is low not only because of management's divide-and-rule strategies but also because the structures of interest representation are at odds with dynamic value chains and fragmented employment, in particular in continental countries such as Germany and Austria.

This chapter has shown that (admittedly rare) incidences of workers' resistance can be found in unlikely places: highly individualized self-employed workers take industrial action without any union support. These actions may target an obvious contradiction within the organization of parcel delivery and the management control strategy it implies, namely the technical superfluity of some entities within the cascade of subcontractors. Yet, workers' collective action remains unlikely in a setting of high competition between each other and with a view to the remoteness of those actors who actually set out the conditions under which people work in this sector: the transnational third party logistics companies. While workers in a standard employment relationship with a subcontractor may at least lodge claims for due wages when they terminate the employment, self-employed workers are powerless in this respect. What is more, often being migrants, not all of whom possess a work permit, they find themselves locked in irregular working environments.

In this context and for the time being, workers in parcel delivery do not seem likely to be able to transfer their high level of positional power resources into actual bargaining power. However, under particular circumstances associational power may be gained relatively quickly even though this can be expected to remain transitory and local. Established institutions of workers' representation do provide associational power, yet they show high levels of inertia in adapting to new economic structures. This not only limits the support they can provide to parcel delivery workers; is also actually restricts the spontaneous resistance of workers against their intolerable employment and working conditions. Yet, this also means that institutional and organizational adaptation may greatly enhance workers' associational power and thus better position them to take advantage of the fact that the logistics processes are not only inherently vulnerable but also economically crucial for entire global production networks that span various business processes and sectors.

Where does this leave us in terms of the connection between value chain research and Labour Process Theory? Regarding the link between the immediate labour process and the wider political economy (Thompson and Vincent, 2010), the findings in the delivery sector clearly show how the labour process of the subcontractors within the delivery industry is being shaped by the strategies of the few big transnational companies dominating the industry on a global scale. What is more, the fierce price competition between the small and medium delivery subcontractors in a context of not only dominant, large logistics companies but also easy market access is crucial to understanding employment relations in the sector (Weil, 2009). What need to be further explored are processes of value capture (Breznitz et al., 2011) along the chains and their consequences for bargaining relations and employment conditions.

The second point we addressed above, the importance of inter-firm relations to the labour process, is also very well illustrated by the findings on the delivery industry. Crucial features in our case are clearly asymmetric inter-firm power relations, short-term contracts and strong competition among subcontractors. In view of accelerated business processes, flexibility becomes a crucial issue in service labour processes (Flecker et al., 2013). In the parcel delivery industry, the 'flexibility and risk transfer chain' (Frade and Darmon, 2005) seems to be a good label for the subcontracting relationships. It might even be misleading to speak of capital-capital relations in this context because some of the small subcontractor companies can be seen as vulnerable self-employed brokers rather than established employers. What is more, because of relatively easy market entry it is not impossible that workers and their 'employers' will change roles or that workers will collectively eliminate their employer and directly work for a subcontractor one tier further up, as was reported in one case. There is thus a tension between the actual organization of the labour process and the fragmented employment structures that can be addressed by workers' resistance.

The fact that the actual labour process is spread over several organizations does have important consequences. In parcel delivery the labour process is clearly under control of both the employer and the employer's client organization (Rubery, 2006). This goes so far that different companies take over immediate managerial functions relating to delivery work: core companies closely control and monitor workers using ICT-systems and appliances, and often define uniforms and other aspects of workers' appearance, while subcontracting companies determine pay and other employment conditions. It is obvious that core companies dictate patterns of labour organization and usage as in other sectors such as retailing (Newsome *et al.*, 2009). As the workers are separated from the core company by two or more tiers of subcontracting, influencing the rules seems clearly out of reach. Workers' struggles with their immediate employers then focus on issues such as timely payment of wages.

The analysis has shown a marked contrast between workers' positional power in highly vulnerable delivery processes and their actual powerlessness in influencing their working conditions. It is still important to conceive of labour not simply as a passive victim in networked economic relationships, but to take account of labour agency. We therefore agree that we should be occupied with the gap between workers' 'objective potential power and the subjective ability, or willingness, to exercise it' (Taylor and Bain, 2008: 150). However, the rare cases of workers' resistance and influence showed that in the case of the delivery industry there are a number of structural conditions that seem to overdetermine the weakness of labour. These relate to the industry structure, combining an oligopoly of transnational logistics companies with high levels of competition between subcontractors or workers' representation and trade unions ill-suited for such business structures, to name just a few of them. Nevertheless, the contradiction between the highly integrated logistics process and its crucial role in global capitalist production and circulation on the one hand and, on the other, the highly fragmented employment system, challenge labour and provoke resistance. The question, then, is how some of the structural impediments to labour agency on the side of trade unions may be overcome by better adapting workers' representation and trade union structures to dynamic transnational inter-firm relations.

Note

1 'Social Dialogue and Participation Strategies in the Global Delivery Industry: Challenging Precarious Employment Relations' (SODIPER), funded by the European Commission, DG Employment and Social Affairs (VP/2010/001/0226).

REFERENCES

Barrientos, S., Gereffi, G. and Rossi, A. (2011) 'Economic and social upgrading in global production networks: a new paradigm for a changing world', *International Labour Review*, 150(3–4): 319–340.

Batt, R., Holman, D. and Holtgrewe, U. (2009) 'The globalization of service work: comparative institutional perspectives on call centers', *Industrial & Labor Relations Review*, 62(4): 453–488.

Bonacich, E. and Wilson, J. (2008) *Getting the Goods*, Ithaca/London: Cornell University Press.

Breznitz, D., Kenney, M., Rouvinen, P., Zysman, J. and Ylä-Anttila, P. (2011) 'Value capture and policy design in a digital economy', *Journal of Industrial Competition and Change*, 11: 203–207.

Coe, N. M. (2014) 'Missing links: logistics, governance and upgrading in a shifting global economy', *Review of International Political Economy*, 21(1): 224–256.

Coe, N. M., Dicken, P. and Hess, M. (2008) 'Global production networks: realizing the potential', *Journal of Economic Geography*, 8(3): 271–295.

Cumbers, A., Nativel, C. and Routledge, P. (2008) 'Labour agency and union positionalities in global production networks', *Journal of Economic Geography*, 8(3): 369–387.

D'Cruz, P. and Noronha, E. (2009) 'Experiencing depersonalised bullying: a study of Indian call centre agents', *Work Organisation, Labour and Globalisation*, 3(1): 26–46.

Dicken, P. (2011) *Global Shift,* London: Sage.

Doellgast, V. and Greer, I. (2007) 'Vertical disintegration and the disorganization of German industrial relations', *British Journal of Industrial Relations*, 45(1): 55–76.

Edwards, R. (1979) *Contested Terrain: The Transformation of the Workplace in America*, New York: Basic Books.

Flecker, J. (2010) 'Fragmenting labour: organizational restructuring, employment relations and the dynamics of national regulatory frameworks', *Work Organization, Labour and Globalisation*, 4(1): 8–23.

Flecker, J. (ed.) (2012) *Arbeit in Ketten und Netzen. Die dynamische Vernetzung von Unternehmen und die Qualität der Arbeit*, Berlin: Edition Sigma.

Flecker, J. and Meil, P. (2010) 'Organizational restructuring and emerging service value chains – implications for work and employment', *Work, Employment & Society*, 24(4): 1–19.

Flecker, J., Haidinger, B. and Schönauer, A. (2013) 'Divide and serve: the labour process in service value chains and networks', *Competition & Change*, 17(1): 6–23.

Frade, C. and Darmon, I. (2005) 'New modes of business organization and precarious employment: towards the recommodification of labour?' *Journal of European Social Policy*, 15(2): 107–121.

Gallie, D. (2007) *Employment Regimes and the Quality of Work*, Oxford: Oxford University Press.

Gereffi, G., Humphrey, J. and Sturgeon, T. (2005) 'The governance of global value chains', *Review of International Political Economy*, 12(1): 78–104.

Haidinger, B. (2012) *On The Move in Global Delivery Chains: Labor Relations and Working Conditions in the Parcel Delivery Industries of Austria, Germany, the Czech Republic and Hungary*, SODIPER Synthesis Report, FORBA: Vienna.

Haidinger, B., Schönauer, A., Flecker, J. and Holtgrewe, U. (2014) 'Value chains and networks in services: crossing borders, crossing sectors, crossing regimes?' in M. Vidal and M. Hauptmeier (eds) *The Comparative Political Economy of Work and Employment Relations*, Basingstoke: Palgrave Macmillan, pp. 98–118.

Hall, P. A. and Soskice, D. (2001) *Varieties of Capitalism: The Institutional Foundations of Comparative Advantage*, Oxford: Oxford University Press.

Hermann, C. and Flecker, J. (eds) (2012) *Privatisation of Public Services: Impact on Employment, Working Conditions and Service Quality*, New York/London: Routledge.

Holst, H. and Singe, I. (2011) *SODIPER National Research Report Germany*, FORBA: Vienna.

Huws, U., Dahlmann, S. and Flecker, J. (2004) *Outsourcing of ICT and Related Services in the EU. A Status Report*, Luxembourg: Office for Official Publications of the EC.

Huws, U., Dahlmann, S., Flecker, J., Holtgrewe, U., Schönauer, A., Ramioul, M. and Geurts, K. (2009) *Value Chain Restructuring in Europe in a Global Economy*, Leuven: HIVA.

Jürgens, U. and Naschold, F. (1983) *Arbeitspolitik. Materialien Zum Zusammenhang von Politischer Macht, Kontrolle und Betrieblicher Organisation der Arbeit*, Opladen: Westdeutscher Verlag.

Marchington, M., Grimshaw, D., Rubery, J. and Willmott H. (eds) (2005) *Fragmenting Work. Blurring Organizational Boundaries and Disordering Hierarchies*, Oxford: Oxford UP.

Meil, P., Tengblad, P. and Docherty, P. (2009) *Value Chain Restructuring and Industrial Relations. The Role of Workplace Representation in Changing Conditions of Employment and Work*, Leuven: HIVA.

Neilson, B. (2012) 'Five theses on understanding logistics as power', *Distinktion: Scandinavian Journal of Social Theory*, 13(3): 322–339.

Newsome, K. (2010) 'Work and employment in distribution and exchange: moments in the circuit of capital', *Industrial Relations Journal*, 41(3): 190–205.

Newsome, K., Thompson, P. and Commander, J. (2009) 'The forgotten factories: suppliers, supermarkets and dignity at work in the contemporary economy', in S. Bolton and M. Houlihan (eds) *Work Matters: Critical Reflections on Contemporary Work*, Basingstoke: Palgrave Macmillan, pp. 145–161.

Rubery, J. (2006) *Segmentation Theory Thirty Years On*, Discussion paper, European Work and Employment Research Centre, University of Manchester.

Selwyn, B. (2012) 'Beyond firm-centrism: re-integrating labour and capitalism into global commodity chain analysis', *Journal of Economic Geography*, 12(1): 205–226.

Taylor, P. (2010) 'The globalization of service work: analysing the transnational call centre value chain', in P. Thompson and C. Smith (eds) *Working Life: Renewing Labour Process Analysis*, Basingstoke: Palgrave Macmillan, pp. 244–268.

Taylor, P. and Bain, P. M. (2008) 'United by a common language? Trade union responses in the UK and India to call centre offshoring', *Antipode: A Radical Journal of Geography*, 40(1): 131–154.

Thompson, P. (1993) 'Postmodernism: fatal distraction', in J. Hassard and M. Parker (eds) *Postmodernism and Organizations*, London: Sage, pp. 183–203.

Thompson, P. and Ackroyd, S. (1995) 'All quiet on the workplace front? A critique of recent trends in British industrial sociology', *Sociology*, 29: 615–633.

Thompson, P. and Vincent, S. (2010) 'Beyond the boundary: labour process theory and critical realism', in P. Thompson and C. Smith (eds) *Working Life: Renewing Labour Process Analysis*, Basingstoke: Palgrave Macmillan, pp. 47–69.

Thompson, P., Newsome, K. and Commander, J. (2013) 'Good when they want to be: migrant workers in the supermarket supply chain', *Human Resource Management Journal*, 23(2): 129–143.

Wallace, M., Griffin, L. and Rubin, B. (1989) 'The positional power of American labor, 1963–1977', *American Sociological Review*, 54(2): 197–214.

Weil, D. (2009) 'Rethinking the regulation of vulnerable work in the USA: a sector-based approach', *Journal of Industrial Relations*, 51(3): 411–430.

Wright, E. O. (2000) 'Working-class power, capitalist-class interests, and class compromise', *American Journal of Sociology*, 105(4): 957–1002.

Labour and Segmentation in Value Chains

CHAPTER 5

Nikolaus Hammer and Lone Riisgaard

The appeal of the Global Value Chain (GVC) approach to labour process research consists in its explanatory framework for the relations between firms and workers in a global division of labour. So far, however, a substantial integration of GVC and labour process analyses has proved difficult as the former has primarily been concerned with the impact of different forms of GVC *governance* and has largely neglected the contested nature of the labour process as well as labour markets. Over recent years, a number of researchers have tried to address this gap and have gone beyond a concern with labour as an input factor.

While differences exist across GVC perspectives (Gibbon *et al.*, 2008), debates on the social embeddedness of GVCs (Bair, 2008; Palpacuer, 2008; Coe *et al.*, 2008) have helped with the recognition of labour as a collective actor trying to shape the entry barriers of value chains through, for example, social and labour standards, as well as an agent in the very process of production (e.g. Riisgaard and Hammer, 2011; Robinson and Rainbird, 2013). Geographers and development scholars (e.g. Henderson *et al.*, 2002; Barrientos *et al.*, 2003; Lund and Nicholson, 2003) and, more recently, labour process and industrial relations scholars have begun to widen notions of labour in GVCs and started to 'put labour into value chains' (e.g. Taylor *et al.*, 2013).

The case for integrating GVC analysis with labour has been made with regard to different areas of work and employment as well as from different theoretical premises: regarding the role of social institutions and skill formation (Ramirez and Rainbird, 2010); inter-firm relations and employment relations (Lakhani *et al.*, 2013); space and embedded production networks (Rainnie et al., 2011). This chapter builds on these debates. Yet, rather than starting from the impact of governance on work and employment, its entry point lies in an acknowledgement of the *interdependencies* of the social relations at the workplace and GVCs, thereby aiming to highlight how the *labour process and the social relations in which they are embedded impact on GVCs*. The argument put forward here is that, while market and coordination structures within GVCs are relevant, it is the indeterminacy of labour (its social and political intractability as a production factor) that is fundamental when it comes to explaining agency at various levels within GVCs. It is important to note that different strands of value chain analysis (e.g. Gibbon et al., 2008) are, implicitly or explicitly, based on different concepts of labour and the labour process. For example, the global production networks perspective (e.g. Coe et al., 2008) is explicit in viewing labour as a contested social relation and the basis of *value* creation; our discussion below, however, focuses on what might be called the GVC mainstream (as in Gereffi et al., 2005) which looks at labour, skills and employment as input factors.

In this chapter, we emphasize two aspects of contemporary factory regimes that help to underscore the importance of a broad perspective on the labour process and social relations of production, as well as their role for GVC dynamics. First, there is a wide range of production relations that have been brought into the centre of GVCs – from formal employment to informal outwork to dependent self-employment (Chen, 2005; Barnes, 2012). The restructuring of GVC governance has not only affected how different production relations and factory regimes are coordinated or compete across the global economy. Rather, it is the outcomes of GVC restructuring and struggles at the point of production that have restructured and re-segmented those production relations and factory regimes themselves. Increasingly, the same product can, for example, be produced by formal and informal employees as well as casual and day labourers working side by side in an exporter's production facilities, as outwork/homework, or by independent informal 'entrepreneurs', who often are own-account workers who own neither their means of production, nor the production inputs. Second, in analysing the role of the labour process within GVCs, it is important to bring in the social relations those labour processes draw on: how, for example, the increasing informalization of formal employment, particular forms of worker mobility, and the autonomy of workers over their own reproduction are part of the struggles over the extraction of labour from labour power. These social relations give a concrete form not only to the indeterminacy of labour but also to the methods of control within the labour process. And beyond their role in the extraction of labour from labour power, these social relations shape notions of solidarity and forms of collective action, and, in this process, generate renewed dynamics of GVC restructuring.

Three areas, we argue, need to be recognized in particular, in making the social relations under which value is produced and distributed more explicit. First, an emphasis on the indeterminacy of labour recognizes that the purchase of labour power alone does not secure a predefined quality and quantity of labour, and that the latter needs to be extracted through ever-contested mechanisms of control (e.g. Thompson and Newsome, 2004). This inherent contestation at the point of production accords the labour process a relative autonomy from market (and GVC) structures. Second, building on such a concept of the labour process, we need to recognize that the outcomes of management-labour relations have implications for dynamics of cooperation and competition between firms, as well as between different groups of workers or different production relations. Thus, struggles between management and labour at the workplace impact on the dynamics of segmentation in both product and labour markets (Grimshaw and Rubery, 2005). Third, we feel it is useful to expand the notion of factory regimes not only by a recognition of the role of the employment contract (Nichols and Cam, 2005) but also by relations of reproduction, as elements of particular solidarity, gender and migration regimes are reconfigured into GVCs.

The chapter proceeds in two sections. The first section discusses some of the elements that link the labour process with the broader political economy. It takes up arguments from within labour process theory about moving 'beyond skills and control' or even 'beyond the workplace' and argues how the contingent nature of workplace struggles influences the configuration of labour and product markets. The second section shows how GVC restructuring, while deriving advantages from relocation and outsourcing, also entails a considerable re-segmentation of the workforce along the lines of the employment contract, worker mobility and the living arrangements of workers. Thus, what labour process theory offers to GVC analysis is a concept of GVCs that links different labour processes, production relations and factory regimes. It is only through recognition of the contingent nature of workplace dynamics, as well as their wider social relations, that we can flesh out specific forms of GVCs' social and institutional embeddedness (Bair, 2008; Taylor, 2010; Selwyn, 2013).

The Labour Process, Power and Governance

The emphasis GVC analysis has placed on different forms of inter-firm governance has become a focus of critique and has been countered by calls to socially 'embed' GVCs and to 'bring the social back in'

(Bair, 2008; Palpacuer, 2008). In the first instance, the problem with GVC analysis is less that work and employment, or labour as an agent, do not figure, than that the workplace only figures as a dependent variable that absorbs the constraints stemming from particular forms of governance. This treatment of labour highlights the paradox that forms of inter-firm governance are seen as socially constructed, yet that the very processes through which the actors within the firm are constituted are neglected. We argue, in a first step, that the indeterminacy of labour and the specific workplace dynamics that arise out of that are central in fleshing out this social, and therefore contested, embeddedness of GVCs. The acknowledgement of the *interdependencies* between the social dynamics at the workplace and market dynamics allows developing accounts of the changing division of labour and associated organizational forms that draw on politics and power rather than notions of efficiency (as is the case when forms of governance are seen as a function of the complexity and costs of the transaction between firms; e.g. Gereffi *et al.*, 2005).

Approaches that have a conception of the contested nature of the labour process have for some time tried to analyse its implications beyond the workplace, that is, for the labour and product market. The common assumption in those approaches is that the contestations over the labour process (over the extraction of labour from labour power as well as mechanisms of control) have consequences for workers and employers with regard to their respective abilities to compete in labour and product markets as well as regarding their ability to organize collectively. Different authors within the labour process tradition have conceptualized this link between the workplace and product market competition in different ways, by emphasizing their contingent relations (Edwards, 1986; Brown, 2008) or by conceiving of them as part of a circuit of capital (Kelly, 1985). While these arguments, as we will see below, do not differentiate between horizontal and vertical forms of competition, and thereby do not say much about the functional division of labour, their basic point should also hold for forms of cooperation and competition across GVCs. Thus, struggles over the labour process, as they underlie both the balance of power at the workplace as well as that of organized actors, shape not only how firms compete in product markets but also the way they can build their forward and backward linkages or pursue strategies of industrial upgrading.

Brown (2008) and Edwards (1986), for example, have both insisted on the indeterminate and interdependent nature of the links between product markets, technology and work organization. While workplace struggles take place under constraints set by product markets and technology, they 'develop logics of their own' and result in collective organization that is able to challenge 'some of the "external" conditions of its activity' (Edwards, 1986: 275). Historically, workplace struggles have established public goods (e.g. in the form of collective bargaining that underlies industrial peace and the sharing of productivity gains) and thereby shaped the organization of production and product markets (Brown, 2008).

While this argument shows how labour process dynamics can shape product markets, Kelly (1985) has argued from a Marxist perspective that the analysis of the labour process needs to go beyond the capital-labour relationship and that the real subordination of labour is not solely achieved through control in the labour process. Kelly's point is that, rather than examining particular factors impacting on the labour process, it is important to analyse the *articulation* of different parts within the circuit of capital.

> To account for observed changes in the division of labour we must ... consider the possible role of competition between capitals, as well as conflict between labour and capital ... we need to consider the full circuit of industrial capital as the starting point for analyses of changes in the division of labour: purchase of labour power; extraction of surplus value within the labour process; realisation of surplus value within product markets. There is no sound theoretical reason for privileging one moment in this circuit – the labour-capital relation within the labour process – if our objective is to account for changes (or variations) in the division of labour.
>
> (Kelly, 1985: 32)

The indeterminacy of labour also underlies approaches of labour market segmentation that try to spell out the resulting dynamics across capital-labour, capital-capital, and labour-labour relations (Rubery, 2007). Looking at work and employment from an inter-organizational perspective, Grimshaw and Rubery (2005), for example, argue that product market competition puts constraints on management at the same time as, in reverse, workers' strategies have important implications for product market dynamics. As differences within labour have an immediate impact on the competitive relations between different capitals it is difficult to confine the analysis of the employment relationship to a management-labour issue on the wage-effort bargain, separate from inter-capital relations. From a labour market segmentation perspective, organizational change and the dynamics of the employment relationship are intricately related:

> [S]ince, as organisations adapt their boundaries, new tensions and contradictions between capital (the contracting organisations) and labour

(the different workforces) arise that, in turn, may act as a brake on organisational change or a pressure for further transformation and diffusion.
(Grimshaw and Rubery, 2005: 1038)

The core assumptions of labour process theory as well as analysis beyond the workplace are important not only insofar as they place capital-labour relations in a broader political economy but also because they offer an analytical foundation for social- and power-based explanations of market structures, competitive dynamics and ultimately also of value chain governance. Restructuring processes within the global economy clearly impact on the way production and labour processes are organized, yet, as production is fragmented, labour processes are broken up and re-linked, workforces re-segmented, and new contradictions emerge for management. Compromises over the labour process co-constitute the range of strategies firms can reasonably pursue within the functional division of labour, in specific product markets, as well as in labour markets. Given the way they rest on the labour process, firms' competitive strategies are as unstable and inherently contested.

GVC analysis has looked at changing forms of economic coordination primarily from the angle of value chain or inter-firm governance, that is, forms of coordination across the functional division of labour or forms of inter-firm coordination beyond market and hierarchy. Insofar as relations between firms occupy centre stage, the approach privileges a firm-centric (Selwyn, 2013) and managerial perspective. This leaves two options for the way labour is conceived: either it is at the receiving end of major restructuring processes such as changing trade policies or the rise of buyer-driven GVCs that affect work and employment, or it appears as a stakeholder/campaigner in exactly those restructuring processes. Either way, strategies of control and resistance over the labour process (that is, the contested nature of value production) are not part of *value* chain analysis.

A strong formulation that looks more to transaction cost- rather than power-based explanations of value chain governance can be found in Gereffi *et al.* (2005), where different forms of governance are developed on the basis of the following dimensions: the complexity of transactions, the ability to codify those transactions and the capabilities in the supply base. Against this framework, however, it can be argued that organizational or strategic change is part and parcel of management and there is no reason to assume that the labour process and workplace relations are neutral as regards different forms of governance. In fact, it might be difficult to argue that the labour process and the organization of work have no bearing on the complexity of transactions, the ability to codify those transactions and the capabilities in the supply base. Lakhani *et al.* (2013) have aimed to bring these implications to the fore more explicitly with regard to employment relations but remain too close to the transaction cost foundations of this approach to grant a fundamental role to social struggles at or around the workplace.

In contrast, there is a growing sense that the contested nature of workplace relations and the labour process, as the locus where labour is extracted, are important in explaining the dynamics of GVC restructuring. For example, when Barrientos and Kritzinger (2004) discuss the increase in contract labour in the South African fruit export sector as it became more integrated into GVCs, they also point to the downsides the externalization of employment can have for the labour process: 'Problems can arise ... given the producer is less able to control skill, incentives, commitment or employment conditions of contract workers to meet the quality standards set by global buyers' (Barrientos and Kritzinger, 2004: 84). Thus, drawing on Kelly's circuits of capital framework, one might say that the requirements of buyer-driven value chain governance can create problems in the labour process that, ultimately, might lead to a disarticulation between the GVC and the labour process.

The arguments presented above show how a labour process perspective allows for broadening our concepts of cooperation, coordination, competition and control within GVCs beyond a focus on firm networks in the functional division of labour. The struggles over the labour process, that is, over the organization of production, over productivity and quality, over management's control strategies, over labour's resistance, etc., are central to the way firms compete and position themselves within a value chain. The articulation of the labour process with those product and process standards through which governance is exerted is contingent on the social relations at work. In other words, the ability of employers to manage the indeterminacy of labour establishes their competitive bid regarding firms in the same sector, as well as access to the functional division of labour in the first place. However, as Burawoy's factory regimes, as well as feminist work, would have it, struggles over the extraction of labour extend to terrains beyond the workplace.

In fact, the second step of our argument on the interdependencies between the labour process and GVCs is to highlight not only the work intensification and increasing segmentation of the workforce within the labour process but also the extent to which a range of factory regimes in the Global South are defined by a weakening of established protections in terrains outside the workplace. For example, it can often be observed that management strategies in the context of GVC restructuring create complex divisions: between groups of workers performing the same tasks (establishing different 'tiers' – Barrientos, 2013); between those performing different aspects of the labour process (what would conventionally fall under segmentation); as well as between different relations of production. Such lines of division often overlap, for example when formal and informal employees work side by side, and allow us to return to the two aims introduced in the beginning. First, the reconfiguration of GVCs underlies the fragmentation of production and re-segmentation of production relations in a range of interlinked labour processes (e.g. Basole and Basu, 2011 on India). Second, management mobilizes aspects such as contract, mobility and reproduction as controlling devices in such interlinked labour processes. Those dimensions thereby constitute important terrains on which GVCs' factory regimes compete. In discussing these aspects in more detail below with regard to GVCs, we find it useful to look at Burawoy's factory regimes (1985), Smith's division between the effort-wage bargain and the effort-mobility bargain (2006) as well as the work of ethnographers and development researchers on informal employment (e.g. Breman, 2010).

The Fragmentation of Production and the Segmentation of Workers

The restructuring of global value chains highlights a range of interlinked processes of differentiation. First, the fragmentation of production resets the basis on which different labour processes are linked and compete with each other; second, such changes often come with a re-segmentation of the workforce insofar as upgrading or outsourcing pose new competitive challenges and focus on reorganizing the relevant labour processes; third, as management responds to GVC restructuring, we can observe a 'tiering' of the workforce within the firm whereby workers essentially perform equivalent tasks, yet are divided by a range of different employment statuses (Barrientos, 2013). On the one hand, these different aspects of GVC restructuring indicate how it is socially and politically contested at the workplace. For example, as captive arrangements between firms and cost pressures become stronger, firms may refocus their core activities, intensify the labour process, and change the composition and terms of their workforce. However, the viability of this form of governance is dependent on the social relations and resistance at work, as well as the extent to which the organization of the labour process can be successfully articulated within labour and product markets, as well as the functional division of labour. On the other hand, the fragmentation of production highlights strategies of control in restructured labour processes that go far beyond the fairly regulated terrain of the workplace and the employment relationships of the Global North. While GVC analysis promises a perspective on how different labour processes are recombined across global value chains, such insights have been hampered by narrow concepts of work, employment and the broader social relations they are embedded in (Taylor, 2010). In this respect, research from labour process, anthropological and feminist perspectives has been able to open up important questions around work and household production (Yeates, 2004), migration and informalization (Breman, 2010) or the role of work space-living space linkages in the formation of solidarities and collective action (Hammer, 2010; Jenkins, 2013). In the following sections we discuss such extensions with regard to contracts, living arrangements and mobility.

Contracts and the Employment Relationship

Efforts to externalize labour and to weaken the institutions of hegemonic factory regimes that supported labour's bargaining power in the workplace can be broken down into three different moments of segmentation and tiering: along a range of precarious employment contracts; on the basis of different production relations; as well as through the supply and management of labour through third party labour contractors. These elements have become central features in factory regimes of the Global South.

Exploring labour control in factory regimes of the Global South, Nichols and Cam (2005) build on Burawoy's concept of factory regimes but highlight the specific role different forms of material support and contract play in the segmentation of the workforce. This contrasts with the support afforded through a range of welfare benefits in hegemonic regimes. On the one hand, it concerns the role of firm-level provisions in 'employees' subordination, making them dependent on the enterprise welfare system for housing, pensions, sickness benefits, and so on' (Burawoy, 1985: 144). On the other hand, the increasing segmentation of the workforce according to different contracts is linked back to aspects of material support and reproduces divisions. Examples can be found in the way contractual status gives access to housing, or paternalist contributions to health and industrial accident costs, or even the education of workers' children.

Nichols and Cam (2005: 222), in their study of the global white goods industry, found that, as regards labour control, elements of the 'ideological apparatus of hegemonic despotism are well in place, [yet] ...

the dismantling of established labour is also well under way'. This is expressed in reductions of relatively privileged workers in favour of more precarious contracts or outsourcing, as well as a reduction in the (historically often fairly considerable) material support. They conclude on an interesting note that underlines the variation in management strategies as well as the forms of management-labour accommodations at the workplace: whereas factories in China, Taiwan and South Korea have seen a rapid and massive shift towards fixed-term and agency labour, the overwhelming part of the workforce in Turkish and Brazilian white goods factories remained on permanent contracts. In the context of a global industry, this suggests a certain autonomy of the labour process; in consequence such differences are relevant in firms' competitive positioning in product markets as well as value chains.

This emphasis on workforce segmentation on the basis of a range of 'non-standard' contracts corresponds with concerns to differentiate between different production relations that have come out of research on the informal economy (see e.g. Chen, 2005; Barnes, 2012). Against the background of an increasing informalization of formal employment, it is crucial to distinguish independent forms of self-employment from those that are based on the authority relations of an employment relationship; to distinguish between different forms of informal employment; as well as to analyse the deeply gendered nature of the informal economy (e.g. Chen, 2005). Even in multinational corporations' (MNCs') subsidiaries (rather than any outsourced production units) we can observe a strongly segmented and tiered order, observed, for example, in Hammer's (2010) study on MNCs in Greater Delhi. These cases showed that beneath a small layer of permanent employees existed a tier of so-called apprentices. These apprentices were essentially fully skilled migrant workers who, through this classification, were denied the wage rates and the employment security as well as the status that come with permanent employment within an MNC. Further sources of flexibility stemmed from segments of so-called 'contract workers' (in fact, outsourced workers), 'company casuals' as well as casual employees. The last three tiers represented informal employees, with 'company casuals' effectively constituting a labour pool that could count on more regular opportunities than casual employees.

A crucial contribution of these debates on informality lies in their *relational* treatment of informal employment which emphasizes the complex dynamics between informal and other forms of employment, the discontinuous character of informal employment and the way it operates around regulated economic activity (Harriss-White and Gooptu,

2001; Agarwala, 2009; Breman, 2010). Crucially, it locates informality in the context of contemporary forms of economic organization and management strategies:

> In contrast to definitions based on modernisation and neoliberal assumptions, a relational definition does not view the informal economy as an isolated remnant of a feudal past that will automatically disappear under the market influence of industrialisation ... Once such interdependencies between the informal economy, formal economy, the state, and civil society are unearthed, the relational definition can be operationalised to include the entire range of informal workers.
> (Agarwala, 2009: 336)

Another important aspect of the shift towards 'non-standard employment' lies in the increasing mediation of employment through 'third party labour contractors'. In this case, the risk that is displaced through the outsourcing of production is paralleled in the outsourcing of different aspects of the management of labour, which can combine internal and externalized functions in different ways. Barrientos (2013), for example, brings this out clearly, differentiating between different labour intermediaries depending on the extent to which they perform functions of supplying, paying, supervising labour. These dynamics result in a situation where the workforce is not only segmented but also 'tiered', in that workers on different contracts perform the same tasks next to each other.

Returning to our theme of the interdependencies between the labour process, product markets and the functional division of labour, one can see how multiple lines of segmentation and 'tiering' might weaken labour's influence, particularly in the way market pressures underlie hegemonic despotic factory regimes. However, a factory regime built on such fine divisions might be difficult to sustain, and be inherently unstable, when it comes to articulating the labour process with quality standards in GVCs.

Living Conditions

Differentiations along contractual lines are often closely paralleled by access to a continuum of more or less coercive and decent living conditions. They reinforce control at the workplace in different ways at the same time as they give rise to particular forms of resistance: depending on the context, labour camps or compounds at the same time are a site of control as well as a terrain to organize labour process resistance.

The politics around living arrangements are closely intertwined with those over mobility choices which we will discuss below; however, they deserve to be kept analytically separate.

In a study on the development of the compounds in the South African mining industry, Bezuidenhout and Buhlungu (2011) present a useful differentiation of aspects of control: spatial control, reproductive control, associational control and political control. This differentiation relates to restrictions on the movement of workers as they migrate, as well as how they can move around compounds and the adjacent localities; the institution of single-sex compounds as well as the firm's monopoly on selling provisions; the regulation of union and other associational activities amongst workers; as well as the policing and coercive side of mining firms' control over workers and their living areas. During the mid-1980s, however, a combination of factors, such as mounting international pressure, a high gold price and changes in the labour process, led to more formalized industrial relations and allowed the National Union of Mineworkers (NUM) to organize the compounds and, subsequently, organize collective discipline during strikes. As established forms of control were transformed in the transition to post-apartheid South Africa, though, living areas have spread geographically and become more segmented as the 'company-state is making way for the market as the key mechanism of control. The logic of coercion is fading, and the logic of choice intersects with class and citizenship status'. (Bezuidenhout and Buhlungu, 2011: 254) Needless to say these developments have challenged the foundational solidarities of NUM's power. Interestingly, the combination of market control with segmentation along class, ethnicity, caste and citizenship lines is a central organizing logic of living areas in hegemonic despotism as it entrenches the link between 'promotion' in the contractual hierarchy at work and an 'upgrading' in living arrangements.

Differences across forms of dormitory labour regimes or constellations between work and living spaces need to be recognized and, following Pun and Smith (2007), it is instructive to link these arrangements, both to societal aspects and to the functional division of labour. While there is no mechanistic correspondence between dormitory labour regimes and the position in the value chain, there are clear interdependencies between the labour process, the forms of control within living arrangements, and the drivenness of global value chains (and therefore the visibility and political opportunities afforded by those living arrangements). The state, clearly, is an important actor in the regulation as well as provision of living arrangements and communal services (or the withdrawal from social protection as detailed in Pun et al., 2010). Where workers have little leverage at the workplace they at times see the state as a target for class-based demands that are expressed as improvements in living conditions, a social wage and expanded forms of citizenship (e.g. Agarwala, 2009).

Mobility

Against the background of capital mobility in the restructuring of global value chains, it is probably surprising that the mobility of labour has received relatively scant attention, particularly in the construction or hospitality sectors where migrant labour constitutes the reverse of off-shoring. However, going beyond the specific mobility form of labour migration, labour process theory has integrated mobility into the core of its considerations. Central here is Smith's (2006) differentiation of two aspects of the indeterminacy of labour: while the effort-wage bargain is concerned with the extraction of labour from labour power in the labour process, what he calls the effort-mobility bargain is concerned with the substitutability of labour and the ownership over mobility choices. Even though mobility within the capitalist employment relationship is owned by the worker, employers can use a range of strategies in order to influence actual mobility choices.

Management strategies over recruitment, contracts and living arrangements all come together in segmenting and tiering the workforce and in structuring the labour process. For example, in his research on labour in South and South-East Asia, Breman (2010) shows how the informalization of labour is developed and reproduced through mechanisms of circular migration. In such a regime, employers in quarries or the textile industries in Western India preferred hiring migrant workers from far-away regions despite an oversupply of labour in their own region. In turn, workers from those regions had to look elsewhere for their survival. In this process, mobility and recruitment on the basis of ethnic or caste lines combine to structure the workforce into fragmented solidarities and collectivities. At a different level, research on Indian construction sites has also pointed to the practice of rotating groups/gangs of workers around sites in order to prevent the formation of strong social contacts and collective organization. Rather than being the outcome of supply and demand factors on the labour market, these processes are the result of changing social relations of production in the wake of the expulsion of rural, landless/land-poor labour, the integration into global value chains, as well as the re-segmentation of product and labour markets through outsourcing.

As argued above, mobility choices can be shaped in a number of ways as well as in different directions. At the workplace level, workers are often tied in/locked in through advance payments, and at times through withheld wages or the confiscation of identity and/or residency documents. Breman (2010: 343–345), for example, argues that forms of debt bondage are shaped by capitalist relations rather than earlier forms of servitude in the sense that neo-bondage is governed through a contract dominated by its economic dimension (for 2005 he estimates that 40 million workers were caught in such relations of unfree labour in India). Neo-bondage has developed as a genuine social relation in the emergence of the market-based political economy and therefore cannot be seen as a residual of earlier forms of agrarian bondage. Neo-bondage is based on the migrant, ethnic, caste and gender relations that inform the segmentation of the labour force, and is overlaid by the contractual cascades of which labour contractors are a central part (Barrientos, 2013). However, depending on the power balance at work and the wider labour market, such devices can also be turned into their opposite. For example, underlining the point about capitalist forms of neo-bondage, Breman (2010) reports an instance where workers were originally tied in through advance payments. As skilled labour became scarce, though, and the power balance between employers and workers shifted, these advance payments came to be seen as a sunk cost to the employer, and effectively became a 'signing-on fee'.

In many cases, the structure of mobility choices and the particular strategies they are based on are supported by the state, insofar as they directly result from regulatory gaps and inconsistencies. For example, for both migrants from former Soviet republics to Russia and internal migrants in China, the regulated relation between work, social protection and residency permits established a more or less grey or illegal space, severely restricting or even abolishing workers' mobility choices (Pun et al., 2010). The few examples given above should also sharpen our perspectives on forms of neo-bondage and their relationship with other segments of the workforce. Equally, at the core of Smith's (2006) distinction between two aspects of the indeterminacy of labour lies an appreciation that struggles within the labour process are interdependent with ownership over mobility choices. In the same sense, the extent to which labour is substitutable in the restructuring of GVCs and the particular forms such struggles can take, needs to be recognized.

Conclusion

GVC analysis has paid considerable attention to the determinants of value chain governance and has, in the process, focused on transactions between firms at the expense of the struggles over the labour process that are central to any inter-firm transaction. Referring back to labour process debates, this chapter has argued that conflict at the point of production cannot be reduced to a management-labour issue alone but has implications for the structure of labour and product markets, too. In the same way, the labour process, it is argued, is not trivial with regard to firms' positioning within the functional division of labour. The ability to organize the labour process is crucial not only for firms' vertical and horizontal competitiveness but also for their ability to develop inter-firm cooperations. The restructuring of GVCs breaks up labour processes but immediately reconnects them through struggles at the workplace level and the implications they have for labour and product markets. A conception of value chains as interlinked sets of horizontally and vertically competing labour processes can play an important part in a social explanation of GVC dynamics.

The chapter has also argued that GVC restructuring has led to an expansion of the terrains of control strategies of the labour process beyond the workplace. The fragmentation of production has come with complex forms of tiering and/or segmenting workforces along precarious employment contracts and different forms of informal employment, the structuring of mobility choices, and living arrangements. These terrains of control are a systemic element of the way GVCs are reorganized: they form part of the social foundations on which Taylorist and flexible forms of production are recombined and reconnected in GVCs (Pun and Smith, 2007). While there is space for more detailed analyses of the interrelations between the fragmentation of production processes, the internal tiering of the workforce, and the re-segmentation of the labour market, we feel that they are important elements in a power-based account of GVC restructuring as opposed to one that is based on firm strategy. Furthermore, the focus on the labour process and struggles over control beyond the workplace allows us to account for new terrains that shape global forms of economic organization.

REFERENCES

Agarwala, R. (2009) 'An economic sociology of informal work: the case of India', in N. Bandelj (ed.) *Economic Sociology of Work*, Bingley: JAI Press, pp. 315–342.

Bair, J. (2008) 'Analysing global economic organization: embedded networks and global chains compared', *Economy and Society*, 37(3): 339–364.

Barnes, T. (2012) 'Marxism and informal labour', *Journal of Australian Political Economy*, 70: 144–166.

Barrientos, S. (2013) '"Labour chains": analysing the role of labour contractors in global production networks', *Journal of Development Studies*, 49(8): 1058–1071.

Barrientos, S. and Kritzinger, A. (2004) 'Squaring the circle: global production and the informalisation of work in South African fruit exports', *Journal of International Development*, 16(1): 81–92.

Barrientos, S., Dolan, C. and Tallontire, A. (2003) 'A gendered value chain approach to codes of conduct in African horticulture', *World Development*, 31(9): 1511–1526.

Basole, A. and Basu, D. (2011) 'Relations of production and modes of surplus extraction in India: part II – "Informal" industry', *Economic and Political Weekly*, 46(15): April 9, 63–79.

Bezuidenhout, A. and Buhlungu, S. (2011) 'From compounded to fragmented labour: mineworkers and the demise of compounds in South Africa', *Antipode*, 43(2): 237–263.

Breman, J. (2010) *Outcast Labour in Asia – Circulation and Informalization of the Workforce at the Bottom of the Economy*, New Delhi: Oxford University Press.

Brown, W. (2008) 'The influence of product markets on industrial relations', in P. Blyton, N. Bacon, J. Fiorito and E. Heery (eds) *The SAGE Handbook of Industrial Relations*, London: Sage, pp. 113–128.

Burawoy, M. (1985) *The Politics of Production*, London: Verso.

Chen, M. A. (2005) *Rethinking the Informal Economy: Linkages with the Formal Economy and the Formal Regulatory Environment*, http://www.wider.unu.edu/publications/working-papers/research-papers/2005/en_GB/rp2005-10/_files/78091752824112453/default/rp2005-10.pdf: UNU-WIDER Research Paper 2005/10.

Coe, N. M., Dicken, P. and Hess, M. (2008) 'Global production networks: realising the potential', *Journal of Economic Geography*, 8(3): 271–295.

Edwards, P. K. (1986) *Conflict at Work: A Materialist Analysis of Workplace Relations*, Oxford: Basil Blackwell.

Gereffi, G., Humphrey, J. and Sturgeon, T. (2005) 'The governance of global value chains', *Review of International Political Economy*, 12(1): 78–104.

Gibbon, P., Bair, J. and Ponte, S. (2008) 'Governing global value chains: an introduction', *Economy and Society*, 37(3): 315–338.

Grimshaw, D. and Rubery, J. (2005) 'Inter-capital relations and the network organisation: redefining the work and employment nexus', *Cambridge Journal of Economics*, 29(6): 1027–1051.

Hammer, A. (2010) 'Trade unions in a constrained environment: workers' voices from a new industrial zone in India', *Industrial Relations Journal*, 41(2): 168–184.

Harriss-white, B. and Gooptu, N. (2001) 'Mapping India's world of unorganized labour', *Socialist Register*, 37: 89–118.

Henderson, P., Dicken, P., Hess, M., Coe, N. and Yeung H. W.-C. (2002) 'Global production networks and the analysis of economic development', *Review of International Political Economy*, 9(3): 436–464.

Jenkins, J. (2013) 'Organising "Spaces of Hope": union formation by Indian garment workers', *British Journal of Industrial Relations*, 51(3): 623–643.

Kelly, J. (1985) 'Management's redesign of work: labour process, labour markets and product markets', in D. Knights, H. Willmott and D. Collinson (eds)

Job Redesign: Critical Perspectives on the Labour Process, Aldershot: Gower, pp. 30–51.

Lakhani, T., Kuruvilla, S. and Avgar, A. (2013) 'From the firm to the network: global value chains and employment relations theory', *British Journal of Industrial Relations*, 51(3): 440–472.

Lund, F. and Nicholson, J. (eds) (2003) *Chains of Production, Ladders of Protection. Social Protection for Workers in the Informal Economy*. Durban, South Africa: School of Development Studies, University of Natal.

Nichols, T. and Cam, S. (2005) 'Labour in a global world – some comparisons', in T. Nichols and S. Cam (eds) *Labour in a Global World: Case Studies from the White Goods Industry in Africa, South America, East Asia, and Europe*, Basingstoke: Palgrave Macmillan, pp. 206–238.

Palpacuer, F. (2008) 'Bringing the social context back in: governance and wealth distribution in global commodity chains', *Economy and Society*, 37(3): 393–419.

Pun, N. and Smith, C. (2007) 'Putting transnational labour process in its place: the dormitory labour regime in post-socialist China', *Work, Employment and Society*, 21(1): 27–45.

Pun, N., King, C. C. C. and Chan, J. (2010) 'The role of the state, labour policy and migrant workers' struggles in globalized China', *Global Labour Journal*, 1(1): 132–151.

Rainnie, A., Herod, A. and McGrath-Champ, S. (2011) 'Review and positions: global production networks and labour', *Competition and Change*, 15(2): 155–169.

Ramirez, P. and Rainbird, H. (2010) 'Making the connections: bringing skill formation into global value chain analysis', *Work, Employment and Society*, 24(4): 699–710.

Riisgaard, L. and Hammer, N. (2011) 'Prospects for labour in global value chains: labour standards in the cut flower and banana industries', *British Journal of Industrial Relations*, 49(1): 168–190.

Robinson, P. K. and Rainbird, H. (2013) 'International supply chains and the labour process', *Competition and Change*, 17(1): 91–107.

Rubery, J. (2007) 'Developing segmentation theory: a thirty year perspective', *Economies et Sociétés*, 26(6): 941–964.

Selwyn, B. (2013) 'Social upgrading and labour in global production networks: a critique and an alternative conception', *Competition and Change*, 17(1): 75–90.

Smith, C. (2006) 'The double indeterminacy of labour power: labour effort and labour mobility', *Work, Employment and Society*, 20(2): 389–402.

Taylor, P. (2010) 'The globalisation of service work: analysing the transnational call centre value chain', in P. Thompson and C. Smith (eds) *Working Life. Renewing Labour Process Analysis*, Basingstoke: Palgrave Macmillan, pp. 244–268.

Taylor, P., Newsome, K. and Rainnie, A. (2013) '"Putting Labour in its Place": global value chains and labour process analysis', *Competition and Change*, 17(1): 1–5.

Thompson, P. and Newsome, K. (2004) 'Labour process theory, work, and the employment relations', in B. E. Kaufman (ed.) *Theoretical Perspectives on Work and the Employment Relationship*, Ithaca/New York: ILR Press, pp. 133–162.

Yeates, N. (2004) 'Global care chains', *International Feminist Journal of Politics*, 6(3): 369–391.

CHAPTER 6

Articulation of Informal Labour: Interrogating the E-waste Value Chain in Singapore and Malaysia

Aidan M. Wong

Introduction

The global production of e-waste is estimated to be around 40 million tonnes per annum and growing at a rate of 3–5 per cent annually, ranking it as one of the fastest growing waste streams (Cui and Forssberg, 2003; Schluep *et al.*, 2009; Nnorom *et al.*, 2011). A corollary of this growth in e-waste has been the exponential increase in the global e-waste trade, where around '80 per cent ends up being shipped (often illegally) to developing countries to be recycled by hundreds of thousands of informal workers' (Lundgren, 2012: 5, 16). While e-waste contains toxic elements that are hazardous (Robinson, 2009), it also consists of materials that are valuable and that can be recycled.

Recognizing surplus value to be the product of social relations of production, with the *labour process* being at the core of the creation of value, this chapter interrogates the activities and practices that enable the revalorization of 'waste', and unpacks the strategies employed by wholesalers and recycling firms to expand their influence on the network, particularly in terms of increasing their ability to create, enhance and capture value in the network. In this sense, this chapter contributes to a more nuanced understanding of the role of labour in structuring global production networks (Smith *et al.*, 2002; Selwyn, 2007; Barrientos *et al.*, 2011; Rainnie *et al.*, 2011; Taylor *et al.*, 2013; Herod *et al.*, 2014), and looks not at the movement per se of the commodity in question (i.e. the movement of e-waste across space), but rather seeks to understand the social relations engendered in its production network through the movement of value(s) that is/are embodied in the commodity.

This chapter analyses the role of the informal sector in globalized production (Phillips, 2011), focusing in particular on *karung guni* (a local term for the itinerant rag-and-bone traders) and their articulations with the regional e-waste recycling network in Malaysia and Singapore. Informal labour is constitutive of this e-waste recycling production network, as demonstrated by the pivotal role of *karung guni* to the creation of value through their collection and primary processing of e-waste. The chapter analyses how the informal sector is intimately linked with the formal sector in multiple ways, as demonstrated through an examination of the practices of *karung guni*, in particular on their collection and primary processing of e-waste which forms the basis for the (re)creation, enhancement and capture of value by subsequent downstream actors. Informal labour is thus central to e-waste recycling.

Waste in Theory

Recent scholarly interest has examined the significance of waste and recycling industries (Crang *et al.*, 2013; Herod *et al.*, 2013; Herod *et al.*, 2014; Pickren, 2014a), and the constitutive role of labour (Coe, 2013; Coe and Hess, 2013; Rainnie *et al.*, 2013; Taylor *et al.*, 2013) in shaping globalized production. An investigation into waste sheds light on the processes, politics and possibilities surrounding value (re)creation in production networks and provides an avenue for advancing the Global Value Chain (GVC) approach to take into better consideration processes beyond the present emphasis on the points of production-distribution-consumption. An interrogation of the role of informal labour – in addition to considering an otherwise overlooked group of actors in GVC studies – highlights the constitutive and pivotal role of informal labour in regional e-waste recycling networks in Malaysia and Singapore through their primary processing of e-waste that is otherwise not undertaken by formal e-waste recycling firms or wholesalers.

At present, the GVC approach has been operationalized to understand the processes of production, distribution and consumption, with more empirical and theoretical emphasis placed on the first two processes. However, to view consumption as the end point of a GVC signals a premature end to the potential contributions of the GVC framework. Indeed, Bair (2009: 15) argues that 'what may be the last link in one chain is itself an input or intermediate link to another'. She emphasizes how a commodity must be traced, even after the product is consumed.

This may be understood in two ways. First, it links together what might otherwise be thought of as an incomplete commodity chain by bringing the end products (after consumption) back into the productive realm as 'raw material'. Second, through the processes of recycling, what is deemed 'worthless' is found to embody value once again through the labour process. The by-products of consumption can form the beginnings of another GVC. The ability to integrate a GVC perspective in understanding the recycling industry is fruitful because it incorporates a view towards commodities and resources beyond consumption; and through the analysis of the (re)generation of value in waste, discarded and disposed materials can be conceptualized as the beginning of a new value chain (Herod et al., 2013; Herod et al., 2014; Pickren, 2014a; 2014b).

Labour – in particular informal labour – while increasingly recognized in GVC research, still requires much more interrogation, analysis and research before it is recognized for its constitutive role vis-à-vis 'firms' and 'states' (Selwyn, 2009; Phillips, 2011; Rainnie et al., 2011; Lund-Thomsen et al., 2012; Barrientos, 2013; Taylor et al., 2013). Labour has often been viewed as a passive factor of production, with limited agency in shaping the networks in which it participates (Coe and Jordhus-Lier, 2011; Coe, 2013). When considered in GVC research, labour is analysed through a geographically localized lens that sees it as subordinated to the demands of hyper-mobile capital (Castree et al., 2004). Furthermore, labour is most often considered through the lens of organized labour and formal employment, thus overlooking a significant portion of the population that is involved in the informal economy or in forms of self-employment (Lund and Nicholson, 2003; Phillips, 2011). To this end, the GVC approach stands to benefit from the enriching presence of informal labour in its conceptualization by taking into consideration the constitutive role of informal labour in shaping and structuring globalized production and challenging the conventional conceptualization of labour in capitalist relations of production.

The informal economy is important in two ways. First, up to 45 per cent of urban employment is found in the informal sector in 'developing countries' (Harriss-White and Gooptu, 2001; Breman, 2010). Even in 'developed countries', the informal sector is an important component of the urban economic fabric (Williams and Windebank, 1998; Williams and Windebank, 2002; Williams, 2009), and is 'embedded in richer as well as poorer regions and societies of the world' (Phillips, 2011: 311). Second, the informal sector is linked with the formal sector and globalized production through a myriad of articulations and relationships (Cheng and Gereffi, 1994; Alter Chen, 2006), for example, through the provision of sanitation, recycling and waste management services, and services that support social reproduction including childcare and housecleaning services (Roy, 2005; Wilson et al., 2006). Phillips (2011: 381) has argued that '[d]espite the wealth of scholarship on informality and informal economies across the social sciences, however, theoretical and empirical attention to informality remains rather limited'. It is this void that this chapter addresses through the case of *karung guni* in Malaysia and Singapore.

Methodology

A qualitative methodology was identified as the most suitable means to achieve the aims of this chapter, and comprised formal semi-structured interviews, informal unstructured interviews (particularly with *karung guni*) and field observation. Sturgeon (2006: 47; emphasis mine), reflecting on GVC research methodologies, argued that '[a]n understanding of ... industry-specific factors, and their interaction, requires deep knowledge of specific industries and occupations that *can only be gained through qualitative research methods*'. Wherever possible, data was triangulated across interviews and field observations.

Fieldwork and data collection was carried out in Kuala Lumpur – the federal capital and largest city in Malaysia; Penang – a state in northwest Peninsular Malaysia that has a high concentration of electronics manufacturing firms and e-waste recycling facilities; Putrajaya – the federal administrative centre and seat of government of Malaysia; and in Singapore. Fieldwork was conducted between July 2011 and July 2012, with a repeat visit to Singapore made in December 2012. A total of 201 interviews were carried out, comprising 38 in Kuala Lumpur; 57 in Penang; four in Putrajaya; and 102 in Singapore.

E-waste Circuit of Capital

Figure 6.1 is informed by Marx's circuit of capital (Marx, 1956). This approach was adapted to understand the flows of capital within this segment of the e-waste recycling network in Malaysia and Singapore, with the explicit aim of highlighting the integral role of labour and the labour process in the creation and capture of value (Smith et al., 2002; Herod et al., 2013; Herod et al., 2014). Labour, and in particular informal labour, is integral to the processes of value creation, especially with regard to the initial collection of e-waste from households and small businesses. The

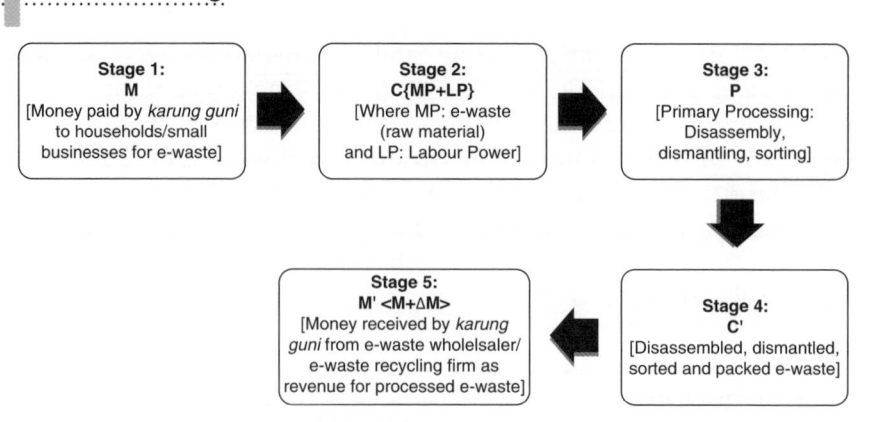

```
Stage 1:           Stage 2:              Stage 3:
   M              C{MP+LP}                  P
[Money paid by   [Where MP: e-waste    [Primary Processing:
karung guni       (raw material)         Disassembly,
to households/    and LP: Labour Power]  dismantling, sorting]
small businesses
for e-waste]

         Stage 5:
       M' <M+ΔM>                    Stage 4:
[Money received by karung            C'
guni from e-waste wholesaler/   [Disassembled, dismantled,
e-waste recycling firm as        sorted and packed e-waste]
revenue for processed e-waste]
```

Figure 6.1 E-waste circuit of capital

e-waste circuit of capital represents the flows of capital that exist in this segment of the e-waste recycling network, and highlights the relationships between various actors, while also stressing the functions carried out by each group of actors in facilitating the creation of value.

To situate the concrete value relations investigated in this chapter in a wider theoretical context, Figure 6.1 illustrates the circuit of capital as observed in the regional e-waste recycling network in Malaysia and Singapore. In Stage 1: (M), money is paid by *karung guni* to households and small and medium firms for their e-waste. In this way, capital moves from the money form into the commodity form as purchased e-waste. This transaction between *karung guni* and households and small businesses is akin to the purchase of means of production (raw materials) by capitalists in the market. In Stage 2: (C{MP+LP}), capital in the commodity form as e-waste (means of production) is combined with the *karung guni*'s own labour power – which s/he does not purchase, since s/he owns his/her own labour power – and enters into the production process. In Stage 3: (P), primary processing takes place and capital moves into the production form. In this instance, *karung guni* use their own labour to dismantle and disassemble e-waste, and subsequently sort it, before packaging it together. In Stage 4: (C'), capital once again moves into the commodity form as primary processed e-waste that is available to be sold to e-waste wholesalers. In Stage 5: (M' <M+ΔM>), capital in the money form is paid to *karung guni* who sell their primary processed e-waste to wholesalers. At this stage, ΔM indicates the surplus value that *karung guni* have produced and, in part, captured. Stage 5 marks the point at which e-waste has been taken out of the hands of *karung guni* and is further processed by other economic actors in the value chain. The process of recycling continues with these other actors, and culminates in the re-introduction of recycled precious metals into the production process. Figure 6.1 illustrates the flows and transformations of capital from the money form, into the commodity form, and the production form, to be returned to commodity form and money form. This cycle is repeated through the e-waste circuit of capital. The importance of the labour process in the creation of value is seen in the movement of M ... M'. The surplus value – which is the difference between M ... M' (i.e. ΔM) – is the product of the combination of abstract labour (i.e. *socially necessary labour time*) with the means of production (Marx, 1956; Elson, 1979). In this sense, labour power is a necessary, but not sufficient factor that needs to be combined with means of production to create surplus value. Without this combination, no surplus value can be created. The exchanges that occur at M-C and C-M are pivotal junctures that present actors with the opportunity to extract more value from the network, through various strategies.

Waste and Value

As 'waste', commodities are sold on to *karung guni*. This serves as the starting point for a series of processes that allow for the discarded and seemingly useless commodities to be broken down and subsequently reused or recycled – a process that may be conceived of as their re-birth as a commodity. These previously unwanted commodities and materials are given a new lease of life, and are once again articulated in networks of production-distribution-consumption.

E-waste, when discarded by owners and recycled by others – regardless of whether through municipal garbage collection, collection by *karung guni*, or other means – embodies value, and should not be regarded as detritus and devoid of any value(s). In this regard, e-waste is not the opposite of value, but rather, 'waste' still embodies value – value that may not be perceived by the original owners who have discarded the 'waste' (Figure 6.1, Stage 1). Reiterating Marx's (1990) conception of value, commodities possess use value, exchange value and importantly, surplus value. In this e-waste circuit of capital, surplus value is created through the labour process from the activities of concrete labour. Value is inherent in waste, and a commodity is discarded only because it is seen to be of minimal or no value to the original owner. The creation of surplus value relies on the *labour process* to transform what is presently 'waste' to that which is of value once again.

Waste is not in opposition to value, but rather is constituted by it. When does a commodity become 'waste'? This transformation from commodity to 'waste' occurs the moment a consumer decides that the commodity is to be replaced, discarded or is obsolete – hence creating e-'waste' (see Lepawsky and Billah, 2011). 'Waste' is created when a commodity has become something of no or little value to the owner simply because it is no longer desired or wanted or indeed no longer performs a use. This marks the beginning step in the process of 'waste' production, and is the precursor to the next step of collection by *karung guni*. Indeed, *karung guni* – who are armed with a particular way of valuing – view e-waste through a lens different from that of the consumers who discard their obsolete and/or broken electronic and electrical products. For *karung guni*, e-waste – in spite of being discarded or unwanted by previous owners – embodies value, and this is demonstrated in two distinct ways. First, in the very act of wanting to acquire the e-waste from owners who wish to discard their e-waste, *karung guni* demonstrate that there is an already existing value to e-waste. The value of e-waste is seen in the economic potential that *karung guni* identify in e-waste, either to be sold on as cannibalized reusable components or as recyclable e-waste components. Second, through the act of purchasing e-waste from the owners for a nominal sum of money, *karung guni* value e-waste. In this regard, the purchase of e-waste may be conceptualized in a similar manner as the purchase of raw material for production. This recognition of value embodied within e-waste is aptly understood by Sheppard and Barnes (1990: 37) as 'validation through exchange', a process which supports Marx's (1956) conception of exchange value, since a commodity is of no exchange value until it is actually traded through the market. In a similar way, *karung guni*, through their purchase of e-waste from households and small and medium firms, validate the exchange value of e-waste when they pay an amount of money in return for e-waste. For example, Roy, a *karung guni* in Singapore, argued that he is very careful in his purchase of e-waste, and tries to look out for those that he knows will give him a higher return:

> Of course I don't buy e-waste that has little value to me! I am not crazy you know … I am also not a garbage collector. Sometimes people sell computers with Pentium 3 or Pentium 2 processors. Those are so old, there is little value in them, except for scrap. What I really want are CPUs that are only about three years old, complete with the hard drive. These often have salvageable components that I can sell on to component refurbishing shops, or to computer servicing shops in Sim Lim Square. They are much more valuable.
>
> (Interview with Roy, Singapore, 12 July 2011)

According to Roy, the more up to date the technology of the CPU, the greater the amount he is willing to pay. Roy further explained that for computers running on processors that are more than five years old, he would pay around SGD 10–15 (≈ USD 8–12) for the unit, whilst those running on more up-to-date processors would be valued around SGD 35–40 (≈ USD 28–32).

Value in e-waste is derived from the previous rounds of congealed labour that is still embodied in e-waste (Herod *et al.*, 2013, 2014). Exchange value can still be found in e-waste from the point when *karung guni* purchase e-waste from its owners. Latent use value – which is the basis of the exchange value – is found within e-waste, and it is this latent use value that is acted upon by labour (*karung guni*) to create more value in e-waste. *Karung guni* who purchase e-waste from households and small commercial offices cart the e-waste to their homes to disassemble, sort and package in sufficient quantities to sell on to e-waste wholesalers. In addition, *karung guni* cannibalize e-waste to salvage various components that are still in a working condition to sell on to electrical and electronic repair shops, including computer servicing shops, and mobile phone repair shops. Richard, a *karung guni* in Penang, argued that the sale of working components to local electronics and electrical repair shops was a good source of revenue, and provided even higher returns than if he sold the components to e-waste wholesalers:

> I sell the working parts to a couple of repair shops in the city centre. It is a good source of money since they pay more to me compared to just selling it to e-waste wholesalers. The difference is between 15 per cent to 20 per cent more than what I would be paid if I sold it as recycled materials. But I must also make sure that the parts are working. If they are not, then the repair shops will not buy from me any more.
>
> (Interview with Richard, Penang, 15 January 2011)

Although the sale of working components to repair shops yields greater returns, technical ability to test the components is required. The requisite knowledge concerning electrical circuitry and the functioning of electrical and electronic products, and the ability to decipher which components of e-waste are working, is a complex skill set that not all *karung guni* possess. Out of 46 *karung guni* interviewed in Singapore, 42 were engaged in the sale of working components to repair shops, whilst only 26 out of the 41 *karung guni* interviewed in Malaysia actively sold to repair shops.

An analysis of the e-waste circuit of capital finds its foundation in an appreciation of the labour process as crucial to the creation of value (see Figure 6.1). Without the labour process – focused around the collection, dismantling and sorting of e-waste by *karung guni* – the functioning of the regional e-waste production network in Malaysia and Singapore would not be possible.

Informal Labour

The informal sector, replete with its diverse forms of production, is articulated in many ways within the capitalist mode of production (Guha-Khasnobis *et al.*, 2006; Williams, 2009; Williams and Windebank, 2002). The activities that the informal sector performs are significant to the functioning of the e-waste recycling network. *Karung guni* are dominant in the activities of collecting, disassembly and sorting of e-waste components, and the downstream actors in the regional e-waste recycling production network in Malaysia and Singapore are heavily dependent on the labour of *karung guni*. Although the articulation of the informal sector in the e-waste recycling network in Malaysia and Singapore varies slightly between the two contexts (due mainly to different socio-political environments in Malaysia and Singapore), their core activities are similar, and can be understood in two main areas which are central to the very functioning of the regional e-waste recycling network: (1) collecting; and (2) primary processing – disassembling, dismantling and sorting.

Collecting

The collection of e-waste by itinerant waste buyers is the pivotal point in understanding the revalorization of waste by *karung guni* (see Figure 6.1, Stage 1). E-waste produced by households and small commercial firms is purchased by *karung guni*, who, through the exchange, highlight the latent value in the e-waste that they purchase. This collection of e-waste by *karung guni* is essential for the subsequent processes in the e-waste recycling network, and several e-waste recycling firms have attempted to copy the collection geographies of *karung guni*, but with very low levels of success (see Bunnell *et al.*, 2011). Without *karung guni* going around to purchase e-waste from households and small and medium firms, there is a significant pattern of either discarding e-waste indiscriminately, or keeping the e-waste in homes and offices in drawers and in corners, thus losing out on the recycling potential of these materials.

Karung guni are essential to the process of collection because they have an established foothold in the community as purchasers of waste and are the preferred people to whom e-waste is sold. Many households refuse to pass their recyclable materials to municipal solid waste firms or commercial recycling firms, choosing instead to sell to *karung guni*. Indeed, *karung guni* perform a critical function in the regional e-waste recycling network through their collection of e-waste. George, a director of a Singapore-based e-waste recycling firm shared that they had attempted to operate their own collection rounds, but gave up after their pilot project, due to poor responses from the public:

> *Karung guni* do very important work in collecting old televisions and other electronic products from households. We do not have the same network that they have, and they are already familiar with the residents who are willing to sell to them.
>
> (Interview with George, Singapore, 21 November 2011)

The difficulties involved with attempts at copying the collection networks of itinerant waste buyers were similarly highlighted by three other managers of e-waste recycling firms in Singapore, and two in Malaysia. In addition, any attempts at copying *karung guni* collection networks would also increase the operating costs for e-waste recycling firms by requiring increased manpower and the purchase of tools and machinery, however rudimentary. This point underscores the established nature of the collection networks of *karung guni*, and how they have managed to become socially embedded within the communities that they serve. In addition to the collection networks, *karung guni* also visit very frequently, since each housing estate is not serviced by only one *karung guni*, but rather has several of them going through an estate at different times of the day throughout the week. This is in contrast to the collection routines of municipal solid waste collectors in Singapore who only collect recyclable paper, glass and plastics (not e-waste), and who do so only once a week or fortnight. Similarly, Neo (2010) found that many government-led recycling initiatives in Singapore, under the auspices of the National Recycling Programme, did not take into account the role of informal itinerant waste buyers. Jonathan, a Singapore government official, recounted the difficulties faced by municipal solid waste collectors:

> They [*karung guni*] provide a service that we cannot. We tried encouraging households with our door-to-door fortnightly collections, but then *karung guni* go every week, and there are so many of them, that one home can get multiple *karung guni* going there in a week, even in

a day. They [the households] also rather sell it to them since they get money for selling their discarded items ... they get no money from us.
(Interview with Jonathan, Singapore, 27 November 2011)

The sale of e-waste and recyclable material to *karung guni* does not present itself as a problem to the government, and has in fact been seen in a positive light, leading to the relaxed enforcement of regulations and licensing requirements on *karung guni* by authorities in Singapore. One of the most distinct effects of regular visits by *karung guni* has been the lower levels of rubbish collected by municipal solid waste collectors. From the perspective of the government, the activities of itinerant waste buyers aid in reducing the amount of waste that is sent to landfill or incineration, and because it is separated at source, provides valuable materials that can be recycled and re-introduced into manufacturing and production. In addition, it was suggested by several e-waste wholesalers, both formal and informal, that itinerant waste buyers are their primary source of e-waste, and this ranges from 85 per cent to all of the e-waste that they sell wholesale subsequently. Aaron, a formal e-waste wholesaler in Singapore, encapsulated the sentiments of eight of the 11 e-waste wholesalers in Singapore, and 12 of the 14 e-waste wholesalers in Malaysia when he argued:

My e-waste ... if not for *karung guni*, I might as well close down. They are the backbone of my supply. If they stop collecting, I will lose between 90 per cent to 95 per cent of my supply. I know there are other wholesalers who are entirely dependent on a group of *karung guni* ... they have a special relationship, and it is hard to 'steal' *karung guni* away from another wholesaler once they have a strong business relationship.
(Interview with Aaron, Singapore, 14 August 2011)

This finding is similar to that of Hieronymi *et al.* (2012, see also Streicher-Porte *et al.*, 2005; Chi *et al.*, 2011; Kreibe, 2012), who highlight the importance of the informal sector in the collection of e-waste on a global scale.

Disassembly, Dismantling and Sorting

After collecting e-waste from households and small commercial firms, *karung guni* disassemble and dismantle – in their homes or along the roadside – the e-waste into its component parts, and then sort them accordingly (see Figure 6.1, Stage 2 to Stage 4). The geography of *karung guni* activities is important and is a potential source of tension because of the interwoven nature of home-space and work-space. E-waste is generally separated into categories such as plastic casings, aluminium casings, copper wires, circuit boards, capacitors, resistors and silicon chips. These are then placed in bags or boxes until a sufficient volume is accumulated, or until individual *karung guni* need to sell the primary processed e-waste so as to ensure sufficient cash flow to continue purchasing 'raw' e-waste. This process of dismantling and sorting is very important for downstream actors in the e-waste recycling network, as it improves the efficiency and productivity of the e-waste recycling firms. For example, Shekdar (2009) emphasizes the importance of the hand sorting of solid waste in Asia, arguing that this practice has formed the basis for more efficient practices of recycling and reuse because the waste materials have been separated into distinct streams and can be managed more effectively and efficiently. This practice of dismantling and sorting by *karung guni* can be conceptualized as contributing to the profitability of the e-waste recycling firms, while remaining outside the direct employment of these firms. Mark, a manager in a full-recovery e-waste recycling firm in Singapore, argued that *karung guni* are vital to his business as they manually dismantle and sort e-waste, a process that reaps far superior output compared to mechanical processors:

> There is a great amount of cost-saving for us from the sorting that *karung guni* do ... They essentially make it easier for us to put e-waste into our crushers, and be assured that the crushed materials that emerge are of a high quality. Hand sorting is something that can never be replicated by mechanical sorting methods, even today. If we were to do the dismantling and sorting in-house, our operational costs would rise significantly.
> (Interview with Mark, Singapore, 21 August 2011)

Indeed, the dismantling and sorting that is performed by *karung guni* is a significant value creation process, and reduces the financial commitment by e-waste recycling firms. This arrangement in effect permits the e-waste recycling firm to engage in significant cost-savings as it does not need to pay wages and pensions, negotiate with unions, or provide employment benefits to the *karung guni*. A key concern highlighted by many interviewees was the potential need to employ many more staff if *karung guni* were not involved in the disassembly, dismantling and sorting of e-waste. Christopher, general manager of an e-waste recycling firm in Singapore, suggested:

> Without what *karung guni* do for us, we would have to employ many more staff to manually dismantle all the e-waste that we receive. That

would not only be time-consuming, but also very labour intensive ... What they [*karung guni*] do is really essential for us, and it increases our downstream productivity since we save on having to go through more rounds of sorting.

(Interview with Christopher, Singapore, 13 November 2011)

The functions of *karung guni* are thus quite considerable, especially in the processes of dismantling and sorting of e-waste. In addition, *karung guni* do not function merely as providers of means of production for e-waste recycling firms, but occasionally serve as outsourced labour for e-waste recycling firms when they manage to attain large orders of e-waste for disposal. In the first instance, *karung guni* are disguised wage labour for e-waste recycling firms by selling the collected, dismantled, disassembled and sorted e-waste to wholesalers who subsequently sell this on to e-waste recycling firms. In the second instance, *karung guni* are occasionally paid by e-waste recycling firms as outsourced wage labour to perform the same duties of dismantling, disassembly and sorting. However, the difference in this instance is that *karung guni* have sold their labour power to the e-waste recycling firms, and in effect are receiving a wage for their work. Also, this second instance removes from *karung guni* the ownership of the means of production (i.e. e-waste), since the e-waste is owned by the recycling firm and not by *karung guni* themselves.

Disassembly, dismantling and sorting of e-waste is thus a critical function performed by *karung guni* that is considered to be of high value by actors in the e-waste recycling network. The relations of *karung guni* with e-waste recycling firms are not as straightforward as simply selling them dismantled, disassembled and sorted e-waste, but also includes the sale of their labour power when recycling firms outsource the dismantling, disassembly and sorting functions to them.

Conclusion

Waste is the linchpin that links together two (seemingly) disconnected production networks by bridging the gap between consumption on the one hand, and a new round of production and value creation on the other. Waste embodies value, and this is demonstrated through an analysis of the e-waste circuit of capital. Rather than analysing the regional e-waste recycling network through an investigation into the movement per se of the commodity itself, Marx's (1956) circuit of capital has been adopted to focus on the flows of value within the network, and has hence illuminated the processes that enable the creation, enhancement and capture of value. These processes include the collection and primary processing of e-waste by *karung guni*, the bulk collection and further sorting of e-waste by wholesalers, and the extraction of recovered precious metals by e-waste recycling firms.

The payment of money by *karung guni* to households which they collect from is a validation of the value that *karung guni* perceive in the e-waste that they purchase, in what has been termed 'validation through exchange' (Sheppard and Barnes, 1990: 37). All subsequent transactions between economic actors in the regional e-waste recycling network, whereby e-waste (at various levels of processing) is traded, similarly demonstrate this validation of value embodied in e-waste. *Karung guni*'s validation of value in e-waste is the crucial moment at which what is waste is reconceptualized as a raw material for subsequent rounds of production and value creation. Second, this process of (re)valuation by *karung guni* through their purchase and collection of e-waste, and the subsequent disassembling, dismantling and sorting, brings to light the process of value creation. I have argued that *karung guni* are the pivotal actors (through their collection and primary processing of e-waste) that enable the creation, enhancement and capture of value by other downstream actors.

Karung guni are crucial in the regional e-waste recycling network in Malaysia and Singapore because of the core functions that they perform in terms of the collection and primary processing of e-waste. The informal sector is constitutive of the regional e-waste recycling network, and needs to be considered in the analysis. To this end, the examination of the relationships of *karung guni* with the regional e-waste recycling network has demonstrated that the informal sector is articulated with this production network as a key source of 'raw material'. The examination of *karung guni* has also revealed the importance of considering the labour process in the analysis of global production. With reference to Figure 6.1, surplus value in this network is produced through the labour process, as demonstrated for example by the concrete labour of *karung guni* who collect, dismantle, disassemble and sort the e-waste.

REFERENCES

Alter Chen, M. (2006). 'Rethinking the informal economy: linkages with the formal economy and the formal regulatory environment', in B. Guha-Khasnobis, R. Kanbur, and E. Ostrom (eds) *Linking the Formal and Informal Economy: Concepts and Policies*, Oxford: Oxford University Press, pp. 75–92.

Bair, J., 2009. 'Global commodity chains: genealogy and review', in J. Bair (ed.) *Frontiers of Commodity Chain Research*, Stanford, CA: Stanford University Press, pp. 1–34.

Barrientos, S. (2013). '"Labour chains": analysing the role of labour contractors in global production networks', *The Journal of Development Studies*, 49(8): 1058–1071.
Barrientos, S., Gereffi, G. and Rossi, A. (2011) 'Economic and social upgrading in global production networks: a new paradigm for a changing world', *International Labor Review*, 150(3–4): 319–340.
Breman, J. (2010) *Outcast Labour in Asia: Circulation and Informalization of the Workforce at the Bottom of the Economy*, New Delhi: Oxford University Press.
Bunnell, T., Miller, M., Marolt, P., Li, H. and Yeo, V. (eds) (2011) *Inter-Asia Roundtable 2011: Recycling Cities*, Singapore: Asia Research Institute, National University of Singapore.
Castree, N., Coe, N., Ward, K. and Samers, M. (2004) *Spaces of Work: Global Capitalism and Geographies of Labour*, London: SAGE Publications.
Cheng, L. L. and Gereffi, G. (1994) 'The informal economy in East Asian development', *International Journal of Urban and Regional Research*, 18(2): 194–219.
Chi, X., Streicher-Porte, M., Wang, M. Y. L. and Reuter, M. A. (2011) 'Informal electronic waste recycling: a sector review with special focus on China', *Waste Management*, 31(4): 731–742.
Coe, N. M. (2013) 'Geographies of production III: making space for labour', *Progress in Human Geography*, 37(2): 271–284.
Coe, N. M. and Hess, M. (2013) 'Global production networks, labour and development', *Geoforum*, 44: 4–9.
Coe, N. M. and Jordhus-Lier, D. C. (2011) 'Constrained agency? Re-evaluating the geographies of labour', *Progress in Human Geography*, 35(2): 211–233.
Crang, M., Hughes, A., Gregson, N., Norris, L. and Ahamed, F. (2013) 'Rethinking governance and value in commodity chains through global recycling networks', *Transactions of the Institute of British Geographers*, 38(1): 12–24.
Cui, J. and Forssberg, E. (2003) 'Mechanical recycling of waste electric and electronic equipment: a review', *Journal of Hazardous Materials*, 99(3): 243–263.
Cumbers, A., Nativel, C. and Routledge, P. (2008) 'Labour agency and union positionalities in global production networks', *Journal of Economic Geography*, 8(3): 369–387.
Elson, D. (1979) 'The value theory of labour', in D. Elson, (ed.) *Value: The Representation of Labour in Capitalism*, London: CSE Books, pp. 115–180.
Guha-Khasnobis, B., Kanbur, R. and Ostrom, E. (2006) 'Beyond formality and informality', in B. Guha-Khasnobis, R. Kanbur and E. Ostrom (eds) *Linking the Formal and Informal Economy: Concepts and Policies*, Oxford: Oxford University Press, pp. 1–20.
Harriss-White, B. and Gooptu, N. (2001) 'Mapping India's world of unorganised labour', in L. Panitch and C. Leys (eds) *The Socialist Register 2000: Working Classes, Global Realities*, London: Merlin Press, pp. 89–118.
Herod, A., Pickren, G., Rainnie, A. and McGrath-Champ, S. (2013) 'Waste, commodity fetishism and the ongoingness of economic life', *Area*, 45(3): 376–382.
Herod, A., Pickren, G., Rainnie, A. and McGrath-Champ, S. (2014) 'Global destruction networks, labour and waste', *Journal of Economic Geography*, 14(2): 421–441.

Hieronymi, K., Kahhat, R. and Williams, E. (eds) (2012) *E-waste Management*, London: Routledge.

Kreibe, S. (2012) 'Current and new electronic waste recycling technologies', in K. Hieronymi, R. Kahhat and E. Williams (eds) *E-waste Management*, London: Routledge, pp. 25–48.

Lepawsky, J. and Billah, M. (2011) 'Making chains that (un)make things: waste–value relations and the Bangladeshi rubbish electronics industry', *Geografiska Annaler: Series B, Human Geography*, 93(2): 121–139.

Lund, F. J. and Nicholson, J. (eds) (2003) *Chains of Production, Ladders of Protection: Social Protection for Workers in the Informal Economy*, Durban, South Africa: School of Development Studies, University of KwaZulu Natal.

Lundgren, K. (2012) *The Global Impact of E-waste*, Geneva: International Labour Organization.

Lund-Thomsen, P., Nadvi, K., Chan, A., Khara, N. and Xue, H. (2012) 'Labour in global value chains: work conditions in football manufacturing in China, India and Pakistan', *Development and Change*, 43(6): 1211–1237.

Marx, K. (1956) *Capital Volume II*. F. Engels, ed., Moscow, USSR: Progress Publishers.

Marx, K. (1990) *Capital Volume I*, London: Penguin.

Neo, H. (2010) 'The potential of large-scale urban waste recycling: a case study of the national recycling programme in Singapore', *Society & Natural Resources*, 23(9): 872–887.

Nnorom, I. C., Osibanjo, O. and Ogwuegbu, M. O. C. (2011) 'Global disposal strategies for waste cathode ray tubes', *Resources, Conservation and Recycling*, 55(3): 275–290.

Phillips, N. (2011) 'Informality, global production networks and the dynamics of "adverse incorporation"', *Global Networks*, 11(3): 380–397.

Pickren, G. (2014a) 'Geographies of E-waste: towards a political ecology approach to e-waste and digital technologies', *Geography Compass*, 8(2): 111–124.

Pickren, G. (2014b) 'Political ecologies of electronic waste: Uncertainty and legitimacy in the governance of e-waste geographies', *Environment and Planning A*, 46(1): 26–45.

Rainnie, A., Herod, A. and McGrath-Champ, S. (2011) 'Review and positions: global production networks and labour', *Competition & Change*, 15(2): 155–169.

Rainnie, A., Herod, A. and McGrath-Champ, S. (2013) 'Global production networks, labour and small firms', *Capital & Class*, 37(2): 177–195.

Robinson, B. H. (2009) 'E-waste: an assessment of global production and environmental impacts', *Science of the Total Environment*, 408(2): 183–191.

Roy, A. (2005) 'Urban informality: toward an epistemology of planning', *Journal of the American Planning Association*, 71(2): 147–158.

Schluep, M., Hagelueken, C., Kuehr, R., Magalini, F., Maurer, C., Meskers, C., Mueller, E. and Wang, F. (2009) *Recycling – E-waste to Resource*, Final Report [Online], Geneva: UNEP.

Selwyn, B. (2007) 'Labour process and workers' bargaining power in export grape production, North East Brazil', *Journal of Agrarian Change*, 7(4): 526–553.

Selwyn, B. (2009) 'Labour flexibility in export horticulture: a case study of northeast Brazilian grape production', *Journal of Peasant Studies*, 36(4):761–782.

Shekdar, A. V. (2009) 'Sustainable solid waste management: an integrated approach for Asian countries', *Waste Management*, 29(4): 1438–1448.

Sheppard, E. and Barnes, T. J. (1990) *The Capitalist Space Economy: Geographical Analysis After Ricardo, Marx and Sraffa*, London: Unwin Hyman.

Smith, A., Rainnie, A., Dunford, M., Hardy, J., Hudson, R. and Sadler, D. (2002) 'Networks of value, commodities and regions: reworking divisions of labour in macro-regional economies', *European Urban and Regional Studies*, 26(1): 41–63.

Streicher-Porte, M., Widmer, R., Jain, A., Bader, H.-P., Scheidegger, R. and Kytzia, S. (2005) 'Key drivers of the e-waste recycling system: assessing and modelling e-waste processing in the informal sector in Delhi', *Environmental Impact Assessment Review*, 25(5): 472–491.

Sturgeon, T. J. (2006) 'Conceptualizing integrative trade: the global value chains framework', *Trade Policy Research*, 6: 35–72, http://www.international.gc.ca/economist-economiste/assets/pdfs/research/TPR_2006/Chapter_3_Sturgeon-en.pdf (accessed: 8 June 2012).

Taylor, P., Newsome, K. and Rainnie, A. (2013) '"Putting labour in its place": global value chains and labour process analysis', *Competition & Change*, 17(1): 1–5.

Williams, C. C. (2009) 'Formal and informal employment in Europe: beyond dualistic representations', *European Urban and Regional Studies*, 16(2): 147–159.

Williams, C. C. and Windebank, J. (1998) *Informal Employment in the Advanced Economies: Implications for Work and Welfare*, London: Routledge.

Williams, C. C. and Windebank, J. (2002) 'The uneven geographies of informal economic activities: a case study of two British cities', *Work, Employment & Society*, 16(2): 231–250.

Wilson, D. C., Velis, C. and Cheeseman, C. (2006) 'Role of informal sector recycling in waste management in developing countries', *Habitat International*, 30(4): 797–808.

Unpacking Labour: Power, Agency and Standards

PART II

CHAPTER 7

Global Production and Uneven Development: When Bringing Labour in isn't Enough

Jennifer Bair and Marion Werner

In spite of the veritable efflorescence of work on global production networks (GPN) during the last decade and a half, there is a resounding consensus that questions of labour continue to be marginalized in this literature (Bair, 2005; Coe *et al.*, 2008; Cumbers *et al.*, 2008; Taylor, 2010; Rainnie *et al.*, 2011; Stringer *et al.*, 2014). The fact that this conclusion has been reiterated so frequently is somewhat surprising, given the proliferation of contributions during roughly the same period that would appear to fill this very lacuna (Collins, 2003; Hale and Wills, 2005; Coe and Jordhus-Lier, 2010; Hough, 2010; Ramamurthy, 2011; Werner, 2012; Kelly, 2013). This leads us to ask if repeated calls to 'bring labour in' may be less a lament of labour's absence from this work than an expression of dissatisfaction with the way that labour is being conceptualized in analyses of global production. Consider, for example, that many of the recent interventions calling for the incorporation of labour into the GPN literature express a critical if not sceptical attitude towards this approach, and its central conceit of 'upgrading', even as the authors draw eclectically from that same conceptual framework. Although we sympathize with these critiques, we argue that there is much to be learned from the study of GPNs (by which term we mean to include the varied traditions of global chains/network research, including the global commodity chain (GCC), global value chain (GVC), and GPN frameworks). *Specifically, the value of the GPN perspective lies in its largely hitherto unrealized potential to inform our understanding of capitalism as a process of combined and uneven development* (cf. Coe *et al.*, 2008).

It is from this central concern for harnessing GPN insights towards elaborating a broader analysis of capitalist uneven development that we engage here in a consideration of the labour process in global circuits of production. As the diversity of chapters in this volume demonstrates, there is no a priori way to apply the GPN approach to questions of labour. We observe, however, that much of the work on GPNs and labour falls, more or less neatly, into two broad streams. The first and largest of these asks how labour (sometimes understood collectively, but more often as a particular group of workers) is affected by the dynamics of a particular GPN. The primary research question orienting this stream is what impact efforts to improve a firm's performance and position within the chain – that is, to upgrade – have on labour. In contrast to this first body of work, in which labour is an *object of* GPNs, the second area of research foregrounds labour as an *agent in* GPNs, and considers the degree to which the form and content of the labour process, shaped by labour struggles, is co-constitutive of global production arrangements.

In this chapter, we engage critically with both these approaches to the labour question in GPNs as part of our ongoing effort to think through contemporary forms of uneven development in light of observable GPN dynamics (see Werner and Bair, 2011 and the essays collected therein). While GPN-based labour studies have yielded detailed analyses of changes in the labour process, and highlighted the structures of opportunity for shaping that process from the social position of labour, we believe that critical engagements should consider labour process changes in GPNs as concrete determinations of the global restructuring of labour-capital relations. In foregrounding uneven development and what elsewhere we have called a 'disarticulations perspective' (see Werner and Bair, 2011; Bair *et al.*, 2013), we aim to reorient the conversation about global production, which we feel is becoming mired in a set of internecine debates over network conceptualizations (GPN, GCC, GVC, etc.) that may miss the global economy 'forest' for the network 'trees' (see also Dussel Peters, 2008).

In what follows, we argue that while the two strands of literature on labour and GPNs – labour as object and labour as agent – appear to offer complementary correctives to one another, the privileging of network forms in both variations limits how their respective insights can be brought to bear upon our understanding of the ongoing social and territorial reworking of capitalist accumulation. Because capitalism is not reducible to discrete networks of particular firms, GPNs and labour's mobilization within these circuits cannot stand in for political economic analysis in toto. It is not simply a matter of 'extending' the network to include additional non-firm actors and institutions such as labour unions. Rather, we argue for an understanding of the cycles of network formation charted by scholars of GPNs – the emergence, maintenance and eventual reconfiguration of global production arrangements, and labour's role in each of these moments – as a process that contributes to the reproduction of capitalist accumulation along existing and new contours of uneven development.

Two Extant Approaches to Labour and GPNs

We began our chapter by observing that GPN research has been widely faulted for ignoring labour. Nevertheless, we identified two broad, but rather distinct streams of work on labour in GVCs and GPNs.

Labour as object: Scholars of development pioneered the study of global production networks as a way to understand how new forms of economic integration and trade liberalization challenged the previous model of industrialization and economic growth in the global South. During the 1990s, as the field consolidated into what was then called the global commodity chains framework (to be joined later by the GVC and GPN approaches), its central research question became how functionally integrated but spatially dispersed production networks shaped development trajectories (Gereffi, 1994; 1999; Kaplinsky, 1998; Humphrey and Schmitz, 2001). In practice, this meant narrowing the optic from the national economy – the default unit of analysis during the developmentalist era – to sets of inter-firm relationships that stretch across developed and developing economies. This shift, in turn, necessitated a similar rescaling of development to one that could be accommodated by, and evaluated in, the context of the network ontology. Thus, while development remained the ultimate (if underdetermined) end of participation in commodity chains, as an object of analysis, development was largely displaced by the concept of industrial upgrading, defined as the process whereby an actor (typically a firm or producer) moves up the chain to a more secure, profitable, or otherwise preferable position within it. Although there was little dedicated attention to labour in the first generation of upgrading research, some studies suggested that upgrading at the organizational level affected the quality and quantity of employment in the export sector, and in some cases, reshaped the labour process within the upgraded enterprise (Carrillo and Hualde, 1998; Bair and Gereffi, 2001; Dolan and Humphrey, 2001).

Over time, commodity chain research came to centre increasingly on how the upgrading prospects of network participants were shaped by the power dynamics, or governance structure, of the GPN. Originally defined as the 'authority and power relationships that determine how financial, material, and human resources are allocated and flow within a chain' (Gereffi, 1994: 97), multiple conceptualizations of governance have been proposed since the term was debuted in Gereffi's typology of buyer-driven and producer-driven governance (Gibbon et al., 2008). Some scholars, drawing from transaction cost economics, view governance as the coordination of exchanges, which can take place within the firm, on the market, or via one of several hybrid modes (modular, relational, captive) (Gereffi et al., 2005). Others, influenced by convention theory, see governance as a form of normalization or justification in which activities along the chain are understood and brought into alignment with broader normative environments (Gibbon and Ponte, 2005). In a recent review of the governance literature, Ponte and Sturgeon explain that:

> [t]he idea of governance ... rests on the assumption that, while both disintegration of production and its re-integration through inter-firm trade have recognizable dynamics, they do not occur spontaneously ... Instead these processes are 'driven' by the strategies and decisions of specific actors. The relevance of GVC governance is that it examines the concrete practices, power dynamics, and organizational forms that give character and structure to cross-border business networks. (2014: 200)

Several of the first studies of governance and upgrading focused on the apparel industry – a classic case of what Gereffi (1994) called a buyer-driven chain. Gereffi argued that the sourcing networks connecting foreign brands and retailers to developing country-exporters represented 'potentially dynamic learning curves' through which suppliers could be educated about the demands of producing (and perhaps eventually designing) for foreign markets (1999: 39). This model of upgrading in buyer-driven industries was supported by subsequent research on garment producers in Latin America, which were found to be moving up from basic assembly subcontracting to more complex activities and more sophisticated products (Kessler, 1999; Bair and Gereffi, 2001; Schrank, 2004). Yet many studies also suggested that the consequences of upgrading have proven disappointing, whether in terms of the unit value of exports (Schrank, 2004), the financial position and overall health of the firm (Pickles et al., 2006; Tokatli, 2013), the well-being of workers (Gibbon and Ponte, 2005; Raworth and Kidder, 2009), or even the firm's very survival (Werner and Bair, 2011). Collectively, this research underscored the need to reappraise the concept of industrial upgrading. Specifically, GPN scholars were called upon not just to better specify the conditions under which economic upgrading occurred, but also the factors affecting whether it benefited workers.

One solution to this problem that has been posed by leading scholars of GPNs is to reconceptualize upgrading as two analytically separate processes: economic upgrading, which refers to the firm-level process of increasing value capture or moving to higher value-added activities, and social upgrading, which refers to the process of securing workers' 'rights and entitlements and improving the quality of their employment' (Barrientos et al., 2011: 324). These two dimensions of upgrading are now seen as bi-directional, with recent contributions to the GPN literature emphasizing that movement within a network does not always go in the direction of increased competitiveness, better working conditions, greater security, etc. Downgrading, as well as upgrading, is a theoretical possibility and, as we are learning from this work, an empirical regularity.

Applying this revised down/upgrading schema to analyses of GPNs represents one of the current frontiers of work in this field. A particularly ambitious example is the Capturing the Gains research network, an international, interdisciplinary team of scholars studying upgrading (or its absence) in four GPNs: apparel, tourism, cellular phones and horticulture.[1] The ultimate goal is to develop indicators of each dimension of upgrading that are relevant to different industry and country contexts and yet general enough to yield comparable data. Collection and analysis of this data would enable the relationship between the economic and social dimensions of upgrading, first assumed and later problematized in various case studies, to be examined empirically (Milberg and Winkler, 2011). Operationalizing social upgrading is particularly challenging when it comes to measuring enabling rights of freedom of association and collective bargaining – core labour standards that have nonetheless proven elusive to measure (let alone safeguard) via typical inspection and monitoring regimes.

Research on upgrading has already contributed to our understanding of how the labour process within an industry or workplace is shaped by the dynamics of the larger GPN in which it is embedded. Introducing a separate social dimension to the upgrading schema, and considering instances of downgrading, undoubtedly improves the analytical toolbox of GPN research, and moves it in the direction of grappling with the complicated and contingent nature of network restructuring. While the early GPN literature might be faulted for an excessively optimistic tone regarding the prospects for network participants to upgrade, this enthusiasm has been curbed by the sobering findings that continue to accumulate from a wealth of case studies.

Among the key conclusions are that upgrading, even at the level of the firm, is by no means a guaranteed outcome of GPN participation; that successful upgrading – at the level of improved efficiencies, expanded capabilities, etc. – does not always secure greater value capture for the firm; and that the gains from upgrading, when they do occur, are not necessarily shared by workers.

From the vantage point of a labour process analysis, however, there are also shortcomings to this stream of work. The overriding criticism to date is that conventional GPN research treats labour as little more than a factor of production. Specifically, at least in some versions of the GPN approach, the framework flirts with a kind of technological determinism that would reduce the labour process to a function of industry characteristics. For example, Gereffi et al. (2005) predict that inter-firm governance results from the nature of the production process and the supply base: is product architecture integral or modular? How complex is the information that needs to be exchanged between the links in the chain, and to what degree can it be codified? If this view of governance is extended to the analysis of labour, we run the risk of assuming that particular industries necessitate (strong version) or correlate with (weak version) particular distributions of the labour force in terms of skills, employment status and conditions of work (e.g., Figure 1 in Barrientos et al., 2011). The upshot is that GPN analyses in this vein frame techno-managerial interventions as the drivers of the process to achieve higher relative returns. Short shrift is given to how relations of production shape the upgrading outcomes for firms and the role that labour plays in determining this process.[2]

Labour as agent: In large part, this stream emerged as a critical engagement with some of the early work on globalized production systems, especially Gereffi's global commodity chain approach. Authors sympathetic to the thrust of GPN analysis nevertheless objected to the tendency to either ignore workers or treat them 'as passive victims' of capital's search for cheap labour (Smith et al., 2002). Part of this problem is that the study of global production networks tends to focus on the relationships among firms, and the ways in which powerful firms could exercise control over, or govern, others. But as Smith et al. argued, GPN researchers largely neglected what happened inside the firm, ignoring the degree to which both the *intra-firm organization of work* and *worker organization* had recursive effects on the dynamics of the broader chain:

> We would contend that labour process dynamics strongly influence wealth creation and work conditions within any one node and across

a chain. In addition, we would argue that organized labour can have an important influence upon locational decisions within and between countries, thereby determining in part the geography of activities within a value chain.

(2002: 47)

Thus, the agentic nature of labour matters for GPNs in two interconnected, but analytically distinct ways that are well summarized by Cumbers *et al.* (2008: 370).

[L]abour, in both the abstract sense of the work required to produce surplus value, and the more institutional sense of attempts by workers to organize collectively to improve its share of surplus value, remains a fundamental component of GPNs. From the perspective of capital, the labour problem sooner or later reasserts itself into the logic of accumulation. That problem – in its simplest terms – is threefold: first, the need to successfully incorporate labour into the production process; second, the need to exercise control over labour time in the production process; and third, stemming from this second point, the imperative to exploit labour as part of the process of commodification to realize surplus value.

Thus, while the governance structure of a GPN may create particular opportunities and pressures for firms at various network nodes, these inter-firm dynamics are not divorced from the dynamic of the labour-capital relation within each node. What this stream of research on GPNs and labour suggests is that the distribution of value along the chain – i.e. between firms – is at least partly contingent upon the distribution of the surplus within the firm – i.e. between capital and labour.

Workers' collective efforts to increase their share of the surplus can be understood, in this sense, as a cause of social upgrading. Rather than treat social upgrading as a (potential) effect of economic upgrading on workers, as is typically the case in the labour-as-object stream described above, this second stream centres labour agency as a condition of social upgrading. This argument has been articulated most clearly by Ben Selwyn (2013) in his contribution to a special issue of *Competition and Change* on global value chains and labour process analysis. The export-oriented grape industry that Selwyn studied via fieldwork in northeast Brazil is a prime example of the kind of buyer-driven commodity chain found in the horticultural sector, where supermarkets in the global North set exacting standards regarding myriad aspects of a product – in Selwyn's case, the size, shape and sugar-levels of grapes. Product criteria for fresh fruits and vegetables have implications for the labour process, such as requiring more frequent and more skilled operations during the harvest cycle. While the ability of developing country-farms to adopt more complex production processes and meet the demanding criteria of global buyers might be considered a form of upgrading, GPN research suggests that economic upgrading has been accompanied by social downgrading for those labouring on farms and in packhouses (Barrientos, 2001; Raworth and Kidder, 2009).

In contrast, Selwyn finds that a successful campaign by the local rural workers' union, STR, was critical for securing social upgrading for grape workers in Brazil, including higher pay and better working conditions. Specifically, the union wielded the threat of strike, which was powerful because the buyer-driven nature of the grape GPN included strict production schedules on local farms that increased the vulnerability of exporters to a work stoppage. While economic upgrading created pressures for changes in the labour process of the GPN, social upgrading resulted from labour's agency; the union's ability to translate workers' structural power in the chain into associational power in the labour-capital relation is 'a core determinant of the relationship between economic and social upgrading' (Selwyn, 2013: 83).

Selywn's study is notable for being among the first to apply the language of upgrading to the analysis of labour's agency within GPNs, but a similar concern is implicit in much of the work in this stream. Just as scholars of GPNs and development seek to identify opportunities for organizational learning and upgrading for firms, scholars of GPNs and labour ask what kind of opportunity structures exist (or can be created) for labour to exercise collective power to achieve gains for workers. Where are the pressure points or critical junctures in the chain that create structural and/or associational power for workers (Cumbers *et al.*, 2008; Rainnie *et al.*, 2011; Riisgaard and Hammer, 2011)?

Ultimately, the degree of labour agency within the various nodes of a GPN, and the degree to which labour can shape the organization, geography and distribution of surplus within a chain is an empirical question (Coe and Hess, 2013; also Thompson *et al.* in this volume). In arguing for a closer dialogue between GPN analysis and labour geography, Coe and Jordhus-Lier argue that the latter can benefit from the former because, in revealing 'the fragmented yet tightly coordinated organization of capital at the global scale, GPN analysis can simultaneously serve to reveal the variegated landscape for agency potential across different sectors' (2011: 221). In a trajectory parallel to the social upgrading literature discussed above, work in this stream has also moved in the direction of a more sober analysis of the possibilities that GPNs create for forms of labour agency that benefit workers.

When Adding Labour isn't Enough

Our own perspective draws on the insights of these two approaches, while taking their shortcomings as an opportunity to explore what we consider to be undertheorized aspects of global production circuits and new avenues for research. While the labour-as-agent literature offers its approach as a corrective to the labour-as-object stream, both suffer from a key shortcoming which hampers our ability to gain further purchase on the dynamics of uneven development: network essentialism. On the one hand, in the literature that endeavours to add labour via the notion of social upgrading, we concur with other scholars that the possibilities for down/upgrading to be determined by labour's associational power are downplayed. Nonetheless, the labour-as-agent literature continues to focus largely on workforces that have the capacity to exert associational power, that is, workforces that are or could be structurally positioned to shape the labour process through collective action. In short, both streams treat the question of labour in GPNs as stable and self-evident. The network ontology determines the set of actors and characteristics – specifically, who is labour and what form labour takes – a priori, rather than as an outcome of critical analysis. This is what we mean by network essentialism (cf. Taylor, 2007); in GPN analysis the network functions as both the object to be explained and the structure of the explanation, as explicandum and explicans. To overcome this problem, we propose that production networks – and labour's form within them – are best considered as, on the one hand, conjunctural expressions of uneven development and, on the other hand, organizational and social arrangements that reshape the geographies of uneven development, thereby hastening new network arrangements. Here, then, we seek to answer the following question: *what elements of a labour process analysis allow us to understand the capacity for GPN creation and maintenance, as well as the dynamics that eventually lead to network restructuring?*

The first task of such an analysis, we argue, is to unsettle what we think of as the 'distribution fallacy' of labour and GPNs, evident most strongly in the literature on upgrading. *Despite empirical evidence to the contrary*, the literature on upgrading offers types of work (e.g., high- and low-skilled, knowledge-intensive) and statuses of employment (e.g., temporary, permanent) as relatively stable categories into which workers are distributed. Consider Arianna Rossi's work on the Moroccan garment industry. On one hand, Rossi (2013) found ample evidence that apparel firms producing for US and European clients were upgrading, and that some of this economic upgrading was likely to benefit workers. Reorganizing the shopfloor to improve product flow and shorten through-put times enabled managers to estimate production schedules more accurately, thus reducing excessive overtime and the wage and hour violations associated with it. Simultaneously, however, Rossi found that some forms of upgrading had divergent outcomes for workers, benefiting some but creating heightened vulnerability for others. For example, as firms expanded into additional activities beyond basic production, such as sourcing materials, and packing and shipping finished garments, they found themselves dealing with sharply fluctuating demand for workers in these new links of the chain. This demand was met by creating a new set of temporary workers who enjoyed less job security and protection than the 'upgraded' regular workforce.

Thus, although exporters were becoming the highly flexible, 'full-package' suppliers sought after by clients, this transition was enabled by the development of a secondary labour force whose employment conditions were irregular and precarious. In this sense, Rossi argued, economic upgrading was linked to social downgrading, at least for a segment of the workforce:

> The simultaneous presence of regular and irregular workers is the result of the contradictory pressures that suppliers receive from their buyers: on the one hand, brands' purchasing practices, exacerbated in the fast fashion segment, demand low cost, high flexibility, and ever shrinking lead times; on the other hand, the fast fashion model also requires high quality, reliable production, and compliance with labour standards. In order to cope with this tension, supplier firms resort to employing a mix of regular and irregular workers to respond simultaneously to both sets of requirements.
>
> (Rossi, 2011: 231; see also Werner, 2012)

Rossi's findings are fascinating for an analysis of uneven development. Like other work on upgrading, including that of Selwyn discussed here, her research suggests that we are seeing relatively new arrangements amongst global suppliers in the South of 'core' and 'precarious' workers, often organizationally unified in the same firm and tiered hierarchically by social difference (e.g., gender, migrant status, etc.), not unlike arrangements observed in the global North from the 1970s onward (Harrison, 1994). And yet, hinged to the social upgrading framework, this observation and its implications for thinking about novel arrangements and social forces at play in the creation of surplus value are not interrogated. Instead, GPNs are sketched out along the two axes of social and economic upgrading, and the mixed labour outcomes Rossi so ably documents are imputed therein.

Yet, it is clear from Rossi's own and other such studies of upgrading that permanent, stable employment exists in tension with multiple forms of precarious employment. The combination of these forms of employment is the outcome not only of buyers' demands in a particular GPN, but also of the broader social relations determining the conditions of labour's exploitation at a particular place and time. Nonetheless, in the upgrading literature it is presumed that these are separate categories representing different stages of development in a process of linear improvement. Social upgrading, so conceived, involves workers moving from a more precarious category of work to a less precarious one.

Now, as we noted above, the revised down/upgrading schema allows for the possibility that this progress will not be achieved, and that the share of workers experiencing insecure and irregular employment will persist or even grow. Our point, however, is that this conceptual formulation of down/upgrading does not apprehend what GPN research itself shows us: that these forms of work always exist in relation to one another, albeit in different proportions and to different degrees. Rather than focus upon this relational co-constitution of types of work and status of employment, the distribution fallacy instead allows proponents of upgrading frameworks to gloss the obvious conclusion that the 'social upgrading' of some groups of workers is only ever achieved in part through the 'social downgrading' of other workers. If indeed many companies 'adopt a mixed approach of high quality and low-cost employment which facilitates both standards and cost flexibility' (Barrientos et al., 2011: 333), then it seems to us that what GPNs can help us theorize are the shifting uneven social relations that are expressed through globalized production arrangements, and the ways in which gendered and racialized workers are enrolled within new hierarchies of the labour process. To be sure, we recognize that this is not necessarily the only, or even the primary, project that motivates scholars of GPNs. Our point is simply that the up/downgrading framework does not do enough to elucidate the shifting, structured hierarchies of the labour process, given its commitment to defining a fixed set of categories in order of 'increased returns' (for economic upgrading) and 'decent work' (for social upgrading) and framing empirical findings in terms of movement along these paths.

The second task of resituating the GPN/labour literature within the ambit of uneven development is to consider worker agency beyond the network optic. We suggest that this can be done by interrogating how we define structural/associational power, on the one hand, and how we understand labour as a category, on the other. Authors in the labour-as-agent stream are aware of the limitations of its strong emphasis on associational power and formal employment within the network. As Coe and

Jordhus-Lier acknowledge, the literature 'tends to focus on employees within GPNs whose position offers them the potential to exert effective pressure on their employers '(2011: 222). In the analysis of structural and associational power in GPNs, the former is conceived primarily in terms of the social location of workers in relation to the organizational form and governance dynamics of any given chain or network.[3] While regional and national conjunctures are not ignored, the weight of explanation can fall too strongly upon the network position of workers. A desire to find a silver lining in the otherwise brutal assault on labour since the 1970s – an assault that was largely effected through the very processes of outsourcing and offshoring that network frameworks were created to explain – may be clouding our ability to ask basic questions. For example, is structural power within networks a necessary condition for workers to exert associational power in GPNs? Can other elements such as labour market-based structural power (i.e., tight labour markets) and specific political conjunctures (i.e., hegemony) ever be more important to the outcomes of the associational efforts of workers in GPNs? And if so, what are the implications for how we theorize worker agency in production networks?

Beyond these questions, a focus on collective worker agency, while obviously important, is nonetheless insufficient to grasp the role played by labour in the reciprocal structuring of GPNs and uneven development. To restate our central question, what aspects of labour create the conditions for GPNs to reconstitute the conditions for surplus value extraction? One important element here is the intersection between workers and what Marx called the reserve army or relative surplus population. In many locations, the rapid growth of GPNs has been concomitant with the rise of under- and unemployment, indicating the creation of a large 'reserve army'. Thus, when we talk about GPNs and class relations, we must consider these relations in a broad sense, not simply as they are manifest in the particular embodiments of labour and capital within the network. As Marx wrote, 'the relative surplus population is … the background against which the law of demand and supply of labour does its work' (1976: 792).

Various authors are contributing to the conceptual challenge and political imperative to focus upon these constitutive outsides of the wage relation. Some observe, for example, what Nicola Phillips (2011) calls 'a dynamic *structural blending* of informality with formality in GPNs' (quoted in Rainnie *et al.*, this volume). Such intercalations of forms of work are both cause and consequence of GPN formation, maintenance and restructuring, and have gained more attention as of late, as scholars have increasingly turned to notions of dispossession and devaluation in light of an intensification of market forces worldwide (e.g. Hough, 2010; Wilson, 2013). Our own work on 'disarticulations' in commodity chains represents an initial attempt to theorize this problematic. We argue for the central analytical and political importance of processes that enrol and expel workers in/from GPNs, and contend, further, that these are not shaped by capital alone. Labour shapes GPNs through everyday practices and struggles over value, relations of power that emerge empirically in phenomena such as 'tight' labour markets (as in parts of China today) and worker 'turnover' as evidence of mobility between formal and informal forms of work. As numerous feminist scholars have long argued, the processes that create labour for what we now call GPNs must be interrogated. In short, how does living, embodied labour *become* value for capital, how is this value realized via incorporation into (and expulsion from) GPNs and, to paraphrase Diane Elson (1979), how are political conjunctures and possibilities for strengthening labour's power forged through this process?

These were the questions that motivated us to study global production networks in the first place, even though we came to formulate them, via the disarticulations concept, largely through a critique of the extant GPN literature. In our view, the critical task of grappling with how the socio-spatial unevenness of the world economy spurs network formation (and abeyance) has been neglected in favour of a narrower form of analysis focused on the dynamics and consequences of specific network formations. This kind of analysis may well have value for answering questions about the position of labour in a chain and/or for informing strategies by which labour can exploit this positional power, but it is nevertheless inadequate for understanding the broader landscape of uneven development out of which these networks take shape. The conceptual forerunner of the GPN – the commodity chain – was developed as a heuristic, a way to make comprehensible and tractable the territorial expansion of a capitalist world economy that cannot be reduced to any particular chain. Likewise, GPN analysis can inform our study of the labour process, but only if we take care not to confuse our understanding of that process with the particular configurations of work and employment that the network ontology of the GPN framework renders visible. For us, the question of GPNs and labour, then, is first and foremost the question of how we understand the shaping of the capital-labour relation with respect to variation over uneven geographies of capitalism. This may be less a matter of 'bringing labour in' to the GPN than it is of moving beyond the network.

Notes

1 See http://www.capturingthegains.org/ for more information about the Capturing the Gains research project and numerous research outputs from this group.

2 Proponents of social upgrading might argue that their conceptualization of social upgrading, which examines whether workers in GPNs are secure in their 'rights and entitlements as social actors' goes some way towards addressing this objection (Barrientos *et al.*, 2011: 325). Nonetheless, we concur with Selwyn (2013) that the dominant conceptualization of social upgrading found in the GPN literature implies that it will be achieved through 'top down' approaches to monitoring and enforcement, and/or multi-actor collaborations, as opposed to altering the balance of forces between capital and labour.
3 Silver (2003) divides structural power into two categories: labour market-based power and workplace-based power. The GPN literature tends to pay far more attention to the workplace-based forms of power that arise through buyer-driven imperatives such as just-in-time delivery and 'choke points' in distribution (see Selwyn, 2012).

REFERENCES

Bair, J. (2005) 'Commodity chains and global capitalism: looking back, going forward', *Competition and Change*, 9(2): 153–180.

Bair, J., Werner, M., Berndt, C. and Boeckler, M. (2013) 'Dis/articulating producers, markets, and regions: new directions in critical studies of commodity chains' (Editor's introduction to special issue, 'Critical perspectives on commodity chain studies'), *Environment and Planning A*, 45(11): 1–9.

Bair, J. and Gereffi, G. (2001) 'Local clusters in global chains: the causes and consequences of export dynamism in Torreón's blue jeans industry', *World Development*, 29(11): 1885–1903.

Barrientos, S. (2001) 'Gender flexibility and global value chains', *IDS Bulletin*, 32(3): 83–93.

Barrientos, S., Gereffi, G. and Rossi, A. (2011) 'Economic and social upgrading in global production networks: a new paradigm for a changing world', *International Labour Review*, 150(3–4): 319–340.

Carrillo, J. and Hualde, A. (1998) 'Third generation maquiladoras? the Delphi-General motors case', *Journal of Borderland Studies*, 13(1): 79–97.

Coe, H. and Hess, M. (2013) 'Global production networks, labour and development', *Geoforum*, 44: 4–9.

Coe, H. and Jordhus-Lier, D. (2011) 'Constrained agency: re-evaluating the geographies of labour', *Progress in Human Geography*, 35(2): 211–233.

Coe, N., Dicken, P. and Hess, M. (2008) 'Global production networks: realizing the potential', *Journal of Economic Geography*, 8(3): 271–295.

Collins, J. (2003) *Threads: Gender, Labour and Power in the Global Apparel Industry*, Chicago: University of Chicago Press.

Cumbers, A., Nativel, C. and Routledge, P. (2008) 'Labour agency and union positionalities in global production networks', *Journal of Economic Geography*, 8: 369–387.
Dolan, C. and Humphrey, J. (2001) 'Governance and trade in fresh vegetables: the impact of UK supermarkets on the African horticulture industry', *Journal of Development Studies*, 37(2): 147–176.
Dussel Peters, E. (2008) 'GCCs and development: a conceptual and empirical review', *Competition and Change*, 12(1): 11–27.
Elson, D. (1979) 'The Value Theory of Labour' in D. Elson (ed.) *Value: The Representation of Labour in Capitalism*, London: CSE Books, pp. 115–180.
Gereffi, G. (1994) 'The organization of buyer-driven global commodity chains: how U.S. retailers shape overseas production networks', in G. Gereffi and M. Korzeniewicz (eds) *Commodity Chains and Global Capitalism*, Westport, CT: Praeger, pp. 95–122.
Gereffi, G. (1999) 'International trade and industrial upgrading in the apparel commodity chain', *Journal of International Economics*, 48(1): 37–70.
Gereffi, G., Humphrey, J. and Sturgeon, T. (2005) 'The governance of global value chains', *Review of International Political Economy*, 12(1): 78–104.
Gibbon, P., Bair, J. and Ponte, S. (2008) 'Governing global value chains: an introduction', *Economy and Society*, 37(3): 315–338.
Gibbon, P. and Ponte, S. (2005) *Trading Down: Africa, Value Chains, and the Global Economy*, Philadelphia: Temple University Press.
Hale, A. and Wills, J. (2005) *Threads of Labour: Garment Industry Supply Chains from the Workers' Perspective*, Malden, MA: Wiley Blackwell.
Harrison, B. (1994) *Lean and Mean: The Changing Landscape of Corporate Power in the Age of Flexibility*, New York: Basic Books.
Hough, P. (2010) 'Global commodity chains and the spatial-temporal dimensions of labour control: lessons from Colombia's coffee and banana industries', *Journal of World Systems Research*, 16(2): 123–161.
Humphrey, J. and Schmitz, H. (2001) 'Governance in global value chains', *IDS Bulletin*, 32(3): 19–29.
Kaplinsky, R. (1998) 'Globalization, industrialisation and sustainable growth: the pursuit of the Nth Rent.' IDS Discussion Paper 365, University of Sussex.
Kelly, P. (2013) 'Production networks, place and development: thinking through global production networks in Cavite, Philippines', *Geoforum*, 44: 82–92.
Kessler, J. (1999) 'The North American free trade agreement, emerging apparel production networks and industrial upgrading: the Southern California/Mexico connection', *Review of International Political Economy*, 6(4): 565–608.
Marx, K. (1976) *Capital, vol. 1*, London: Penguin.
Milberg, W. and Winkler, D. (2011) 'Economic and social upgrading in global production networks: problems of theory and measurement', *International Labour Review*, 150(3–4): 341–365.
Phillips, N. (2011) 'Informality, global production networks and the dynamics of "adverse incorporation"', *Global Networks*, 11(3): 380–397.

Pickles, J., Smith, A., Roukova, P., Begg, R. and Bucek, M. (2006) 'Upgrading and diversification in the East European industry: competitive pressure and production networks in the clothing industry', *Environment and Planning A*, 38(12): 2305–2324.

Ponte, S. and Sturgeon, T. (2014) 'Explaining governance in global value chains: a modular theory-building effort', *Review of International Political Economy*, 21(1): 195–223.

Rainnie, A., Herod, A. and McGrath-Champ, S. (2011) 'Global production networks and labour', *Competition and Change*, 15(2): 111–169.

Ramamurthy, P. (2011) 'Rearticulating caste: the global cottonseed commodity chain and the paradox of smallholder capitalism in south India', *Environment and Planning A*, 43(5): 1035–1056.

Raworth, K. and Kidder, M. (2009) 'Mimicking "lean" in global value chains: it's the workers who get leaned on', in J. Bair, (ed.) *Frontiers of Commodity Chain Research*, Stanford: Stanford University Press, pp. 165–189.

Riisgaard, L. and Hammer, N. (2011) 'Prospects for labour in global value chains: labour standards in the cut flower and banana industries', *British Journal of Industrial Relations*, 49(1): 68–90.

Rossi, A. (2013) 'Does economic upgrading lead to social upgrading in global production networks? evidence from Morocco', *World Development*, 46: 223–233.

Schrank, A. (2004) 'Ready-to-wear development: foreign investment, technology transfer, and learning-by-watching in the apparel trade', *Social Forces*, 83(1): 123–156.

Selwyn, B. (2012) *Workers, State and Development in Brazil: Powers of Labour, Chains of Value*, Manchester: Manchester University Press.

Selwyn, B. (2013) 'Social upgrading and labour in global production networks: a critique and an alternative conception', *Competition and Change*, 17(1): 75–90.

Silver, B. (2003) *Forces of Labour: Workers' Movements and Globalization Since 1870*, New York: Cambridge University Press.

Smith, A., Rainnie, A., Dunford, M., Hardy, J., Hudson, R. and Sadler, D. (2002) 'Networks of value, commodities and regions: reworking divisions of labour in macro–regional economies', *Progress in Human Geography*, 26(1): 41–63.

Stringer, C., Simmons, G., Coulston, D. and Whittaker, D. H. (2014) 'Not in New Zealand's waters, surely? linking labour issues to GPNs', *Journal of Economic Geography*, 14: 739–758.

Taylor, M. (ed.) (2010) *Renewing International Labour Studies*, London: Routledge.

Taylor, M. (2007) 'Rethinking the global production of uneven development', *Globalizations*, 4(4): 529–542.

Tokatli, N. (2013) 'Toward a better understanding of the apparel industry: a critique of the upgrading literature', *Journal of Economic Geography*, 13(6): 993–1011.

Werner, M. (2012) 'Beyond upgrading: Gendered labour and the restructuring of firms in the Dominican Republic', *Economic Geography*, 88(4): 403–422.

Werner, M. and Bair, J. (2011) 'Commodity chains and the uneven geographies of global capitalism: a disarticulations perspective' (Editor's introduction to special issue, 'Losing our chains: Rethinking commodities through disarticulations'), *Environment and Planning A*, 43(5): 988–997.

Wilson, B. (2013) 'Breaking the chains: coffee, crisis, and farmworker struggle in Nicaragua', *Environment and Planning A*, 45(11): 2592–2609.

CHAPTER 8

Understanding Labour's Agency under Globalization: Embedding GPNs within an Open Political Economy

Andrew Cumbers

Introduction

There has been a growing interest in recent years in the concept of global production networks (GPNs) for theorizing the global economy and in particular for thinking about the relations between different social actors that are brought together across diverse and extended geographies in the process of production (Coe *et al.*, 2004; Coe and Hess, 2013). As part of this developing debate, there has been a renewed call for interrogating the way labour is enrolled in GPNs (Cumbers *et al.*, 2008). As the author has pointed out elsewhere, GPNs are ultimately networks of 'embodied labour' (Cumbers *et al.*, 2008: 372) in the sense that labour is the essential element in the production and reproduction of GPNs through its centrality in the labour process. No amount of technological innovation or financialization of the global economy changes this central point. As such, it is important that labour and its different meanings are taken seriously in understanding both its changing role and positionality in relation to the globalization of work and corporate practices therein, and in the prospects for its own agency in shaping underlying global economic processes.

The purpose of this chapter is to contribute to the ongoing debate on these issues by developing further our thinking with respect to the complex geographies of labour in relation to other social actors in GPNs. The focus here is on using and extending the GPN framework, suggesting that it has considerable, and as yet largely unrealized, potential for understanding the changing relationships between capital, the state and labour in the global economy. Other recent conceptualizations such as the global commodity chains (GCC) and global value chains (GVC) literatures, despite their revisions and newer incarnations, tend to have a flatter ontology. The GPN framework in its initial conception adds value to our understanding precisely because it combines a relational perspective on the way local places and actors are embedded in broader global networks whilst integrating a sense of the continuing importance of vertical territorial relations, such as the role of states and local labour control regimes (Kelly, 2013), in shaping economic and social outcomes.

The chapter argues that one of the key contributions of the GPN literature could be a more sophisticated approach to how we think about economic globalization and labour's place within it. GPN's essential contribution lies in its deployment of a networked approach as a perspective on globalization alongside its emphasis upon the multi-scalar dynamics of political economic governance processes. By combining a networked approach embedded within a multi-scalar geographical political economy, the GPN account has always offered the promise of moving beyond existing firm-centric GCC-GVC approaches to focus upon how different social actors are connected in the construction of global economic relations and the possible implications for social agency and power.

Nevertheless, there remains an important issue here in how labour is conceived, both as a complex and differentiated category in its own right, and in its relations with other social actors – notably state and capital but also the broad spectrum of civil society groups – through which effective global accumulation processes are mediated and effectively stabilized. Ontological and political issues therefore arise here that a more developed GPN framing situated within a broader political economy approach can help resolve. The chapter does this through using Wright's (2001) distinction between structural and associational power as a means of conceiving of labour within GPNs.

The chapter is in four parts. The first section considers some of the key issues highlighted by labour geographers in response to earlier narratives of globalization which consider the role, agency and power of labour in GPNs. This literature emphasizes the importance of situating labour, both individually and collectively, within wider processes of uneven development and political economic restructuring. A second section suggests that a GPN conceptual framing can be important in theorizing the role of labour in the global economy.

It develops one of the original intentions, to understand how labour, capital and state actors co-produce global economic structures and outcomes through action which connects global networks with place-centred activities. A third section produces an indicative sketch of how a more labour-sensitive GPN might be operationalized through the lens of a series of different cases, before a fourth section, the conclusion, draws together the strands of the argument.

Labour, GPNs and Issues of Agency and Power

There has been an interesting and productive confluence of ideas in recent years between critical labour scholars, so-called labour geographers, and researchers working under the label of GPNs (e.g. Cumbers *et al.*, 2008; Rainnie *et al.*, 2010; 2011; Coe and Hess, 2013; Helfen and Fichter, 2013; Kelly, 2013). The most significant outcome of this engagement has been the recognition of labour's continued agency in processes of global economic restructuring. This acknowledgement contrasts with earlier analyses of economic globalization, especially those concerned with global value chains where labour was largely written off as a serious agent in political and economic processes (e.g. Bair, 2005; Gereffi *et al.*, 2005). Subsequently, there is a growing amount of work by both labour geographers and critical labour scholars that has explored the changing positionality and agency of labour in GPNs (e.g. Cumbers *et al.*, 2008; Selwyn, 2011, 2013) and the theoretical and political implications stemming from this.

A key element is distinguishing between a perspective of labour agency as always present in production processes and a specific concern with the collective organization of workers, both through unions and other forms of organization. In earlier work, Wright (2001) usefully referred the difference between workers' structural power and their associational power. In relation to GPNs, and drawing on the basic insight from Marx that labour and work are the source of all value, workers' structural power is reflective of the fact that GPNs are fundamentally networks of 'embodied labour' (Cumbers *et al.*, 2008). At different points within and across a GPN, workers, both individually and indeed collectively, hold considerable latent power by virtue of being the key to the production process. Their ability to translate this power into effective collective action to improve working conditions and raise labour standards is an important theoretical and empirical question (Taylor and Bain, 2008; Selwyn, 2013).

The structural power of workers varies enormously across space and is contingent on diverse factors, not least the nature of the production process, its associated labour processes, driven by the type of product market, levels of technology and skill requirements. Labour process theorists, while recognizing the importance of these factors, have been a little slower at appreciating the implications that geography – as an active dimension in shaping the economic landscape – has for workers' differentiated structural power. What Massey (1984) famously referred to as 'spatial divisions of labour' are critical in framing the relative structural power of differently located groups of workers within GPNs. Typically, in many GPNs, a continuing international division of labour often means that workers in developed economies are more highly skilled, more unionized and better able to leverage improved conditions than less skilled and less organized and more fragmented workers in the global south. Historically, labour organizations in the global north have of course often been complicit in the repression of labour unions in parts of the global south, especially during the Cold War period when the international labour movement was much more riven with ideological differences (Thomson and Larson, 1978).

Of course, these two types of agency are inter-related in the sense that workers' 'associational power' is often strongly predicated upon their 'structural power'. One example might be the contrast between the recent fortunes of unions in the UK's rail industry with those in lower paid service sectors (Wills, 2005; Cumbers *et al.*, 2010). Rail unions have been able to harness the deeply embedded knowledge of workers and their understandings of the working of complex transport networks, infrastructure and logistics to great effect. In contrast, unions representing less skilled workers in many parts of the service sector (notably cleaning and security services) face the problem of the disposability and replaceability of workers through new technologies and cheaper sources of labour, notably recent immigrant groups and agency-based workforces.

A third aspect critical to thinking about labour agency in GPNs is bound up in their 'relational power' (Allen, 2003), in terms of broader questions of transnational solidarity (Featherstone, 2012). Relational here refers to the way that the actions of workers in one place can have impacts on those in another location within a GPN. How can associational and structural power be mobilized relationally to the benefit of all workers in a GPN rather than restricted to gains for workers in particular places that may have negative effects for workers elsewhere? Thinking relationally about labour agency therefore involves developing a broader and more dynamic perspective on the relations between workers and other actors and institutions within GPNs. This necessitates an awareness of the ongoing forging of connections between workers operating out of uneven and variegated terrains of capitalism in different places.

In this respect, a common critique levelled at labour geographers is that they tend to pay too much attention to the associational power and the collective agency of unionized workers without a more thorough-going assessment of labour more generally. Thus positive accounts of labour agency in selected disputes are developed at the expense of both the broader structural conditions and relations underpinning labour agency and the diverse experiences of labour and work in a global economy (e.g. Castree, 2007; Coe and Jordhus-Lier, 2012). Peck, for example, has recently written that in their determination to 'rebuff ... the victimization script embedded in more orthodox forms of political-economic geography ... this agency-first perspective has had the unintended consequences of resurrecting a (new) kind of structure-agency binary, in order to locate the project [of labour geography] unambiguously on the side of unbounded political possibility'. (Peck, 2013: 109). As Peck himself acknowledges, there has been considerable self-reflection and a more critical response to this charge, and indeed many of those labour geographers researching GPNs show considerable awareness of the multifaceted and complex relations of labour both in formal employment, informal work, slavery and social reproduction processes in constituting the production of GPNs (e.g. Selwyn, 2011; Carswell and de Neve, 2013; McGrath, 2013).

Framing GPNs within a Broader Spatial Political Economy

The key contribution from the GPN formulation, that gives it greater analytical purchase than earlier GCC and GVC approaches, is its greater attentiveness to the relations between local and national actors and broader global production relations. This is achieved both through the use of a networking concept to theorize power and relationality within a global economy, but also through its recognition of the importance of territorialized social relations and institutional structures (Sunley, 2008) in shaping global processes (Cumbers et al., 2008).

The genesis of the GPN concept lies in Dicken's authoritative and longstanding commitment to theorizing global business dynamics from a more sophisticated geographical perspective than many standard business school texts. His work has evolved significantly over time but has developed from an earlier concern with mapping the globalization of business and its strategic imperatives – particularly in manufacturing sectors – to a more expansive project that seeks to understand the workings of the global economy through an analysis of key actors and institutions and their socio-spatial relations.[1] Although Dicken's magisterial work

Global Shift (GS) has remained heavily focused on transnational business activity, from a very early stage it was committed to an analysis of the state in its different forms and the way geography complicates globalization processes. His approach was in stark and refreshing contrast to much of the hyperglobalization literature of the 1990s (e.g. Ohmae, 1990; Frank, 2007). Dicken was also cognizant of the existence of varieties of capitalism and the multi-scalar nature of economic and political processes and relations driving the global economy. In the 1998 edition of GS, Dicken engaged with international relations scholarship – notably Stopford and Strange (1991) – to recognize the way that GPNs are enmeshed within a 'nexus of relationships' between states and firms (1998: 10).

Dicken's work then developed through his collaboration with Henry Yeung, Neil Coe, Martin Hess and others into what has become known as their distinctive GPN approach. The key element and innovation in their approach has been the use of the network concept to emphasize the relationality and more open-ended sense of power relations at work in the GPN between firms and states in particular. Critical to this understanding, drawing on economic sociology but providing a critical geographical dimension, is the appreciation of economic activity as being both socially and spatially embedded (Hess, 2004).

Two important implications of the embeddedness perspective are significant for the analysis here. First, multinational corporations (MNCs) are not all powerful and hypermobile but need bespoke locational strategies and a degree of embeddedness in particular places to make accumulation happen. 'Spatial fixes' (Harvey, 1982) are required that connect different places in global flows of capital, information, managerial control and strategy, and labour processes to produce commodities to realize surplus value. Second, and following from the importance of this 'spatial fix', is recognition of the contribution of diverse non-business actors including national states, local and regional development institutions and organizations, civil society organizations, such as workers and trade unions, to global productive activity. Within the confines of a capitalist mode of production, the role of national states and local and regional actors in this schema is to try to 'embed' and tie down productive activity in particular places, in other words, effectively embedding local places for the longer term (rather than as a quick fix, low-cost haven) in the network of the MNC. This leads the GPN proponents to deploy the important concept of 'strategic coupling' in recognition of the way these relations are mutually constructed. MNCs need stable and compliant local places but places also need to attract and more importantly secure foreign direct investment, as MacKinnon's useful recent paper reminds us

(2012). The original purpose of the much-cited article (Coe *et al.*, 2004) in a leading geography journal was an intervention into debates in economic geography about local and regional economic development, reflected in the title 'Globalizing regional development'. Specifically, the article developed a critique made by the present author and colleagues (MacKinnon *et al.*, 2002) of the new regionalist discourse emerging around the innovation and learning strategies of regional actors in the 1990s. The essence of the critique was that regionalist accounts over-celebrated the autonomy and collective agency of regions at the expense of a recognition of the broader spatial processes that have driven economic development.

Leaving aside the origins of the concept, in an earlier and now less cited article (Henderson *et al.*, 2002), there is a sense of the potential of the GPN concept to develop a more open-ended, relational and dynamic sense of the different power relations at work in structuring the global economy: 'we must understand how places are being transformed by flows of capital, labour, knowledge, power, etc. and how, at the same time, places (or more specifically their social and institutional fabrics) are transforming these flows as they locate in place-specific domains' (Henderson *et al.*: 438). In particular, there is an important emphasis here upon processes of value creation, enhancement and capture, and the way that these processes involve business and non-business actors at multiple geographical scales through webs or networks of economic governance.

The big omission from the GPN school, which they have subsequently recognized (e.g. Coe and Hess, 2013), was with regards to labour as a critical social actor within GPNs. GPN analysis remains heavily capital-centric although constrained and indeed regulated by state agency at a range of scales – from the local, through the national to the supranational (EU, IMF, World Bank, etc.). Labour is certainly present as the ultimate creator of value but the focus around which actors and places 'capture the value' implies a rather passive form of agency. The attention instead is on how regions – as collective ensembles – deal with the 'focal firms' that drive GPNs: 'regional institutions may mobilize their region-specific assets to bargain with these focal firms such that their power relations are not necessarily one-way in favour of the latter' (Coe *et al.*, 2004: 475). Whilst this is an important departure in terms of regional actors, it says little about the independent agency of labour, in the sense of the ability of workers and trade unions to act autonomously from the interests of capital (Cleaver, 2000). Labour action is reduced to the enlisting of local trade unions as part of regional coalitions seeking to attract FDI by mobilizing regional resources, here referred to as 'assets', of which a compliant labour force is presumably one. The emphasis overall is the importance of developing institutions and assets that are complementary to the interests of the MNC:

> The bargaining position of these regional institutions is particularly high when their region-specific assets are highly complementary to the strategic needs of focal firms – these regional institutions become really powerful through their relational interaction with focal firms in selected global production networks. (Coe *et al.*, 2004)

In this much-cited paper, the case of the relationship between BMW and its host region, Bavaria, is used to suggest how regions can successfully embed capital locally through regional strategies that can produce beneficial support environments. In this case the development of a flexible production system involved a deal with the local unions on wages and conditions that actually went against the wishes of the national union to preserve national collective bargaining structures (Coe *et al.*, 2004). In both theoretical and political terms this is a very limited way of thinking about labour agency, the essence of which is captured in the following quote: 'The likelihood of value capture in specific regions is therefore greatly enhanced by a cooperative set of state, labour and business institutions that offer region-specific assets to focal firms on global production networks' (Coe *et al.*, 2004).

Instead of realizing its original ambition and recognizing the more complex web of social and scalar relations that govern GPNs, the outcome is a set of local, regional and national actors, including labour, that remain in dependent power relations with MNCs, and at the same time place-dependent, lacking their own broader spatial networks or agency. Labour's agency is ultimately severely 'constrained' (Coe and Jordhus-Lier, 2012). Not only does this framing belie the reliance of MNCs on both home and host regions as sites for realizing surplus value but it also underplays the relational aspects of other economic actors. Whatever the relative capacities of capital and labour to exercise their spatial connections and global reach, it is important to recognize labour's own historic ability to forge its own transnational connections and practices (Featherstone, 2012). It also understates the potential for labour to use its own broader spatial networks to both resist capital and open new 'generative' possibilities of its own that can 'articulate political presents and futures beyond neoliberalism' (Featherstone, 2012: 254).

A further criticism made of the GPN perspective is that it diminishes the continuing importance of the state as a mediator of capital-labour relations (Smith, 2014). More generally, and despite its potential, it has, as Glassman notes, 'so far largely steered clear of forms of political and geo-political contestation that illustrate some of the worst violence and messiness of "actually existing globalization"' (Glassman, 2011: 162). Riisgaard and Hammer (2011) have made the important point that workers' associational power is shaped as much by local and national institutional and governance contexts as it is by GPN structure or relations. While this critique is well-made, the potential of the GPN concept in its original form was to construct a framework that acknowledged the integral role of the state as a key institution through which social relations are built into it, rather than regarding it as an external influence. A productive way forward here is to engage with Jessop's strategic-relational perspective (e.g. Jessop, 2008; Smith, 2014), which essentially sees the state as a relatively autonomous institution, operating at and across different geographical scales, always ultimately bound up with securing capital accumulation but open to competing struggles by different social groups. Labour actors can be on opposing sides in these struggles, in the shape of social democratic impulses to become part of local and national state development projects which can have the direct effect of intensifying exploitation in the labour process conditions for grassroots workers. Such ambiguities within labour are often deeply gendered and racialized (see Cumbers *et al.*, 2014; Ince *et al.*, 2014).

At the same time, the GPN framework cannot be a theory of everything and it is not a meta theory (such as, for example, a Marxist political economy perspective). Instead it is best perceived as offering a number of 'middle-range' concepts that allow us to align concrete empirical phenomena (e.g. export processing zones) to more abstract concepts (the creation of surplus value). It offers a conceptual framing device that usefully allows us to see how global production and distribution is organized by connecting places and people as social actors within advanced global capitalism. As Coe says: 'labour agency needs to be re-embedded in state formations as much as it does in the global structures of capital' (2013: 274). It is important in this sense to still place GPN analysis within a broader Marxist perspective where the production of surplus value (see Starosta, 2010) remains at the core of the underlying process of accumulation.

In short, if the GPN perspective retains its original sense of a relational ontology in recognizing the way different social actors, acting at and across multiple scales, co-produce GPNs, it has the analytical superiority over GCC/GVC perspectives (Coe, 2012). Indeed, the GPN framework can usefully explore the productive tensions that exist between places and networks, particularly in the sense of how particular local labour control regimes are constructed to stabilize labour-capital-state relations in particular places as part of broader GPNs (Kelly, 2013). As Coe has argued in a recent defence of the GPN perspective: 'a central concern of GPN analysis is not to consider the networks in an abstracted manner for their own sake, but to reveal the dynamic developmental impacts that result for both the firms and territories that they interconnect' (Coe, 2012: 390). The overall strength of this approach is weakened by attempts to capture everything within the GPN's network ontology, which underplays the importance of underlying structural conditions and processes (see Sunley, 2008; Coe, 2012).

Consequently, a more useful starting point is to frame the GPN perspective within a more open evolutionary political economy perspective (see MacKinnon *et al.*, 2009; MacKinnon, 2012) which incorporates capital and labour as both autonomous agents and inter-dependent dialectically through capitalist social relations and processes of value creation which materialize in distinct and variegated labour processes across the global economy (Cleaver, 2000). Seen in this light, the GPN concept offers a conceptual device for exploring the ongoing multi-scalar and networked relations between labour, capital and the state within the context of uneven development and the shifting dynamics of the global economy.

The Value of a GPN Perspective to Thinking about Labour Embeddedness in Economic Globalization

A particularly important insight is that the social and spatial embeddedness of actors within GPNs is two-way. Following Massey (2005), places and the actors within them shape broader global processes as well as being shaped by them. GPN analysis sometimes misses the more nuanced but critical implications of this reciprocal set of relations with an emphasis upon 'focal firms' (i.e. key MNCs as the most powerful forces within networks) as the main players within GPNs. But being attentive to the relational and dynamic nature of GPNs results in a much broader sense of the social actors operating both within but also through particular places. This perspective means appreciating the way that state actors (at different geographical scales from the local through to the global), labour unions, civil society groups, business associations and broader constellations of economic governance – including the role of financial interests – all come together to facilitate different constellations of social, economic and political power through GPNs.

From a perspective of labour agency, a GPN framework can be useful for thinking through how business corporations emerging from and embedded within particular spatial contexts might develop very different configurations of social relations within their GPNs as they internationalize (see for example Helfen and Fichter, 2013). The author's own work in the energy sector points to important contrasts between European MNCs, where strong domestic labour movements are able to use their national positions to develop global framework agreements (GFAs), compared with the situation in UK and US MNCs, which tend to remain resolutely anti-union in their overseas operations (Cumbers, 2004). Such operations do not suggest that such GFAs automatically deliver labour solidarity and improved global labour standards and conditions, but they do highlight the very different social-spatial configurations that are evident in GPNs (Cumbers et al., 2008).

A GPN perspective can also shed light on the opportunities and limitations of labour organizing. This section now considers two examples of labour agency in the sense of associational power (Wright, 2001) in the most unpropitious of conditions. The first considers the recent efforts by Chinese workers to organize in the multinational production enclaves of south east China. The dramatic escalation of labour disputes in the period since 2000 challenges the notion of a compliant and increasingly alienated global south workforce in the face of multinational capital and a repressive state (Howells, 2006). A wave of strike activity in the summer of 2010 in the country's industrial heartland of southern Guandong is characteristic of the growing trend for grassroots workers to organize collectively in protest at poor wages and working conditions, particularly in the factories that employ predominantly migrant workers who have moved to the city from the countryside. The most celebrated instance has been the struggle at Foxconn (Chan et al., 2013), a Taiwanese electronics firm employing a massive 400,000 people in the city of Shenzhen, supplying iPhones and iPads for Apple, along with other well-known brand names. Foxconn was forced to double the wage rates of workers following an all-out strike. The appalling working conditions facing many employees was brought to light by a spate of suicides by many young recent migrants (Chan, 2013); it was common for people to be working for ten hours per day on just USD 1 per hour and under harsh disciplinary and supervisory conditions (BBC News, 2010).

Such developments forced the employers to dramatically increase wages and have led to the state controlled union federation, the All China Federation of Trade Unions (ACFTU), to organize in the workplaces of foreign corporations such as Wal-Mart and MacDonald's, and after a period of decline, union membership has actually risen in recent years (Quinjun, 2010). The ACFTU is also under pressure to decentralize and provide greater autonomy to local workers rather than continuing to be a state-dominated organization more concerned with maintaining social stability than representing workers' interests against employers. While the ability of the nascent labour uprisings to avoid co-option by a powerful state remains an open question, the emergence of mass collective labour resistance in China brings to mind Karl Polanyi's point about the limitations of a free market utopia and what he termed the 'double movement', where labour and other social actors at some point fight back to attempt to regulate and constrain market forces.

Not only does the action of Chinese workers serve as a reminder of the continued agency of labour, but a broader point is the usefulness of a GPN concept in interrogating the diverse spatial and scalar politics at work within a dynamic and evolving global political economy (see MacKinnon, 2012). The networked and multi-scalar framing of a GPN allows an appreciation of the way local labour control regimes (Chinese local production enclaves) are constructed as part of broader global accumulation processes between national and local state actors on the one hand, and multinational actors on the other. A GPN lens also allows us to see how labour is able to mobilize locally and transnationally, through supportive wider civil society networks (including transnational labour advocacy and ethical consumer groups) to shift both state practices (in the form of the ACFTU) and global corporate responses.

The second example is of the recent successes of dock workers' unions in Egypt in signing collective agreements with foreign transport and logistics MNCs (Anderson, 2013). A GPN approach illuminates the potential for multi-scalar labour organizing in the context of an acute national political and geopolitical crisis. Although the International Transport Foundation (ITF) had been undertaking a long painstaking campaign to organize in the Middle East, there had been little success in the country's ports in Egypt prior to 2011. A repressive political regime had been able to keep unions at bay for over a decade. However, the 2011 Tahrir Square uprisings that led to the overthrow of the Mubarak regime opened up a national political space within which local organizers and the ITF could mobilize. In a climate of political uncertainty, strike action by 1,500 workers at the Suez Canal Container Port facility led to the Danish management company quickly signing a collective bargaining agreement for the first time. A similar agreement was subsequently struck with Dubai-based firm DPW at the port of the Sokhna. In the face of threats by the company to bring in the army to deal with strikers in this instance, the ITF was able to mobilize its workforce at other DPW sites in Asia and Europe to threaten escalation. The threat of wider industrial action led to the company backing down and conceding a collective agreement (Anderson, 2013).

Politically, of course, such gains are contingent and highly fragile given the continuing crisis and uncertainty. As Anderson says:

> Egypt's docks, then, have become a key space of contest; one where workers, along with assistance from their international allies, have sought to transform the Tahrir revolt into political and economic gains in the workplace; but equally a site where the both traditional and emerging forces hostile to this movement are vigilant. The Port Said and Sokhna disputes show that dockers' unions are well placed to capitalise on these links. Whether Egypt will continue to be viewed as the latest advance in the ITF's POC [Ports of Convenience] campaign is likely to depend on the developing strength of dockers' unions both within and beyond Egypt's borders. (Anderson, 2013: 132)

Conceptually, though, the GPN approach adds value here in understanding how the extended global social connections of both labour and capital fuse with national political structures and processes in a dynamic, open-ended fashion to shape both labour agency and the potential for progressive outcomes. Like the other two examples, the value of the GPN approach here is in setting labour struggles within a much broader global political economic canvas which is sensitive to variegated local political and social contexts.

Conclusions

Labour geographers and critical labour scholars have made great strides in reversing the neglect of the role played by workers and trade unions in the construction of the global economy. However, the accusation has been made that in reasserting labour into broader global processes, the perspective is often partial and over-celebratory about agency without a sense of the limits and tensions arising from deeper underlying power structures. I have argued here that one of the ways of addressing these issues could be to position labour agency within a broader political economy framing, which is at the same time sensitive to the issues of space, place and scale. In other words, critical labour research on global restructuring needs to address how labour responds to globalizing economic processes to deal with the complex dynamics of capital accumulation and value creation.

Global capital links places, communities and workers together in ever more elaborate chains of production and value creation. This goes hand in hand with the ongoing production of uneven development across space and the continuing sharp differentiation of places in terms of their social, political and economic make-up. While existing approaches in the GCC/GVC traditions have their strengths, it has been argued that the GPN approach offers more potential because of its greater sensitivity to the relational and multi-scalar nature of global political economy. Reflecting its origins in the economic geography literature, concerned specifically with going beyond the deficiencies of the new regionalism literature on the one hand, and the excesses of hyper-globalization narratives on the other, its conceptual framing allows a productive tension between places and networks without giving ontological primacy to either.

However, to realize this potential, it is necessary to go beyond some of the more recent emphases on 'focal firms' and business-state dynamics to develop a more rounded conception of agency that recognizes the co-production of the global economy by capital and labour within a context of changing processes of state regulation. A useful way of doing this is to use Wright's distinction between labour's structural power and its associational power (2001) to explore how workers are able to both exploit their embodied position with the labour process of GPNs and to mobilize broader spatial solidarities. Attention to the relational power of workers also helps to understand how labour agency has differential implications across space.

Framed within an open political economy approach, and embedded within underlying structures and processes of capital accumulation – rather than given its own primacy in explaining everything – the GPN concept is a useful device for understanding the changing power relations of the global economy and the shifting balance between capital and labour. It does this through its ability to better represent the complex spatialities of labour, capital and state actors and the way these are entangled in particular instances. From the point of view of labour politics and labour organizing, a GPN approach allows us to see how labour agency and ultimately success and failure are linked to a broader set of structures, institutions and processes. By recognizing the dynamic set of relations that exist between local, national and multinational actors, it helps us to understand not only the constraints but also the opportunities for progressive politics.

Note

1 Compare for example the first edition with the third edition and the most recent sixth edition (Dicken 1986; 1998; 2010). A seventh edition is now on the way.

REFERENCES

Allen, J. (2003) *Lost Geographies of Power*, Oxford: Blackwell.

Anderson, J. (2013) 'Intersecting arcs of mobilization: the transnational trajectories of Egyptian dockers' unions', *European Urban and Regional Studies*, 20: 128–133.

Bair, J. (2005) 'Global capitalism and commodity chains: looking back, going forward', *Competition and Change*, 9: 153–180.

BBC News (2010) China's factories hit by wave of strikes. www.bbc.co.uk/news/10434079, last accessed, 18th December 2014.

Carswell, G. and de Neve, G. (2013) 'Labouring for global markets: conceptualising labour agency in global production networks', *Geoforum*, 44: 62–70.

Castree, N. (2007) 'Labour geography: a work in progress', *International Journal of Urban and Regional Research*, 31(4): 853–862.

Chan, J. (2013) 'A suicide survivor: the life of a Chinese worker', *New Technology, Work and Employment*, 28: 84–99.

Chan, J., Pun, N. and Selden, M. (2013) 'The politics of global production: Apple, Foxconn and China's new working class', *New Technology, Work and Employment*, 28: 100–115.

Cleaver, H. (2000) *Reading Capital Politically*, London: AK Press.

Coe, N. (2012) 'Geographies of production II: a global production network A–Z', *Progress in Human Geography*, 36(3): 389–402.

Coe, N. (2013) 'Geographies of production III: making space for labour', *Progress in Human Geography*, 37: 271–284.

Coe, N. and Hess, M. (2013) 'Global production networks, labour and development', *Geoforum*, 44: 4–9.

Coe, N. M. and Jordhus-Lier, D. C. (2012) 'Constrained agency? re-evaluating the geographies of labor', *Progress in Human Geography*, 35(2): 211–233.

Coe, N., Hess, M., Yeung, H. W. C., Dicken, P. and Henderson, J. (2004) 'Globalizing regional development: a global production networks perspective'. *Transactions of the Institute of British Geographers NS*, 29: 468–484.

Cumbers, A. (2004) Embedded internationalisms: building transnational solidarity in the British and Norwegian trade union movements. *Antipode*, 36(5): 829–850.

Cumbers, A., Nativel, C. and Routledge, P. (2008) 'Labour agency and union positionalities in global production networks', *Journal of Economic Geography*, 8(2): 369–387.

Cumbers, A., MacKinnon, D. and Shaw, J. (2010) 'Labour, organisational rescaling and the politics of production: union renewal in the privatised rail industry', *Work, Employment and Society*, 24: 127–144.

Cumbers, A., Featherstone, D., MacKinnon, D., Ince, A. and Strauss, K. (2014) 'Intervening in globalisation: the spatial possibilities and institutional barriers to labour's collective agency', *Journal of Economic Geography*, doi:10.1093/jeg/lbu039, available at http://joeg.oxfordjournals.org/content/early/recent.

Dicken, P. (1986) *Global Shift: Industrial Change in a Turbulent World*, London: Paul Chapman.

Dicken, P. (1998) *Global Shift: Transforming the World Economy*, London: Paul Chapman.

Dicken, P. (2010) *Global Shift: Mapping the Changing Contours of the World Economy*, London: Sage.
Featherstone, D. (2012) *Solidarity: Hidden Histories and Geographies of Internationalism*, London: Zed.
Frank, T. (2007) *The World is Flat: The Globalised World in the Twenty First Century* (2nd edition), London: Penguin.
Gereffi, G., Humphrey, J. and Sturgeon, T. (2005) 'The governance of global value chains', *Review of International Political Economy*, 12: 78–104.
Glassman, J. (2011) 'The global geopolitical economy of global production networks', *Geography Compass*, 5: 154–164.
Harvey, D. (1982) *Limits to Capital*, Oxford: Blackwell.
Helfen, M. and Fichter, M. (2013) 'Building transnational union networks across Global Production Networks: conceptualising a new arena of labour–management relations', *British Journal of Industrial Relations*, 51(3): 553–576.
Henderson, J., Dicken, P., Hess, M., Coe, N. and Yeung, H. W-C. (2002) 'Global production networks and the analysis of economic development', *Review of International Political Economy*, 9: 436–464.
Hess, M. (2004) '"Spatial" relationships? Towards a reconceptualisation of embeddedness', *Progress in Human Geography*, 28(2): 165–186.
Howells, J. (2006) *New Democratic Trends in China? Reforming the All-China Federation of Trade Unions*, IDS Working Paper 263, Brighton: Institute of Development Studies.
Ince, A., Featherstone, D., Cumbers, A., MacKinnon, D. and Strauss, K. (2014) 'British jobs for British workers? Negotiating work, nation, and globalisation through the Lindsey oil refinery disputes', *Antipode*, doi: 10.1111/anti.12099.
Jessop, B. (2008) *State Power: A Strategic Relational Approach*, Cambridge: Polity.
Kelly, P. (2013) 'Production networks, place and development: thinking through Global Production Networks in Cavite, Philippines', *Geoforum*, 44(1): 82–92.
MacKinnon, D. (2012) 'Beyond strategic coupling: reassessing the firm-region nexus in global production networks', *Journal of Economic Geography*, 12(1): 227–245.
MacKinnon D., Cumbers A. and Chapman K. (2002) 'Learning, innovation and regional development: a critical appraisal of recent debates', *Progress in Human Geography*, 26(3): 293–311.
MacKinnon, D., Cumbers, A., Pike, A., Birch, K. and McMaster, R. (2009) 'Evolution in economic geography: institutions, political economy, and adaptation', *Economic Geography*, 85(2): 129–150.
Massey, D. (1984) *Spatial Divisions of Labour: Social Structures and the Geography of Production*, Basingstoke: Macmillan.
Massey, D. (2005) *For Space*, London: Sage.
McGrath, S. (2013) 'Fuelling global production networks with slave labour?: Migrant sugar cane workers in the Brazilian ethanol GPN', *Geoforum*, 44: 32–43.
Ohmae, K. (1990) *The Borderless World*, London: Collins.
Peck, J. (2013) 'Making space for labour' in D. Featherstone and J. Painter (eds) *Spatial Politics: Essays for Doreen Massey*, Oxford: Wiley-Blackwell, 99–114.

Quinjun, W. (2010) 'Establishing trade unions within foreign companies in China', *Employee Relations*, 32(4): 349–363.

Rainnie, A., Herod, A. and McGrath-Champ, S. (2010) 'Workers in space', in S. McGrath-Champ, A. Herod and A. Rainnie (eds) *Handbook of Employment and Society*, Northampton: Edward Elgar Publishing, pp. 249–272.

Rainnie, A., Herod, A. and McGrath-Champ, S. (2011) 'Review and positions: global production networks and labour', *Competition and Change*, 15(2): 155–169.

Selwyn, B. (2011) 'Beyond firm-centrism: re-integrating labour and capitalism into global commodity chain analysis', *Journal of Economic Geography*, 12: 205–226.

Selwyn, B. (2013) 'Social upgrading and labour in global production networks: a critique and an alternative conception', *Competition and Change*, 17: 75–90.

Smith, A. (2014) 'The state, institutional frameworks and the dynamics of capital in global production networks', *Progress in Human Geography*, Online Publication, doi: 10.1177/0309132513518292 (accessed 20 August 2014).

Starosta, G. (2010) 'Global commodity chains and the Marxian law of value', *Antipode*, 42: 433–465.

Stopford, J. M. and Strange, S. (1991) *Rival States, Rival Firms: Competition for World Market Shares*, Cambridge: Cambridge University Press.

Sunley, P. (2008) 'Relational economic geography: a partial understanding or a new paradigm?', *Economic Geography*, 84: 1–26.

Taylor, P. and Bain, P. (2008) 'United by a common language? Trade union responses in the UK and India to call centre offshoring', *Antipode*, 40: 131–154.

Thomson, D. and Larson, R. (1978) *Where Were You Brother? An Account of Trade Union Imperialism*, London: War on Want.

Wills, J. (2005) 'The geography of union organising in low-paid service industries in the UK: Lessons from the T&G's campaign to unionise the Dorchester Hotel, London', *Antipode*, 37(1): 139–159.

Wright, E. O. (2001) 'Working-class power, capitalist-class interests, and class compromise', *American Journal of Sociology*, 105: 957–1002.

CHAPTER 9

Social Downgrading and Worker Resistance in Apparel Global Value Chains

Mark Anner

This chapter explores labour control and resistance at the point of production in apparel Global Value Chains (GVCs). It argues that, since the mid-2000s, structural transformations in the global apparel industry have engendered pricing and sourcing dynamics conducive to three systems of labour control: (1) increased work intensity and control through the piece rate system, (2) employer control over workers through company unions, and (3) the use of violence and threats of violence against independent unionism. Yet, workers are also engaging in a range of resistance strategies, notably work stoppages and strategic corporate campaigns. For these strategies to be truly transformative, labour activists need to achieve coordinated bargaining with buyers and suppliers across countries.

The first section of this chapter explores the literature and develops the argument. The second section of the chapter looks at changes in the apparel Global Value Chain (GVC) structures that created competitive pressures conducive to adverse pricing and sourcing practices. Using El Salvador as an illustrative case study of an apparel export country facing extreme cost-cutting pressures since 2005, the third section of the chapter draws on field research to examine how GVC dynamics have resulted in three adverse forms of workplace labour control, what I am labelling as 'social downgrading'. The final section explores patterns of worker resistance.

Labour Control and Global Value Chains

Labour process analysis has contributed to the field of labour studies by emphasizing the dynamics of control, consent and resistance at the point of production (Thompson and Smith, 2010). Its conceptualization of workers as complex social actors helps to explain variations in how, why and when workers may consent to or resist exploitation (Hyman, 1995; Edwards, 2010). Labour process analysis explores the complexities and multiple influences on class consciousness (Hudson, 1991). It sees workers' struggles as ones not only for economic demands but also for a sense of fairness (Friedman, 2004). The literature on Global Value Chains begins with a more macro-structural approach (Taylor, 2010). Recent literature has contributed to the GVC approach by incorporating labour into the chain and network analyses (Herod, 2001; Rainnie et al., 2011; Riisgaard and Hammer; 2011). For Riisgaard and Hammer, the governance structure of Global Value Chains helps to explain labour's strategic options (2011). Notably, the authors emphasize the power of lead firms to shape rules along value chains.

Early models of labour control often focused on advanced industrial economies (Braverman, 1974; Burawoy, 1979). But as competitive pressures shifted low wage production segments of GVCs to the Global South, more pernicious patterns of labour control have emerged. In the lowest wage countries like Bangladesh and Indonesia, unfavourable labour market conditions force workers to stay in poorly paid jobs with abusive working conditions in what scholars refer to as 'market despotism' (Webster *et al.*, 2008). Latin America has been notorious for more violent forms of worker control (Levenson-Estrada, 1994).

While labour remains integral to the production process, Rainnie *et al.* argue that the literature on labour activism in global value chains has 'failed to consider labour as an active agent capable of shaping such chains' structure and geographical organization' (Rainnie *et al.*, 2011). Yet, labour has often influenced GVC dynamics, as the spatial, technological and product fixes suggest. Because of labour activism, capital moves location, changes technology or shifts to new products (Silver, 2003). This dynamic is well illustrated by Jeff Cowie's research on the Radio Corporation of America (RCA), which shows how worker resistance through strikes, union formation, and collective bargaining improved workplace conditions but then led to shifting production sites within the United States and then eventually to Mexico (Cowie, 1999). The question is whether worker activism is capable of shaping GVCs to achieve sustainable benefits for labour.

In the 1990s, literature on international labour solidarity tended to assume a limited ability of workers to address abuses locally, while providing for a larger role for cross-border alliances. In this framework, the main axis of conflict shifted from workers and employers at the point of production to consumer activists and GVC lead firms in northern markets (Gordon and Turner, 2000). This literature tended to focus on cross-border, macro-level sources of power. Workplace abuses were turned into framing tools to leverage upstream buyers by shaming brand-sensitive firms in the Global North (Anner, 2000).

However, there was also an emerging scepticism of excessive reliance on transnational over domestic activism. Research showed that campaigns that turn very quickly to cross-border activism are far less sustainable than campaigns that first develop strong domestic strategies, most notably plant-level activism (Anner, 2011). Recent literature on transnational labour campaigns is further redirecting our focus by exploring how transnational campaigns impact local movements (McCallum, 2013). Other scholars remind us that, despite increased reference to global labour solidarity, the history of organized labour has been deeply linked to the nation-state and domestic labour struggles (Erne, 2008).

This chapter builds on this literature by examining the impact of upstream lead firm consolidation and shifts in international trade rules on forms of labour control at the site of production. It does so by examining a case of an apparel exporting country, El Salvador, which has faced particularly sharp cost-cutting pressures since 2005. Work intensity, company unions and the threat of violence have been used to control costs, increase worker discipline and lessen the likelihood of collective resistance. However, these extreme measures are engendering strong within-plant worker solidarity that is complemented, but not supplanted, by transnational campaigns that target lead firms in GVCs. The challenge is to transform these efforts into strategies capable of providing more sustainable benefits for labour.

Methodology

To explore the argument presented above, this study uses case study analysis in one country and one sector. It focuses on apparel because apparel GVCs provide a clear example of dramatic and recent restructuring in a buyer-driven GVC. The country level case study approach allows for an in-depth exploration of the evolving dynamics of labour control in one national context. For my country case, I have selected El Salvador because it offers a case of an apparel exporting country facing extreme cost-cutting pressures. Drawing on theoretical arguments from labour process analysis, I hypothesize that apparel GVC restructuring will contribute to new and intensified labour control practices. I then turn to field research to explore the evolution of specific labour control mechanisms in the sector. This process-tracing method allows for researchers to

Social Downgrading and Worker Resistance | 155

go beyond correlation analysis to explore the precise mechanisms that link causes and outcomes (Collier, 1993).

The findings presented in this report are based on three trips to the field between September 2012 and March 2013.[1] During those trips, I conducted approximately 35 interviews with workers, unionists, labour researchers and activists, government representatives, labour lawyers, private factory auditors and factory owners. Phone interviewers were conducted with two major apparel brands. This research project entailed delicate matters such as death threats received by worker activists in apparel export factories. To protect their identities, I have not used their names or other information that could potentially identify them, including factory names. Factories are referred to as Factory A, Factory B and Factory C.

Apparel Global Value Chain Restructuring

The global economy is increasingly shaped by Global Value Chains (GVCs), understood here as a range of activities involved in the design, production and marketing of a product. Multinational Corporation coordinated GVCs account for 80 per cent of global trade, and the income from trade flows within GVCs doubled between 1995 and 2009 (OECD, 2013). In buyer-driven value chains such as apparel, large retailers, marketeers and branded manufacturers exert greatest governance control over decentralized production networks (Gereffi and Memedovic, 2003). The question is whether recent shifts in GVC dynamics in the apparel sector have resulted in greater compliance with international labour standards and better conditions for labour – what some scholars refer to as 'social upgrading' (Gereffi and Memedovic, 2003; Barrientos *et al.*, 2011). One World Bank report argues that recent global consolidation in the sector has meant that 'firms are only able to enter supply chains of global buyers if they can offer high manufacturing capabilities, *including low costs, high quality, short lead times, production flexibility, and labour compliance*' (Staritz, 2011; emphasis mine).

This chapter argues that labour compliance has not improved precisely because of increased exigencies for low costs, short lead times and flexible production schemes. Firms are increasingly looking for new ways to reduce costs, increase worker discipline, and improve the rate of production by controlling labour. In a 2013 Organisation for Economic Co-operation and Development (OECD)/World Trade Organization (WTO) survey, the top five responses for the most influential factors in sourcing and investment decisions in textiles and apparel were production costs, labour skills and productivity, quality standards, labour costs and order delivery time. Only 8 per cent of responses indicated that respect for labour standards was important (Fukunishi et al., 2013). Buyers are particularly wary of labour standards compliance programmes that include a strong defence of freedom of association rights (Anner, 2012).

This chapter does not dispute that social upgrading is possible when the appropriate public and private sectors policies are implemented. However, in many cases the state and the private sector have failed to pursue policies conducive to social upgrading. At the same time, four important and inter-related developments have adversely altered the structure of the global apparel industry for labour: (1) The phase-out of the Multi-Fibre Agreement, (2) The entry of China and then Vietnam into the World Trade Organization, (3) The consolidation and growing market power of retailers relative to suppliers. (4) The global recession that began in 2008–2009. These factors have contributed to an increase in worker rights violations, or 'social downgrading'.

In 2001, global competitiveness in apparel faced a significant transformation when the World Trade Organization (WTO) admitted China as a member. China's position was enhanced as WTO member states negotiated the Agreement on Textiles and Clothing (ATC) that, on 1 January 2005, phased out the system of quota-based trade in apparel based on the Multi-Fibre Agreement (UNDP, 2003). Asian competitiveness increased further with the US-Vietnam Bilateral Trade Agreement of 2001. Like China, Vietnam offered labour control through state controlled unions, yet with much lower wages. China and Vietnam have been the largest exporters of apparel to the United States since 2008.

An additional factor shaping competitiveness dynamics in the apparel sector is brand and especially retailer concentration relative to suppliers. Since start-up costs in apparel are relatively low, apparel production has been greatly dispersed to a very large number of factories in numerous developing countries. By 2006, there were a total of 3,500 export processing zones (each with many independent factories within them) employing 66 million workers in 130 countries (Milberg and Amengual, 2008). No doubt, the phase-out of the Multi-Fiber Arrangement (MFA) has facilitated the consolidation of suppliers. Yet retailers concentrated their power more through advances in logistics and technology (Abernathy et al., 1999). The result was a net increase in value chain monopsony, the power consolidation of lead firms relative to downstream suppliers. In such a context, retailers and other buyers can often dictate the price they will pay per garment. And, as Richard Locke notes, even as many suppliers grow in size, their power remains weak relative to that of upstream buyers. He adds, 'many of the workplace problems we observe ... also are the result of a set of policies and practices designed and implemented *upstream* by large retailers and global buyers' (Locke, 2013; emphasis in original).

These macro-level political and structural changes have had two dominant effects on workplace dynamics. The ability of lead firms to set the price paid to less powerful production contractors has generated a cost-crisis for suppliers. Notably, the real dollar price per square metre of apparel entering the US market *declined by 46.2 per cent* from 1989 to 2011 (Anner *et al.*, 2013). This indicates that apparel suppliers are indeed producing under increasingly tight economic margins as competitiveness at the supplier level intensifies. In Central America, countries established lower minimum wages for apparel export workers. They also, as we will see below, increased their efforts to weaken or eliminate independent unionism. And the push for lead firms to demand just-in-time inventory has generated a work-intensity crisis in workplaces.

Apparel and Labour Control in El Salvador

Measured in terms of volume and value, most apparel production in El Salvador is located in Export Processing Zones. Apparel export factories located outside EPZs tend to be small and locally owned. The first EPZ was built in the 1970s, but production stagnated due to social unrest and then civil war. It was in the post-war 1990s, with their broad range of fiscal incentives, that production soared, surpassing all other Salvadoran exports. The main apparel exports in the sector include cotton knit shirts, blouses and undergarments (about 49 per cent of apparel exports in 2013) and knit shirts, blouses, trousers and undergarments made with synthetic fibre (about 33 per cent of apparel exports).

The labour-intensive, assembly dynamic of the sector in El Salvador can be observed by comparing exports with imported inputs for apparel production. While in 2013, El Salvador exported USD 1,158.2 million in apparel, that year it also imported USD 725.2 million in apparel production inputs, most notably fabric. Thus, the dynamics of the apparel sector can best be seen by examining the value added generated within the country (exports-imports), and not by measuring the total value of apparel exports. What the data indicate is that the industry grew from 1992 until 2008. Then there was a dramatic drop in 2009. Some 85 per cent of Salvadoran apparel exports go to the US, and when the US entered a recession in 2009, the apparel sector in El Salvador entered into a crisis that remained through 2013. Value added in the sector declined by 37.2 per cent (see Figure 9.1).

The post-2009 crisis escalated a cost-squeeze dynamic that has characterized the sector since its inception. Between 1990 and 2009, in the manufacturing sector (which is dominated by the apparel sector), while labour productivity rose by 78.1 per cent, unit labour costs in real dollars declined by 60.8 per cent between 1990 and 2009 (Alvarado Zepeda, 2010). In 2003, El Salvador began a differentiated minimum wage system where EPZ workers are paid less than workers in the service sector or non-EPZ manufacturing sectors. In 2013, the hourly minimum wage rate for the service sector was USD 1.01, USD 0.99 for non-apparel export manufacturing, and USD 0.85 for apparel manufacturing. The total value of salaries paid in 2013 in the apparel export sector, including management salaries, amounted to USD 300 million.[2] That year, value added in the sector was USD 406 million. Thus, labour costs made up 74 per cent of the value added, which suggests that this remains a labour-intensive sector.

International Financial Institutions (IFIs) continue to emphasize the role of the apparel export sector in generating jobs, reducing poverty and contributing to GPD growth, and El Salvador is one of the three top Latin American apparel exporters. Yet, in a country of 6.3 million people, employment in the sector in 2013 stood at 72,744 jobs. Value added in the EPZ sector never contributed significantly to GDP growth or poverty reduction. Rather, the economy has grown and is maintained as a result of the billions of dollars that enter each year in family remittances. In 2013, remittances brought in USD 3.9 billion and accounted for 16.27 per cent of GDP. This is 9.7 times more than the contribution of

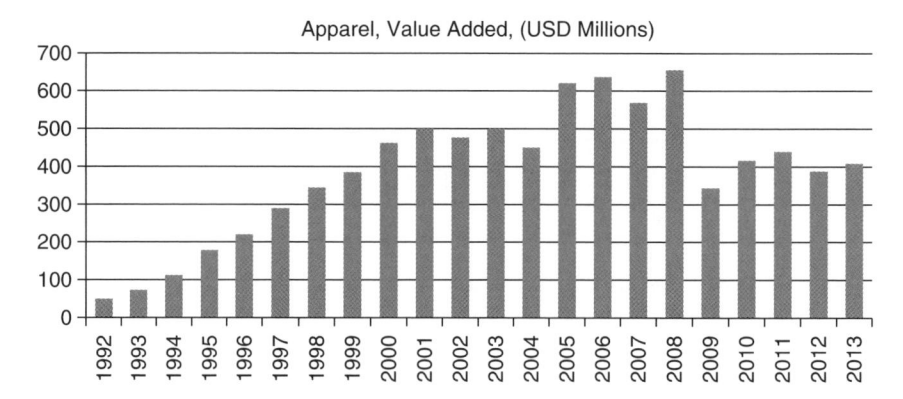

Figure 9.1 Apparel, value added

Source: Author's calculations.

Table 9.1 GDP, apparel and remittances (USD millions)

	GDP Growth Rate	Value Added, Apparel	Value Added, Apparel/GDP	Remittances	Remittances/GDP
1995	6.40%	174.0	1.83%	1,063.0	11.19%
2001	1.71%	489.0	3.54%	1,910.5	13.84%
2005	3.56%	616.5	3.61%	3,017.1	17.64%
2009	−3.13%	340.5	1.64%	3,387.1	16.36%
2013	1.68%	406.0	1.67%	3,953.4	16.27%

Source: Author's calculations based on World Development Indicators and Central Bank of El Salvador annual data.

the apparel export sector (See Table 9.1.). And while 73,000 Salvadorans received income from apparel export jobs, 1.2 million adult immigrants sent on average USD 2,939 per year to their families (Cohn et al., 2013). What these data suggest is that it is not the export of apparel but rather the export of people that has contributed most significantly to GDP growth and poverty reduction.

The economic context and a long, harsh history of political and labour repression have left the Salvadoran labour movement weak and highly fragmented. According to Ministry of Labour data, by 2012, the country had 405 unions and 170,837 union members. That is, the average union had 422 members. These unions were divided into seven national confederations and 34 federations. Many of these federations are multi-sector, independent national organizations that act like labour centres. Unions can be formed with 35 workers, but the majority of workers in an enterprise must be members of a union in order to obligate employers to bargain collectively. Apparel export workers have not had a single collective bargaining agreement since the sector began to grow in the early 1990s (Anner, 2011).

It is in this context of post-MFA, global recession, consolidating buyer power, and rising Asian exports that apparel producers in El Salvador have sought to compete by repressing workers' rights (social downgrading). This general trend is illustrated by an annual workers' rights measure provided by the Cingranelli-Richards (CIRI) Human Rights Dataset. CIRI scores countries on a three-point scale from '0' for bad to '2' for good. From 1992 to 2001, the average yearly workers' rights score in El Salvador was 0.9. From 2002 to 2011, the average yearly workers' rights score was 0.4.[3] This indicates that respect for workers' rights has declined by 56 per cent.

To better grasp the precise mechanisms used by employers to control labour by curtailing workers' rights, I turned to process tracing conducted during three trips to the field to interview workers and other stakeholders in the sector. What I found was that employers are reinforcing old labour control practices and implementing new ones. They are: (1) The piece rate system to increase worker discipline and production; (2) The promotion of company unions to achieve collective control over labour; and (3) The use of gangs to threaten independent trade unionists, to limit the possibility of workers organizing efforts that might increase costs and reduce the ability of managers to control workers.

Piece Rate System: an Old System of Labour Control in New Bottles

One of the most notorious and contested systems of labour control in the apparel industry is the piece rate system. The system has varied across countries and time, but the general premise remains the same: to pay workers by how much they produce and not by how long they work. Given the development of minimum wage laws, a straight piece rate system is less common now. One approach is for employers to require workers complete a certain number of operations per eight-hour shift in order to keep their job and earn the minimum wage, such as sewing 1,000 collars on shirts per shift. Workers are then paid bonuses based on how far above the daily quota they go. The price squeeze resulting from upstream buyer consolidation and changing global trade rules means factory owners are paid less in real dollar terms by buyers. But they cannot cut wages if they are already paying the minimum wage. The piece rate system is used in these circumstances to maintain the economic viability of the firm.

What this means is that employers might respond to a 10 per cent government mandated wage increase and a 5 per cent buyer price reduction by requiring a 15 per cent increase in the piece rate. For example, workers would now be required to sew 1,150 collars per straight shift as opposed to 1,000. The result of this work intensification can be seen when visiting factories during field research. In addition to working at a faster pace, workers will forgo lunch, water and bathroom breaks in order to meet their production quota. Supervisors, under such a system, do not need to shout orders to work faster. The workers discipline themselves by the need to make the quota in order to keep their jobs or exceed the quota in order to increase their disposable income to cover their basic living needs.

Garment production is particularly conducive to an individual piece rate system because the pliant nature of cloth and the constantly changing seasons and fashion make mechanization difficult. Most garments today are still produced by a worker sitting behind a sewing machine performing one operation in the production of a garment. What has changed is the intensity of the system. A field research visit to Factory A revealed that as competition from Asia increased, workers were instructed that they needed to increase the pace of their production in 2013 by 27 per cent over their production rate in 2012. As one worker noted, 'the old rate was hard; the new rate was impossible' (interview San Salvador).

In another attempt to increase production, some firms experimented with 'team' work, in which team members are each paid the same bonus based on the overall team's rate of production. Worker interviews indicated that, in the process of setting up the teams, workers at Factory A were told by their manager to 'yell at other team members and insult them if they are not working hard enough because you will all suffer for the loss of production bonuses caused by one slow worker' (interview San Salvador). In this case, production increases are achieved through peer pressure based on a co-dependence on bonus income. Workers at Factory B, also visited by the author in 2013, were told that if they did not meet production goals, they would be ordered to stay late without receiving overtime pay. Interviews with workers indicated that most workers find the system repressive, but they need the bonuses (assuming they are properly paid) because the minimum wage is too low to meet basic family needs. Yet, as we will see ahead, when production quotas are pushed to unbearable levels, the majority of workers may join forces and strike.

Company Unions

Interviews with workers and worker advocates indicate that, at some worksites, employers require their workers to join a pro-management union as a condition of employment. By favouring a pro-management union, employers seek to reduce the risk of strikes and collective bargaining agreements with an independent union that would raise costs. Interviews with workers at Factory C indicated that, in order to grow a pro-management union and weaken an independent union, employers give pro-management union leaders the ability to circulate and talk to production workers at any time during their shifts. In contrast, unionists belonging to independent unions are denied free mobility and access to the workforce. In one case, a new worker who was still under her probationary period was fired because she was seen associating with members of the independent union.

Interviews with workers from Factory C also suggested that, to facilitate pro-management union access to the workforce, the plant-level leaders of these organizations were assigned a position that either required little or no production work or that required them to move around the plant and to speak with all of the workers. Employers also grant small personal loans to workers contingent upon affiliation to the pro-management organization while workers who were affiliated to an independent union are denied such loans. The loans are dispersed and supervised by a plant-level leader of the pro-management union. El Salvador has an open shop system that allows for multiple production worker unions in one factory, but it does not allow for double union affiliation. The result is that when the employer pressures workers to join the company union, they must first require disaffiliation from the independent union. To facilitate the process, when workers apply for loans, they are given three forms. The first form is to disaffiliate from the independent union, the second form is to join the company union, and the third form is to secure the loan. Given the low salary levels in the factory, many workers need loans. As a result, a significant share of the workforce end up affiliated to the company union.

Company unions are not a new dynamic in the garment industry. Yet, what field research suggests is that this practice has escalated as cost pressures have increased. The rise of company unions in some ways is also a response to a practice of some Corporate Social Responsibility programmes that certify compliance with freedom of association criteria simply as a result of union presence. These programmes often do not check if the union is funded or otherwise controlled by employers. The existence of the union, no matter how it was formed, controlled or funded, is taken as a sign that the freedom of association requirement in the company code of conduct has been met. In many ways, company unions are an ideal form of employer collective control over the workforce, because they provide a direct mechanism for employers to manipulate workers' interests while also allowing employers to appear union friendly.

Violence and the Threat of Violence

After a violent civil war (1981–1992) and what appeared to be a transition away from violence against unionists toward somewhat more sophisticated forms of labour control, targeted anti-union violence has been on the rise in El Salvador. This violence is part of a larger wave of gang-related violence sweeping the country. The United Nations Office on Drugs and Crime (UNODC) reported in 2011 that El Salvador had the second highest homicide rate in the world, at 69.2 per 100,000 inhabitants. Salvadoran gangs have been shown to have links to organized crime and receive support from the police and other structures of power (Pedraza Fariña *et al.*, 2010).

A particularly worrisome trend is a growing number of reports by trade unionists that they faced threats from gangs after leading protests in apparel export processing zones. In January 2013, a union leader was approached as she was leaving work by a gang member near the gates of her factory, the F&D Factory in the San Marcos Free Trade Zone.[4] One gang member pointed a gun at her and told her that he didn't want to see her at the factory again. As the young man threatened her, he raised the sleeve of his jacket to reveal more gang tattoos and said, 'You know we don't mess around'. Immediately following this incident, the union leaders received multiple anonymous threatening telephone calls. The union leader saw a factory manager sitting inside his parked car about one half block from where this incident at the time took place (Federación Sindical de El Salvador, 2013).

Another example of these gang-related threats occurred at Factory B. Workers who went on strike in support of an independent union in early 2012 were beaten by gang members who workers believed were tied to the company union. One worker at the factory reported that on the day the strike began a member of the company union handed her his mobile phone. On the phone, a man told the worker that he was in her neighbourhood, standing outside her house, and could see her two children inside. He then told the worker that if she did not want anything to happen to her children, she should not participate in the strike.

The question these cases present is why would violent street gangs care if young workers want to form a union at their garment factory. The answer to this question begins in analysing the relationship between gangs and factory owners. Gangs extort local factory owners by requiring that they make monthly payments to the gangs or risk gang retaliation. What this suggests is that, through regularized 'protection' payments, gang leaders and factory owners develop an institutionalized relationship. And when faced with pressure from independent trade unions, some employers may request the services of gang members to threaten or harm trade union members. That is, they may increase the amount they pay in protection money to request that gangs provide them with protection from independent trade unionists. The system of labour control thus has not progressed unambiguously from its most violent manifestation in the 1980s to increasingly sophisticated forms of labour control in the current period. Rather, labour control practices can shift back, and in some case have, to their more repressive, albeit more targeted, forms.

Worker Resistance

Given such systems of labour control, what is labour's capacity for resistance? And when there is resistance, what form does the resistance take? I have written elsewhere about the impact of GVC governance, state structures and labour ideologies on patterns of resistance (Anner, 2011). In that work, I suggested that value chains with stronger buyer power are more conducive to transnational activist campaigns, and value chains with stronger producer power are more likely to engender transnational labour networks. Moreover, the degree of transnationalism is influenced by labour ideologies and labour's inability to access state institutions (Anner, 2011).

In the cases illustrated here, the GVC and state structures are held constant; all examples of worker resistance involve the apparel sector and El Salvador. What field research revealed is that when the piece rate system is excessively burdensome, workers may quickly coalesce in protest. This is what happened in the case of Factory A when managers announced in January 2013 that the piece rate would go up by 27 per cent. The independent union, which by that point had become small and isolated due to the management strategies outlined above, opposed the change, but did not speak out immediately. Representatives of the company union tried to talk management into reducing the burden, but to no avail. Management was helpful when workers in this union wanted funds to organize social events and resources to recruit members away from the independent unions, but it was not responsive when the company union wanted to modify a policy that increased work intensity.

At this point, workers from the company union and workers with no union affiliation approached the independent union and asked it to organize a strike. The independent union leaders responded that they would, but only if all the other workers fully supported the strike. They agreed, and in January the entire workforce shut down operations for three days, forcing the company to rescind the piece rate increase. It was one of the more significant protest events in the apparel sector in years, and it displayed the fluidity of worker identities and interests, and the limitations of the use of the piece rate system and company unions as systems of labour control.

Often, however, the use of company unions fragments worker resistance. This was the case at Factory C, where factory owners fired a worker who was completing her probationary period for associating with the independent union. This provoked a strike by the unionists in March 2013. About 100 workers joined the strike, which represented the minority of the workforce. In contrast with the strike at Factory A, which involved an issue that affected all workers, this was an issue that could be seen as affecting only one worker. The independent union, however, saw it as a violation of basic workers' rights and knew that they would never grow if workers saw that joining the union could result in termination. For the company union, not only was the issue one that they believe did not directly affect them, but from their perspective, actions that helped to keep the independent union weak could only strengthen the company union. Indeed, in response to the strike, the company union began handing out flyers outside the factory calling on workers to return to their jobs. The flyers noted that, if they did not, the company could lose a contract, which would result in a 30 per cent cut in production and thus employment. The workers returned to their jobs and the strike failed.

The use of violence against unionists is the harshest system of labour control, and it may appear to be the most difficult to address. Yet it is the very extreme nature of the threat of bodily harm that allows activists the ability to frame the issue in a way that resonates with larger social values of human decency (Keck and Sikkink, 1998). It is this normative frame that gives workers power and shapes this form of resistance. Because the framing approach is effective in the countries of large consumer markets, Salvadoran garment workers have reached out beyond national borders and formed alliances with activists elsewhere, most notably in the United States, Canada and Europe. Thus, the concrete experience of the threat of violence against them for their union activities is communicated via transnational activist campaigns in order to shame the upstream GVC lead firms to instruct their suppliers to accept the union.

This dynamic has been successfully used in El Salvadoran cases such as Mandarin and Do All Enterprises, where worker tours facilitated the re-hiring of dismissed union activists (Anner, 2011). More recently, in early 2014, 1,066 workers at Manufacturas Del Rio (MDR) lost their jobs when the factory closed after workers formed a union and demanded that the employer bargain collectively with them. Cross-border campaigns demanding payment of lost wages, benefits and severance were then organized, targeting the firm's buyers, which included Fruit of the Loom, Adidas, Lacoste and Levi's. In July 2014, the campaign was successful in that the workers were paid what they were owed.

The challenge facing labour is making the gains from these factory-focused campaigns into transformative changes in GVCs. Indeed, even the 'successful' campaigns outlined above are defensive. In one case the piece rate was returned to the previous year's rate, which was already unbearable. In other cases, fired workers got their jobs back, but their union remained weak. In another case, workers who were fired without back pay or severance received what they were owed, but the workplace was closed and the union was destroyed. So long as the pricing and sourcing mechanisms outlined above continue, it will be difficult to find sustainable solutions to the problems they create.

With my co-authors, Jennifer Bair and Jeremy Blasi, I have argued that what is needed is a form of cross-border, triangular bargaining of binding agreements among buyers, suppliers and labour (Anner *et al.*, 2013). Such an approach has both contemporary and historic antecedents. In the mid-twentieth century, 'jobbers agreements' in the US based on triangular negotiations largely eliminated sweatshop practices for decades; and the 2013 Accord on Fire and Building Safety in Bangladesh brought buyers and labour together to address building safety through a binding agreement (Anner *et al.*, 2013). Salvadoran workers are realizing they need to pursue such an approach. For the last several years they have participated in a network of unionists and labour activists known as the International Union League for Brand Responsibility. One of its first major campaigns is targeting the Adidas corporation and demanding that Adidas enter into direct negotiations with this coalition of unionists from 11 countries to provide living wages and stable contracts.[5] It is too early to determine if this campaign will succeed, but the strategy does hold the promise of a more sustainable solution to the problems facing workers in GVCs.

Conclusions

Incorporating Global Value Chain literature insights into labour process analysis allows for a more complete understanding of systems of labour control and patterns of worker resistance at the point of production and throughout the value chain. What this chapter has illustrated is that upstream buyer consolidation and changing global trade rules pushed apparel industry employers into deeper and more extreme systems of labour control, including an increased intensity of the piece rate system, more aggressive promotion of company unions, and the use of violence against independent unionists.

Yet the examples presented here also illustrate patterns of labour resistance. In the case of Factory A, the company union strategy fell apart when members of the company union could not take the intensity of the increased piece rate system and were not able to convince management to reduce it. Their allegiances quickly changed, and they found themselves out on strike alongside a combative independent trade union. And in their moment of unity, they were successful. Other independent unions have turned to transnational activist campaigns to further circumvent systems of workplace control. Indeed, they have used the threat of violence to mobilize consumer outrage in the Global North. And they have broadened their demands to include respect for the right to independent unionization and decency at work. Companies such as Gap, Liz Claiborne and Adidas have all been the targets of transnational activist campaigns for workers' rights in El Salvador, often with important, if short-lived, successes.

The broader question is whether these campaigns have fundamentally altered workplace and GVC practices for the benefit of labour. The evidence is mixed. Lead firms who argued in the 1990s that they were not responsible for the conditions of labour at suppliers now realize that argument is no longer acceptable. Yet much remains to be done, as illustrated by the threat of violence against unionists in El Salvador (in addition to the horrific building fires and collapses in Asia – notably the Rana Plaza collapse that killed over 1,000 workers). It appears that for more sustained transformations, neither workplace strikes nor value chain campaigns will be sufficient. Rather, what is needed is for labour to achieve cross-border, binding collective agreements with suppliers and buyers that address the pricing and sourcing dynamics that are the source of labour abuses. Such a strategy, combined with more effective and uniform laws and enforcement mechanisms, will go a long way to ensuring that 'social downgrading' is transformed to 'social upgrading'.

Notes

1 Tara Mathur, a researcher with the Workers' Rights Consortium, travelled with me to El Salvador in December 2012, and we conducted numerous factory visits and stakeholder interviews together on that trip. I benefited significantly from our conversations about those factory visits.
2 Cámara de la Industria Textil, Confección y Zonas Francas de El Salvador (CAMTEX), http://camtex.com.sv/.
3 See http://www.humanrightsdata.com/p/data-documentation.html.
4 Since the case reported in this section was publicly denounced by a trade union federation, the name of the factory is provided. The author did interview the workers that received the threats, who

confirmed the veracity of the report presented on the federation's website.
5 See International Union League for Brand Responsibility, www.union-league.org/ (Accessed 9 August 2014).

REFERENCES

Abernathy, F. H., Dunlop, J. T., Hammond, J. H. and Weil, D. (1999) *A Stitch in Time: Lean Retailing and the Transformation of Manufacturing: Lessons from the Apparel and Textile Industries*, New York: Oxford University Press.

Alvarado Zepeda, C. A. (2010) *Análisis de la Productividad y los Costos Laborales Unitarios Reales en El Salvador 1990–2009. Aspectos Teóricos e Implicaciones en la Competitividad*, San Salvador: Banco Central de Reserva de El Salvador.

Anner, M. (2000) 'Local and transnational campaigns to end sweatshop practices,' in M. E. Gordon. and L. Turner (eds) *Transnational Cooperation Among Labor Unions*, Ithaca, NY: ILR Press, pp. 238–255.

Anner, M. (2011) *Solidarity Transformed: Labor's Responses to Globalization and Crisis in Latin America*, Ithaca: ILR Press, an imprint of Cornell University Press.

Anner, M. (2012) 'Corporate social responsibility and freedom of association rights: The precarious quest for legitimacy and control in global supply chains', *Politics & Society*, 40(4): 604–639.

Anner, M., Bair, J. and Blasi, J. (2013) 'Toward joint liability in global supply chains: Addressing the root causes of labor violations in international subcontracting networks', *International Labor Law & Policy Journal*, 35(1): 1–43.

Barrientos, S., Gereffi, G. and Rossi, A. (2011) 'Economic and social upgrading in global production networks: A new paradigm for a changing world', *International Labour Review*, 150(3–4): 319–340.

Braverman, H. (1974) *Labor and Monopoly Capital*. New York: Monthly Review Press.

Burawoy, M. (1979) *Manufacturing Consent: Changes in the Labor Process under Monopoly Capitalism*. Chicago: Chicago University Press.

Cohn, D. V., Gonzalez-Barrera, A. and Cuddington, D. (2013) *Remittances to Latin America Recover, but Not to Mexico*, Washington, DC: Pew Research Center.

Collier, D. (1993) 'The comparative method,' in A. W. Finifter. (ed.) *Political Science: The State of the Discipline*, Washington DC: The American Political Science Association, pp. 105–119.

Cowie, J. R. (1999) *Capital Moves: RCA's 70-Year Quest for Cheap Labor*, Ithaca: Cornell University Press.

Edwards, P. (2010) 'Developing labour process analysis: Themes from industrial sociology and future directions,' in P. Thompson and C. Smith (eds) *Working Life: Renewing Labour Process Analysis*, Basingstoke: Palgrave Macmillan, pp. 29–46.

Erne, R. (2008) *European Unions: Labor's Quest for a Transnational Democracy*, Ithaca, NY: ILR Press, an imprint of Cornell University Press.

Federación Sindical de El Salvador. (2013) Amezan a Muerte a Secretaria General de Seccional de la Empresa F&D del Sindicato de la Industria Textil Salvadoreña, SITS, Miembro de FESS, Available: http://fedesindicalsal.blogspot.com/2013/01/amezan-muerte-secretaria-general-de.html.

Friedman, A. L. (2004) 'Strawmanning and labour process analysis.' *Sociology* 38: 573–91.

Fukunishi, T., Goto, K., and Yamagata, T. (2013). 'Aid for Trade and Value Chains in Textiles and Apparel' Washington, DC: World Trade Organization, IDE-JETRO, Organisation for Economic Co-operation and Development.

Gereffi, G. and Memedovic, O. (2003) *The Global Apparel Value Chain: What Prospects for Upgrading for Developing Countries*, Vienna: United Nations Industrial Development Organization.

Gordon, M. E. and Turner, L. (2000) 'Going global', in M. E. Gordon. and L. Turner (eds) *Transnational Cooperation Among Labor Unions*, Ithaca, NY: ILR Press, 3–25.

Herod, A. (2001) *Labor Geographies: Workers and Landscapes of Capitalism*, New York: Guilford Press.

Hudson, R. (1991) 'Good soldiers, smooth operators, and saboteurs' *Work and Occupation* 18(3): 271–90.

Hyman, R. (1995) 'Industrial relations in Europe: Theory and practice', *European Journal of Industrial Relations*, 1(1): 17–46.

Keck, M. E. and Sikkink, K. (1998) *Activists Beyond Borders: Advocacy Networks in International Politics*, Ithaca: Cornell University Press.

Levenson-Estrada, D. (1994) *Trade Unionists Against Terror: Guatemala City 1954–1985*, Chapell Hill: The University of North Carolina Press.

Locke, R. (2013) *The Promise and Limits of Private Power: Promoting Labor Standards in a Global Economy*, New York: Cambridge University Press.

McCallum, J. K. (2013) *Global Unions, Local Power: The New Spirit of Transnational Labor Organizing*, Ithaca: ILR Press, an imprint of Cornell University Press.

Milberg, W. and Amengual, M. (2008) *Economic Development and Working Conditions in Export Processing Zones: A Survey of Trends*, Geneva.

OECD, W. UNCTAD (2013) 'Implications of Global Value Chains for Trade, Investment, Development and Jobs', *Prepared for the G-20 Leaders Summit*, Saint Petersburg: Russian Federation, September.

Pedraza Fariña, L., Miller, S. and Cavallaro, J. L. (2010) *No Place to Hide: Gang, State, and Clandestine Violence in El Salvador*, Cambridge, MA: Human Rights Program, Harvard Law School.

Rainnie, A., Herod, A. and McGrath-Champ, S. (2011) 'Review and positions: Global production networks and labour', *Competition and Change*, 15(2): 155–169.

Riisgaard, L. and Hammer, N. (2011) 'Prospects for labour in global value chains: Labour standards in the cut flower and banana industries', *British Journal of Industrial Relations*, 49(1): 168–190.

Silver, B. J. (2003) *Forces of Labor: Workers' Movements and Globalization Since 1870*, New York: Cambridge University Press.

Staritz, C. (2011) *Making the Cut? Low-Income Countries and the Global Clothing Value Chain in a Post-Quota and Post-Crisis World*, Washington, DC: The World Bank Group.

Taylor, P. (2010) 'The globalization of service work: Analysing the transnational call centre value chain,' in P. Thompson. and C. Smith (eds) *Working Life: Renewing Labour Process Analysis*, Basingstoke: Palgrave Macmillan, pp. 244–268.

Thompson, P. and Smith, C. (2010) 'Debating labour process theory and the sociology of work', in P. Thompson and C. Smith (eds) *Working Life: Renewing Labour Process Analysis*, Basingstoke: Palgrave Macmillan, pp. 11–28.

UNDP (2003) *Making Global Trade Work for People*, Sterling: Earthscan.

Webster, E., Lambert, R. and Bezuidenhout, A. (2008) *Grounding Globalization: Labour in the Age of Insecurity*, Malden: Blackwell Publishing.

CHAPTER 10

Labour and Global Production Networks: Mapping Variegated Landscapes of Agency

Neil M. Coe

An Important Conversation, Just Starting to Unfold...

Even as recently as six or seven years ago it was still valid to say that the by-then burgeoning literature on global value chains (GVCs)/global production networks (GPNs) had paid remarkably little attention to issues of labour and work (Coe *et al.*, 2008; Cumbers *et al.*, 2008). At that point, there remained a perceptible gap between work concerned with the firm and industry level dynamics of global production systems, and work that sought to chart the impacts of those systems on workers and/or to consider potential worker responses to those impacts. As Barrientos *et al.* (2011a: 300) depict, until recently 'these two bodies of literature have tended to remain separate, either confined within specific academic disciplines and conceptual frameworks, or proceeding at different levels of analysis'. As of today, such an assertion is thankfully far less accurate, with a recent burst of contributions from various perspectives that are seeking to close this gap and bring labour genuinely into the fold of global production network analysis. Such work encompasses, inter alia, attempts to explore the connections between modes of economic upgrading and notions of social upgrading (e.g. Barrientos *et al.*, 2011b), work from a 'disarticulations' perspective that seeks to reveal the place-specific social relations that underpin (dis)connections to GPNs (e.g. Bair and Werner, 2011), studies that advocate a renewed focus on labour process theory to understand labour's place in global production systems (e.g. Rainnie *et al.*, 2011), research that explores the potential agency of workers within such systems (e.g. Coe and Jordhus-Lier, 2011), and accounts of how labour organizations are responding to the challenges posed by new, networked forms of economic globalization (e.g. Bieler and Lindberg, 2011).

An important conversation, then, has started to take place about the conceptual incorporation of labour, as a multi-faceted phenomenon, into GPN theory. Although still in its early stages, the dialogue is productively bringing together scholars from a wide range of disciplinary perspectives, including, most centrally, economic geography, economic sociology, political science, development studies and international labour studies. A common concern is not just to put labour 'on the map' as a crucial constituent of GPNs – although that is an important first step both politically and conceptually – but also to create analytical space for the potential *agency* of workers and their organizations as active shapers of the structures and strategies inherent to GPNs. This chapter seeks to contribute to these emerging debates by staging a dialogue between the literatures on GPNs and labour geography to try to further theorize the notion of labour 'agency' in the contemporary global economy. This is a critical analytical task in seeking to understand the perils and possibilities of worker action within GPNs, allowing us to move beyond generally optimistic (e.g. Evans, 2010) or pessimistic (e.g. Burawoy, 2010) accounts to offer nuanced readings of how particular groups of workers, in particular places and at particular times, may or may not be able to effect progressive change in their terms and conditions of work. I use the term *variegated landscapes of agency* to capture the highly differentiated positionality of workers within GPNs.

Two points of clarification are important at this stage. First, my intention in this chapter is not to belabour the differences between the GVC and GPN approaches. Although I write from within the latter perspective and would argue that (a) the GPN approach has been explicit from the outset that workers, their collective organizations, and their civil society partners are an integral part of GPNs (see Henderson *et al.*, 2002) and (b) its multi-scalar and multi-actor sensibilities are well attuned to interpreting the positionality of labour in GPN structures, here I am more concerned with speaking to the GVC/GPN literatures in general. My use of the term GPN, then, while reflective of my own positionality, is here intended as shorthand for the research field as a whole. Second, labour geography, a subfield of economic geography, is a multi-stranded endeavour covering a range of perspectives and theoretical traditions. Here I employ the term to refer to the particular strand that has been concerned, since the 1990s, with revealing the agency of labour as an active geographical agent that can shape economic landscapes (see Coe and Jordhus-Lier, 2011, for more). This body of work is itself relatively porous, with connections to, and overlaps with, fields such as working class studies, labour studies, labour history and industrial relations (e.g. Ellem and McGrath-Champ, 2012; Fine and Herod, 2012).

The ensuing analysis proceeds in three stages. First, and taking my cue from the initial exchanges between GPN and labour geography analyses, I will consider the crucial question of what exactly labour agency is, and provide an initial multi-dimensional mapping of the concept. Second, I will seek to demonstrate how both GPN and labour geography approaches can learn from deeper interaction. In particular, combining insights from the two perspectives can help us to re-embed a multi-dimensional view of labour agency within the structures and strategies of GPNs. Third, I will then argue that these insights in turn need to be combined with an appreciation of how worker agency is also heavily conditioned by the *territorial* institutional and regulatory formations within which people live and work. A dynamic and multi-scalar institutional perspective is required to understand the intersections of GPNs and the particular places in which they touch down, and how those intersections in turn shape the potential for worker agency. I will posit that the incorporation of labour process theory – a key theme in this volume – can contribute to this but will not on its own be sufficient, due to the rise of the increasingly complex and overlapping forms of transnational labour regulation that characterize contemporary GPNs. While labour regulation is always ultimately experienced within the workplace, the forces that shape that workplace regulation have increasingly complex and distanciated geographies.

Framing the Agency of Labour

What, then, is labour agency? One of the benefits of the initial dialogue between GPN and labour geography researchers has been recognition of the need for more precise delineations of this concept. Simply evoking the concept of labour agency in abstract and general terms is ultimately of limited utility. Instead I want to suggest that labour agency should be seen as a multi-dimensional concept that can be delimited along six axes of variation. This usefully expands labour agency beyond the traditional concern of labour geography, and labour studies more generally, for collective action undertaken through unions and other formal organizational structures. It starts to tackle the concern of Das (2012: 21) that labour geography 'fails to properly theorize agency, which is a complex category'. It also reflects a world in which, as Bezuidenhout and Buhlungu (2011: 257) succinctly put it, 'worker agency can be informal or formal, individual or collective, spontaneous or goal directed, sporadic or sustained, and it can operate on different scales'.

First, it is important to be clear about the level or type of labour agency that is under consideration. Put another way, what counts as agency? Of course, in a fundamental sense, labour agency is inherent to the capitalist labour process and the generation of surplus value. In labour geography, however, the term is usually invoked in relation to attempts to change the *status quo* of capital-labour relations. In this context, and following Katz (2004), worker agency can be thought of as a multi-level concept, ranging from strategies of *resilience* (everyday coping practices), through *reworking* strategies (efforts to materially improve the conditions of existence) to *resistance* strategies (direct challenges to capitalist social relations). Read from this perspective, it seems that many of the case studies that have been the bread and butter of the labour geography project fall into the domain of reworking strategies, in that they profile time- and place-specific attempts to tilt capitalist relations in favour of workers. Of course the three strategies are not mutually exclusive, and at times will overlap and be used in combination. They will also vary in the degree to which the aims of strategies are explicit or implicit, and are conscious or unconscious. There are different views on the desirability of viewing agency in such multi-level terms. While for some scholars encompassing everyday practices of resilience is important in order to demonstrate the quotidian nature of labour agency, for others, for instance Das (2012), this perspective is antithetical to developing meaningful strategies of resistance grounded in class politics. Analytically, however, making such distinctions seems an important and necessary first step.

Second, and drawing upon one of the seminal contributions of labour geography, is the need to precisely delineate the geographies of labour agency, which are many and varied. In a recent review, for instance, Herod (2012: 343) highlights and exemplifies five geographical approaches:

(1) [C]ontrol the geographical location of work; (2) control the spatial scale at which contract bargaining takes place and what this means for their efforts to engage with the unevenly developed geography of capitalism; (3) cross space as they seek to develop relations of solidarity; (4) defend place rather than class in the face of capital restructuring; and (5) shift the geographical terrain of their struggle so as to seek advantage in their battles with employers.

Other approaches are to distinguish spatial strategies over a global-local spectrum (Munck and Waterman, 2010), or to intersect the domain of action (local versus global) with the target of action (local versus global) to develop a four-fold typology of action ranging from the defence of place, through consumer campaigns and worker migration, to transnational union campaigns (Castree *et al.*, 2004). This latter typology has the advantage of bringing migration – a generally neglected topic in labour geography and indeed GPN analysis – firmly into the fold as a spatial strategy of labour. More generally, labour geography research has shown that workers are active architects of spatial strategies and in that way 'construct' scales of action in a similar way to states and firms, but also, that 'upscaling' is but one of several strategies that workers can pursue. Local action remains a potentially potent strategy within GPNs (Padmanabhan, 2012). Indeed, the literature on transnational unions is replete with examples of the severe challenges of constructing campaigns across territories with 'contrary political, social and institutional logics' (Fichter and Sydow, 2012: 8; see also Cumbers *et al.*, 2010). As with the different levels of agency, the different geographies at play are often easier to parse in theory than in practice. Drawing upon Tufts (2007), it is perhaps better to think in terms of the inherent yet variable *multiscalarity* of all worker campaigns and to appreciate the non-deterministic and reinforcing interconnections between interventions at different spatial scales (see Taylor and Bain, 2008, for a concrete example of this multi-scalarity).

Third, the temporalities of agency require elucidation. As an approach, labour geography has sometimes been portrayed as a loose collection of case studies of successful moments in labour struggles that has failed to place those case studies in their temporal context. Were those successes the exceptions that prove the general rule of labour concessions and worsening terms and conditions? Were they brief bright spots in a general process of neoliberal downward levelling? Worker agency, therefore, needs to be placed in historical context and seen as part of longer-term struggles. This matters analytically, as the timing of agency, in relation both to political context and to other worker actions, successful or otherwise, has a non-trivial influence on the likelihood of success. It is also important in terms of judging any gains from successful action, and the extent to which they can be protected from subsequent erosion. Moreover, different groups of workers may have different stakes in the sustainability of progressive conditions, e.g. full time workers versus migrant labour and short-term employees whose time horizons may be shorter. This broader temporal perspective will reveal failures as well as successes. As Das (2012) persuasively argues, failures may actually be more revealing about the prevailing structural conditions in which workers operate than successes. In short, we need 'to understand how contemporary political practice [worker agency] intertwines with previous actions and activities – themselves structured by the way in which the economic landscape has been made – as part of a locale's spatial path dependency' (Rainnie *et al.*, 2010: 252).

Fourth, it is important to distinguish the balance of individual versus collective action inherent to different forms of labour agency. As noted above, labour geography has tended to focus, particularly in its formative years, on action coordinated through trade unions. As of today, however, the project is much broader, incorporating a range of new modes of action, mobilization and organization (Coe and Jordhus-Lier, 2011). Rogaly (2009), for instance, considers what agency might mean to groups of unorganized migrant workers. De Neve and Carswell (2013), in a study of the Tiruppur garment cluster in Tamil Nadu, South India, show how worker agency has important individual dimensions that are embedded in local social relations, livelihood strategies and the reproductive sphere, and which are heavily shaped by gender, age and caste. Harking back to the seminal work of Burawoy (1979), we need to keep in view the multiple subject positions on which workers act.

Fifth, and relatedly, where collective action is involved, we need to be clear on the mode of collective action that is being invoked. As noted above, this in part means being explicit about the geographical dimensions of agency (e.g. local, national or transnational campaigns). Equally, however, it concerns the extent to which traditional modes of business unionism are being replaced or at least complemented by forms of community or social movement unionism. Jordhus-Lier (2013) offers an overview of the rich multidisciplinary literature on community unionism, which has demonstrated how unions have increasingly extended their activities into new community sites of recruitment and new domains of mobilization in partnership with other civil society actors. This 'community turn' may also reemphasize the importance of locally based and coordinated worker actions. Tufts (2009), however, cautions against simple distinctions, identifying a model of 'Schumpeterian' unionism in Toronto's hotel sector that falls somewhere between the ideal-types of business unionism and social movement unionism.

Sixth, and finally, it is important to consider how worker agency is influenced by the form of employment relations involved. This may mean distinguishing between formal and informal employment relations. Research is increasingly showing how GPNs are not only constituted by formal workers; lower tiers of the subcontracting process may incorporate informal workers who lack a formal contract with an employer, with obvious ramifications for their agency potential. Moreover, GPNs may also incorporate workers who are 'unfree' in that they are unable to exercise the choice to not work (Phillips and Sakamoto, 2012), although this should not be read as necessarily negating agency. McGrath (2013), for example, in a fascinating study of the on-the-ground complexities of unfree labour in Brazil's sugar cane and garment industries, demonstrates multiple elements of agency, both individual and collective (see also Stringer et al., 2014, on the agency of seemingly 'invisible' workers in the fishing industry). Another important aspect is whether there is a third party – i.e. a labour market intermediary – involved in the employment relationship. The landscape of labour market intermediaries that supplies and in part reproduces the workforce for GPNs is still poorly understood. In a pioneering study, Barrientos (2013) reveals the prevalence of intermediary use and advances a typology of labour agents, quasi-labour agents, labour contractors and *ad hoc* labour contractors, with such intermediaries providing coordination, information and efficiency benefits for 'squeezed' employers inserted into GPNs. As she argues, this complicates notions of worker agency and how it might be targeted and coordinated:

> [L]abour contracting fulfils its functions through a separation between the productive engagement of the worker in commercial activity (engaged in production of goods and services) and the 'contractual' engagement of the worker ('employment' by a separate labour contractor). At its core, this compounds a dislocation in the twofold character of labour as a factor of production, and as workers with social agency and rights.
>
> (Barrientos, 2013: 1066)

This more refined vocabulary of labour agency helps us to pin down in a given context exactly what it is, who it is aimed at, what its goals are, who is involved, and which organizational structures are being mobilized. In the next section we will see how these starting points can provide the foundation for a deeper integration between the ideas of GPN analysis and labour geography, and a reconnecting of the notion of labour agency into the structures of capital in which it is unavoidably embedded.

Deepening the Dialogue between GPN Analysis and Labour Geography

A central premise of this chapter is that there is much to be gained from furthering the initial dialogue between GPN analysts and researchers who have foregrounded the potential agency of labour within contemporary capitalism, and most notably labour geographers. These benefits can be viewed from both sides of the relationship. First, and following the trailblazing work of Andrew Herod in the 1990s (e.g. Herod, 1997), labour geography has grown into a thriving and broad endeavour (for recent overviews, see Bergene *et al.*, 2010; McGrath-Champ *et al.*, 2010; Coe, 2013) that arguably contains several important lessons for GPN analysis.

Most obviously, labour geography research serves to illustrate the futility of obscuring the role of labour and worker politics in GPN research. Such an argument can be developed on three levels. First, conceptually, there is by now a small but growing chorus of voices arguing that GPNs are nothing if not labour systems. Put another way, GPNs are networks of embodied labour just as much as they are meshes of value adding corporate connections (Smith *et al.*, 2002; Cumbers *et al.*, 2008; Rainnie *et al.*, 2011; Riisgaard and Hammer, 2011; Selwyn, 2012). To not give labour due weight in our theoretical architecture is therefore analytically dubious, even if we must remain realistic about the relative power of labour *vis-à-vis* other actors in contemporary capitalism (cf. Dicken, 2011). Second, the geographies of labour, even in a passive sense, are clearly a hugely important shaper of the structures and strategies of GPNs. The uneven availability of an 'appropriate' workforce – most notably in terms of the intersecting attributes of skills, productivity, cost and controllability – across different places is perhaps the single most important factor driving GPN formation and subsequent patterns of locational shift and organizational reconfiguration. And yet many accounts remain silent on how the workforces that underpin GPN activities are produced and reproduced through the activities of a wide range of organizations of which the key actors in much GPN research, firms and states, are but two of several. The role of migration processes in underpinning such labour needs is also underplayed (although see Zhu and Pickles (2013) for an excellent study on the role of migrant labour in China's garment industry, and Azmeh's (2014) research on the same industry in Egypt and Jordan). Third, and foregrounding labour geography's focus on agency, it is important to create space for workers as *selectively* important 'reshapers' of GPN structures and strategies. This entails the incorporation of labour in a more active sense into GPNs, i.e. not just in terms of workers' availability and attributes, but rather as an agent of change with its own strategies and objectives which, under certain conditions, can cause GPN actors to alter and adapt their organizational configurations. As Smith *et al.* (2002: 47) argue, 'organized labour can have an important influence upon locational decisions within and between countries, thereby determining in part the geography of activities within a value chain'.

The strength of labour geography thus has been in demonstrating the need to bring labour and its collective organizations 'into the fold' as an integral and fundamental part of the value processes that are at the heart of GPN analyses. Moreover, as a field it has judiciously used case studies to demonstrate the potential for successful worker actions, under certain conditions, within contemporary GPNs. It has arguably been less successful, however, in theorizing systematically about those conditions and how they relate to the wider structures of capital (i.e. GPNs) in which workers are embedded. This is where GPN analysis comes into its own. By mapping the multi-scalar configurations of intra-, inter- and extra-firm networks that underpin the production, circulation and consumption of goods and services, GPN analysis provides a functional overview of the global production systems in which many workers labour. In so doing, it helps us to interpret more systematically GPNs as variegated landscapes of agency potential. Put another way, it enables us to reveal how certain groups of workers at certain times and places *may* have the potential to take action that results in progressive change in their terms and conditions of employment. Rather than simply asserting the agency of labour in general terms, such an approach can detail the variable levels of potential agency *within* functionally integrated economic networks.

On a practical level, this may be about using the insights of GPN analysis to reveal the weak points in tightly integrated transnational production networks that are vulnerable to disruption, for example, logistical choke points, areas of potential exposure to consumer campaigns or a high dependence on workers with unique skills that are in limited supply. The rise of increasingly fragmented GPNs with complex patterns of ownership and increased temporal and spatial flexibility has created a range of inherent vulnerabilities (Anderson, 2009), for instance associated with the lead times inherent in just-in-time production networks. One of Herod's (2000) most famous labour geography case studies, for example, explores how the United Auto Workers were able to exploit the weaknesses inherent to the General Motors production system in the late 1990s. Understanding the operations of GPNs thus becomes a key target for labour organizations, which may over time become embedded in an iterative relationship with GPN structures in which the two develop symbiotically. Helfen and Fichter (2013: 569) for instance, describe how, in the context of transnational union networks (TUNS),

> [H]ow such TUNs are organized and governed will depend on the contingencies of GPN structures, on the associational power and the dynamics of power relationships among collective actors in the network ... the impact of TUNs on the governance of GPNs may induce restructuring or policy changes subsequently affecting the organization and governance of TUNs.

GPN analysis may also have two other advantages for labour advocates. First, its systematic overview may help reveal lines of solidarity between workers occupying similar positions in subcontracted production networks. Second, it can also serve to predict and/or interpret the 'geographical dilemmas' likely to be raised by worker action, i.e. the knock-on consequences, either intentional or unintentional, for workers in other localities (Castree et al., 2004). In this regard, Sweeney and Holmes (2013) offer an illustrative case study drawn from the British Columbian pulp and paper sector.

More analytically, notions of power and governance from GPN analysis can usefully be used to frame understandings of labour agency. In particular, power within GPNs can be thought of as: (a) relational in that it is practised rather than stored and accrued as an asset; (b) transaction-specific in the sense that a GPN actor may be more or less powerful depending on which other GPN actors are being considered; (c) co-existing with relations of dependency in that GPNs are systems of reciprocal relations at the same time as they are systems of contest and struggle; and (d) being exercised by a range of actors, be they corporate, state or civil society organizations. Such a perspective gels nicely with the notion of *structural power* from labour studies (Selwyn, 2012), which looks at the extent to which workers can derive power from their position within the wider production process (e.g. due to the scarcity of their skills and/or the commodities they produce). Silver (2003) further breaks down the notion of structural power into *marketplace* bargaining power deriving from tight labour markets, and *workplace* bargaining power emanating from the strategic position of workers within the wider production system (we will discuss in the next section whether or not such structural power can be translated into the *associational* power often required for effective action).

Following Riisgaard and Hammer (2011), we can also think about the extent to which the prevailing *governance regime* within different GPNs serves to shape agency. They observe, for instance, that tightly integrated and coordinated GPNs are more vulnerable to the collective action of workers compared to more loosely coordinated GPNs that may contain, for example, several market-based relationships. They further argue that buyer-driven GPNs involving large, well-known brands are also more sensitive due to their need to protect their brand and to maintain an 'ethical' reputation in the eyes of consumers. It is also important to recognize the wider importance of global market conditions, as transmitted through GPN structures. For example, in a study of the football manufacturing industry in Pakistan, Lund-Thomsen and Coe (2014) found that a collapse in global demand severely hampered efforts to improve workers' terms and conditions in a context where many suppliers were simply seeking to secure orders and stay afloat.

In sum, using the tools of GPN analysis, the notion of worker agency can be reconnected to the structures of capital in order to explain and understand the variegated landscape of labour agency. Important though this step is, however, on its own it is not enough, for labour agency potential is not only shaped by the positionality of groups of workers within wider GPN structures – it is also determined by the territorial socio-economic formations in which they are simultaneously embedded. It is to this dimension that I turn in the next section.

Intersecting GPNs and Territorial Formations

A deepened dialogue between labour geography and GPN analysis, I have argued, can lead to more nuanced readings of the potential for labour agency within GPN structures. While considering how workers 'plug in' to what we can term – following Neilson and Pritchard (2010) – the 'vertical' dimension of GPNs (i.e. transnational corporate connections) is vital, it will not fully explain the potential for, and success or not, of worker actions without due consideration of the *territorial* spaces in which workers simultaneously live and work. In other words, the 'horizontal' dimension of GPNs, or how they are embedded in particular institutional and regulatory spaces, with particular histories and trajectories, is an equally crucial component of the landscape of agency potential. Arnold (2013), for example, charts how the potential for worker agency in Cambodia's garment industry is shaped by four interlinked forces encompassing both dimensions: the workers' position within the global garment industry, the repressive nature of the state, the nature of their employment contracts (many are fixed term), and the highly fragmented nature of the local labour movement. 'Outside in' perspectives on labour agency in GPNs thus need to connect with 'inside out' accounts that foreground the socio-economic histories and realities of the places incorporated into GPNs. As Neilson and Pritchard (2009: 131) argue (in the particular context of ethical trading initiatives), 'the mutual structuring of value chain governance with the institutional environments associated with particular places ... all too rarely do we hear about how these agendas are enmeshed within regional producer communities; the bottom-up perspective of how these agendas are made manifest in economic landscapes' (see also Wilson, 2013).

There are already several studies that show the potential for positioning labour agency at the intersection of network structures (i.e. GPNs) and territorial formations (i.e. places). Riisgaard and Hammer's (2011: 183) research on the cut flower and banana sectors, for instance, suggests that 'the governance of inter-firm linkages, while crucial in structuring the terrain for labour, is always mediated by the specific social relations of local production and labour control regimes'. Selwyn's (2009) work on export grape production in northeast Brazil demonstrates the complex and state-mediated bargaining processes between capital and labour that are played out in every locality connected into GPNs (see also Taylor, 2010, for a service sector case). De Neve and Carswell's (2013) Tiruppur study highlights that employment choices which intersect with GPNs are just one part of the wider livelihood strategies of workers embedded in multi-dimensional local labour markets. In another South Asian study, Lund-Thomsen (2013) similarly argues for a notion of labour agency that is shaped by the intersection of the 'horizontal' and 'vertical' dimensions. His research on workers in the football manufacturing industry of Sialkot, Pakistan demonstrates how agency potential is shaped both by the governance structures of GPNs and the local socio-economic contexts of work and employment as manifested in the gendered nature of work, the spatial location of workers, livelihood strategies and patterns of labour recruitment.

Understanding these complexities requires recognition that the social regulation of labour within GPNs is an inherently *multi-scalar* phenomenon. While regulation is always ultimately experienced by workers in the workplace, the dynamics shaping that experience of regulation have complex, multi-layered geographies, ranging from the micro-scale of workplace politics to the global landscape of GPN regulation. I will briefly introduce this global landscape before moving on to consider how it intersects with other scales of regulation. It has been well charted that the rise of GPN structures over the past 20 years or so has been accompanied by the emergence of a 'world of standards' constituted by a wide range of forms of private and quasi-private governance targeting many aspects of GPNs, but often with a particular focus on labour (for excellent overviews of this increasingly complex terrain, see Nadvi and Wältring, 2004; Ponte *et al.*, 2011). More specifically, Pries and Seeliger (2013: 27, emphasis in original) describe how 'an increasing entanglement of mechanisms, levels and collective actors of labour regulation is emerging as *cross-border texture of work and employment regulation*'. As Table 10.1 depicts, this 'texture' encompasses a wide range of regulatory forms, actors, geographical configurations and modes of enforcement. It is an 'emerging constellation into which measures of cross-border labour regulation are being brought about by a spectrum of actors which reaches beyond the classical triangle of (nationally segmented)

Table 10.1 Types of transnational labour regulation

Form of regulation	Main actors	Geographic scope and implementation	Extent of enforcement	Examples
Minimum standards	United Nations, International Labour Organization, labour unions, employer associations	Universal status of human rights	Ratification, monitoring, blaming, no legal penalties	International Labour Organization core conventions: 29, 87, 98, 100, 105, 111, 138, 182
Supranational governance	Supranational bodies, international organizations, nation-states	International organization of nation-states	Supranational Court of Human Rights, national legislation	European Union, European Works Councils
International Framework Agreements	Global Union Federations, international corporations	Collective negotiation across individual branches or entire organizations	No legal administration; dependent on voluntary declaration	Volkswagen, Leoni, Arcelor, Public Services International
Labels, certifications	Labelling and certification organizations, producers, consumers	Scale of organization: global, product or organization related	No accreditation; dependent on producers' public status and/or consumer choices	Fairtrade International, International Organization for Standardization
Multinational guidelines	International organizations, companies, national agencies	Companies with headquarters located in nation-states involved in signing	National reports, public criticism	Organization for Economic Co-operation and Development multinational guidelines
Voluntary disclosure	Independent monitoring organizations, companies, media	Level and geographic extent of public involvement	Public status, public relations, monitoring reports	Independent Monitoring Commission, United Nations Global Compact, Corporate Social Responsibility
Campaigns, protests	Nongovernmental organizations, media, public	Limited in time and issue	Discursive regulation, public criticism	Nestlé boycott (1977), Corporate Watch

Source: Modified from Pries and Seeliger, 2013.

states, capital and labour representatives' (Pries and Seeliger, 2013: 29). Importantly, they argue that while there is a tendency for studies to focus on particular mechanisms and their motivations and impacts, equally important is the need to look at how the interplay and reinforcing between different elements may serve to create new contours to the transnational texture of regulation.

The literature on the *impacts* of such transnational regulatory initiatives, which in effect are designed to 'travel' between different nodes of GPNs, is, however, replete with examples of muted, uneven and unintended outcomes across different localities (e.g. Locke, 2013). As Neilson and Pritchard lucidly argue (2010: 1834), again with respect to ethical trade initiatives, such schemes 'tend to selectively inhabit regional production spaces. Some producers and communities may be enrolled and benefit from such schemes, but others may be bypassed'. These on-the-ground variations can only be understood with reference to territorial institutional and regulatory contexts. Table 10.2 offers an admittedly very crude window onto this topic. It seeks to make the simple observation that transnational regulatory initiatives are only likely to foster progressive change when they are in alignment with the 'local' institutional context – putting to one side for a moment what the 'local' might mean – i.e. the situation in the bottom-right cell. In this vein, Locke's (2013) impressive book-length analysis demonstrates that meaningful improvements in labour standards in the context of global production seem to require productive *intersections* of firm-level initiatives, labour schemes emanating from the wider production network, and government efforts at effective and enforced legislation.

Much of the empirical evidence collected on the impacts of different kinds of transnational initiatives seems to fit more into the top-right cell, however, in that the actual impacts are uneven due to a relative lack

Table 10.2 Intersections of transnational and 'local' labour regulatory contexts

		Transnational regulation initiatives	
		Absent	Present
'Local' Institutional Context	Restrictive	No potential for progressive change	Limited/uneven potential for improvements
	Supportive	Unlikely and suggests limited GPN engagement	Decent potential for worker agency/ improvements in conditions

of alignment with local institutional conditions. These variable institutional factors might include: local, regional and national policies and regulations; rates, modes and cultures of worker collective organization; NGO and private sector consultant activities; media activities and representations; local labour market structures including gender divisions of labour, levels of informality and degrees of labour market intermediation; and different modes of engagement with GPNs. With respect to the first of these, for instance, studies often highlight the futility of labour provisions in transnational initiatives that are not backed up by local laws and regulations, or where those strictures cannot be effectively enforced. Importantly, and following Selwyn (2012), the extent to which workers are able to marry their structural power within GPNs with *associational* power will to a great degree be determined by the local institutional and regulatory context (e.g. laws and norms regarding collective organization). Considering the interface between transnational imperatives and local conditions can also serve to reveal how, in some cases, 'such initiatives may ... inadvertently exacerbate social and economic tensions within producer regions' (Neilson and Pritchard, 2010: 1834). Moreover, they may not interact productively with locally initiated projects to improve labour standards – there is an implicit assumption in some corners of the literature, it seems, that progressive labour interventions will always originate from 'downstream' in GPNs terms. By contrast, Lund-Thomsen and Wad (2014) profile the emergence of national and subnational corporate social responsibility initiatives from *within* the BRIC economies.

The question becomes, then, how best to frame this regulatory interface in conceptual terms. Riisgaard and Hammer (2011) suggest resurrecting the notion of the local labour control regime (LLCR) (taken from Jonas, 1996) as one possible avenue. The LLCR is indeed a rich theoretical formulation for understanding the place-specific accommodations that develop between capital and labour and, importantly, shines light on the spheres of consumption and reproduction as constituent elements of the LLCR. There are concerns, however, about its adaptability to the multi-scalar nature of contemporary regulatory landscapes. Instead, therefore, I want sketch out five parameters of the broad *kind* of analytical approach that will be required in this context.

1. **Territorial-cum-relational:** As described above, we need to keep in view both the imperatives impacting upon workers from wider GPN structures, and the local regulatory and institutional contexts within which they work. It is the intersection and interplay of these two sets of forces that will ultimately determine the extent to which particular

groups of workers embedded in particular places are able to exercise their agency through combinations of structural and associational power. The interface needs to be seen as two-way, with initiatives to improve the conditions of workers having both local and non-local origins.

2. **Multi-scalar:** The interface has to be seen as multi-scalar, encompassing scales ranging from the workplace all the way up to the 'global' scale of the GPN as a whole. As Bridi (2013: 1086), describes, labour control 'is conditioned exogenously by multi-scalar factors, and generated endogenously at the point of production ... the structuring of the labour process in the workplace is shaped by the geographic connections and broader economic landscapes in which workers are located'. Importantly, the 'local' institutional and regulatory context needs to be unpacked into at least three levels to reveal the overlapping local, regional and national influences that are in play. Indeed in countries with complex, multi-layered institutional geographies, such as China and India, an even more refined scalar vocabulary may be required. In any discussion of labour regulation, the national scale will inevitably require foregrounding. Indeed, 'the national context of governance remains the strongest predictor of improved working conditions in the supply chain' (Locke *et al.*, 2012: 1; see also Oseland *et al.*, 2012, on the importance of *national* labour networks, regulation and work discourses in conditioning the agency of aquaculture workers in Chile).

3. **Institutional:** The analytical approach will need to be broadly institutional in nature, encompassing both the formal (rules and regulations) and informal (local business cultures and practices) relationships in which particular groups of workers are embedded. Local work cultures, for instance in relation to gender norms, constructions of class and collective organization conventions, therefore need to be incorporated in addition to multi-scalar legal frameworks.

4. **Evolutionary:** Clearly the framing of the GPN/territory interface also needs to be dynamic in order to examine how local and non-local actors together drive institutional change (or not) in particular nodes within GPNs. In particular, it is important to consider how transnational labour regulatory initiatives are 'refracted' – i.e. adapted, translated and selectively appropriated – through local institutions, creating uneven landscapes of improvements in conditions and agency potential. Hughes *et al.* (2014) describe this phenomenon in terms of how transnational initiatives are 'strategically re-articulated' in particular contexts. As Brown (2013: 2587) shows in the context

of Fairtrade banana growing in the Urabá region of Colombia, such initiatives are not conjured up in a regulatory vacuum but rather are 'superimposed onto a complex institutional framework'. The language of evolutionary economic geography may be helpful in framing the processes of institutional change that result. Martin (2010), for instance, distinguishes between processes of layering, conversion and recombination as a first step in parsing different processes and outcomes of institutional change.

5. **Intermediated:** Finally, it is important to develop a multi-actor/multi-stakeholder perspective that highlights the role of non-firm, non-state organizations that help to translate 'back and forth' between relatively abstract transnational regulatory forms and local norms and practices. These may include worker organizations, NGOs, charities, industry associations, monitoring organizations and others. They may be locally based, regional, national or international in scope. These are key agents in the processes of institutional refraction and strategic re-articulation described above.

Clearly these five characteristics do not represent a tightly integrated framework or theory of worker agency in GPNs; indeed, such an aspiration is perhaps too ambitious. They do, however, I hope, give an impression of the theoretical sensibilities that will be required to understand the complex interface between particular places and networks at which labour agency is ultimately forged.

Finally, and following the urging of Rainnie *et al.* (2011), Selwyn (2012), Taylor *et al.* (2013) and Goger (2013), among others, it is important to consider the potential role of labour process theory (LPT) – one of the central themes of this book – in such a theoretical framing. The time for forging such connections appears ripe; in a recent review of LPT, for instance, Thompson (2010) noted a long-standing interest in notions of worker power and agency, and also a growing desire to enhance appreciation of the wider structures of capitalism within which the labour process is forged. The core strength of LPT remains in helping us to understand the workplace as an arena of labour regulation, and how the nature of particular employer-employee relationships evolves in response to wider imperatives. Burawoy's (1985) seminal work on factory regimes and his distinction between the labour process and the political apparatuses of production, for instance, remain insightful for thinking through processes of workplace struggle and change. As depicted above, however, contemporary landscapes of labour regulation are increasingly complex (Burawoy, for instance, essentially looked at factories within bounded national contexts), and hence the insights of LPT need to be embedded in an avowedly multi-scalar framework that recognizes, among others: the multi-scalar nature of the state, the fragmented-yet-coordinated nature of GPNs, the complex geographies of the regulatory impulses affecting particular workplaces (e.g. originating elsewhere in the GPN), and the rise of intermediated employment relations, all of which serve to complicate the forces shaping workplace politics (cf. McKay, 2006). A labour-geography infused GPN approach would seem to offer conceptual connections to LPT theory that would be of mutual benefit. From the perspective of LPT, a multi-scalar and multi-actor theory of fragmented production systems is necessary to help discern the disparate forces shaping contemporary workplace labour dynamics. For GPN theory, LPT provides a window onto the fundamental labour dynamics which underpin the processes of value creation, enhancement and capture that are central to such theory, but are often obscured and taken for granted in this genre of work (Smith *et al.*, 2002).

Conclusion

This chapter has attempted to do three things. First, building on recent literature, I have sought to distil and refine a multi-dimensional and 're-embedded' conceptualization of labour agency as a necessary first step towards understanding worker agency in GPNs. Second, I have argued for the potential of deepening the still embryonic dialogue between GPNs scholars and those working in the traditions of labour geography and labour studies. This conversation will be of mutual benefit, and is crucial to deeper theorization of the position and possibilities of labour in GPNs. Third, I have argued that such theorization will need to embed labour not only within GPN structures, but also within the places and territories in which it is incontrovertibly 'grounded'. Understanding this territory-network interface will require conceptualizations that are institutional, evolutionary and multi-scalar in nature.

This is perhaps the nub of the chapter, namely that workers in GPNs are subject to complex, multi-scalar landscapes of regulation that shape their agency potential. Understanding how these multi-scalar forces intersect and interact from the perspective of particular groups of workers in particular places is a key challenge in terms of both theory and praxis. As this volume suggests, labour process theory can play an important part in this emerging conversation through the tools it offers for understanding the workplace capital-labour dynamics that are the on-the-ground manifestations of these complex interactions.

REFERENCES

Anderson, J. (2009) 'Labour's lines of flight: rethinking the vulnerabilities of transnational capital', *Geoforum*, 40(6): 959–968.

Arnold, D. (2013) *Workers' agency and re-working power relations in Cambodia's garment industry*, Capturing the Gains Working Paper 24, University of Manchester. Available from: http://www.capturingthegains.org/publications/workingpapers/wp_201324.htm.

Azmeh, S. (2014) 'Labour in global production networks: workers in the qualifying industrial zones (QIZs) of Egypt and Jordan', *Global Networks*, 14(4): 495–513.

Bair, J. and Werner, M. (2011) 'Commodity chains and the uneven geographies of global capitalism: a disarticulations perspective', *Environment and Planning A*, 43(5): 988–997.

Barrientos, S. (2013) '"Labour chains": analysing the role of labour contractors in global production networks', *The Journal of Development Studies*, 49(8): 1058–1071.

Barrientos, S., Mayer, F., Pickles, J. and Posthuma, A. (2011a) 'Decent work in global production networks: framing the policy debate', *International Labour Review*, 150(3–4): 299–317.

Barrientos, S., Gereffi, G. and Rossi, A. (2011b) 'Economic and social upgrading in global production networks: a new paradigm for a changing world', *International Labour Review*, 150(3–4): 319–340.

Bergene, A. C., Endresen, S. B. and Knutsen, H. M. (eds) (2010) *Missing Links in Labour Geography*, Farnham: Ashgate.

Bezuidenhout, A. and Buhlungu, S. (2011) 'From compounded to fragmented labour: mineworkers and the demise of compounds in South Africa', *Antipode*, 43(2): 237–263.

Bieler, A. and Lindberg, I. (eds) (2011) *Global Restructuring, Labour and the Challenges for Transnational Solidarity*, London: Routledge.

Bridi, R. M. (2013) 'Labour control in the tobacco agro-spaces: migrant agricultural workers in South-Western Ontario', *Antipode*, 45(5): 1070–1089.

Brown, S. (2013) 'One hundred years of labor control: violence, militancy, and the Fairtrade banana commodity chain in Colombia', *Environment and Planning A*, 45(11): 2572–2591.

Burawoy, M. (1979) *Manufacturing Consent*, Chicago: University of Chicago Press.

Burawoy, M. (1985) *The Politics of Production*, London: Verso.

Burawoy, M. (2010) 'From polanyi to pollyanna: the false optimism of global labor studies', *Global Labour Journal*, 1(2): 301–313.

Castree, N., Coe N. M., Ward, K. and Samers, M. (2004) *Spaces of Work: Global Capitalism and the Geographies of Labour*, London: Sage.

Coe, N. M. (2013) 'Geographies of production III: making space for labour', *Progress in Human Geography*, 37(2): 271–284.

Coe, N. M. and Jordhus-Lier, D. (2011) 'Constrained agency? re-evaluating the geographies of labour', *Progress in Human Geography*, 35(2): 211–233.

Coe, N. M., Dicken, P. and Hess, M. (2008) 'Global production networks: realizing the potential', *Journal of Economic Geography*, 8(3): 271–295.

Cumbers, A., Nativel, C. and Routledge, P. (2008) 'Labour agency and union positionalities in global production networks', *Journal of Economic Geography*, 8(3): 369–387.

Cumbers, A., MacKinnon D. and Shaw, J. (2010) 'Labour, organisational rescaling and the politics of production: union renewal in the privatised rail industry', *Work, Employment and Society*, 24(1): 127–144.

Das, R. J. (2012) 'From labor geography to class geography: reasserting the Marxist theory of class', *Human Geography*, 5(1): 19–35.

De Neve, G. and Carswell, G. (2013) 'Labouring for global markets: conceptualising labour agency in global production networks', *Geoforum*, 44: 62–70.

Dicken, P. (2011) *Global Shift: Mapping the Changing Contours of the World Economy* (6th edition), London: Sage.

Ellem, B. and McGrath-Champ, S. (2012) 'Labor geography and labor history: insights and outcomes from a decade of cross-disciplinary dialogue', *Labor History*, 53(3): 355–372.

Evans, P. (2010) 'Is it labor's turn to globalize? Twenty-first century opportunities and strategic responses', *Global Labour Journal*, 1(3): 352–379.

Fichter, M. and Sydow, J. (2012) Union and Networks: Unions as Networks. Paper to the ILERA (IIRA) World Congress 2012, Philadelphia, USA.

Fine, L. M. and Herod, A. (2012) 'Introduction', *Labor History*, 53(3): 329–333.

Goger, A. (2013) 'From disposable to empowered: rearticulating labor in Sri Lankan apparel factories', *Environment and Planning A*, 45(11): 2628–2645.

Helfen, M. and Fichter, M. (2013) 'Building transnational union networks across global production networks: conceptualising a new arena of labour–management relations', *British Journal of Industrial Relations*, 51(3): 553–576.

Henderson, J., Dicken, P., Hess, M., Coe, N. M. and Yeung, H. W.-C. (2002) 'Global production networks and the analysis of regional development', *Review of International Political Economy*, 9(3): 436–464.

Herod, A. (1997) 'From a geography of labor to a labor geography', *Antipode*, 29(1): 1–31.

Herod, A. (2000) 'Implications of just-in-time production for union strategy: lessons from the 1998 General Motors-united auto workers dispute', *Annals of the American Geographers*, 90(3): 521–547.

Herod, A. (2012) 'Workers as geographical actors', *Labor History*, 53(3): 335–353.

Hughes, A., McEwan, C., Bek, D. and Rosenberg, Z. (2014) 'Embedding fairtrade in South Africa: global production networks, national initiatives and localized challenges in the Northern Cape', *Competition and Change*, 18(4), 291–308.

Jonas, A. E. G. (1996) 'Local labour control regimes: uneven development and the social regulation of production', *Regional Studies*, 30(4): 323–338.

Jordhus-Lier, D. C. (2013) 'The geographies of community-oriented unionism: scales, targets, sites and domains of union renewal in South Africa and beyond', *Transactions of the Institute of British Geographers*, 38(1): 36–49.

Katz, C. (2004) *Growing Up Global: Economic Restructuring and Children's Everyday Lives*, Minneapolis, MN: University of Minnesota Press.

Locke, R. (2013) *The Promise and Limits of Private Power: Promoting Labor Standards in a Global Economy*, Cambridge: Cambridge University Press.

Locke, R., Distenhorst, G., Pal, T. and Samel, H. M. (2012) 'Production goes global, standards stay local: private labor regulation in the global electronics industry', *MIT Political Science Department Research Paper No. 2012–1*, MIT, Boston.

Lund-Thomsen, P. (2013) 'Labor agency in the football manufacturing industry of Sialkot, Pakistan', *Geoforum*, 44: 71–81.

Lund-Thomsen, P. and Coe, N. M. (2014) 'Corporate social responsibility and labour agency: the case of Nike in Pakistan', *Journal of Economic Geography*, 14, doi: 10.1093/jeg/lbt041.

Lund-Thomsen, P. and Wad, P. (2014) 'Introduction to theme issue on global value chains, local economic organization, and corporate social responsibility in the BRICS countries', *Competition and Change*, 18(4): 281–290.

Martin, R. (2010) 'Roepke lecture in economic geography – rethinking path dependency: beyond lock-in to evolution', *Economic Geography*, 86(1): 1–27.

McGrath, S. (2013) 'Many chains to break: the multi-dimensional concept of slave labour in Brazil', *Antipode*, 45(4): 1005–1028.

McGrath-Champ, S., Herod, A. and Rainnie, A. (eds) (2010) *Working Space: Handbook of Employment and Society*, Cheltenham: Edward Elgar.

McKay, S. C. (2006) *Satanic Mills or Silicon Islands? The Politics of High-Tech Production in the Philippines*, Ithaca: Cornell University Press.

Munck, R. and Waterman, P. (2010) 'Global unions versus global capital: or, the complexity of transnational labour relations', in S. McGrath-Champ, A. Herod and A. Rainnie (eds) *Working Space: Handbook of Employment and Society*, Cheltenham: Edward Elgar, pp. 275–289.

Nadvi, K. and Wältring, F. (2004) 'Making sense of global standards', in H. Schmitz (ed.) *Local Enterprises in the Global Economy: Issues of Governance and Upgrading*, Cheltenham: Edward Elgar, pp. 53–94.

Neilson, J. and Pritchard, B. (2009) *Value Chain Struggles: Institutions and Governance in the Plantation Districts of South India*, Chichester: Wiley-Blackwell.

Neilson, J. and Pritchard, B. (2010) 'Fairness and ethicality in their place: the regional dynamics of fair trade and ethical sourcing agendas in the plantation districts of South India', *Environment and Planning A*, 42(8): 1833–1851.

Oseland, S. E., Haarstad, H. and Floysand, A. (2012) 'Labor agency and the importance of the national scale: emergent aquaculture unionism in Chile', *Political Geography*, 31(2): 94–103.

Padmanabhan, N. (2012) 'Globalisation lived locally: a labour geography perspective on control, conflict and response among workers in Kerala', *Antipode*, 44(3): 971–992.

Phillips, N. and Sakamoto, L. (2012) 'Global production networks, chronic poverty and "slave labour" in Brazil', *Studies in Comparative International Development*, 47(3): 287–315.

Ponte, S., Gibbon, P. and Vestergaard, J. (eds) (2011) *Governing Through Standards: Origins, Drivers and Limitations*, Basingstoke: Palgrave Macmillan.

Pries, L. and Seeliger, M. (2013) 'Work and employment relations in a globalized world: the emerging texture of transnational labour regulation', *Global Labor Journal*, 4(1): 26–47.

Rainnie, A., McGrath-Champ, S. and Herod, A. (2010) 'Working spaces', in S. McGrath-Champ, A. Herod and A. Rainnie (eds) *Handbook of Employment and Society: Working Space*, Edward Elgar: Cheltenham, pp. 61–86.

Rainnie, A., Herod, A. and McGrath-Champ, S. (2011) 'Review and positions: global production networks and labour', *Competition and Change*, 15(2): 155–169.

Riisgaard, L. and Hammer, N. (2011) 'Prospects for labour in global value chains: labour standards in the cut flower and banana industries', *British Journal of Industrial Relations*, 49(1): 168–190.

Rogaly, B. (2009) 'Spaces of work and everyday life: labour geographies and the agency of unorganised temporary migrant workers', *Geography Compass*, 3(6): 1975–1987.

Selwyn, B. (2009) 'Disciplining capital: export grape production, the state and class dynamics in northeast Brazil', *Third World Quarterly*, 30(3): 519–534.

Selwyn, B. (2012) 'Beyond firm-centrism: re-integrating labour and capitalism into global commodity chain analysis', *Journal of Economic Geography*, 12(2): 205–226.

Silver, B. (2003) *Forces of Labour: Workers' Movements and Globalisation Since 1870*, Cambridge: Cambridge University Press.

Smith, A., Rainnie, A., Dunford, M., Hardy, J., Hudson, R. and Sadler, D. (2002) 'Networks of value, commodities and regions: reworking divisions of labour in macro-regional economies', *Progress in Human Geography*, 26(1): 41–63.

Stringer, C., Simmons, G., Coulston, D. and Whittaker, D. H. (2014) 'Not in New Zealand's waters, surely? Linking labour issues to GPNs', *Journal of Economic Geography*, 14(4): 739–758.

Sweeney, B. and Holmes, J. (2013) 'Problematizing labour's agency: rescaling collective bargaining in British Columbia pulp and paper mills', *Antipode*, 45(1): 218–237.

Taylor, P. (2010) 'The globalization of service work: analyzing the transnational call centre value chain', in P. Thompson and C. Smith (eds) *Working Life: Renewing Labour Process Analysis*, Basingstoke: Palgrave Macmillan, pp. 244–268.

Taylor, P. and Bain, P. (2008) 'United by a common language? Trade union responses in the UK and India to call centre offshoring', *Antipode*, 40(1): 131–154.

Taylor, P., Newsome, K. and Rainnie, A. (2013) '"Putting labour in its place": global value chains and labour process analysis', *Competition and Change*, 17(1): 1–5.

Thompson, P. (2010) 'The capitalist labour process: concepts and connections', *Capital and Class*, 34(1): 7–14.

Tufts, S. (2007) 'Emerging labour strategies in Toronto's hotel sector: toward a spatial circuit of union renewal', *Environment and Planning A*, 39(10): 2383–2404.

Tufts, S. (2009) 'Hospitality unionism and labour market adjustment: toward Schumpeterian unionism?' *Geoforum*, 40(6): 980–990.

Wilson, B. R. (2013) 'Breaking the chains: coffee, crisis, and farmworker struggle in Nicaragua', *Environment and Planning A*, 45(11): 2592–2609.

Zhu, S. and Pickles, J. (2013) 'Bring in, go up, go West, go out: upgrading, regionalization, and delocalization in China's apparel production networks', *Journal of Contemporary Asia*, 44(1): 36–63.

Sector Studies

PART III

CHAPTER 11

The Significance of Grass-Roots Organizing in the Garment and Electrical Value Chains of Southern India

Jean Jenkins

Introduction

The expansion of global capital into developing economies has seen labour-intensive global value chains (GVCs) increase the opportunities for paid employment among new constituencies of labour. Significant increases have been recorded, for example, in the employment of women and rural migrants who are new to paid industrialized work outside the home (Barrientos and Visser, 2012: 7). Yet while labour-intensive industrialization may well bring employment to developing regions and growth to their economies, it stands accused of having 'largely ignore[d] ... [safeguarding] ... the improvement in quality of life of those employed' (Warouw, 2006: 183). In this chapter, it will be argued that the lack of economic and social upgrading accruing to workers – where *economic upgrading* is defined as a move from 'low value to high value activities' by economic actors (including workers) and *social upgrading* is defined as the 'improvement in the rights and entitlements of workers as social actors' (Barrientos and Visser, 2012: 7) – is a predictable consequence of rent-seeking behaviour by commercial interests in the value chain. The chapter considers the significance of workers' independent collective organization at workplace level, and concludes that local activism is an essential factor in the defence of workers' interests and enforcement of regulation. It is further argued that organising at the local level must be complemented by a network of external allies, in order for workers to secure leverage and pressurize local employers for substantive change at the workplace (see Quan, 2008; Merk, 2009).

The chapter draws upon primary research into workers' and activists' experiences in the export-facing garment factories of Bangalore and the mobile phone factories located in the Special Economic Zone (SEZ) of Chennai, Southern India. Qualitative enquiry was conducted in Bangalore in 2009 and 2012 and a short period of fieldwork was undertaken in Chennai in 2012. The main research methods involved semi-structured and unstructured interviewing of workers and labour activists, labour lawyers, union leaders, public officials, managers and consultants, and scrutiny of local reports on conditions on the ground. The condition of garment workers was studied across both periods of fieldwork, and in 2012 interviews were undertaken with some of the same respondents interviewed in 2009. Research with activists and workers on the mobile phone SEZ of Chennai took place in 2012, and these findings offer additional insights into the experiences of workers employed in low-skill, labour-intensive production environments.

The chapter is divided into four main sections. The first broadly considers early definitions of the value chain, and focuses on labour's interests vis-à-vis the rent-seeking motivation of firms. In section two, we examine the dynamics of the garments and electrical value chains in more detail and consider workers' experiences at the workplace. The third section of the chapter considers the potential for public and private regulation to remedy conditions for workers in the absence of effective enforcement mechanisms, such as independent collective organization, at the workplace. In conclusion, the chapter suggests that attempts to suppress grass-roots organization at the local level should be seen as a deliberate employer strategy which is at once both a function and consequence of inter-firm relationships in the value chain, rather than the aberrant behaviour of a few rogue employers. Concerted employer opposition to collective organization at the local level is explained in this context, and the need for external alliances between local activists and campaigners for workers' rights at the international level is emphasized.

Labour and the Value Chain

A commodity chain broadly comprises all the material, labour, technology and processes involved in the production of a finished commodity (Hopkins and Wallerstein, 1986). In the era of the multinational corporation, a *global* commodity chain is an interlinked global network, built on the premise that the fragmentation of a production process (or service provision) between different providers – or suppliers – will improve overall productive capacity and efficiency. Depending on the exact configuration of the value chain, suppliers may be subsidiaries or semi-autonomous units *within* the boundaries of the multinational corporation (MNC), or they may be external providers. Decisions by MNCs as to which activities are outsourced, kept in-house or relocated, determine relationships within and between firms along the value chain. The central focus and function of the lead firm is concentrated on the integration of activities and the control of resources and production standards across the value chain (Barrientos and Visser, 2012: 7). Surplus value is created along the different stages of the fragmented production network, and is expressed as different kinds of 'economic rents', depending on the product or service and the type of chain (Gereffi, 1999: 43).

In early conceptualizations of the supply chain, Gereffi (1994) distinguished between 'buyer-driven' and 'producer-driven' commodity (supply) chains, differentiated by the degree to which the lead (buyer) firm exercised integrated control and co-ordinated the activities of its supplier firms. Producer-driven chains exercised relatively greater control over the co-ordination of production and integration of activities along the chain, and as such were generally dominated by integrated transnational manufacturers in capital- and technology-intensive industries, such as automobiles and advanced electronics. Buyer-driven chains, on the other hand, were dominated by retailers or brands which concentrated on design and marketing but did not own their own manufacturing capacity, and sourced finished articles from supplier factories. Buyer-driven chains, as broadly defined, are typically found in sectors characterized by low-skill and labour-intensive, highly dispersed production, such as the garment sector and the low-skilled electronics sector – the focus of this chapter.

As value chain analysis has evolved, Gereffi *et al.* (2005: 78–83) have proposed a five-fold typology to provide a 'more complete typology of value chain governance'. The authors formulated a framework of analysis around three main variables which could be assigned either high or low values, dependent on the *complexity* of information involved in transactions between a lead firm and supplier firm, the ability to *codify* (standardize and specify) the information required for those transactions, and the *capabilities* in the supplier firm. Our discussion will return to the significance for labour of Gereffi *et al.*'s (2005) chosen variables, but at this point in our discussion it is sufficient to note that they provide the basis for closer categorization of lead firms' control strategies in their dyadic relationships with supplier units, and allow for more detailed insight into inter-firm relations along the chain.

Inevitably, the rent-seeking behaviour of firms leads to the squeezing of margins for suppliers along the chain in the process of 'capturing value' (Barrientos and Visser, 2012). In general, the global brand will be able to secure the greatest economic rent as they capture the highest share of value at the 'consumer end of the chain' (Nathan and Sarkar, 2011: 55; Barrientos and Visser, 2012: 7). But inter-firm relationships are structured on the basis that firms will seek to maximize their share of surplus value wherever they sit within the value chain. It follows that the rent-seeking motivation of firms, right along the chain, must have significance for the experience of workers at its base, particularly where labour is a significant element of total costs for local producers. However, in its concentration on explaining and analysing inter-firm relationships, workers are the very actors the GVC framework has hitherto tended to neglect. Even proponents of the GVC approach have acknowledged that there has been a concentration on theorizing the distribution of wealth and power across the value chain, to the exclusion of an analysis of the distribution of economic wealth across society (Gereffi *et al.*, 2005: 98–100; Palpacuer, 2008: 393–394).

The neglect of socio-political-economic context in GVC analysis has been deliberate, in the interests of theoretical clarity, and in an attempt to 'provide a general explanation for the co-ordination of inter-firm exchanges in value chains that is not dependent on territorial or institutional context, and is therefore "placeless" in some sense' (Bair, 2008: 357). The absence of context distinguishes the GVC approach from the (complementary) global production network approach (GPN), which places commercial relationships very firmly in their geo-political, socio-economic context (for example, Dicken *et al.*, 2001).[1] Nevertheless, from both the GVC *and* GPN approach, labour was originally theorized as little more than an 'endogenous factor of production' (Barrientos *et al.*, 2011: 322). It was left to a separate body of academic work from different disciplines, such as, for example, the political sciences, anthropology, human geography, the labour process debate and industrial relations, to examine workers' position and interests in the value chain (Barrientos and Visser, 2012: 7). Thus, alongside theoretical developments in GVC analysis sits a multi-disciplinary and broad literature which highlights that 'low margins and stiff competition' between manufacturers supplying global brands have generally resulted in lax environmental practices and poor, sometimes appalling, working conditions, in a range of international settings (Locke *et al.*, 2013: 520).

While accepting that Gereffi *et al.*'s (2005) theoretical framework for understanding contemporary value chains is intended to explain the nuances of *inter-firm* relationships, we can perhaps bring labour in to the analysis by adapting the variables of complexity, codification and capability to focus on labour's value at the bottom of the chain. Where technology facilitates the organization of complex information into a codifiable form, automates the labour process and allows for the standardization of work-related information and skill, it follows that the value of the worker as a repository of distinct capabilities and tacit knowledge is minimized. Individuals become increasingly interchangeable and therefore dispensable, particularly where labour is in plentiful supply. Thus, when we focus on the labour process at the bottom of the value chain, the early GVC theorization of labour as 'an endogenous factor of production' lends a certain clarity, emphasizing as it does labour's status as little more than a disembodied, calculated cost. Labour has hitherto been ignored in value chain *theory* in the interests of clarity, but in *practice*, the interests of workers in low-skilled, labour-intensive environments are also largely ignored. While it was not the intention of global value chain theory to do so, arguably, its early focus highlights what labour has been and *is* for local producers – a dispensable commodity, whose interests are worthy of attention only as far as is necessary to facilitate its effectiveness in the capturing of value by the firm. Suppliers, intent on minimizing costs in the context of tight margins, commodify workers as part of the process of creating wealth. Global corporations thus secure competitive advantage through cost savings derived from suppliers in developing economies, where the share of economic rents for local employers, and wages and working conditions for local labour, will 'tend towards market-based minima' (Nathan and Sarkar, 2011: 53).

In this context, solutions to the economic and social upgrading of labour have been sought in statutory rights and 'soft law', such as private regulation in the form of corporate social responsibility (CSR) initiatives, intended to advance workers' rights and control 'bad' employers (Locke *et al.*,). Yet, on the international stage, private and statutory regulation alike 'have not function[ed] effectively in isolation', due to poor enforcement (Locke at al., 2013: 520; see also, for example, Esbenshade, 2004; Bartley, 2011; Barrientos and Visser, 2012; Jenkins, 2013). As the firms along the value chain are probably best placed to ensure enforcement of both private and statutory regulation on labour rights at their workplaces, we might ask, why is labour's position failing to improve? The answer, though simplistic, would appear to be that (hitherto, at least) it has not been in employers' interests, to support enforcement of regulation, be that private or statutory, that results in the loss of their control over the cost or-day-to day management of labour. There is a wealth of evidence, for example, that local employers at the base of value chains, in a range of international settings, deliberately target specific categories of labour, such as women and migrants, for their reputation as being cheap and easy to control. Furthermore, employers engage in systematic attacks on any nascent grass-roots organization aimed at changing labour's experience of work and society (for example, Caraway, 2007; Gunawardana, 2007; Jenkins, 2013).

In the next section of the chapter, in understanding the current context for labour, the particular examples of the garments and electrical value chains are discussed in more detail.

The Garment and Electrical Value Chains

The value chain in garments was profoundly influenced by the import and export quotas imposed by the 1974 Multi-Fibre Agreement (MFA). The industry restructured and global brands pursued production sites in global regions known to be *less efficient* overall producers than existing manufacturing sites, but which had the attraction of lower labour costs. In this context there was what Birnbaum (2005: 6) has described as '"nomadic sourcing" – the search for quota-free countries with the cheapest workforce'. Similar 'races to the bottom' in search of the attractive combination of cheap labour, favourable fiscal policies and regulatory regimes were to be found in the labour-intensive, low-skilled, electronics value chains (for example, Caraway, 2007; Locke *et al.*, 2013: 524). Today's international dispersal of supplier units is the legacy of this strategic approach by global brands.

The garment sector, and the low-skilled electronics sector, then, provide two prime examples of the 'highly aggressive pattern of global sourcing' by international brands and retailers who have directly targeted 'lower-cost production sites' (Gereffi, 1999: 40). In those locations pursuing foreign direct investment, it became part of international 'common sense' that cheap *and* compliant workforces were necessary pre-conditions for the 'inflow of outward-oriented transnational operations' (Rasiah, 2001: 93). The pre-existing low socio-economic status of women in such settings fed the stereotype of them as being both cheap and docile, and they became the workforce of choice in many labour-intensive operations. This was particularly the case in the garments and low-skilled electronics sectors, where gendered perceptions of women's 'dexterity ... [and] ... high tolerance for monotonous work' also prevailed (Caraway, 2007: 49). Thus it is that many thousands of young women now labour in the garment factories of Bangalore and the mobile phone production units in Chennai.

The garment factories of Bangalore supply a range of international retailers and brands and are generally Indian-owned. While most of the larger, tier-one type units ('tier one' because they have the most direct links with the lead firms) are located in distinct garment factory areas of the city, they are not located on a designated export-processing zone. Today, there are estimated to be some 500,000 garment workers in Bangalore and although bespoke tailoring for the home market was formerly a male preserve, the mass production of garments for export is overwhelmingly female dominated (Jenkins, 2013). To the south, in Chennai, mobile phone production for a large and well-known international brand takes place on its own SEZ. Five major supplier factories, owned by international companies such as Foxconn, are sited on the zone, clustered around the lead firm's own plant. It seems that proximity of location is very important to this configuration, as in recent years one of the largest, key suppliers moved a relatively small distance within the same SEZ, so that factory units could be even closer together. The total number of workers on the mobile phone zone is around 30,000, and 80 percent of these workers are female (Cividep, 2010: 23).

Tier one factories in both sectors are large and modern, with highly automated shop floors. Assembly line workers are classed as low-skilled. In sourcing their labour, both the garment factories and mobile phone zones look outside their immediate environs, preferring to recruit workers, the majority of whom will be socio-economically disadvantaged, young and female, from rural village communities some distance from the factory areas. Generally, the young women will initially expect to work for a five-year period before returning to their village to be married, and will rent multiple occupancy accommodation (from private landlords) near to the SEZ while employed. The same life pattern was repeated in garments, where first and second generation rural migrants live in areas dominated by factory workers' accommodation (mainly small dwellings rather than large, shared multiple-occupancy houses). The employers' practice of sourcing labour from outside the garment factory areas and away from the SEZ was said by labour activists to be a deliberate aspect of managerial control strategies, intended to isolate workers from social networks of support, making them more vulnerable to managerial control at the workplace.

On production lines in both sectors, female assembly workers will usually be managed and controlled by male supervisors. Patriarchal social hierarchies pertaining outside the workplace are replicated within the factory walls (see also, Bhowmik 2009: 134–135; Taylor *et al.*, 2009), inasmuch as the supervisory relationship is set against the context of the multiple layers of socio-economic disadvantage that characterize women's domestic lives. This is the very context, said one union leader interviewed, that feeds perceptions of women as 'less trouble' than men, and therefore 'easier to control' at the workplace. A senior public official commented that young unskilled women were targeted by employers because there was a perception (underpinned by the neglect of women's issues and low-skilled work by the hitherto male-dominated, established labour movement) that their gender and their economic and social deprivation meant that they were unlikely to gain access to formal unions or collective bargaining. They were thus seen as less likely to challenge managerial authority (see Jenkins, 2013). In that sense, the respondent said, the feminized nature of the labour force 'well suits the requirements of employer'.

Minimum wage rates in the garment sector, already inadequate for more than bare subsistence, are regularly contravened by employers (Jenkins, 2013). The average wage for a garment worker in 2012 was around 4,000 Indian Rupees (Rs.) per month,[2] which at that time did little more than cover the rising costs of food and rent. It is important to note that even if wage rates rise, experience shows that to date they have not kept pace with price inflation in environments where minimum wages are often as much as 70–80 percent below what is calculated as a 'living wage'. Wages for workers on the mobile phone SEZ varied according to length of service and which exact factory they worked for. A labour activist explained that a skilled worker at the highest paying unit (run by the global brand itself) could earn as much as 11,000 Rs.[3] per month, but at supplier factories situated nearby, the rate for the same skilled work could fall as low as 5,500 Rs.[4] The exact exchange value of these wages may change according to time and the financial markets, but the varying rates for similar jobs with different firms illustrate the wider potential for manipulation of costs within the value chain. Conceivably, the global brand (intent on capturing value but with an eye on its reputation with consumers as a 'good' employer) can claim to be paying relatively good wages, while benefiting, directly or indirectly, from costs savings along the value chain derived from less favourable rates paid by suppliers with whom it shares very close working relationships. A young female respondent working at a supplier unit to the brand earned around 4,000 Rs. per month after three years' employment and a labour activist confirmed that this was a typical wage for young women workers. He commented that her earnings were far too low to be considered a 'living wage' and said of the SEZ, 'the ratio of unemployment [in Chennai] is very low, but yet the lifestyle … it is very bad … earnings are too low'.

In both sectors studied, a worker's experience of managerial relations *within different sections of the same factory* could vary, and highlights the significance of the worker's relationship with first-line supervision in a context where it could be very risky to challenge your manager. A respondent working on the mobile phone SEZ, said '[*my*] supervisors are] friendly, but they are not all so good'. The essence of this comment was repeated by workers in the garment sector and might be expected in any workplace, but had greater significance in the context of this setting. A supervisor who is not 'good' to work for can terrorize an individual worker with de facto impunity. One garment worker summed up her feelings about being watched by her supervisors by saying '[I] felt like a rat in front of cats'. In these factory environments bullying and sexual harassment is rife, with sexual favours often being demanded of young and vulnerable workers in return for the allocation of better working patterns or less abusive treatment on the assembly line (see Jenkins, 2013).

Thus, respondents gave many first and second hand accounts of women driven to desperation by their factory life. For example, the word 'torturing' is used by garment workers, to describe the verbal abuse and harassment they can experience on the assembly line. Respondents told of a range of insults and daily pressures at the hands of their supervisors, from name calling and the throwing of cloth at machinists' faces, to insults like a male supervisor catching hold of a woman's marriage necklace and jerking it at her neck, which is considered a grossly disrespectful form of behaviour. There were also many examples of unexplained deaths, suicides and rapes. Less serious but nevertheless distressing examples of violations of human dignity involved workers being locked in rooms or made to stand in front of fellow workers in enforced silence for several hours, as sanctions for failing to make targets or for expressions of dissent. Respondents also spoke of the widespread abuse of working time, in the form of long hours working in the garment sector and Sunday overtime on the SEZ. In practice, workers said that they often had no real choice over whether to work or not.

Statutory Rights, Private Regulation and Independent Collective Organization – the Remedies for Worker Exploitation?

The working conditions described above emphasize labour's lack of worth as living, breathing individuals with interests, needs and aspirations of their own, in the labour-intensive sectors studied. What potential is there for remedy from statutory rights or private regulation? In answering this question, we should begin by acknowledging that at workplace level, within the value chain, it is *'local capital* that imposes control at the point of production … [and in doing so, it will] … make use of the space created by the free mobility of global capital' in its control strategies (Padmanabhan, 2012: 976, emphasis in original). Employers and managers use the threat of capital flight to serve their rent-seeking imperatives in a variety of ways – to influence public policy, manage individual workers, undermine the enforcement of statutory regulation and deter collective organization.

In terms of statutory employment rights, garment workers on large factory sites are among the 7 per cent of Indian workers who have formal sector status. In theory, this gives them access to statutory protections against dismissal and access to health insurance and provident funds. But as in the case of other examples from developing countries (see Barrientos and Visser, 2012), the laws on the statute book are poorly understood by the ordinary worker, are labelled as anti-competitive rigidities by the business lobby, and are weakly enforced (see for example, Srivastava, 2011). Thus it is that, for the typical female garment worker, beset by poverty, socially disadvantaged and often overwhelmed by the dual burden of domestic and paid work, formality is little guarantee of access to the institutional protections of the state (Sankaran and Madhav, 2011: 9; Jenkins, 2013). India's SEZs, on the other hand, are specifically *created* to be 'spaces of exception' and are exempt from regulation (Gunawardana, 2007; Sippola, 2012). In these spaces, special incentives not only provide cheap (or free) sources of land and utilities for international business, but also fund tax concessions and allow inward investors and exporters to bypass labour laws (Ghosh, 2009: 72–73). Thus, in the quest to attract investment and impress potential investors with its business-friendly credentials, the state has ensured that mobile phone workers in Chennai are unable to depend on statutory labour rights and must rely instead on the employer's code of good practice. In contrast, garment workers have a range of statutory employment rights, but as an individual worker, it is almost impossible to access them.

If statutory rights go unenforced or are inaccessible, we may ask whether workers are more likely to be able to access remedy for poor working conditions through voluntary codes of social responsibility promoted by international brands in their role as lead firms. As Bartley (2011: 522) highlights, private regulation based on corporate codes can become 'deeply intertwined' with pre-existing structures of power, and in light of the gendered social relations of the workplace, there is much scope for this to happen. Interviews with labour activists in Bangalore affirmed that increased reliance on private codes had been a major contributor to the marginalization of statutory protections such as, for example, the state system of factory inspection. Testimony of workers and activists suggested that private monitoring of factories was just as weak and open to abuse as the discredited and corrupt state system. They spoke of bogus monitors, of coaching of workers by managers to give correct answers, and of private codes 'making no difference' to conditions on the ground. These comments reflect the findings of a range of empirical studies which note the weak enforcement of private and statutory regulation in defence of workers in global value chains (for example, Esbenshade, 2004; Caraway, 2007; Gunawardana, 2007; Lynch, 2007; Bartley, 2011; Barrientos and Visser, 2012; Locke et al., 2013). Respondents to this research were clear that *in and of themselves* corporate codes and statutory rights made little difference to the daily experiences of workers on the ground, as individuals were extremely unlikely to be able to enforce them. However, for activists, private and statutory regulation did at least provide published standards which could be used as a basis for bargaining.

This brings our discussion to the new paradigm for better conditions in value chains as suggested by Barrientos *et al.* (2011). In their theoretical framework for economic and social upgrading for workers, they argue it should be based on three pillars: statutory rights, voluntary corporate codes *and* independent union organization. The latter they deem necessary for the enforcement and representation of workers' rights in the value chain. The proposition seems entirely valid, and is supported by the argument being made in this chapter – in the absence of collective voice at the workplace, any private code or statutory regulation may be undermined as individual workers are in no position to challenge managerial authority. Workers' collective power is arguably the one element with the potential (however limited or small) to shift the balance of employers' unilateral power and roll back the frontier of control in workplace relations. Perhaps for that reason, independent autonomous collective organization is fiercely, and generally, opposed by the employers and commercial interests that dominate global value chains. Oppression of independent collectivism is widespread and systematic and, rather than being the exceptional behaviour of a few 'bad' employers, research suggests it is the norm (for example, Hutchinson and Brown, 2001; Hale, 2005; Merk, 2009; Jenkins, 2013). While it is unlikely that firms and international brands would agree – most if not all codes of corporate responsibility champion freedom of association, for example – it is difficult to overestimate the challenges posed by employers to grass-roots organization at workplace level.

First, taking the new constituency of labour targeted by employers for their reputation for compliance and turning them into organized bodies of workers is extremely difficult. A range of studies (for example, Hutchinson and Brown, 2001; Caraway, 2007; Gunawardana, 2007; Jenkins, 2013; Merk, 2009) all point to the challenges involved in organizing such workers – hence their attractiveness to employers as new recruits. Various established labour movements have been somewhat tardy in addressing these challenges, yet in many locations around the world we see evidence of 'pre-union' associations, workers' centres, micro-saving groups and community-based structures acting to bring people together around their shared domestic and work-based interests. Such initiatives have been particularly effective with women and other types of socio-economically disadvantaged workers (for example, Bhatt; 2006; Fine 2006; Milkman, 2006) and such tactics are being successfully employed by labour activists in Bangalore and Chennai. It is, however, a slow process. Activists spoke of the need for great patience in cultivating workers' confidence to speak aloud and 'hear their own voices' in workers' meetings. They gave examples of women who had taken not weeks or months but *years* of attendance at workers' gatherings to make their first comment.

Second, activists have to contend with the direct and systematic opposition of employers to independent collective organization. Respondents to this research asserted that one of the most immediate responses to any suggestion of unionization was – 'if you join a union, this factory will close'. The associated victimization of workers identified as union members – for example, by isolating them from their fellow workers and targeting them with abuse – was widespread (see Jenkins, 2013). In a contrasting strategy of incorporation, on the mobile phone SEZ, a company-sponsored union was the only recognized form of consultation with workers. Any form of dissent outside that forum was treated harshly. For example, in response to a spontaneous walk-out by workers in 2010 (over an altercation between a worker and a supervisor), some 1,700 workers on the SEZ were arrested and imprisoned on charges ranging from criminal damage to trespass. The same event also highlighted employers' use of paternalistic social structures outside the workplace as tools of control (see Taylor *et al.*, 2009: 23–25; also, Bhowmik, 2009: 134–135; Bartley, 2011), as managers wrote letters to the village homes of workers who went on strike, asking their parents to call their unruly children to order and instruct them to return to work.

Alongside such strategies, activists also spoke of the existence of local protection rackets among employers seeking to avoid unionization, where local firms pay a regular fee in return for the services of thugs employed to keep bona fide organizers away from workers. The president of a small women's garment union in Bangalore, for example, told how she was followed and threatened with physical harm by several such thugs for many months while leading a long-running local dispute over the physical beatings meted out to male workers at a factory supplying a global brand. In connection with the dispute, the same activist and her colleagues were charged with 'civil defamation' by the state, on the basis that they had been communicating with campaigners and foreign media about poor working conditions. The case was eventually dropped and the activists were exonerated of the charges against them, but the process took no less than two years. Such examples highlight the very real threat that workers face as they struggle towards a voice in their own destinies, both at the individual and collective level.

Local employers' repertoire of opposition to independent collective organization on the ground is thus systematic, varied and highly effective as a tool of fear. As such it is difficult to see attempts to suppress the collective worker voice as anything less than a part of a conscious strategy on the part of local employers, and it would seem to be a very effective corporate tool, implemented locally but within the framework of the value chain. By these various means, local employers suppress the worker voice, retain maximum capacity for unilateral decision-making and maintain a tight grip on the control of *their* costs and production schedules at the workplace level.

In response to such concerted opposition, it is remarkable that workers mobilize and challenge their employers, and yet they do. The exertion of leverage at the workplace is, however, difficult. Numbers of trade union members are low in relation to the working population – for example, one garment union in Bangalore, a city with around 500,000 garment workers had 500 members, another 1,800, another 2,500. Union membership of independent unions in the SEZ was significantly increased after workers were imprisoned during the 2010 dispute (no fewer than 6,000 workers joined an alternative union to the company forum) but it still did not have bargaining rights in 2012. Thus, for a fragmented labour movement, exerting leverage often relies on securing the enforcement of private and statutory regulations on pain of exposure of local abuses which might be damaging to the reputation of the global brand – something Esbenshade (2004: 54) has represented as the 'triangle of power'. As part of their quest to bring labour into plain sight, then, labour organizers pressurize local suppliers through their relationships with international brands, and use the value chain structure to their advantage. This tactic allows local activists to have more influence than their numbers might suggest were possible.

Respondents to this study, for example, had cultivated relationships beyond the local and relied in no small measure on support from external organizations, such as the wider union movement, Oxfam and other campaigning organizations. In their local bargaining strategies, activists aimed to hold firms to account on basic statutory rights like the minimum wage, where redress was relatively simple and straightforward to achieve. They also used the global brands' own corporate social responsibility policy statements to great effect, reaching out to international consumers through the media network provided by their relationships with campaigning groups. One example of the use of the 'triangle of power' given by respondents to this research related to a heavily pregnant woman who was denied medical attention by her managers and whose baby died as she gave birth alone, after being turned out of the factory gates. Local unions and activists united with international campaigners such as the Clean Clothes Campaign and Labour Behind the Label to target the reputation of the global brand being supplied by the factory – which was an international retailer of baby clothes. In fear for its reputation, the brand pressurized the local employer to pay compensation to the woman and institute better medical facilities at the workplace. Small gains, perhaps, but an illustration of local activism gaining leverage through the value chain structure.

In Quan's (2008: 90–94) work as an organizer, she explains how representations of the value chain were used to educate workers, in basic pictorial terms, about their position in modern capitalism, and as a means of identifying other suppliers, workforces and potential allies. Quan argues that by reaching out to a range of social and political actors the local labour organizer can create their own version of a GVC – one that constitutes 'a dynamic flow of organizing towards worker power' (Quan, 2008: 95; see also Merk, 2009). In the cases outlined in this chapter, the workers' situation at the bottom of the value chain would have been largely invisible without external allies, and access to consumer-facing publicity would have been even more difficult. Furthermore, and crucially, in the absence of external links, the value chain configuration would leave workplace activists as the only actors operating and bargaining at a local level, at the mercy of a network of firm-centric, rent-seeking behaviours that traverse the globe, with the ultimate threat of capital flight at their disposal.

Conclusion

Even where national economies are booming, there is overwhelming evidence of the dearth of economic and social upgrading for workers, particularly in low-skill, labour-intensive value chains (see, for example, Gereffi *et al.*, 2005; Barrientos *et al.*, 2011). Remedies for exploitative working conditions and poverty wages have been sought through the options of private regulation, in the form of voluntary codes of corporate social responsibility (so-called 'soft law') and statutory regulation. However, weak enforcement has meant that neither statutory nor private regulation has proved effective (see Gereffi *et al.*, 2005; Barrientos *et al.*, 2011; Locke *et al.*, 2013: 520).

It is argued here that the continued absence of economic and social upgrading for workers should be understood not as an aberrant by-product of internationalized production, but rather as a predictable outcome of inter-firm relationships founded in the rent-seeking motive and the capturing of value (see Nathan and Sarkar, 2011; Barrientos and Visser, 2012: 18). The cases discussed here highlight that local employers' resourcing strategies are designed *from the outset* to take advantage of the socio-economic deprivation of young women in their society. Disempowerment is perceived as a desirable feature of the ideal worker, being associated not only with women's low-cost and supposed compliance at the workplace, but also their greater distance from access to representation or employment rights. In essence, her vulnerability is the female worker's unique selling point. Thus local employers target labour of minimal socio-economic 'value' to maximize their control and economic rents at their position on the value chain.

In this context, the enforcement of private codes and statutory rights is at the mercy of powerful vested interests, and in the absence of independent workplace organization, there is enormous scope for employers to hide from scrutiny and avoid or subvert regulation. Workers' own independent collective organization has the potential to be a constant presence in workplace relations, unlike other forms of auditing which come and go. But in the context of a value chain where the weight of employers' power is directed at preventing collective organization, and capital flight is a potent threat (even if more imagined than real), it is unlikely that organization at a purely local level would be in a position to secure significant leverage with local employers. In a hostile climate for collective organization, it is all the more important that workers and activists at the workplace have access to a network of external allies which can help to target different levels of the value chain and develop a network of support for local activism. In low-skilled, labour-intensive settings like the cases discussed in this chapter, local organization is often relatively fragmented and weak in relation to the power of local employers. But its position can be reframed by the support of external allies if they facilitate a triangle of (admittedly limited) power, in the form of access to consumers and the reputation of the global brand. In this way leverage can be attained within the value chain, and pressure can be exerted to enforce the provisions of statutory and private regulation at the local level.

In conclusion, perhaps we can measure the potential of local organization by the amount of effort devoted to suppressing it, which is considerable. Private codes and statutory regulation may provide a necessary structure of rights for labour but it is grass-roots organizing, complemented by a network of external allies, which holds most promise for the empowerment of workers and the enforcement of more decent standards of life and work at the bottom of the value chain. Evidence thus far suggests it is a task that most certainly cannot be left in the hands of global brands and their suppliers.

Notes

1 A detailed account of each analytical approach is beyond the scope of this chapter, but for a comprehensive summary of their distinctive features, Bair (2008: 354–359) is to be recommended.
2 Around £39 or USD 66 at the time of writing.
3 Around £107 or USD 182 at the time of writing.
4 Around £53 or USD 91 at the time of writing.

References

Bair, J. (2008) 'Analyzing global economic organization: embedded networks and global chains compared', *Economy and Society*, 37(3): 339–364.

Barrientos, S., Gereffi, G. and Rossi, A. (2011) 'Economic and social upgrading in global production networks: a new paradigm for a changing world', *International Labour Review*, 150(3–4): 319–340.

Barrientos, S. and Visser, M. (2012) *South African horticulture: opportunities and challenges for economic and social upgrading in value chains*, Capturing the Gains: economic and Social Upgrading in Global Production Networks Working Paper Number 12, University of Manchester, UK.

Bartley, T. (2011) 'Transnational governance as the layering of rules: intersections of public and private standards', *Theoretical Inquiries in Law*, 12(2): 517–542.

Bhatt, E. R. (2006) *We are Poor but So Many: The Story of Self-Employed Women in India*, South Asia Series. New York: Oxford University Press.

Bhowmik, S. K. (2009) 'India: labor sociology searching for a direction', *Work and Occupations*, 36(2): 126–144.

Birnbaum, D. (2005) 'Sourcing: a must for clothing suppliers', *International Trade Forum* Issue 3, (3–8) Geneva, International Trade Centre.

Caraway, T. L. (2007) *Assembling Women: The Feminization of Global Manufacturing*, Ithaca, NY and London: Cornell University Press.

Cividep-India (2010) 'Changing industrial relations in India's mobile phone manufacturing industry', *Stichting Onderzoek Multinationale Ondernemingen, Centre for Research on Multinational Corporations (SOMO)*, The Netherlands: Amsterdam.

Dicken, P., Kelly, P., Olds, K. and Yeung, H. W. (2001) 'Chains and networks, territories and scales: towards a relational framework for analyzing the global economy', *Global Networks*, 1(2): 89–112.
Esbenshade, J. (2004) *Monitoring Sweatshops: Workers, Consumers and the Global Apparel Industry*, Philadelphia: Temple University Press.
Fine, J. (2006) *Worker Centres: Organizing Communities on the Edge of the Dream*, Ithaca, NY and London: ILR Press, Cornell University Press.
Gereffi G. (1994) 'The organization of buyer-driven global commodity chains: how U.S. retailers shape overseas production networks', in G. Gereffi and M. Korzeniewicz (eds) *Commodity Chains and Global Capitalism*, Westport, CT: Praeger, pp. 95–122.
Gereffi, G. (1999) 'International trade and industrial upgrading in the apparel commodity chain', *Journal of International Economics*, 48(1999): 37–70.
Gereffi, G., Humphrey, J. and Sturgeon, T. (2005) 'The governance of global value chains', *Review of Political Economy*, 12(1): 78–104.
Ghosh, J. (2009) *Never Done and Poorly Paid – Women's Work in Globalising India*, feminist fine print series, New Delhi: Women Unlimited.
Gunawardana, S. (2007) 'Struggle, perseverance, and organization in Sri Lanka's export processing zones', in K. Bronfenbrenner (ed.) *Global Unions: Challenging Transnational Capital through Cross-Border Campaigns*, Ithaca, NY and London: Cornell University Press, pp. 78–98.
Hale, A. (2005) 'Organising and networking in support of garment workers: why we researched subcontracting chains', in A. Hale and J. Wills (eds) *Threads of Labour: Garment Industry Supply Chains from the Workers' Perspective*, Women Working Worldwide, Oxford: Blackwell Publishing, pp. 40–68.
Hopkins, T. K. and Wallerstein, I. (1986) 'Commodity chains in the world economy prior to 1800', *Review*, 1(2): 11–145.
Hutchinson, J. and Brown, A. (eds) (2001) *Organising Labour in Globalising Asia*, London: Routledge.
Jenkins, J. (2013) 'Organising spaces of hope: union formation by Indian garment workers', *British Journal of Industrial Relations*, 51(3): 623–643.
Locke, R. M., Rissing, B.A. and Pal, T. (2013) 'Complements or substitutes? Private goods, state regulation and the enforcement of labour standards in global supply chains', *British Journal of Industrial Relations*, 51(3): 519–552.
Lynch, C. (2007) *Juki Girls, Good Girls: Gender and Cultural Politics in Sri Lanka's Global Garment Industry*, Ithaca and London: Cornell University Press.
Merk, J. (2009) 'Jumping scale and bridging space in the era of corporate social responsibility: cross border labour struggles in the global garment industry', *Third World Quarterly*, 30(3): 599–615.
Milkman, R. (2006) *L.A. Story: Immigrant Workers and the Future of the US Labor Movement*, New York: Russell Sage Foundation.
Nathan, D. and Sarkar, S. (2011) 'A note on profits, rents and wages in global production networks', *Economic and Political Weekly*, 3 September 2011, XLVI: 36.
Padmanabhan, N. (2012) 'Globalization lived locally: a labour geography perspective on control, conflict and response among workers in Kerala', *Antipode*, 44(3): 971–992.

Palpacuer, F. (2008) 'Bringing the social context back in: governance and wealth distribution in global commodity chains', *Economy and Society*, 37(3): 393–419.

Quan, K. (2008), 'Use of Global Value Chains by Labor Organizers', *Competition & Change*, 12(1): 89–104.

Rasiah, R. (2001) 'Labour and work organization in Malaysia's proton', in J. Hutchinson and A. Brown (eds) *Organising Labour in Globalising Asia*, London: Routledge, pp. 90–107.

Sankaran, K. and Madhav, R. (2011) *Gender equality and social dialogue in India*, International Labour Office Working Paper 1/2011, Geneva (ISBN 978-92-2-123910-9).

Sippola, M. (2012) 'The restructuring of the Nordic labour process and the variegated status of workers in the labour market', *Competition & Change*, 16(3): 243–260.

Srivastava, M. (2011) 'In India, 101 employees pose big problems', *Bloomberg Businessweek*, 17 January 2011, 4212: 13–14.

Taylor, P., D'Cruz, P., Noronha, E. and Scholarios D. (2009) 'Indian call centres and business process outsourcing: a study in union formation', *New Technology, Work and Employment*, 24(1): 19–39.

Warouw, N. (2006) 'Community-based agencies as the entrepreneur's instruments of control in post-Soeharto's Indonesia', *Asia Pacific Business Review*, 12(2): 193–207.

CHAPTER 12

Human Security in Evolving Global Value Chains: Reconsidering Labour Agency in a Livelihoods Context

Lee Pegler

Introduction

The debate about the adequacy of conditions applying to people supplying many of the products we consume on a daily basis is now very commonplace. Drawing from and building on recent work (Pegler, 2015) which analyses the labour processes/human security of workers at the beginning of these chains of value, this chapter considers the degree to which labour is able to shape their situation – to exhibit agency? Such questions are quite specific in agricultural situations, where the focal point of interest is not only workers but also family farmers.

What seems to be fairly clear is that labour conditions and agency to change them are often found to be negative at the beginning of buyer-driven and agricultural GVCs. Various studies point to a disjuncture between economic upgrading by producers in the Global South, when they enter chains, and the conditions facing their workers (Knorringa and Pegler, 2006; Barrientos et al., 2011). Even when it does occur, economic upgrading may sometimes even lead to social downgrading (Barrientos et al., 2011; Pegler, 2011).

One important theme of enquiry is what do we mean by social upgrading and how useful is labour process theory for evaluating it? When will we have confidence to say that labour is involved such that economic and social upgrading might occur simultaneously (Selwyn, 2013)? This takes us back to a consideration of the labour-capital relation, to the subjective responses production generates and to the spaces it allows for labour agency. This is the central gap this chapter addresses – that of agency and its subjective basis – with data from an evolving chain.

The subjects of this chapter are the river dwellers (*ribeirinhos*) of the Amazon in Brazil who pick and sell the açaí berry. The market for açaí is rapidly evolving[1] but there are questions about whether *ribeirinhos* will gain due to issues such as the role of traders (river transporters – Brondízio, 2008) and the desire by various agencies to regulate the market. There are spaces for agency yet the attitudes of *ribeirinhos* are not uniform (Pegler, 2015). Despite similarities as a group, *ribeirinhos* exhibit varied perspectives and strategies. This is a function of their position in social hierarchies but also of their multiple tasks.

This analysis of labour processes, and *ribeirinhos*' varied reactions to those vying to 'represent' them, makes an important addition to labour process theory. The indeterminacy of labour power is a particularly complex process in contexts where labour is also farmer/producer and spread across various locations/products. Inherent antagonisms between capital and labour are also more dissipated. Yet the frontiers of control and resistance to them can be delineated, especially through the addition of constructs such as Human Security (to labour control considerations – this chapter; Pegler, 2015) and governmentality (to the consideration of agency – this chapter). The following section summarizes the chain and product context for the study (Pegler, 2015) and this further analysis.

Açaí and its (Global) Value Chain

Açaí is a black berry that grows on a palm tree (mainly from the Amazon) which has formed part of the staple diet of Amazonian river dwellers (*ribeirinhos*) for centuries (Pereira, 2012). It is traditionally eaten as a pulp or as a liquid. Variants of the product are now being eaten by a rapidly growing consumer base, in Brazil and internationally (especially the USA but also Europe). Açaí has always been seen to have medicinal qualities (Heinrich et al., 2011). Its more recent 'discovery' as a healthy, cleansing antioxidant has served to bolster its demand by this broader range of consumers (Colapinto, 2011).

Strong demand is bringing about changes to the governance of the chain. At a firm level, the Brazilian market is exhibiting considerable volatility and firms are consolidating (Binios, 2012). At an international level, a more certain line of supply has been established. Açaí juice and ice-cream are being sold in the European and North American markets. Health shops and boutiques offer tea bags and frozen açaí blocks and other firms in Europe are beginning to produce and sell cosmetic/

pharmaceutical lines as has been done in Brazil. Yet this international chain is still somewhat experimental and small scale compared to more established fruits and tropical health products.

From a development perspective, açaí appears to offer substantial opportunities for sustainable production (ADS, 2011). Its evolution raises questions about the impact on workers/communities at source (Castro, 1999). Cultivation is labour intensive and can be managed without significant deforestation. It is a complementary product to other activities (e.g. palm hearts; fishing) and now generates significant added value (Pegler, 2015). For these reasons it has been heralded as a potential 'win-win' case for small-scale producers amongst a mass of largely negative examples of local producer outcomes as a result of their insertion in GVCs (SDS, 2005; Pegler, 2011). The fact that it is at an initial stage of development as a GVC makes it particularly interesting to study as it helps to illustrate that there are different possibilities for how upgrading impacts opportunities for labour. Moreover, labour processes in such informal, family-based primary production contexts illustrate specific social relations of production for consideration (Bernstein, 2010).

This incipient chain situation offers *ribeirinhos* varied but uncertain spaces for value generation/upgrading. *Ribeirinhos'* existing flexibility between tasks and crops (and other activities) means that their labour process derives from multiple points of production, something which requires us to open up our consideration of their subjectivity (Fraxe *et al.*, 2007). Moreover, aside from the various manual, family-based stages of picking, sorting and bagging, the production chain is complicated (Pegler, 2015). It is a perishable product for which various logistical issues (small to large boats; distances; multiple buyers/transporters) underline an uncertain governance process, even before questions of homogenization, freezing and packing are considered.

For example, the typical middlemen/transporters who permeate this system can sometimes be the *ribeirinhos* themselves (or friendly neighbours) whilst at other times these functions are fulfilled by exploitative agents and landowners (something with a strong negative tradition in the Amazon – Brondízio, 2008[2]). The upgrading process thus offers opportunities and constraints to *ribeirinho* inclusion. As an extreme case, the possibility of monoculture açaí plantations would seriously limit any chances of upgrading by these peasant communities in the evolving açaí value chain. Whether or not this occurs, the terrain of contestation may become more problematic if market 'drivers' (key firms) and governments move to develop more regularized systems of supply, certification and management of value-generation, for what has until recently been a largely informal activity.

This is the broader context behind this study (Pegler, 2015). Data was sought which would help improve our understanding of the labour processes of the Amazonian peasants who are collecting and selling açaí to a fast expanding (now global) market. This particular case study took place in the Brazilian state of Amazonas, a presently minor but rapidly growing producer of açaí (Pegler, 2015; Appendix, Tables 1–3). The specific region centred on the Amazonas state açaí 'capital', the town and municipality of Codajás. The local communities (Miuá; Badajós) and township (Tefé), from whom a sample of families were drawn, supply açaí to that centre as well as to the metropolis of Manaus. In total, 23 families were interviewed for over one hour each in relation to their livelihoods, tasks/production-activity, division of labour and sense of wellbeing/security. This was complemented by homestead mapping and focus groups in those areas as well as numerous interviews with producers, transporters, port workers, government officials and açaí company personnel in the broader regions of Codajás and Manaus. This research was spread over a number of periods in 2011–2012.

Drawing the central primary data from small localities supplying the Codajás hub held special empirical and conceptual importance. Seasonal production means that (especially with strong demand) açaí prices fluctuate wildly (from US$ 11.40–US$ 57 per 50kg sack) between early and late season. The case study areas generally produce their berries late in the season, thus attracting higher prices. Yet the logistics of production and supply from these outlying communities to port/processing/sale are particularly complicated. For these two reasons, studying peasants in these areas was seen to have the greatest chance of illustrating the pressures of the market on *ribeirinho* family activity but also the complexities of chain governance and agency dynamics at a local level.

From Labour Control to Social Upgrading?

Understanding the process of labour agency requires a look back through the lenses we use to analyse labour within the production process, at the debate about labour control within the labour process. This section first recounts how the lenses we use may need modification when applied to GVC contexts and in rural situations (Pegler, 2015). Firms and others are actively promoting economic upgrading but whether this leads to social upgrading at source depends on how we define the labour process. Secondly, this section summarizes the case study evidence of what this broadened labour process vision suggests for prospects of social upgrading for *ribeirinhos* (Pegler, 2015).

The need to obtain a minimal level of agreement by labour to carry out tasks is central to the production process, defining the labour process as both an objective and subjective act. Burawoy's (1985/2000) views on labour processes within capitalism hold appeal as they suggest a quite nuanced view of labour control. He argues that labour control is both a workplace and a broader political issue but also that there is significant ambiguity in subjective responses to the pressures of production (to social relations in production). Yet, whilst appealing at an intuitive level (i.e. we are not all duped by capitalism and we do sometimes like our work), there are aspects of this vision of labour control which need adaptation.

First, in agricultural situations the tasks of production take on a broader livelihood and household/community orientation (Kelly, 2002; Harilal *et al.*, 2006). This further reinforces a need to consider social relations at a gendered level (Carswell and De Neve, 2012). In fact, it might (as suggested by Kelly, 2009) be best to think in terms of global reproduction networks, ones that interact with production relations and, together with them, give a more holistic vision of the production context. Labour works, but also goes home, and this brings into play possible conflicts between economic and social spheres in respect of task and reward distribution as well as ecological/sustainability considerations, especially in proximate family-based agricultural contexts.

Secondly, the place of production is not so fixed and value can be added en route and in many locations (Taylor *et al.*, 2013; Kelly, 2012; Newsome, 2010). Thirdly, labour control 'at a distance' within globalized production complicates the consideration of its governance by capital. Labour is local, while capital is not always so fixed – it is 'stretched' across space, searching for spatial fixes to this governance problem (Harvey, 1982). The uncertainties of these considerations of space underline a growing view that a stronger integration of local (horizontal) dynamics with vertical chain considerations is vital for an understanding of labour's position in chains (Neilson and Pritchard, 2010).

Accordingly, the case of Amazonian peasants' (*ribeirinhos'*) inclusion in the açaí GVC highlights the need to modify how we see the terrain of labour control to take account of these agricultural, gendered and community dynamics (Pegler, 2015). The peasants who cultivate and collect the açaí berry live flexible lives working in various locations and with various products. Whilst dominated by men, production is family- and community based. Typical household/community activities include fishing, prawning, vegetable growing, palm heart extraction, wood cutting, boat building and transport. Men and (mainly) boys work with wood, fish and transport and pick açaí. Women and girls tend the house and garden. The growth in demand may be putting pressure on these production processes and social relations.

Aside from the adaptive focus these different spaces require in terms of 'objective' indicators of change, this also seems to suggest a need to open up subjectivity further – not just responses ranging 'from control to consent' but to a broader range of influences on wellbeing in rural livelihood settings. For this reason this study has augmented Burawoy's (1985/2000) ambiguous vision of subjectivity with a Human Security perspective (Pegler, 2015). Drawing inspiration from Sen (1999), the Human Security argument concerns people's material and non-material securities in their livelihoods and measures to protect these (Truong, 2006; Gasper, 2010). Within this school of thought, values and subjectivity are considered to go beyond that specified by a consumption orientation. As with Burawoy's view, wellbeing is not delimited by an alienation perspective.

More specifically, this study builds on Human Security writers' ideas (Gasper and George, 2010) that subjectivities can be elucidated by the use of thematic narratives – the ones added to traditional labour process theory in this study being: challenges to traditional values; and the significance of sustainability and preferences for collectivity (Pegler, 2015). The nature of work may ultimately be driven by consumption demands and capitalist productivity imperatives but along the way it interacts with significant variety in values, feelings and responses.

Based on this expanded view of labour processes and a division of the sample based on a family's degree of engagement with the açaí chain, the study generated quite specific results in respect of labour organization and control.[3] First, in terms of tasks, rising açaí demand has increased production levels yet not in great deviation from a traditional family production model. For instance, whilst women have some role in sorting berries and allocating children to help (in addition to house duties) this is not qualitatively different to traditional processes and any new tasks are not overly recognized or valued by men. Similarly, upgrading to the higher value-added 'wine' product does not place but strictly in accordance with their level of involvement in the açaí market. Decisions on 'wine' production, as with technology acquisition (boats) and the employment of wage labour, seem to be more a function of what the family itself can provide and prefers in respect of its collective work-leisure balance rather than a strictly economic profit-maximizing decision.

On the other hand, within this mixed picture of family production and rising demand, the *ribeirinhos* of Amazonas are presently making quite good seasonal returns from açaí collection and sale.[4] Material gains are good in spite of the distances, fragility of boats and substantial margins made by traders. Yet seasonality and the threat of monoculture production add elements of insecurity to their livelihoods. For instance, while monoculture plantations in the state of Amazonas are still small (around 3 per cent of total acreage), there is some expectation that these will increase substantially, as has occurred in the major açaí-producing state of Para (Pereira, 2012). The sense of insecurity, but also variety of feelings, these developments generate is underlined by other indicators of wellbeing.

As with their varying levels of assets and degree of involvement in commercial activity, there are quite different perspectives taken by *ribeirinhos* in respect of what açaí means to them. For example, many were optimistic about the product and few saw this new market as a threat to their traditional ways. Nevertheless, despite hopes that açaí trading may contribute to sustainable strategies, açaí has not yet served to persuade most peasants to take on this (sustainable) product as an alternative to illegal logging. It is complementary at best,[5] at least until there are clearer signs that açaí can be a stable base for security. In addition, most producers believe traders are not as exploitative as many (e.g. Brondízio, 2008) have suggested. They would often also like to trade and only see traders as a threat if margins seem unfair and if trade relations are not transparent. Market relations are not foreign to them.

More fundamental insecurities emanate from seasonality and the insecurities of service provision and social conditions (i.e. robberies).[6] Collective preferences are also nuanced. Solutions to their insecurities must be local and fair but also have a connection to institutions of power at higher levels where decisions on resourcing are made. Yet they are also wary of formal processes and power structures.

In summary, *ribeirinhos* are flexible in more ways than just their movement between fishing, gardening, cultivation/harvesting and transport (Pegler, 2015). Like many rural workers they move in and out of the formal system of regulation. The encroachment of the market is evident but control is more ambiguous as they live diversified livelihoods encompassing varied points of production, values and views on engagement with this 'new opportunity'. Açaí is a worthwhile engagement for this group but it is still not a very secure activity. Moreover, contrasts exist – subjectivity varies from idealism to pragmatism (e.g. açaí cultivation vs. wood extraction) and from individuality to collectivity (e.g. local vs. broader level voice options) and there remains a dominance of male preferences for production decisions, at least at an explicit level (cf. Simonian, 2001).

The addition of human security concepts to an augmented view of labour processes has provided this more detailed view of this mixed and ambiguous control situation. How this image is reflected in their responses to the growing formal governance of the açaí market, and in terms of their allegiance to other potential agencies of representation, forms the empirical part of the main section of this chapter.

Labour Agency in the Face of Evolving Market Structures and Rules

A widened arena for considering labour which embraces both formal and informal work within and outside the point of production also provides a more varied way of understanding the capacity of labour to shape GVCs (Pegler, 2015). In this regard, recent empirical work on this area of thought highlights a number of parameters for the consideration of agency. First, agency can be evident in the form of outright resistance yet it can also come in the form of a more subtle reshaping of current discourse or, simply, via silent resilience (Katz, 2004). Others underline the fact that agency neither has to be large scale nor contrary to the system per se (Herod, 2001; Bernstein, 2010). Yet all these views underline how agency is a conditioned reaction.

To thus understand whether and how these *ribeirinhos* are able to shape their environment first requires an understanding of what that environment (the power context) is. Furthermore, the context of power should be seen as taking many possible forms. It can be very explicit, such as the use of direct force, or it can be structural and less overtly controlling such as in the nature of the 'rules of the game' (e.g. of rules governing labour action/organization). A more subtle but pervasive vision of power is in the recognition that 'statements' affect the way agents see things, thus their chances and opportunities (Lukes, 1977).

This bringing together of the shades of power and agency helps this chapter's analysis move beyond a vision of chain governance as simply coordination (e.g. of labour use). The environment includes policies and structures yet power relations and hierarchies also drive the process. Moreover, there is a message of what the market and key 'drivers' hope from agents further down the chain (e.g. açaí codification and quality control/more efficient production organization) and this has implications for whether *ribeirinhos* are able to find space – i.e. exercise agency – and actually achieve improved wellbeing (social upgrading).

The following section uses this amplified view of governance (governmentality – Pegler, 2011) to describe the context facing these *ribeirinhos* and their agency. *Ribeirinhos*' preferred mechanisms for agency are thus better contextualized, especially when placed alongside their views of how other contenders (for giving voice to their desires) are seen (Pegler, 2015).

The Terrain for Labour Agency – A Governmentality Perspective

A fundamental human (in) security relates to whether agents feel they have voice (Sen, 1999). Governmentality analysis helps us frame voice options. It is a framework which takes us beyond (chain) governance as one of mere technical coordination (Barrientos *et al.*, 2011). It also makes the relational and contested concept of chain 'drivenness' (Gibbon and Ponte, 2008) more detailed in terms of how power and control are legitimized. Govermentality is about the message and how power acts on all actors to shape views of what is needed and eventuates.

Governmentality analysis first describes the nature of the dominant message – that is, what it is. It is also about explaining how this message is translated into (various/sometimes competing) plans or projects (programmes of government) and then how these are codified, measured and evaluated (technologies of government) (Huxley, 2008). The discourse (the initial message and any competing programmes) shapes legitimacy. The overall context (Foucault's Dispositive (Huxley, 2008)) is the dynamic relation of ideas, actors and agencies which define if and how ideas become 'real'. While this framing is sensitive to the fact that particular actors' views often come to dominate, this context is also defined by locational specifics such as the porosity of the locality to outside ideas and the nature of local values (Coe and Kelly, 2002).

The key analytical questions are therefore: (a) what is the message, nature of programmes and proposed technologies; (b) is the message believed/supported/contested; (c) are all voices heard and; (d) has this process acted to legitimate or modify the message? As such, governmentality goes beyond the concepts of coordination and 'drivenness' in that it more clearly defines the boundaries within which *ribeirinhos* have agency, not only to upgrade but to do this on their own terms. The following paragraphs analyse the dynamics of this dispositive for the case studies.

The town of Codajás is Amazonas state's cultural hub and the symbolic referent for açaí production for the case study communities. The establishment of the 'Planet Açaí' factory in Codajás in 2000 symbolized a local governmental vision to capture more of the value added by the lucrative açaí market. Supported by land, building, technology, management and quality advice from various government agencies,[7] the factory has the capacity to produce eight tons per day in various forms. Up to

2009, this publicly financed plant (and the cooperative of açaí producers who run it) had orders for both regional markets in Brazil (Rio, São Paulo) and (via suppliers, shippers and buyers in Manaus) in Canada and Europe.[8]

While the town had already solidified its regional reputation for the product (e.g. culturally, via their Açaí Festival since 1987), the 1990s–2000s saw a broader surge in national and then international demand. Yet by 2009 much of this reputation, as well as the factory/cooperative project and its effectiveness as an entity, began to wane. The factory lost its quality accreditation and international orders dried up due to disputes over transport and packaging.[9] Internal organizational and representational aspects of cooperative and factory operations also came to be questioned.

The original intention of the cooperative was to be a vehicle by which members' production would be channelled into markets via an organization run by and representing growers.[10] Ideally these members would be drawn from nearby, and from communities such as those in the case studies. Aside from the various technical problems they have had with electricity supply and quality processes, these production and representative goals have never been reached. The majority of local production (70 per cent) runs through Codajás port but not through the factory or cooperative.[11]

Attempts by the cooperative to be collective and redistribute income between seasons have always had problems due to the massive variations in price within each year. Transporters and traders can more easily use partial manufacturing (upgrading) options (e.g. 'wine' making) and preserve the product long enough (i.e. 'wine' in coolers/fruit delivered quickly by public carriers) to get it to clients in other locations, faster, in smaller quantities – still making enough to pay producers and cover costs.[12] This has greatly hampered the ability of the cooperative and factory to guarantee enough output to successfully operate all year round.[13]

As some[14] also note, even when the cooperative's price is adequate it is very slow in paying. Moreover, the cooperative has only ever once redistributed profits and many of the technical assistance and training initiatives they originally suggested have never come to fruition. In addition, most members are not actually producers – they are traders offloading (often excess) produce at the cooperative. Workers at the factory are generally family of those traders or supporters of management.[15] The representativeness of this state-supported model for promoting upgrading possibilities is in question.

There is not only a new election due for cooperative leaders but many new plans for the sector emanating from local and state officials.

A strategy is being developed to attempt to regain factory certification and reassert Codajás as the place for quality (and quantities of) açaí.[16] This involves local producers through attempts to include açaí as a product within schemes which guarantee local small-scale supplier content in (schools) food purchasing.[17] Yet, as with the factory and cooperative, which producers may benefit from this plan is questioned.

The message is clearly one of quality and efficiency for a growing market. This plan includes accessing various schemes[18] as well as broader state and federal government initiatives – to impose quality standards on growers (albeit with technical assistance to those who register), to support large-scale commercial farms and to monitor and codify supply across the region. The message, plans and technologies of governmentality – of formal processes of quality and efficiency – are being rejuvenated. However, these are not supported by most producers and it is not clear which producers may be included and whether the cooperative will really come to be representative of the needs of small-scale family producers.

Institutional supporters of this state-based upgrading and formalization process include various factions. For example, the (now previous) Mayor and the local Secretary of Agriculture (both also producers) support a plan for supply guarantees as well as government-sanctioned quality monitoring, codification and support. The local cooperative presently holds an important place in this plan. Yet the Secretary of Agriculture is more aligned with smaller artisanal producers and the Association of Açaí Growers. State government sustainability agency operatives (e.g. Institute of Development of Amazonas (IDAM)) are more involved in local production initiatives and try to be less involved in local power cliques involved in sector/city promotion. As discussed above, the case study families of this research are sceptical of these Codajás-based initiatives. Moreover, while they would like their representative bodies to hold some weight in those places where power 'resides', they also want their representative processes to be both local and practical.

The dominant message is being driven by local political leaders, who in turn are attempting to retain and harness state and federal agencies of support. All of these factions understand the importance of the level of economic activity due to açaí – sales largely controlled by local traders, regional buyers, processors and retailers. Some of these regional/capital city players have a degree of affinity with the idea of small-scale supplier promotion, inclusion and sustainability goals (e.g. Waku Sese, a prominent processor/retailer in Manaus). Yet the sector is increasingly driven by the commercial 'bottom line' of large-scale operatives. These large corporate interests are also those behind the expansion of monoculture plantation production of açaí beyond central Para state to regions in the case study state of Amazonas.[19] A question, then, is: have local representative bodies provided them with avenues to effectively counter these power structures and assert their agency?

Labour Agency – *Ribeirinho* Voice and Representation

This situation leaves little space for local agencies (e.g. the Rural Workers Union (STR), the Fish Industry Cooperative, the Association of Açaí Growers) to promote the producer voice (Pegler, 2015). For example, the STR is fundamentally an organization of agricultural workers and thus has difficulty getting too deeply involved with this not so easily definable group of workers. Their social security benefits are well recognized and they are trying to extend their agenda to *ribeirinhos*. Yet they see that, while much of the land security issue has been 'resolved',[20] further inroads into developing an active dialogue with local producers will be hard without institutionalized policies supporting local sourcing and local economic development. They are stretched to find the resources to develop a more effective agenda across this extensive region.

On the other hand, the more recent Fish Industry Cooperative has proved itself to be an effective organizer in a short period of time.[21] Riding on a wave of initiatives for fish cultivation (and the popularity of Amazonian varieties), their technical coordination of a successful out-of-season non-fishing subsidy seems to be a clever move. Equally local, but less effective, is the Association of Açaí Growers.[22] Their activities are more centred on the immediate township area. In contrast to these bodies are the networks of local residents' associations[23] – often informal and varied in their focus, activeness, philosophical orientation (some neutral, many Catholic or evangelical) and size. They are by definition local and immediate.

A large majority of producers felt that the cooperative was unreliable, unrepresentative and of little help.[24] In contrast, those involved in fish cultivation were positive about the Fish Industry Cooperative's credit, subsidy and advisory services. Older açaí growers are more likely to be members of the STR. It was the first main representative body in the region and it has social service/retirement benefits.[25] Most producers, on the other hand, prefer the immediate, local service function of community resident organizations, although they are annoyed by those organizations' lack of influence at levels where major resourcing decisions occur.

This analysis shows a large disjuncture between the top-down message coming producers' way and *ribeirinhos*' preferences for representation.

Producers from regions supplying Codajás with açaí are generally happy that the chain is evolving and with the idea of being part of further developments. They are, however, not happy with those who seem to be driving this process. Local political interests (sometimes aligned with larger-scale, downstream commercial operators) are trying to codify, impose rules (e.g. for quality), map the flow of output and formally integrate (thus tax) the sector more fully.

This emerging model of governance comes up against a population who live quite a fluid, flexible and informal existence (Pegler, 2015). The way these producers engage with the chain involves a combination of informal economic activities plus occasional, as-needed reliance on formal institutions. Their preferences for representation are local and social but also reflect a desire that their voice be heard in power circles. Yet most existing forms of representation fail to gather more than occasional, muted support as representatives of their need for practical help in overcoming local insecurities and in fulfilling their desire for açaí to become a more stable source of livelihood.

Even if commercial and NGO interests were to promote açaí as a sustainable livelihood strategy for *ribeirinhos*, their subjectivity highlights that this comes up against variable visions of sustainability and collectivity. The combined use of labour process and human security concepts (Pegler, 2015) has highlighted this variability, one implication being that, if sustainability is to be a driving force behind *ribeirinhos*' attempt to shape their situation, their livelihoods must be given a more secure base. Building on this, this section and chapter has analysed (using a governmentality framework) how their opportunities to upgrade have been constrained by local power structures and by deficiencies of existing representative bodies. *Ribeirinho* voices are not presently being heard nor adequately represented.

Implications – Are Labour-centred Chains Possible?

A central debate within the topical area of 'labour in value chains' is whether social upgrading is possible – what does it entail and how might this be promoted? This particular story (Pegler, 2015) of peasant labourers in an emerging chain highlights how their context has made control more diffuse and subjectivity more ambiguous than that suggested by authors such as Burawoy (1985; 2000). Multiple tasks and points of production plus governance/logistical uncertainties are key reasons for this. A broadened view of labour processes, incorporating insecurities in values, deepened the material and non-material basis upon which we could comment on wellbeing change as a result of chain inclusion.

Inherent conflicts between capital and labour are not so clearly defined. Workers are also producer families, distances are large and the governance of further production flows is in its infancy. Yet by seeing this as a combined process of coordination, formal expression of power and the message of the market, this chapter's further analysis suggests that antagonisms exist and are on the rise. Even now this incipient process leaves space for agency. This is helped by the fact that these peasants are fluid and flexible in their movement and tasks and in terms of their engagement with the market.

A labour-centred chain (one where the 'logic' of the market gives sufficient space for *ribeirinhos* to materially benefit and have a voice) may be possible but will require modalities of representation which are able to articulate the diversity of local needs as well as inspire confidence in their place in broader power structures. This is not only a question of structures and processes but of a will to include *ribeirinhos* by those involved in market development and social policy. A concrete example of this would be a reconsideration of monoculture as the (apparently) preferred future mode for açaí production. Yet this seems a far cry from what is occurring in the state of Para. Whatever emerges, the battle over social upgrading will be based on direct and indirect processes of action and reaction in this complex rural context.

Overall, this study enhances our understanding of concepts of agency, subjectivity and social upgrading. It has also underlined the view that research into, and the promotion of, social upgrading must link vertical chain considerations with local level (horizontal) social realities and viewpoints, including those emanating from a community and household level. This study would be well complemented by research in a number of complementary areas.

First, agency developments in fledgling chain environments could be compared with similar examples in regions where these chains are more fully developed. Secondly, this more variegated conceptualization of subjectivities (i.e. human-security augmented labour processes) could be applied to other regional communities and product studies. Finally, an understanding of such fledgling chains would be greatly enhanced by linking them to research into chain governance processes at the downstream level. That is, how are chain drivers such as logistics agents, buyers, importers and further processors (e.g. those in and around ports/global cities) acting so as to secure an adequate supply of the product, and what possibilities might this permit for production organization at the upstream (source) level?[26] A more integrated vision of governance across chains would give us a clearer picture of sustainability and of the spaces for social upgrading within it.

Notes

1 IBGE – production estimates, various years; while most is still consumed in Brazil (80 per cent), exports are growing fast and key foreign consumers are the US (10 per cent) and the Netherlands (3–4 per cent) (Binios 2012).
2 Debt servitude – a process by which families are kept poor/in debt by the actual landowner who takes part of their produce, charges for its transport and also charges for the return journey with groceries bought from the same landowner's shop.
3 The following (five paragraphs) comments on labour impacts are a summary based on Pegler (2015).
4 For example, estimated seasonal family açaí incomes from açaí range from 4,000–6,000 reais (around 2.5 times the national minimum salary per month over the season).
5 In fact, the more integrated a producer is in the açaí production process the more likely they are to be involved in illegal logging. Most tellingly, the more integrated a producer is in the açaí chain, the less the issue of sustainability is important to them (Pegler, 2015).
6 Pegler (2015); in contrast, fundamental insecurities of land tenure (thus income generation) have been removed for many *ribeirinhos* in recent years as state and federal agencies have declared much of these areas as theirs to use (i.e. as if they owned them/a right to occupy).
7 For example, technical bodies for planning (SUFRAMA), training (SEBRAE), certification (COB), and scientific analysis (EMBRAPA) – interviews, factory workers/Secretary of Agriculture (15 May 2012).
8 Interviews, factory workers/Secretary of Agriculture (15 May 2012).
9 Interviews, factory workers/Secretary of Agriculture (15 May 2012) and interviews with credit cooperative (14 May 2012) and transporters/buyers in region (various days).
10 Interview – cooperative members (14 May 2012).
11 Noted and confirmed by factory staff, governmental personnel and independent operators.
12 Noted in discussions with port traders (July 2012).
13 Interview, Secretary of Agriculture (15 May 2012).
14 Points below noted in various family interviews and in brief discussions with traders/sellers around Codajás.

15 Interviews, factory workers (15 May 2012).
16 Interview, Secretary of Agriculture, Codajás (15 May 2012) for this and the following comments.
17 i.e. via SEDUC – a state equivalent of the national PNAE schools food provision programme, and in applications for technical and financial assistance for growers (ARDS programme). ARDS is run through various banks and government agencies; PNAE and the state SEDUC programme reserve proportions of public purchasing for local and 'small-scale' farmers.
18 Ibid.
19 Noted in company visits in Para and Amazonas, May and July 2012.
20 Noted in interviews with STR (14 May 2012 and 15 May 2012); also see note 6.
21 For interview responses on collectivity, see Pegler 2015.
22 Ibid.
23 Ibid.
24 Ibid.
25 Ibid.
26 As is being done in the ISS/CAPES-NUFFIC project, 'Governance of Labour and Logistics for Sustainability (GOLLS)'.

REFERENCES

ADS (2011) *Agencia de DesenvolvimentoSustentaval do Amazonas*, www.ads.am.gov.br.
Barrientos, S., Gereffi, G. and Rossi, A. (2011) 'Economic and social upgrading in global production networks: a new paradigm for a changing world', *International Labour Review*, 150(3–4): 319–340.
Bernstein, H. (2010) *Class Dynamics and Agrarian Change*, Halifax/Winnipeg: Fernwood.
Binios, D. (2012) 'The obstacles to açaí exportation in Brazil', Unpublished MA in International Management, Sao Paulo: FGV.
Brondízio, E. (2008) *The Amazon Caboclo and the Açaí Palm: Forest Farmers in the Global Market*, New York: New York Botanical Garden Press.
Burawoy, M. (ed.) (2000) *Global Ethnography – Forces, Connections and Imaginations in a Postmodern World*, Berkeley: University of California Press.
Burawoy, M. (1985) *The Politics of Production*, London: Verso.
Carswell, G. and De Neve, G. (2012) 'Labouring for global markets: conceptualising labour agency in global production networks', *Geoforum*, http://dx.doi.org/10.1016/j.geoforum.2012.06.008, 1–9.
Castro, E. (1999) 'Tradição e Modernidade – A Propósito de Processos de Trabalhona Amazônia', *Novos Cadernos NAEA*, 2(1): 31–49.
Coe, N. and Kelly, P. (2002) '"Languages of Labour": representational strategies in Singapore's labour control regime', *Political Geography*, 21: 341–371.

Colapinto, J. (2011) 'Strange fruit – the rise and fall of açaí', *New Yorker*, 87(15).
Fraxe, T. de Jesus Pinto., Pereira, H. S. and Witkoski, A. Carlos (Orgs.) (2007) *Comunida des Ribeirinhas Amazônicas: Modos de Vida e Uso dos Recursos Naturais* (1st edition), Manaus: EDUA, pp. 1, 223.
Gasper, D. (2010) 'Understanding the diversity of conceptions of well-being and quality of life', *The Journal of Socio-Economics*, 39: 351–360.
Gasper, D. and George, S. (2010) *Cultivating humanity? Education and capabilities for a global 'great transition'*, Institute of Social Studies Working Paper 503, The Hague.
Gibbon, P. and Ponte, S. (2008) 'Global value chains: from governance to governmentality', *Economy and Society*, 37(3): 365–392.
Harilal, K., Kanji, N., Jeyaranjan, J., Eapen, M. and Swaminathan, P. (2006) *Power in Global Value Chains: Implications for Employment and Livelihoods in the Cashew Industry in India*, London: IIED, 1–36.
Harvey, D. (1982) *The Limits to Capital*, Oxford: Blackwell.
Heinrich, M., Dhanji, T. and Casseilman, I. (2011) 'Açaí (Euterpeoleracea Mart.) – A phytochemical and pharmacological assessment of the species' health claims' – review article, *Phytochemistry Letters*, 4(1): 10–21.
Herod, A. (2001) *Labor Geographies: Workers and the Landscapes of Capitalism*, New York: Guildford Press.
Huxley, M. (2008) 'Space and government: governmentality and geography', *Geography Compass*, 2(5): 1635–1658.
IBGE/CensoAgropecuário (2006 and 2010), http://www.sidra.ibge.gov.br/.
IBGE – Produção da Extração Vegetal e da Silvicultura, 2012.
Katz, C. (2004) *Growing up Global: Economic Restructuring and Children's Everyday Lives*, Minnesota: University of Minnesota Press.
Kelly, P. (2002) 'Spaces of labour control: comparative perspectives from Southeast Asia', *Trans. Inst Br. Geogr*, 27: 395–411.
Kelly, P. (2009) 'From global production networks to global reproduction networks: households, migration, and regional development in Cavite, Philippines', *Regional Studies*, 43(3): 449–461.
Kelly, P. (2012) 'Labor movement: migration, mobilities and geographies of work', in T. Barnes, J. Peck and E. Sheppard (eds) *The Wiley – Blackwell Companion to Economic Geography*, Oxford: Blackwell Publishing.
Knorringa, P. and Pegler, L. (2006) 'Globalisation, firm upgrading and impacts on labour', *TESG – Journal of Social Geography – Special Issue*, 97(5): 468–477.
Lukes, S. (1977) *Power – a Radical View* (3rd edition), London: Macmillan.
Neilson, J. and Pritchard, B. (2010) 'Fairness and ethicality in their place: the regional dynamics of fair trade and ethical sourcing agendas in the plantation districts of South India', *Environment and Planning*, 42: 1833–1851.
Newsome, K. (2010) 'Employment in distribution and exchange: moments in the circuit of capital', *Industrial Relations Journal*, 41(3): 190–205.
Pegler, L. (2011) *Sustainable value chains and labour – linking chain drivers and 'inner drivers'*, ISS Working Paper 525, The Hague.

Pegler, L. (2015; forthcoming) 'Peasant Inclusion in global value chains: economic upgrading but social downgrading in labour processes?' *Journal of Peasant Studies*.

Pereira, H. S. (2012) Human Security under Globalisation: Value Chains as Opportunities or Constraints? The Case of Açaí, DevISSues, ISS, Den Haag, 4–5.

SDS – Secretaria de Estado do Meio Ambiente e Desenvolvimento Sustentável (2005) 'Cadeia Produtiva do Açaí no Estado do Amazonas', Série Técnica, Manaus.

Selwyn, B. (2013) 'Social upgrading and labour in global production networks: a critique and an alternative conception', *Competition and Change*, 17(1): 75–90.

Sen, A. (1999) *Development as Freedom*, Oxford: Oxford University Press.

Simonian, L. (2001) *Mulheres da FlorestaAmazônica: Entre o Trabalho e a Cultura*, Belém: NAEA/UFPA.

Taylor, P., Newsome, K. and Rainnie, A. (2013) 'Putting labour in its place: global value chains and labour process analysis' – editorial', *Competition and Change*, 17(1): 1–5.

Truong, T. (2006) *Human security and the governmentality of neo-liberal mobility: a feminist perspective*, Institute of Social Studies, Working Paper 432, Den Haag.

CHAPTER 13

The Apple Ecosystem and App Developers: A GPN Analysis

Birgitta Bergvall-Kåreborn and Debra Howcroft

Introduction

Apple Inc. is viewed by many as a unique company with trendy products and quirky inventors, setting it apart from the more staid corporations that typify the IT industry. Historically, the computer industry has provided a clear distinction between hardware and software, yet the Apple business model is based on the interconnection of both elements, which involves distinct global sourcing strategies. Hardware production networks are based on a low-cost manufacturing model that involves outsourcing to developing economies (Froud et al., 2014); software development requires the creation of intangible products by a highly skilled, technical workforce which is predominantly based within Western economies. While success is reflected in the stock market, reports of exploitative working conditions in Asian manufacturing plants have had a negative impact on Apple's brand and reputation (Chan et al., 2013). For Apple, the outsourcing of hardware manufacture represents 'business as usual', but the recent shift to the external sourcing of digital content represents a step-change in Apple's business model.

Given the hyperbole in the ICT industry surrounding firms such as Google, Facebook, and Twitter, understanding how 'new economy business models' (Lazonick, 2009) capture and generate value from delivering services to users/consumers is seen as worthy of study. One approach that enables an in-depth analysis of the connections between globalizing processes, as embodied in the production networks of large firms, concerns how economic activities are coordinated and organized using long chains or networks (e.g. Gereffi, 1994; Dicken et al., 2001). This body of research provides a grounded way to examine globalization in situ and interrogate how power is exercised in transnational firms (Bair, 2005). While a number of variants that fall under the rubric of network/chain approaches exist, this chapter will draw upon the Global Production Network (GPN) perspective to inform the analysis.

A GPN analysis has been selected since it is seen to be particularly advantageous when examining the social relations of production and reflecting upon the condition of labour (Taylor et al., 2013). However, for many GPN scholars, labour is merely one element that comprises a part of the analysis. By contrast, the aim of this chapter is to foreground the labour dimension of the Apple business model by focusing on high-tech labour and the concept of crowdsourcing. Our interest lies in analysing the interconnections between Apple as the lead firm and the multitude of applications developers that provide digital content through the online supply of their labour (known as crowdsourcing). This will enable detailing of the role of the labour force in relation to value capture and enhancement, while recognizing power asymmetries between the lead firm and external content suppliers. The chapter begins by discussing the various network perspectives before outlining the evolution of mobile applications development and distribution (MADD), situating this emerging phenomenon within the context of the IT industry. The next section provides an overview of the research methodology, followed by the empirical observations of the study. Data are analysed using the GPN framework, specifically the focus on value creation, power asymmetries, and embeddedness. Finally, conclusions are drawn.

Networks and Chains

In the frameworks that comprise network/chain approaches, the literature is eclectic and offers distinct intellectual positioning, which is reflected in the different terminologies and differing levels of analysis employed (Bair, 2005). Despite variations, the three approaches of GCC, GVC and GPN constitute a loosely integrated tradition (Levy, 2008) and all three might be better viewed as complementary rather than contending paradigms, given that these approaches share a common interest in 'making visible the structured connections that organize the global economy' (Bair, 2008: 359). Drawing on various elements of GCC and GVC research, the GPN approach provides a more expansive picture.

According to Coe *et al.* (2004: 471), GPN allows us to appreciate 'the globally organised nexus of interconnected functions and operations by firms and non-firm institutions through which goods and services are produced and distributed'. It aims to understand the connections between globalizing processes as embodied in the production networks of transnationals and regional development in specific territorial formations. In this regard, GPNs should be viewed as contested fields, consisting not only of firms but also of a diversity of actors and institutions, each with their own interests (Levy, 2008).

The GPN framework as explicated by Henderson *et al.* (2002) provides three key conceptual categories: how value is created, enhanced and captured (which is pivotal to understanding business models); how power is created and maintained within the production network; and how agents and structures are embedded in particular territories. These three elements facilitate an understanding of Apple, enabling a conceptualization of the production network, yet crucially extending traditional business model analysis, given the attention paid to power and embeddedness. A specifically network focus reveals the complex circulation of capital, knowledge and people that underlies the production of goods and services, and it acknowledges the multiple linkages and feedback loops that are entailed in processes of value capture and creation (Coe *et al.*, 2008). Adopting a GPN perspective recognizes the dynamic nature of production networks, which are in a permanent state of flux. Such an approach emphasizes interdependencies within production networks, enabling us to hone in on issues of control and coordination, and illuminates the processes of network governance and the fluidity of the power relationships that exist between different actors (Cumbers *et al.*, 2008).

Although GPN offers a useful framework for understanding inter-firm networks in the context of globalization, a crucial element that is notably under-researched is labour, which is simply viewed as a commodity and assumed to be intrinsic to the production process (Coe *et al.*, 2008; Cumbers *et al.*, 2008). As Cumbers *et al.* (2008: 372) note, ultimately, GPNs are 'networks of embodied labor' that are embroiled within particular geographies of work and employment, yet the centrality of labour is rarely acknowledged (aside from exceptions such as Taylor, 2010). Indeed, understanding evolving labour-capital relations is vital to the development of GPNs, and researchers argue that investigating how labour may co-determine processes of capitalist development should be placed at the centre of GPN analysis (Rainnie *et al.*, 2011; Selwyn, 2012; Taylor *et al.*, 2013). Given this lacuna in much of the current GPN literature, the labour dimension will be at the forefront of this study.

The Apple Platform and the Evolution of Mobile Applications Development and Distribution

As Apple's product development continues to attract attention, much of the enhanced market share can be attributed to the embedding of artefacts into a platform that links together hardware products with digital content. Apple's product range includes the iPhone, iPod, iPad, iMac and Apple TV, technologies which are enhanced by a variety of services, including the sale of digital content and applications through the App Store, iTunes and iBookstore. The combination of product innovation along with digital content has been complemented by the growing importance of proprietary platforms (Cusumano, 2010). Apple's major inroad into the mobile market is centred on a platform-based ecosystem that comprises hardware and software, and which functions like a market while coordinating supply and demand. The strength of the ecosystem rests on controlling the core platform, which provides a foundation on which third-party firms can develop complementary services and products, thereby generating 'network effects' (Gawer and Cusumano, 2014).

In terms of digital content production, it was not until the launch of the iPhone in 2007 that the market for mobile applications opened up to third-party developers willing to provide applications and services. Apple unveiled its platform in 2008 and released the Software Development Kit (SDK), allowing developers to create applications. Apple sets the parameters for the development environment, and its reputation for tight corporate control and high levels of centralization (Cusumano, 2010) is evident in platform construction and coordination. It regulates the development process via its SDK, which determines precisely the type of software functionality that can be made publicly available. In 2010 Apple bolstered its control with the release of numerous guidelines, which determine which applications will be available for general release. The distribution channel is mediated by Apple, which can halt an application's release if deemed inappropriate or unsuitable.

Between the inception of the App Store in 2008 and 2013, more than 775,000 apps have been made available, with more than 40 billion downloads (Apple, 2013). The App Store provides developers with a link to users; they set their own price for the application and retain 70 per cent of sales and in-app advertising revenues. In January 2013, developers had earned more than USD 7 billion from app downloads which, given that Apple takes 30 per cent of revenues, equates to around USD 3 billion for

Apple (Apple, 2013). These figures translate into developers receiving an average of 17.5 cents per app download, which includes all in-app purchases and revenues. When these transactions are combined, the figures are substantial: the App Analytics firm Distimo cites a 'typical day' in November 2012, when revenues in the App Store generated in excess of USD 15 million, although there is considerable clustering, with seven applications accounting for 10 per cent of revenue (Distimo, 2012).

For consumers, the appeal of Apple's hardware devices is connected with the availability of diverse online content and services, which requires a stream of innovation to sustain interest. In opening up the platform to third-party developers, Apple has outsourced some of its software development to a global base of external contributors, thereby minimizing its own risk while developers create applications that may or may not be successful. This particular form of sourcing has been termed 'crowdsourcing' (Brabham, 2008), which takes place when an organization uses a digital platform to leverage the crowd (as external resources) to contribute to tasks that could alternatively be performed internally by employees or contractors. This usually takes the form of an open call over the Internet, and in the case of Apple, the call is restricted to registered members of the platform. While there are no contractual obligations regarding platform members' productivity, Apple orchestrates a centralized hub that steers the network. Crowdsourcing labour is not necessarily free, although the costs are substantially less than those associated with more traditional forms of employment (Kleeman *et al.*, 2008). However, in Apple's case, there is no direct remuneration provided for the development and supply of mobile applications; instead, development costs are borne entirely by the developers themselves.

Researching Mobile Applications Development

In 2009, a qualitative study of developers' experiences of mobile applications development and distribution (MADD) was undertaken. The study covered Sweden, the UK, and the US, given their significant levels of maturity in the mobile marketplace, and it included both Apple and Google developers. The aim was to capture the everyday working experiences of developers with varying expertise and a mixture of employment contracts. In total 60 developers were recruited using social media channels; this group comprised 22 Apple developers and 38 Google developers, with the former being the focus here. A mixture of face-to-face, co-located interviews, synchronous Skype interviews, and asynchronous online discussion forums were adopted, depending on preferences and geographical location (Table 13.1). Interviews lasted from one to two hours; all were recorded

Table 13.1 Number and type of interviews

ID no.	Number of Apple Developers	Date	Residence	Format
1	One	June 2009 and November 2012	UK	Skype interview
2	One	June 2009	UK	Face-to-face focus group
3–9	Seven	September 2009	USA	Online forum
10–11	Two	September 2009	USA	Online forum
12–13	Two	August 2010	Sweden	Face-to-face focus group
14	One	September 2009	UK	Face-to-face interview
15	One	September 2009	UK	Face-to-face interview
16–17	Two	September 2009	UK	Face-to-face focus group
18	One	September 2009	UK	Face-to-face interview
19	One	September 2009	UK	Face-to-face interview
20–21	Two	September 2009	UK	Face-to-face focus group
22	One	September 2009	UK	Skype interview

and transcribed. Two online forums were created, which lasted for ten days, with a question posted daily. Every participant answered each question and often commented on others' answers, thereby generating debate in a similar way to that of a focus group. Some of the data collection activities (focus groups and forums) involved mixed groups of Apple and Google developers. The participation of Apple developers, either individually or as part of a larger constituency, is reflected in Table 13.1. The ID number of each participant is identified in the direct reporting of the fieldwork.

The Developers' Profile

The developers had extensive platform knowledge, with publishing experience ranging from one to 45 applications, with around half of the developers having published between ten and 40. There were differences in levels of success as the number of downloads for their *most successful* application ranged from over one million to just over 10,000, but there were examples of some applications receiving zero downloads. The amount of revenue generated also varied widely – from USD 150,000 from one application to just USD 50 for a developer with six applications.

Some developers worked on outsourced applications, but the majority 'owned' the product they were developing. The developers represented a diversity of employment types, often experiencing multiple types of employment simultaneously, such as formal employment and subcontracting in their leisure time. More than half of the participants were self-employed, either working as contractors or managing their own start-up. Of interest is the small proportion of developers that are formally employed to develop apps compared with those that are formally employed but develop apps as a sideline, outside the boundaries of the firm. Even for the formally employed, the sector predominantly consists of micro firms and there is an expectation of 'enterprising' behaviour (Barrett, 2001). In the following sections, when presenting the results of our study, quotations will be followed by a number indicating a specific respondent listed in table 13.1.

Findings from the Study: The Organization of Mobile Applications Development and Distribution

In this section, analysis of the fieldwork is presented using a GPN perspective, based on the analytical schema outlined by Henderson *et al.* (2002). This framework covers the three conceptual categories of value creation and enhancement, power, and embeddedness.

Capturing and Creating Value

Henderson *et al.*'s (2002) explication of GPNs suggests that firms are able to capture value from various sources, including product and process technologies, inter-firm relationships, and brand-name prominence. Regarding Apple, the digital platform is crucial to value creation and acts as a conduit that steers the development process, while the App Store serves as a distribution channel through the online marketplace. According to Apple's Annual Report (2011), enhancing the platform is seen as central to its strategy because the provision of 'a strong third-party software and peripherals ecosystem' supports the planned expansion of mobile devices.

Pivotal to value creation is Apple's ability to draw on a crowdsourcing workforce. Employing software developers is costly to firms, and controlling their productivity is notoriously difficult (Barrett, 2001; Marks and Huzzard, 2010). Apple is able to create significant value by avoiding the direct costs of software development, as risk is outsourced to the developers themselves. Crowdsourcing mobile applications entails a move away from salaried forms of exchange within an internal labour market to an external market of competing developers, thus allowing Apple to avoid the incurred costs of the employment contract while profiting from the productivity of what is effectively a volunteer workforce. Handing over to workers the task of transforming their potential into concrete performance is a means of transferring the problem to those who create it, thereby overcoming the indeterminacy of labour. By placing responsibility for productivity firmly at the door of developers themselves, capital is able to reap productivity benefits while eliminating the costs of monitoring and controlling. Apple acknowledges the centrality of externally provided digital content as follows: 'The Company's future performance depends in part on support from third-party software developers'. Although the number of apps currently available seems to imply that the supply of content from third-party developers can be depended upon, averaging revenues of 17.5 cents per download may be unsustainable for developers in the long-term.

Ordinarily, labour is far less mobile than capital, which underlines the importance of place in production processes (see for example, IT offshoring and the temporality of spatial advantages). Within the IT industry, high-skilled technical developers have a tendency to gravitate towards clusters of activity (e.g. Silicon Valley, Amsterdam) (Saxenian, 1992; Gill, 2007), and these clusters tend to materialize as high-cost, city-based labour. While understanding the geographical role of a particular node in a global production network remains important (Rainnie *et al.*, 2011), what is of interest is the way in which the platform operates as the node for organizing app development and distribution, thereby enabling Apple to leverage labour from the crowd workforce, negating spatial restrictions and the costs associated with employing a high-tech, urban labour force.

Apple creates additional value by skimming 30 per cent of the price or in-app advertising revenue from each app that is purchased or downloaded. Apple recommends pricing categories, which impose normative control to the extent that the majority of applications sit within predefined (low-price) categories. Top-slicing 30 per cent does cause resentment, however:

> I find it very unfair that 30% of my application bill goes to a company that had nothing to do with it. Apple gets the money from the actual hardware [iPhone] and even the software [SDK] they created. When you develop apps this makes the phone better, so Apple shouldn't then be making money out of developers as well. (2)

Apple's brand is significant in attracting consumers, which then draws developers to the platform in anticipation of potential earnings: 'They are very successful and their success means our success' (5). For developers, the combination of product features, the online marketplace, and promising consumer demand means that they are willing to invest their time and resources in developing apps:

> The store provides access to a huge marketplace with a real opportunity to make money. This opens up the opportunity to market to millions and millions of people. Because of the App Store and general hype I don't think any other platform comes even close to the revenues you get from your applications. The other platforms are generally missing one or more of those elements. (14)

For Apple, value creation also stems from its low-cost manufacturing model and high levels of profitability on hardware products. For example, net sales in 2010 increased 52 per cent compared with 2009 (USD 22.3 billion), with a further increase of 66 per cent in 2011 (USD 43 billion); the gross margin for 2009–2011 hovers at approximately 40 per cent. For Apple, hardware and software are increasingly interdependent and the growth of hardware sales is interlinked with the provision of software applications and services. While Apple's hardware products may be perceived as innovative, their value enhancement lies in the hosting of external digital content. This is acknowledged by Apple: 'The Company believes decisions by customers to purchase its hardware products depend in part on the availability of third-party software applications and services ... If third-party software applications and services cease to be developed and maintained for the Company's products, customers may choose not to buy the Company's products' (Apple, 2012: 13). Developers provide the intellectual labour and content, which, when aggregated, has a combined value for Apple that is far higher than revenue generated. The platform facilitates access to digital content through online stores, which operate as automated services with low costs and potentially high profit margins (Cusumano, 2010).

In terms of the circulation processes through which the various nodes in the GPN are connected, logistics and the coordination of intricate operations remain of central importance (Coe *et al.*, 2008). A further advantage of the digital platform is that it helps to alleviate logistics problems. The App Store builds on the existing infrastructure of iTunes, which is operational in approximately 120 countries with plans for further expansion (Apple, 2012). Apple's ability to develop efficient circulation processes within the GPN adds to its success and enhances value creation. However, for developers, logistics is about far more than simple distribution. Although the App Store serves as a delivery channel, one developer commented: 'My opinion is that marketing is pretty important. In all cases but the most extreme, if you just put your app on the store and sit, it will fall into the abyss' (3). The importance of marketing was a recurring theme and various strategies were revealed (such as social networking), with one developer suggesting:

> Both the Android market and App Store are bad distribution channels. They yield something, but nothing sizable for sure, not enough for you to get in touch with your customer base. Blogs and other means seem to be much more valuable distribution channels. I think this is the Achilles heel of the mobile app space. (10)

Market structures are such that generating interest from consumers is crucial, but given that the App Store offers limited showcasing beyond the 'top of highlighted popular apps', responsibility for achieving visibility and generating downloads is undertaken by individual developers.

Power Asymmetries: Key Actors and Stakeholders

From a GPN perspective, power asymmetries arise when lead firms have an enhanced capacity to influence decisions and resource allocations – vis-à-vis other firms in the network – consistently in their own interests (Henderson et al., 2002). In the context of the IT industry, sectoral transformation has resulted in a bifurcation, with large firms consolidating their position as the proportion of small firms increases, confirmed by studies in Australia (Barrett, 2001), the Netherlands (Gill, 2007), Sweden (Sandberg et al., 2007), the UK (Marks and Huzzard, 2010) and the US (Batt et al., 2001). These adjustments have resulted in shifting geographies and changing power relationships between actors.

For Apple, the internalization and externalization of functions are in a continuous state of flux, reconfiguring organizational boundaries as they expand third-party sourcing, while maintaining centralized control over development and distribution within the network. Apple's ability to increase its revenue is the outcome of power negotiations with other actors and arises from its market position. It is this strong market position that attracts large numbers of developers:

> Apple ... that's where the market is. I can get the biggest bang for my buck, and rather than spend time porting to additional platforms, I'm focused on enhancing my apps and creating new ones for the Apple platform. (6)

However, actors' power within the network is not simply about relative size and financial clout (Coe *et al.*, 2008); it also depends on the extent to which actors possess assets, the scarcity of these assets, and the extent to which the assets can be controlled. Many developers are in a relatively weak negotiating position with Apple. The commodities being supplied can be easily replaced, they often have a short shelf life, and there is a demand for continuous upgrades, with one developer commenting: 'Another app may come out that offers similar functionality, and the developer has to decide if they can still compete, whether they need to change features, or just scrap the project' (10). Consequently, price-cutting occurs:

> The top 50 list is just flooded with 99-cent applications. Some individual developers say that those prices are too low to get any money, real money. But that's not really Apple's problem – it is the developers' problem. (4)

Developers exist within a crowded and highly competitive marketplace, vying for the attention of both consumers and Apple. The sheer scale of contributions means that third-party content providers have limited bargaining power in this anonymous environment. While some may opt to work on another platform such as Android, overall, they are relatively isolated in terms of network connectivity, occupying a peripheral position. Of particular concern is the process whereby Apple ultimately decides whether applications are permitted in the App Store: 'I have several apps that have spent several months in the approval queue and still aren't approved' (16). A common theme centred around 'the slow and terribly inconsistent app review process' (8), with one developer remarking on his irritation over Apple's ability to curtail his creative freedom: 'I have had to remove features to get an app approved, and the result is less than ideal ... the app is less attractive' (20).

When working in an uncertain market where the future strategy of Apple is undisclosed and with extreme secrecy surrounding product launches, maximizing revenue is key to survival. Neither cost recovery nor income generation can be guaranteed, resulting in unpredictable income levels. Some developers offered their application for free to encourage downloads and stimulate interest, as evidenced in figures suggesting that around one third of applications are available for free (Distimo, 2011a). However:

> Freebies happen in other industries as well, but the difference is that for most industries the free sample is the same as the paid and it is a small

sample that runs out, such as shampoo. Here, the free version is often so good that it stands on its own, it does not run out, have a time limitation, and so it drives up the expectations on the paid app. (18)

GPNs are embedded within multi-scalar regulatory systems (Coe *et al.*, 2008), and their operations can become more seamless if codifiable standards that enable the lead firm to establish dominant forms of governance are created. Different geographical and institutional contexts shape labour conditions and often play a key role in affecting decisions regarding where to locate. In the case of Apple, drawing on crowd-sourced labour means that these regulations are less relevant. However, of significance are the standards that govern the structure of the platform-based network, including the SDK, the approval process, and the distribution mechanism, all of which have been constructed by Apple. These standardizing initiatives have considerable impact in terms of the territories or networks that are being covered. For example, in creating the App Store, Apple was able to build on the legal and financial infrastructure of iTunes, thereby enhancing geographical spread (In December 2009, for example, paid applications for Apple were available in 77 countries, whereas the figure for Android was eight).

When examining power relations, it is important to recognize the cyclical nature of the industry. While many developers have a technical education, continuous competence development is necessary to survive the jobs market. A number of developers commented on the inadequacy of resources and support for iOS development, preferring to look elsewhere: 'I almost never use the Apple-provided resources. If I need help, I'll use Google, then iPhoneDevSDK, then my fellow developer contacts' (12). While wider social networks offer support for experienced developers, they nevertheless acknowledged the difficulties facing those starting out: 'For beginners it might be daunting to find information ... iOS development resources seem a bit scarce to me' (15).

Apple is renowned for extreme secrecy surrounding product launches, but given the interdependence of hardware and software, developers need to quickly adapt when new products are released, amending their apps to ensure compatibility. This lack of transparency is particularly problematic for larger projects:

> Let's say you write an application and it is going to take you six months, then you have to be targeting devices not as they exist now but how they are going to exist in half a year's time. If they [Apple] are not going to tell you how long it is going to take to add that feature, or they are not even going to tell you what they are going to do

within those six months, it becomes very difficult to undertake a project with any sort of confidence (19).

Power differentials extend beyond Apple's opacity, as numerous developers remarked on their sense of powerlessness in relation to Apple's ability to influence their future:

> I mean in a way they are kind of guardians, because they can make or break us. If they decide that they do not like us any more, and that they do not want to promote us, that would make a big difference in how much money we make. They are very much custodians of their marketplace so you've got to be well behaved. (1)

As GPN research informs us, networks are imbued with various types of power relationships and these are not necessarily unidirectional. The network can be comprised of actors that are involved in collaboration and cooperation as well as conflict and competition. There are antagonisms between different sets of actors contingent on their positions in relation to the processes of value capture (Cumbers *et al.*, 2008). Prior to Apple's incursion into the MADD market, there were limited opportunities for accessing this marketplace and so many developers viewed crowdsourcing as opening up opportunities. Yet the primary power dynamic within the GPN is unidirectional, with Apple taking on the role of an industry bottleneck (Parker *et al.*, 2014) as developers endeavour to survive in a climate of intense competition. As the following example shows, Apple chooses to nurture relationships with developers who create popular apps, since attractive content enhances their own market position. This is entirely at their discretion.

> In 2009 the GymFu application suddenly sold very well, making USD 10–20,000 per month ... and the reason it was so successful was that a person at Apple promoted us. Internally, the way it works is that they have a review team and if any of the reviewers think that a new application is really good they escalate it to their managers. And then their managers make a selection of a few applications to be promoted ... If that sort of thing happens to you, you can imagine that it can be pretty intense ... And the great thing with our relationship with Apple is that it's very much a two-way relationship. I mean we speak with them about our development schedule and they recommend new features, ideas and approaches, but this does not change the fact that if they do not like something we've done they will not approve it. (1)

Developers generate work based on respect and recognition from their occupational communities, and the project-based nature of the work means they become reliant on contacts. While developers simply exist as the 'crowd' to Apple, many developers regularly and actively participate in networks since they serve as a key conduit of knowledge about job opportunities, technological developments and firms. Importantly, developers can help neutralize power differentials by creating a form of collective power, relying upon these communities for support in surviving crowdsourcing and sharing experiences of the precarious nature of working life. Social networks help foster collegiality and enable developers to cope with highly fragmented labour markets while being leveraged as a mechanism for work distribution.

The Embeddedness of Mobile Applications

GPNs can be influenced by both territorial embeddedness and network embeddedness. The former refers to how the socio-political context of particular forms of capitalism shapes the territoriality of production networks (Henderson *et al.*, 2002). Firms are grounded spatially, both materially, in terms of fixed assets and headquarters, and also in terms of less tangible aspects, such as their institutionalized and cultural practices. While Apple is geographically extensive, its identity is evidenced in its Annual Report: 'The Company is a California corporation' (Apple, 2013). Apple is firmly anchored in Silicon Valley, and this territorial or societal embeddedness within a regional economy that is renowned for technological innovation remains an important influence. Silicon Valley is also the birthplace of the 'New Economy Business model' (Lazonick, 2009), which is a way of organizing business enterprises that has altered how people are employed, a process that initially affected workers in the US and then filtered through to other regions. This mode of employment is characterized by volatile stock markets, unequal incomes, unstable employment, the offshoring of high-skill jobs and insecurity. It is this shifting labour market that frames the sourcing of digital content to third-party developers and arguably legitimizes this way of working.

Stressing the virtual aspect of the crowdsourced labour force is not intended to negate the spatial elements of MADD. As the mobile apps market has become increasingly internationalized, cultural differences remain important considerations for developers. The majority of apps originate in the US given that the iPhone and App Store were initially launched there, and this region continues to dominate, with UK developers capitalizing on their cultural proximity. In 2012, of the ten most profitable cross-store publishers among 20 of the largest countries for Apple (and Google), five were US-based and three were European (Distimo, 2012). There are clear geographical distinctions regarding the popularity of apps; the proportion of paid versus free apps; the popularity of in-app purchases; the proportion of apps that are regionally, rather than internationally, targeted; and the average price. Much of this reflects economic levels within regions, as well as market maturity (Distimo, 2011b). The Asian market is the fastest growing and is also most sensitized to regionally focused apps, which could have implications for developers in the longer term. The distinction between markets was noted:

> There are numerous app stores and being top at one app store doesn't make you top on the others. There are eight Master App Stores (e.g., the US, Japan, the UK, Australia) and unless you get there, you won't make money. (7)

In terms of network embeddedness, actors participate because they are unable to individually generate the resources and infrastructure that are required for the development and distribution of mobile apps, enabling Apple to maintain control of external complementary assets. Having invested time and resources in participating in the network, there are high switching costs associated with changing platforms, thereby creating lock-in and bolstering Apple's market position. A developer explained the downside of transferring to another platform:

> The domain for mobile apps presents unique needs and solutions. Screen real estate, processing power and data abilities vary across each mobile device. A solution that works and looks good on an Apple or Android phone may not port well to a BlackBerry or other device. The effort to port these apps to new languages and devices could be as much as the effort in developing a new application. (9)

The Apple ecosystem displays high levels of network embeddedness as the platform facilitates the organization of different actors across the network and links products, services, content, and gateways to markets, thereby creating and enhancing value. For consumers, lock-in occurs as they acquire a wide range of complementary products for different functions, and the incompatibility of cross-platform devices solidifies their brand allegiance. Typically, strong network embeddedness arises when a process of trust building occurs between the different actors (Henderson et al., 2002). However, in the case of Apple, the 500 million active accounts on the App Store and the significant number of developers supplying products mean that their central position of control is one that maintains control at a distance. Entrenched network embeddedness does not necessarily arise from a position of trust, but from necessity (in terms of the labour market) as the suppliers of digital content wager on Apple's continuing success. As noted in the previous section, building relationships takes place in an environment of asymmetrical power relations, and the power of Apple is enhanced by its ability to foster high levels of network embeddedness while wielding maximum control.

Conclusion

The aim of this chapter has been to apply a GPN analysis to Apple, with a particular focus on the external sourcing of digital content. Applying the framework reveals the value of not simply adding labour to the mix of our understanding of GPNs, but instead recognizing the critical role played by labour in shaping GPNs. For Apple, profit maximization is primarily realized through hardware sales, which are fuelled by third-party digital content provision. Providing content on such a significant scale crucially rests on the participation of external labour – as recognized by Apple – hence the willingness to open up the platform, creating intense competition among developers, while enhancing central control and market share.

The power base within the mobile industry has adjusted over a relatively short period, with Apple quickly rising to prominence. It controls a centralized platform for development and distribution, constructing a circuit of production whereby micro companies and individual developers create products and market them in vertically disintegrated systems. Apple's success can be attributed to various interrelated elements: the uptake of Internet-enabled devices; enhanced content-driven functionality; Apple's brand reputation and infrastructure; and the success of crowdsourcing. The distinctive aspect of this buyer-seller network is the centralization of control via the platform, which provides the gateway to consumers while leveraging the crowd to boost capital. Developers shoulder the burden of costs while Apple circumvents the investment and resources required for in-house product development and marketing. This is the essence of crowdsourcing, as corporations harness creative labour at little or no cost, while minimizing risk.

By conceptualizing Apple's business activities in GPN terms, it has been possible to examine how and by whom value is captured at various stages of the production network, thus highlighting how development and distribution is controlled by Apple. The platform enables the weaving together of artefacts with a multitude of content, which, when combined, considerably enhance value. Our exploration of the nature of the relationships between the various actors reveals glaring power asymmetries, with Apple maintaining centralized control and keeping a tight grip on the network of development and distribution. These shifts are reflective of wider sectoral trends, as the increasing domination of multinational firms like Apple solidifies their power base. Strong ties and network embeddedness enhance Apple's dominance, as both consumers and third-party developers become increasingly locked into the Apple platform. Placing the strengthening power base of Apple in the broader context of the widespread adoption of mobile devices implies increasing restrictions for both consumers and developers.

REFERENCES

Apple (2011) *Annual Report*, Filed 26 October 2011.
Apple (2012) *Annual Report*, Filed 31 October 2012.
Apple (2013) *Apple Press Info: App Store Tops 40 Billion Downloads with Almost Half in 2012*, http://www.apple.com/pr/library/2013/01/07App-Store-Tops-40-Billion-Downloads-with-Almost-Half-in-2012.html.
Bair, J. (2005) 'Global capitalism and commodity chains: looking back, going forward', *Competition & Change*, 9(2): 153–180.
Bair, J. (2008) 'Analysing global economic organization: embedded networks and global chains compared', *Economy and Society*, 37(3): 339–364.
Barrett, R. (2001) 'Labouring under an illusion? the process of software development in the Australian information industry', *New Technology, Work and Employment*, 16(1): 18–34.
Batt, R., Christopherson, S., Rightor, N. and van Jaarsvald, D. (2001) *Networking: Work Patterns and Workforce Policies for the New Media Industry*, Washington: Economic Policy Institute.
Brabham, D. (2008) 'Crowdsourcing as a model for problem solving, convergence', *The International Journal of Research into New Media Technologies*, 14(1): 75–90.
Chan, J., Ngai, P. and Selden, M. (2013) 'The politics of global production: Apple, Foxconn and China's new working class', *New Technology, Work and Employment*, 28(2): 100–115.
Coe, N., Dicken, P. and Hess, M. (2008) 'Global production networks: realising the potential', *Journal of Economic Geography*, 8: 271–295.
Coe, N., Hess, M., Wai-Chung, H., Dicken, P. and Henderson, J. (2004) 'Globalising regional development', *Transactions of Institute of British Geographers*, 29: 464–484.
Cumbers, A., Nativel, C. and Routledge, P. (2008) 'Labour agency and union positionalities in global production networks', *Journal of Economic Geography*, 8: 369–387.
Cusumano, M. (2010) 'Platforms and services: understanding the resurgence of Apple', *Communications of the ACM*, 53(10): 22–24.
Dicken, P., Kelley, P. F., Olds, K. and Yeung, H. (2001) 'Chains and networks, territories and scales: towards a relational framework for analysing the global economy', *Global Networks*, 1(2): 89–112

Distimo (2011a) *The Battle for the Most Content and the Emerging Tablet Market*, http://www.distimo.com/publications.

Distimo (2011b) *App Distribution Becomes a Global Game: The Shift of Power and Impact for Developers*, http://www.distimo.com/publications.

Distimo (2012) *Year in Review* (App Analytics), http://www.distimo.com/publications.

Froud, J., Johal, S., Leaver, A. and Williams, K. (2014) 'Financialization across the Pacific: manufacturing cost ratios, supply chains and power', *Critical Perspectives on Accounting*, 25(1): 46–57.

Gawer, A. and Cusumano, M. (2014) 'Industry platforms and ecosystem innovation', *Journal of Product Innovation Management*, 31(3): 417–433.

Gereffi, G. (1994) 'The organization of buyer-driven global commodity chains: How U.S. retailers shape overseas production networks', in G. Gereffi and M. Korzeniewicz (eds) *Commodity Chains and Global Capitalism*, Westport: CT.

Gill, R. (2007) *Technobohemians or the New Cybertariat?* Amsterdam: Institute of Network Cultures.

Henderson, J., Dicken, P., Hess, M., Coe, N. M. and Yeung, H. W-C. (2002) 'Global production networks and the analysis of economic development', *Review of International Political Economy*, 9: 436–464.

Kleeman, F., Voß, G. and Reider, K (2008) 'Un(der)paid innovators: the commercial utilization of consumer work through crowdsourcing', *Science, Technology and Innovation Studies*, 4: 5–26.

Lazonick, W. (2009) *Sustainable Prosperity in the New Economy?* Upjohn Institute for Employment Research.

Levy, D. (2008) 'Political contestation in global production networks', *Academy of Management Review*, 33(4): 943–963.

Marks, A. and Huzzard, T. (2010) 'Employability and the ICT worker: a study of employees in Scottish small businesses', *New Technology, Work and Employment*, 25(2): 167–181.

Parker, R., Cox, S. and Thompson, P. (2014) 'How technical change affects power relations in global markets: remote developers in the console and mobile games industry', *Environment and Planning A*, 46: 168–185.

Rainnie, A., Herod, A. and McGrath-Champ, S. (2011) 'Review and positions: global production networks and labour', *Competition and Change*, 15(2): 155–169.

Sandberg, Å., Augustsson, F. and Lintala, A. (2007) *IT and Telecom Companies in Kista Science City, Northern Stockholm* (p. 104). Sweden: National Institute for working Life.

Saxenian, A. (1992) 'Contrasting patterns of business organization in Silicon Valley', *Environment and Planning D: Society and Space*, 10: 377–391.

Selwyn, B. (2012) 'Beyond firm-centrism: re-integrating labour and capitalism into global commodity chain analysis', *Journal of Economic Geography*, 12: 205–226.

Taylor, P. (2010) 'The globalization of service work: analysing the transnational call centre value chain', in P. Thompson and C. Smith (eds) *Working Life: Renewing Labour Process Analysis*, Basingstoke: Palgrave Macmillan, pp. 244–268.

Taylor, P., Newsome, K. and Rainnie, A. (2013) 'Putting labour in its place: global value chains and process analysis', *Competition and Change*, 17(1): 1–5.

CHAPTER 14

Wasted Commodities, Wasted Labour? Global Production and Destruction Networks and the Nature of Contemporary Capitalism

Al Rainnie, Andrew Herod, Susan McGrath-Champ and Graham Pickren

Introduction

This book is evidence of a growing interest in the question of labour in value chains and production networks. However, whilst such interest is welcome it is unfortunate that efforts to more centrally locate labour in analyses of value chains and production networks have tended to focus almost exclusively upon processes of commodity assembly. Little attention has been given to what happens to commodities after their disposal at what are typically seen to be the ends of their lives. This is particularly regrettable because there has been a growing appreciation in other scholarly literatures of the 'ongoingness' of commodities' economic lives beyond their points of initial consumption, that is to say once they have been disposed of as 'waste'. This research upon ongoingness challenges the notion that there is an unambiguous dualism between commodity and waste (i.e. the contention that once a commodity is discarded it becomes, materially and semiotically, 'waste'), arguing instead that the recycling of much of the waste currently being generated by capitalist production can have important impacts upon processes of capital accumulation, as parts retrieved from discarded commodities often serve as inputs into new commodities. What is interesting about the nature of contemporary capitalism, though, is that there seems to be a correspondence between the production of ever greater quantities of wasted commodities as a way to solve crises of accumulation, especially through products' planned obsolescence, and a growth in the proportion of the planet's population which some have argued is being written off by capital, a population which might be called 'wasted labour'.

Given the apparently simultaneous growth in quantities of wasted commodities and wasted labour, the purpose of this chapter is to push Global Production Networks (GPN) analysis to engage with two growing bodies of literature: that which focuses upon the management of waste and that which suggests that there is a large and increasing divide in the global labour market between those workers who are described as formal and those who are described as informal labour, with these terms commonly also equated respectively to included/excluded, valued/not valued, and productive/non-productive (or wasted) labour. Our argument, then, is two-fold. First, we believe that it is important to detail the connections between GPNs and the processes whereby commodities are broken up after they have been discarded. This allows us to interrogate the onward movement of value (here understood in its Marxist sense of 'congealed labour') and so to connect so-called wasted labour to processes of capital accumulation. Second, drawing upon Nicole Phillips's (2011) argument that the dualism of informal/formal labour is a false dichotomy when applied to GPNs, we argue that the same could be said both for understanding the breaking up of discarded commodities so as to retrieve constituent elements that might be re-used in new products, and for understanding the connections between this process of retrieval and the assembling in GPNs of new commodities (i.e. the process of facilitating ongoingness). Thus, Phillips has made the case that:

> informality and formality do not exist as separate (and separated) spheres of economic and social life, but rather are interconnected in complex ways. [Consequently] we need to understand this relationship not simply as the interactions between two supposedly discrete 'spheres' of economic and social life, but rather as a dynamic *structural blending* of informality with formality in GPNs. This structural blending is both a result of the workings of GPNs and a key process in their constitution and evolution.
>
> (Phillips, 2011: 382, original emphasis)

Based upon this we also suggest that viewing large segments of the world's population as permanently non-productive/'wasted labour' is too simplistic, at least when it comes to those workers involved in dismantling discarded commodities. In considering these workers, then, we find Phillips's focus upon the role of GPNs in structuring the relationship between formal and informal labour very helpful. This is because 'ongoingness' scholars who analyse the processing of 'waste' commodities frequently portray those doing this processing, particularly in the Global South, as being informal workers par excellence and imply that their work is largely disconnected from circuits of capital (e.g. see Gidwani and Reddy, 2011), whilst those who work in the GVCs/GPNs in which the commodities are first assembled are seen to be part of the formal labour market.

As a way to challenge these commodity/waste and formal/informal labour dualisms, in this chapter we connect analysis of GPNs with what we have elsewhere (Herod et al., 2013; 2014) described as Global Destruction Networks (GDNs). We take GDNs to be networks of 'waste' product disassembly and component reuse that are companion to, and (can be) integral parts of, new commodity production. Crucially, by putting labour – and specifically the capitalist labour process – at the heart of our analysis, we hope to show that the formal/informal, valued/not valued, productive/wasted dichotomies, when applied to labour and work within GPNs and GDNs, are misleading and unhelpful. In so doing, we have taken up the challenge issued by Bair and Werner (2011: 989) to develop GPN analysis so that it can analyse changing geographies of global production that reflect moments of both inclusion and exclusion. Thus we seek to examine 'the processes that engender the forging and breaking of links between circuits of commodity production, people and places' (Bair and Werner, 2011: 992).

The chapter itself begins by responding to Mike Davis's (2006) work on what current patterns of urbanization and the growth of mega cities and their slums mean for the nature of work and employment under capitalism. Specifically, Davis has suggested that a new section of the urban proletariat is emerging in the mega slums of the Global South, one which is unwanted by, and disconnected from, capital accumulation (see also Yates, 2011). These people's lives are seen to be non-productive of surplus value, such that the activities in which they engage to reproduce themselves can be viewed as 'wasted labour' from capital's perspective. At the same time, some commentators on waste (e.g. Gidwani and Reddy, 2011) have argued that the growth in the quantities of waste produced under capitalism because of the latter's tendency to encourage the planned obsolescence (Slade, 2006) and discarding of commodities which still have use-value is resulting in the emergence of a class of individuals who simply eke out an existence living off these mountains of waste, usually in slums. In the process, it is claimed (e.g. Gidwani and Reddy, 2011: 1652), they lead lives whose economic activities have no consequence for global circuits of capital except as the phagic devourers of last resort of discarded commodities' carcasses, many of which have been exported from the Global North for disposal in the Global South. By way of contrast, we argue that these people are not, in fact, disconnected from the dynamics of capitalist accumulation but, rather, that their activities can feed into circuits of capital in important ways. To show how this is so we argue that it is necessary to focus upon the movement of value, as this allows us to understand how waste can serve as a kind of interior limit to capitalism and a repository of value which can be withheld from circulation but later relaunched into it. This means that waste and the so-called wasted bodies who process it are not permanently cut loose from capitalist processes but, rather, often serve as temporarily superfluous entities that can be re-incorporated and used in ongoing processes of accumulation.

The chapter, then, develops an earlier argument (Herod et al., 2013; 2014) that much recent work on waste has concentrated too much on the semiotic or physical forms of waste and has lost sight of the political-economic and the theorizing of the production, capture and transfer of value. Even Gidwani (2012: 275), one of the few analysts to develop a Marxist approach to making connections between waste and value and who sees waste as 'the recurring other of "value" and, more pointedly, [as] the antithesis of capitalist "value," repeated with difference as part of capital's spatial histories of surplus accumulation', concentrates too much for our taste upon the consumption of goods rather than upon their production, thereby ignoring the labour process. Instead, we argue that it is possible to connect the activities of 'wasted labour' to GPNs through tracing the temporal and geographical movement of value. In order to do so, labour has to be placed at the heart of both GPN and GDN analysis if the links between them, and thus the nature of 'wasted commodities' and 'wasted labour', are to be more fully understood. Through so doing we will show how, then, even these excluded labourers remain connected to processes of value production, capture and transfer. Furthermore, we suggest that a disarticulations perspective (by which we mean a way to connect 'an analysis of global commodities to the politics of disinvestment, devaluation, place-making and subject-making which make their production possible' (Bair and Werner, 2011: 990)) can be used to focus upon the processes through which waste and 'wasted lives' are included/excluded from networks and so challenge perspectives which see these 'surplus populations' as permanent.

The chapter is organized as follows. In the next section we look critically at analysis which proposes a radical division in the labour market based upon consumption rather than production and explore more fully the concept of 'wasted labour'. Our critique is then progressed through an examination of the relationship between GPNs and GDNs, focusing particularly upon the labour process. The next section then offers two examples to illustrate our argument. We end with a brief conclusion.

Planet of Slums – Surplus Humanity?

In 2006 Mike Davis published *Planet of Slums*, a devastating examination of the implications of the urban population of the planet outnumbering the rural for the first time in human history. Davis showed that the world's urban labour force had more than doubled since 1980 and that cities would account for virtually all future world population growth. Furthermore, 95 per cent of this growth will occur in the urban areas of Global South countries (Davis, 2006: 1–2). Davis suggested that this new urban order will be accompanied by increasing inequality within and between cities of different sizes and economic specializations and that, in much of the Global South, urban growth has become decoupled from industrialization, even from development as a whole. As he put it:

> Rather than the classical stereotype of the labor-intensive countryside and the capital-intensive industrial metropolis, the Third World now contains many examples of the capital-intensive countrysides and labor-intensive deindustrialized cities. 'Overurbanization', in other words, is driven by the reproduction of poverty, not by the supply of jobs.
> (Davis, 2006: 16)

Instead of being a focus for growth in the way in which modernization theory would suggest, for Davis myriad Global South cities, then, have become merely dumping grounds for surplus populations who work in unskilled, unprotected and low-wage informal service industries and trade. Such cities appear less the launching pads for Rostovian industrial development and historical progress than modern-day reincarnations of nineteenth-century Dublin, Naples and the East End of London (Davis, 2006: 175). Further surveying the contemporary scene, Davis noted that by the late 1990s a 'staggering' one billion workers, representing one-third of the world's labour force, mostly in the urban Global South, were either unemployed or underemployed (Davis, 2006: 199) and that informal workers now make up around 40 per cent of the economically active population of the Global South. Whereas scholars such as Rostow (1960) suggested that upward mobility in the informal economy would lead to the expansion of the formal economy and so mark the process of capitalist modernization, Davis insists that upward mobility in the informal economy is largely a 'myth inspired by wishful thinking' (see Davis, 2006: 179–185). Rapid urban growth in the context of structural adjustment, currency devaluation and state retrenchment, then, has been a recipe not for stimulating industrialization and modernization but, rather, for the mass production of slums.

Michelle Yates (2011) has picked up on Davis's argument to suggest that contemporary trends under capitalism are leading to the emergence of a population that is permanently surplus to capital's requirements, one which may have no alternative but to try to survive through the black market or 'trash picking' (Yates, 2011: 1680). These populations, she suggests, are little more than humans-as-waste, excreted from the capitalist system. Based upon this, Yates (2011) argues that we have moved into a new phase of capitalism's relationship between system-world and lifeworld. Thus the rise of mega slums, particularly in the Global South, has led to a massive increase in a 'permanent surplus (superfluous) population with little to no possibility of ever being exploited by capital' (Yates, 2011: 1679). This population, though, is not the same as the classic Marxist concept of a reserve army of labour but is, rather, a mass of humanity that is seen as structurally redundant to the processes of global accumulation – it is 'wasted labour' for capital because, unlike Marx's reserve army of labour, these individuals are not seen as ever likely to be a source of surplus value.

A similar dualism (included/valued labour versus excluded/not valued labour) is outlined by McIntyre and Nast (2011: 1465) in presenting their concepts of Biopolis and Necropolis, in which they propose a racialized and gendered reworking of hierarchies that redraw the social and spatial boundaries between hyper-exploited waged work and the people and places excluded from relations of capitalist accumulation. According to them, new kinds of racialized geographies of hyper-exploitation emerge out of two differing regimes of governmentality – the biopolis and the necropolis. Thus the necropolis is 'a space of negation and the socially dead, produced by expropriations and alienations in and outside European nation-states' (McIntyre and Nast, 2011: 1467). The biopolis, by way of contrast, and in opposition to the necropolis, is a form of governmentality that presumes that the sovereign subject must be conserved and shored up for the modern nation-state to survive. McIntyre and Nast then note Marx's division of the modern 'surplus population' into three categories: *latent*, made up of those in insecure employment; *floating*, those moving rapidly in and out of the labour force; and *stagnant*, those only rarely employed. Having done so, they suggest that within the biopolis the majority of the surplus labouring population is either latent or floating, whilst racially denigrated sections of the working class make up most of the stagnant population. In the necropolis the situation is reversed, with most surplus populations being stagnant rather than latent or floating.

Although interesting formulations, we part company with this form of analysis and, more broadly, with much of the work on waste because this work largely views capitalism as characterized by particular forms of *consumption* and therefore focuses on that issue rather than upon labour or the labour process (see Yates, 2011: 1687). For example, the biopolis, McIntyre and Nast (2011: 1467) suggest, is tied to spaces of privileged (and privileging) forms of consumption. This is not to argue that understanding consumption under capitalism is not important. After all, consumption of commodities is what allows capitalists to realize their profits. Rather, the issue is, as Yates (2011) notes, that waste here is approached through an analysis that sees capitalism as being defined as a mode of consumption, not through the characteristics of the labour process. Likewise, in his work Gidwani (2012), although drawing upon Marx, equally focuses upon consumption to the detriment of much consideration of the concrete nature of labour and the labour process. Thus, for him (2012: 282, emphasis added) rising urbanization and consumerism mean that waste has become society's 'internal margin' 'in the form of unending streams of excreta that issue from its voracious *consumption of nature*'. In a vein similar to McIntyre and Nast, Gidwani and Reddy (2011: 1652), in dealing with the issue of the wasting of labour, argue that these processes increasingly give rise to two ecology 'sets':

> on the one side, a way of life that churns out growing quantities of 'waste'; on the other, lives that live off this commodity detritus. On the one side, lives whose labor is valued and rewarded; on the other, lives that are of utter indifference to global circuits of capital. Lives worth preserving, lives easily abandoned ... Valuable lives, wasted lives; and mapped onto these, valuable spaces and spaces designated as wasteful. Colonizing and re-making wasted spaces as valuable spaces, excluding from political citizenship those whose labors are not counted. This is the juggernaut we call 'eviscerating urbanism'.

The result, Gidwani (2012: 285) declares, is that the modern annals of capitalism are a bitter and sometimes bloody struggle between these two 'eco classes' (waste's producers and waste's consumers), as waste in all its forms has come to represent 'a renewing source of jeopardy to capitalism but also a fiercely contested frontier of surplus value production'.

There is much to be valued in Gidwani's Marxist-inspired contribution. His criticism of idealist approaches evident in much of the literature (Gidwani, 2012: 284) and focus on battles over surplus value echo our own approach to thinking through the political economy of waste (Herod et al., 2013; 2014). Furthermore, Gidwani stretches Marx's capitalist dialectic (M-C-M') to hypothesize a 'waste – value dialectic' [W – (M-C-M') – W'], wherein commodity production forms new kinds of waste in the moment of production and the moment of consumption. This is similar to our own formulation (Herod et al., 2014) wherein we suggest a W-NP-W (waste – new product – waste) circuit under capitalism. Both Gidwani's and our approaches locate the analysis of waste and wasted labour in the dynamics of capitalism as a (wasteful) system and both of us see waste as a source of recoverable values and unredeemed profit (Gidwani, 2012: 283). What is different in our approaches, though, is that we believe that rather than there being two, somewhat discrete groups of people, with one being seen as engaging in productive, valued labour and the other not, the two are actually mutually supporting, even as they may be in conflict.

One way to overcome what we feel is problematic in many approaches to considering the nature of waste and wasted labour under capitalism is to develop what Yates (2011: 1681) describes as a production-level theoretical standpoint. The starting point of such an approach is to recognize that capitalism as a mode of production produces both waste objects and waste in human form ('wasted labour'). These two are connected insofar as classic crises of overaccumulation are increasingly linked to crises of social reproduction in which the labour power of millions becomes superfluous to the economic needs of capital. At the heart of this lies a significant contradiction, insofar as labour is the ultimate source of value and yet at the same time is continually and increasingly wasted within the labour process. Thus Yates (2011: 1689) quotes from Volume One of Marx's *Capital*, to the effect that:

> [t]he working population therefore produces both accumulation of capital and the means by which it is itself made relatively superfluous; and it does this to an extent which is always increasing. This is a law of population peculiar to the capitalist mode of production.

Drawing from Marx, then, the distinction between 'wasted' and 'non-wasted' labour/lives can be reformulated. Under capitalism, labour collectively is oppressed but only some workers are subject directly to the extraction and realization of surplus value. This does not mean that other workers (the collective labourer – paid or not paid) are not part of this process. The two categories of workers – excluded and included – are neither hermetically sealed from each other nor are they analytically distinct. The following section develops further this insight.

GPNs, GDNs and Labour

According to Hudson (2012: 389), Marx conceptualizes the capitalist economy as made up of conjoined processes of value creation and material transformation. Under capitalism, value is created via manipulation and transformation within the labour process as materials with use values are produced and, in turn, provide a basis for exchange value and further value creation as they are transformed into new commodities. Furthermore, a concentration on the continuity of material flows, as well as of value, amongst firms and across sectoral boundaries shows how production systems of varying organizational composition, complexity and spatiality are often intimately imbricated – the output of one system becomes the input of another, often in communities quite geographically removed from where it has been produced (Hudson, 2012: 376). A Global Production Network approach is an effective analytical tool for understanding this complexity (Rainnie et al., 2011; 2013). As Coe and Hess (2010: 130) argue, the GPN framework is superior to either that of Global Commodity Chains or Global Value Chains because:

> First, through the explicit consideration of extra-firm networks, it necessarily brings into view the broad range of non-firm organisations – for example, supranational organisations, government agencies, trade unions, employer associations, NGOs, and consumer groups – that can shape firm activities in the particular locations absorbed into GPNs. Second, GPN analysis is innately multi-scalar, and considers the interactions and mutual constitution of all spatial scales from the local/regional to the global. Third, this is an avowedly network[ed] approach that seeks to move beyond the analytical limitations of the 'chain' notion. Production systems are seen as networked 'meshes' of intersecting vertical and horizontal connections in order to avoid deterministic linear interpretations of how production systems operate and generate value. Fourth, the governance characteristics of GPNs are taken to be much more complex, contingent, and variable over time than is suggested in GCC/GVC analyses. Fifth, and finally, a central concern of GPN analysis is not to consider the networks in an abstracted manner for their own sake, but to reveal the dynamic developmental impacts that result for both the firms and territories that they interconnect.

Although GPN analysis has often incorporated analysis of the labour process and how this shapes the dynamics of various GPNs, as we have argued elsewhere (Herod et al., 2013; 2014) one weakness of much GPN analysis has been its failure to put the labour theory of value at the heart of labour process theory. We suggest that so doing is crucial. In this regard, whilst our approach is very different from that of his in many ways, we concur with Paul Thompson (2013), who has taken issue with commentators such as Applebaum et al. (2013) and Vidal (2013) when they have argued that new value creation mechanisms exist outside of the employment relationship. Against this Thompson (2013: 483) suggests that:

> the labour process remains a focal point of productivity gains, restructuring and value capture as part of the delivery of targets to shareholders.

Where we part company with Thompson, however, is in his desire to remove the labour theory of value from labour process theory, whilst retaining a focus on exploitation. This is because, we would suggest, only the labour theory of value can provide an underpinning explanation of surplus value generation within global networks of interdependent and intercompetitive labour processes.

What, though, does this have to do with waste and wasted labour? Well, what we want to suggest is that by tracing the creation and movement of value through the life, death and reclamation of products' constituent elements and their potential reuse as inputs into new GPNs, we can show how the so-called 'wasted labour' which survives by picking through the detritus produced by modern industrialization can actually play a crucial role in shaping the structures of GPNs. To do this we have developed the idea of Global Destruction Networks (GDNs) (see Herod et al., 2013; 2014).

GDNs, we have noted above, are networks of places where products are disassembled and their constituent parts are extracted for processing and reuse. They are therefore intimately entwined with GPNs, though not necessarily in a linear or sequential process. What is important to consider about them here, though, is that the value that was incorporated into commodities and their constituent elements during their fabrication may travel with them through GDNs as these commodities are disassembled. This value may then be carried forward into new commodities as the parts of disassembled commodities – whether recovered whole (as with computer chips) or made into new things (as with melted down metals and plastics) – are used as inputs into new GPNs. Moreover, this value will be added to by the labour of those waste workers involved in disassembly and the process of material recovery, as well as new assembly (for a more detailed outline of this argument, see Herod et al., 2013; 2014). GDNs, then, are conduits of value from commodities in one physical form to commodities in another as, for instance, metals (and the value they contain) retrieved from, say, TVs may be incorporated into new computers.[1] What is especially important to bear in mind about them, though, is that whereas GDNs may be global, local conditions will affect their operation. For example, in the Global North, e-waste is usually disassembled using machinery, but in the Global South it is usually dismantled in a highly labour-intensive (and often dangerous) manner. This means that recovery rates for materials are higher and original components are more reusable when released manually in the Global South, whereas Global North methods yield less reuse grade material but are far safer (Wang et al., 2012). Likewise, whereas ship breaking in India and Bangladesh is a very labour-intensive process largely conducted by gangs of informal workers, in China it is much more capital-intensive, largely because Chinese workers will not accept the low wages and working conditions that Indian and Bangladeshi workers will. The type of labour involved in taking used commodities apart, in other words, has dramatic implications for what kinds of materials can be liberated to become inputs into new GPNs and in what quantities.

The notion of GDNs and a focus upon both how new value is generated within them through the work of dismantling discarded commodities, and how value that was held within discarded commodities can be forwarded onto the new commodities as recycled elements are incorporated into them within GPNs is, we believe, helpful because it allows for several things. First, it provides an opening for consideration of value as more than simply rent extracted along different nodes in a network. Second, although it does not deny the importance of the semiotic and of transformations in the material form of commodities, it does allow for grounding analyses in the political/economic, in what Kirsch (2012: 4) has recently called the 'gritty materialisms' of waste. Third, by concentrating upon value, not to the exclusion of the commodity form but in relation to it, attention can be focused upon the labouring bodies that are crucial to how GDNs and GPNs function and are structured.

Having outlined the concept of GDNs, we now consider two cases of the gritty materialisms of labouring bodies that secure from waste those elements that can be used as inputs into new circuits of surplus value generation.

Waste and Working Lives

As we pointed out earlier, one of the advantages of a labour process theory-informed GPN/GDN approach is that it sensitizes us to the actions of a variety of actors. Hudson (2008: 438) concludes that:

> GPNs highlight the particular spatialities of the global economy and the way in which different spaces and the everyday lives of those that

live and work in them are entangled with or excluded from the processes of production, exchange and consumption through which GPNs are constituted. As a result, they bring together the 'system-world' and the 'life world', the imperatives of the accumulation process with the experienced realities of everyday life for people in varied sites of production, exchange and consumption.

We can see how this maps out by briefly examining two examples of so-called 'wasted' labour.

In a discussion of e-waste scavenging in Accra, Martin Oteng-Ababio (2012) points out that workers in an urban milieu have multiple strategies to earn a living. In Accra this became particularly important as unemployment grew dramatically with the economic crisis of the 1980s. E-scavenging arose for two main reasons. First, the imposition of a Structural Adjustment Programme destroyed jobs and livelihoods and led to a casualization of work, outsourcing and subcontracting that connected formal firms to formal and informal agents, in a circuitry that stretched across the globe in embedded hierarchies, divisions and subdivisions (i.e., the GPN-GDN connection) (Grant and Oteng-Ababio, 2012: 2). Second, because the government removed import duties on the importation of used computers in 2004, Ghana became a destination for much of the world's e-waste, such that by 2011 some 300 to 600 40-foot-long container shipments were arriving each month and 4,500 to 6,000 people were being employed in e-scavenging in Accra alone. However, as Oteng-Ababio points out, this development created not only work but also dynamic entities with linkages between both the formal and informal economies. This finding, he suggests,

> questions whether theoretically, the long held notion that [there is] a segment of the urban society that exclusively participates in informality tells the complete story ... [E-waste processing] demonstrates the functional linkages and fluidity between the formal and informal sector. For example, the reuse of older electronic products is a common practice and the only means through which many formal sector employees can economically access electronic products and participate in the information technology revolution. Also the separation of working components for repairs of faulty electronics has become a common practice. It is also instructive how people move seamlessly from the civil/public sector or the dominant poorly remunerative agricultural sector to participate in this new industry. (2012: 14)

Grant and Oteng-Ababio (2012: 2) conclude, then, that the introduction of liberalization policies in the 1980s allowed informal economies to become more enmeshed in international commodity relations and global economic processes. Most significant for our argument here, though, is that much of the material secured from processed e-waste by these workers will eventually find its way back into the circuits of global capital flow.

We can also re-examine Whitson's (2011) account of waste scavengers (*cartoneros*) in Buenos Aires in this light. Whitson recounts that the number of *cartoneros* working in Buenos Aires jumped from some 10,000 to 40,000 as the Argentinian crisis peaked in 2002 and many formerly formally employed people were forced to turn to waste scavenging to survive. What this highlights is that the divisions between formal and informal work are more porous (in both directions) and less clear-cut than some analysis would suggest and that there is a complex interaction between the role played by *cartoneros*, the state and the restructuring of markets. Thus, the crisis in Argentina produced an escalating predicament in Buenos Aires as waste broke out from its traditional contained areas, provoking an increasingly vocal outcry. At the same time, whilst the value of the Argentinian peso plummeted, the value of recyclable waste material rose 4–5 times. As a result, Argentinian firms were forced to rely increasingly upon domestic sources of supply rather than overseas sources, which led to more opportunities for *cartoneros*. As the number of *cartoneros* rose, so did the output of the six major recycling companies in the city. The increased visibility of the *cartoneros* and scale of the waste issues then forced the local state to pass laws that recognized officially the role of the *cartoneros*. This had the effect of identifying and establishing a clear market for recyclable material, a legal commoditization of recyclable material by informal, non-legal and in many ways unwanted 'waste' labour. However, as Whitson points out, this process of commoditization was complex and contested and based to a large extent on the nature and extent of the *cartoneros*' own labour process. Importantly, during the crisis the work of the *cartoneros* was legitimized, but in the period of recovery support collapsed and pressure came to formalize the market and once again marginalize (in all senses) the *cartoneros*. The result is that, in many ways, *cartoneros* have fulfilled a classic role played by many small firms and independent contractors in identifying and stabilizing a potential market, which then allows large capital to come in and take over. In the GPN literature this is described as providing a pipeline for TNCs (Transnational Corporations) into the 'local buzz' (Rainnie et al., 2013). In this particular case, then, GPNs are locking in to a 'local buzz' identified and developed by an informal element of a GDN. Grant and Oteng-Ababio (2012: 18) make a similar point when they conclude that:

> [e]-waste processing in Accra is a visible imprint of the normalization of informality within global-urban dynamics ... [T]here is the circuitry of the worlds of work within the informal economy and work that intersects with formal industries, international agents, and firms and agents beyond the borders of Ghana ... There is a great diversity within the worlds of work circuitry: some circuits are well integrated and overlap while others are loose, fragile, and isolated – and there are all sorts of combinations in between.

Although both these examples have, in different ways, outlined the role that crisis can have in patterning the extent and shape of GPN-GDN relationships, we are not suggesting, however, that the wasting of labour is only an outcome of crisis. Rather, as Bair and Werner (2011: 991) argue in the case of women workers in Mexico, it is 'an ongoing outcome of reproducing capitalist relations of production within specific historical contexts that are shaped by social difference'.

Conclusion

This chapter has sought to further a value-focused approach to the examination of waste and, in so doing, to challenge forms of analysis which suggest that clear-cut divisions are emerging in the labour market. In particular, we have tried to do three things. First, by developing the concept of GDNs we have provided a way in which to think of ongoingness in terms of the transfer of value rather than simply the physical transformation of materials. This is important because it allows for the retrieval of components from discarded commodities and their potential use as inputs into new GPNs to be linked into the broader rhythms of capitalist accumulation. Thus, if it is profitable to reuse the components they will find their way back into the accumulation process; if not, they will remain outside it, piled on rubbish heaps. As Kirsch and Mitchell (2004: 699) write, 'the networks of association that turn the variegated relations of capital into ossified things – like a commodity ... are directed, if not entirely determined, in *this* world, by the logic and necessity of capital accumulation'. We suggest that the same is true of 'waste'. This means that whereas many analysts have implied an almost infinite ongoingness to waste's reuse, we can instead develop a historical geography of its ongoingness under capitalism – in some times and places waste will be processed to provide materials for reuse and in others it will not.

Second, by focusing upon the different labour processes through which both value and materials circulate, we have highlighted the specifically capitalist qualities of GPNs and GDNs and how the labour process shapes both their structures (as with e-waste processing and ship breaking). The result of this is that, rather than the figure of the recycling labourer being universal, we can instead see how particular kinds of bodies in particular places come to transform materials under conditions created by the uneven development of capitalism. Furthermore, it allows for a view which sees GPNs' and GDNs' structures as the result of conflicts between capital and labour and other social actors and not simply as the outcomes of the dictates of the firms embedded within them.

Third, we have sought to challenge dualistic views which see those workers who retrieve elements from discarded commodities as unconnected to processes of capitalist accumulation and so as engaged in non-productive/wasted labour. In this regard we are in accord with Phillips (2011: 389), who has argued that:

> it is misleading to assume that all informal workers work in something called the 'informal economy' [or] that the 'informal economy' exists as a unitary, singular entity that can be described empirically and used as a basis for theory … Instead, it seems empirically more apposite and theoretically more revealing to think of an economy in which formality and informality structurally blend with one another in complex ways, and in which processes of formalization and informalization proceed simultaneously … The 'informal' thus exists within the 'formal', not simply alongside it, and *vice versa*. Informality sustains the 'formal' economy in its use of informal practices and its appropriation and exploitation of informal workers and small-scale forms of production (including household production) for the purposes of accumulation. Informal workers occupy a position of dependence on the formal economy even while marginalized within it. These relationships shape and constitute production networks at all levels.

At the same time, workers in the formal sector may be 'valued' to varying degrees but still work hours that are too long or too short, in jobs that are insecure, low-paid and often dangerous. Hence, as Yates (2011: 1680) points out, '[t]hose who still have access to wage labor are also embedded in the logic of disposability. The body of the laborer is used up or wasted at accelerated rates in order to secure the most profit'. Lean can be very mean. However, how this manifests itself in practice must start with the concrete conditions of the labour process to be found at various moments in the circuit of capital or at various points within a GPN or GDN. There is, then, as we have stressed throughout this chapter, no clearcut and unbreachable distinction between excluded and included, formal and informal, wasted and non-wasted labour. Instead, we must deal with a dynamic and ever-changing continuum.

Note

1 It is important to note that we are *not* suggesting that all elements are equally and endlessly recyclable and thus we are *not* suggesting that there is an endless degree of value's ongoingness. In fact, the onward movement of value can be stopped for certain elements either by the operation of the market (when it is not profitable to recycle such components) or by nature (when it is physically impossible to recycle them further because of changes in their chemical or physical properties through having been recycled too many times, as is the case with paper and plastic).

REFERENCES

Applebaum, E., Batt, R. and Clark, I. (2013) 'Implications of financial capitalism for employment relations research: evidence from breach of trust and implicit contracts in private equity buyouts', *British Journal of Industrial Relations*, 51(3): 498–518.

Bair, J. and Werner, M. (2011) 'Commodity chains and the uneven geographies of global capitalism: a disarticulations perspective', *Environment and Planning A*, 43(5): 988–997.

Coe, N. M. and Hess, M. (2010) 'Local and regional development: a global production network approach', in A. Pike, A. Rodríguez-Pose and J. Tomaney (eds) *Handbook of Local and Regional Development*, Routledge: London and New York, pp. 128–138.

Davis, M. (2006) *Planet of Slums*, London: Verso.

Gidwani, V. (2012) 'Waste/value', in T. J. Barnes, J. Peck and E. Sheppard (eds) *The Wiley-Blackwell Companion to Economic Geography*, Chichester: Wiley-Blackwell, pp. 275–288.

Gidwani, V. and Reddy, R. N. (2011) 'The afterlives of "Waste": notes from India for a minor history of capitalist surplus', *Antipode*, 43(5): 1625–1658.

Grant, R. and Oteng-Ababio, M. (2012) 'Mapping the invisible and real "African" economy: urban e-waste circuitry', *Urban Geography*, 33(1): 1–21.

Herod, A., Rainnie, A., Pickren, G. and McGrath-Champ, S. (2013) 'Waste, commodity fetishism and the ongoingness of economic life', *Area*, 45(3): 376–382.

Herod, A., Rainnie, A., Pickren, G. and McGrath-Champ, S. (2014) 'Global destruction networks, labour, and waste', *Journal of Economic Geography*, 14(2): 421–441.
Hudson, R. (2008) 'Cultural political economy meets global production networks: a productive meeting?' *Journal of Economic Geography*, 8(3): 421–440.
Hudson, R. (2012) 'Critical political economy and material transformation', *New Political Economy*, 17(4): 373–397.
Kirsch, S. (2012) 'Cultural geography I: materialist turns', *Progress in Human Geography*, 37(3): 433–441.
Kirsch, S. and Mitchell, D. (2004) 'The nature of things: dead labor, nonhuman actors, and the persistence of Marxism', *Antipode*, 36(4): 687–705.
McIntyre, M. and Nast, H. J. (2011) 'Bio(necro)polis: Marx, surplus populations, and the spatial dialectics of reproduction and "race"', *Antipode*, 43(5): 1465–1488.
Oteng-Ababio, M. (2012) 'When necessity begets ingenuity: e-waste scavenging as a livelihood strategy in Accra, Ghana', *African Studies Quarterly*, 13(1–2): 1–21.
Phillips, N. (2011) 'Informality, global production networks and the dynamics of "adverse incorporation"', *Global Networks*, 11(3): 380–397.
Rainnie, A., Herod, A. and McGrath-Champ, S. (2011) 'Review and positions: global production networks and labour', *Competition and Change*, 15(2): 155–169.
Rainnie, A., Herod, A. and McGrath-Champ, S. (2013) 'Global production networks, labour and small firms', *Capital and Class*, 37(2): 177–195.
Rostow, W. W. (1960) *The Stages of Economic Growth: A Non-Communist Manifesto*, Cambridge: Cambridge University Press.
Slade, G. (2006) *Made to Break: Technology and Obsolescence in America*, Cambridge, MA: Harvard University Press.
Thompson, P. (2013) 'Financialization and the workplace: extending and applying the disconnected capitalism thesis', *Work, Employment and Society*, 27(3): 472–488.
Vidal, M. (2013) 'Postfordism as a dysfunctional accumulation regime: a comparative analysis of the USA, the UK and Germany', *Work, Employment and Society*, 27(3): 451–471.
Wang, F., Huisman, J., Meskers, C., Schluep, M., Stevels, A. and Hagelueken, C. (2012) 'The best-of-2-worlds philosophy: developing local dismantling and global infrastructure network for sustainable e-waste treatment in emerging economies', *Waste Management*, 32(11): 2134–2146.
Whitson, R. (2011) 'Negotiating place and value: geographies of waste and scavenging in Buenos Aires', *Antipode*, 43(4): 1404–1433.
Yates, M. (2011) 'The human-as-waste, the labor theory of value and disposability in contemporary capitalism', *Antipode*, 43(5): 1679–1695.

CHAPTER 15

Labour and the Changing Landscapes of the Call Centre

Phil Taylor

Introduction

This chapter builds on previous attempts to integrate labour process analysis with the Global Commodity Chain (GCC), Global Value Chain (GVC) and Global Production Network (GPN) frameworks (Taylor, 2010a). Much early empirical work focused on light manufacturing, electronics, apparel and horticulture to the neglect of service delivery chains and networks. This deficit has been partly overcome through studies of outsourcing and offshoring (e.g. Flecker and Meil, 2010; Feuerstein, 2013; Pawlicki, 2013), which have included research on call centres (Taylor, 2010a; Taylor et al., 2014). Nevertheless, the reluctance to apply chain and network theorizing to the call centre is perhaps surprising given its global dispersion and the considerable attention paid to a new international division of labour centred, principally, on India (e.g. Dossani and Kenney, 2007; Poster, 2007; D'Cruz and Noronha, 2009; Mirchandani, 2012). Even when authors have engaged with explicitly transnational themes, such as multi-scalar union organizing (Taylor and Bain, 2008; James and Vira, 2010) or the contrasting experiences of employees at the different nodes of the call centre 'value chain' (Cohen and El-Sawadi, 2007; Coyle, 2010), authors have failed to employ GVC or GPN concepts. Therefore, this chapter progresses the case for drawing on the GCC, GVC and GPN constructs for deepening our understanding of the call centre value chain (Rainnie et al., 2008). It sees these frameworks as delivering greater analytical purchase than the varieties of capitalist perspectives that informed the Global Call Centre Project (Holman et al., 2007;

2009; Peck and Theodore, 2007). However, two qualifications must be acknowledged.

First, the utility of chain or network theorizing does not lie in privileging one framework to the exclusion of another (Bair, 2009), but in recognizing that different elements of each can be profitably adopted. For example, from the narrower GVC lens of governance it is possible to draw on the notions of the complexity, codifiability and capacity (of suppliers) (Gereffi et al., 2005), to understand some of the constraints on the ability of call centre work to be standardized, transitioned, relocated and then seamlessly delivered from remote geographies. At the same time, from the wider lens of the GPN, the salience of national institutional factors, regulation, labour supply, cost savings and arbitrage, factors associated with territory and place must be embraced (Henderson et al., 2002; Coe et al., 2004). Broader political economic factors exercise a particularly significant influence.

Second, and consistent with the book's core theme, it is argued that integration with labour in general, and with the labour process in particular, is indispensable for more meaningful chain or network analysis. It is now widely acknowledged that the GVC has neglected labour, either as a source of value or as an object of chain dynamics (Smith et al., 2002; Taylor et al., 2013), and while labour is included within the more expansive GPNs and is the preferred framework for many (e.g. Rainnie et al., 2011; Cumbers, in this volume), it does not necessarily assume greater or lesser importance than other factors. Consequently, Cumbers et al. (2008) emphasized that labour should be made central to GPNs, first as the 'abstract labour' that is core to all capitalist production and, second, as labour in collective organizational forms, such as trade unions.

In a literature that often runs in parallel to this GPN research, labour geography has highlighted the difference – first formulated by Wright (2000) – between labour's structural power, derived from workers' position within systems of production, and its associational power (e.g. Coe and Jordhus-Lier, 2011), that implies its exercise, collectively and even individually. Thompson et al., in Chapter 3, accordingly contrasts labour power with labour's power as a means of expressing this distinction. Certainly, the literature has been largely preoccupied with associational power and the need to theorize or 'unpack' labour agency (Taylor et al., Chapter 1 of this book). However, these agential concerns are not the primary consideration here, where the focus rather is on how capital selects, gathers together, organizes and controls call centre workers, in order that they generate a surplus.

The call centre, it is argued, has a unique labour process, a telemediated hybrid of clerical/white-collar work and interactive service work (Boreham *et al.*, 2008). The Information and Communication Technologies (ICTs) that are central to the call centre's operation and distinguish it as an organizational form, shape the systems of managerial control and attempts to overcome labour indeterminacy. It is inextricably a spatial project, and not merely in the obvious sense of offshoring, for its raison d'être lies in connecting organizations and their call-handlers in real time and across space with distant customers. Thus, the call centre raises important questions of geography and the discipline's core concepts of place, space and scale (Castree *et al.*, 2004; Herod *et al.*, 2007).

In the interests of definitional precision and analytical consistency, this chapter separates the call centre from the non-customer facing back office. While the distinction might seem obvious from the perspective of the developed countries of the Global North, the call centre is often conflated with the broader Business Process Outsourcing (BPO) industry in the offshore geographies of the Global South (see Mirchandani, 2012 for a recent example). Based on an understanding of this distinctiveness this chapter seeks to answer related questions. In what ways do the unique characteristics of the call centre structure its value chain, determine the nature of linkages with suppliers and influence the forms of governance adopted? How does this distinctive configuration shape its locational topography, both within the developed countries and to offshored destinations? Substantively, the focus is on the UK and specifically on Scotland's call centre sector and on the UK/Scotland to India call centre 'chain'. However, consideration is given to the broader dynamics of offshoring and, specifically, to call centres in both India and the Philippines as the principal remote geographies for English-language services. The argument is theoretically informed and empirically grounded on extensive data gathered over two decades.

The chapter is structured as follows. First, a summary is given of the sources accessed and the methods utilized. Second, the development of the call centre is situated within appropriate historical, technological, political-economic, organizational and spatial contexts. In the process, inextricably, the distinctive characteristics of its labour process are identified, and contribute to an understanding of the locational decisions within the UK and, particularly, Scotland. Third, following this articulation of the call centre value chain at national and sub-national levels, the dynamics of offshoring are considered. Once again, the nature of the labour process provides an important element in the narrative, facilitating global relocation by lead firms, while simultaneously constraining their propensity to migrate overseas. The conclusion reflects further on labour, the labour process and their integration with GVC and GPN theorizing.

Sources and Methods

Detailed evidence has been gathered in the UK and in Scotland over almost two decades on diverse aspects of the call centre, including corporate strategy, work organization, managerial control, labour utilization, the structure of employment, labour market dynamics, employment relations, technology and locational trends. Similar lines of inquiry have been pursued during fieldwork undertaken annually in India since 2003 and in the Philippines since 2007. Research on developments in Scotland has been near-continuous, and has included five comprehensive sectoral audits (Taylor and Bain, 1997; 2000; 2003; Taylor and Anderson, 2008; 2012) and diverse case studies (e.g. Baldry *et al.*, 2007). Interviews with, and surveys of, senior management have contributed to knowledge of trends in corporate strategy and managerial practice, while quantitative and qualitative research of employee and trade union experiences have complemented such sources.

During thirteen separate periods of fieldwork in India and five in the Philippines, extensive interviews with senior managers and employees have been conducted during site visits. Employee surveys have been implemented in both countries (for India, Taylor *et al.*, 2009; for the Philippines, McDonald *et al.*, 2014). Participation at industry conferences (twenty-one in India, five in the Philippines) and wide-ranging industry and company documentation (e.g. NASSCOM-McKinsey, 2005; NASSCOM, 2012; IBPAP, 2014) have added considerable value. In specific cases (four in financial services, one in telecoms), it has been possible to track the call centre chain from lead firm in the UK to supplier in India through interviews with senior managers at their geographically disparate but connected locations.

The Call Centre and the Spatial Division of Labour

The call centre as a spatial organizational form cannot be understood without reference to the Information and Communication Technologies (ICTs) that are fundamental to its operation. No single technological development accounts for its emergence and widespread diffusion (Miozzo and Soete, 2001), but the digitalization of telecoms and networking and the increase in, and dramatic reduction in the cost of, computing capacity proved hugely influential. Computer Telephony Integration (CTI) has long been recognized as defining the call centre, but the key innovation was Automatic Call Distribution (ACD) switching (Marshall and Richardson, 1996; Taylor and Bain, 1999), enabling calls to be routed, in succession, to agents as they become 'ready' following the conclusion of their previous calls and the completion of required clerical work ('wrap').

Now, call-handlers could be situated within a centre on a single site or, connected in different centres across multiple locations, in 'virtual' centres. The revolutionary spatial aspect lies in the fact that the call centre severs the co-location, or proximate location, of servicing organization and customer (Richardson and Belt, 2001). The 'distance shrinking' technologies permit interactive servicing work to be situated at some distance from the customer, whether at regional/sub-national, national or indeed at the transnational scale.[1] Previously scattered groups of workers could now be gathered in dedicated centres of servicing and sales activities that could be located in, and/or relocated to, regions characterized by pools of available and qualified labour at lower cost.

Hence, as economic geographers first observed (Richardson and Marshall, 1996), the space-shrinking technologies offered opportunities for geographically remote areas to overcome the 'friction of distance', inducing firms to capitalize on the cost advantages of locating there. Thus, in the UK from the mid-1990s, call centre clusters emerged in the 'peripheral' regions of Leeds/Humberside, northeast England and Scotland, with Glasgow particularly prominent (Bristow et al., 2000). Other regions followed, including northwest England, South Wales, the Midlands and Northern Ireland, promising lower costs and skills availability, as labour markets tightened, costs rose and the rate of attrition quickened in the 'first mover' regions. Similar patterns of dispersal to non-metropolitan hinterlands is evident in other developed countries of Europe and in North America and Australasia (Taylor, 2014: 11), although in-country locational patterns differ in the offshore geographies of India and the Philippines.

These new spatial divisions of call centre labour invoked an earlier relocation of back office functions to lower cost regions (Massey, 1984), for both were accompanied, or stimulated, by organizational restructuring and process re-engineering that involved the standardization of processes and job losses. Put bluntly, higher order, professional and managerial functions might remain at, or close to, the head office while, in the interests of cost reduction, large-scale and standardized back office and customer services promising economies of scale could be created and relocated to cheaper locales. In financial services, for example, the 1990s wave that created large contact centres across northern England and Scotland involved a thoroughgoing reconfiguration of customer servicing, the widespread closure of bank branches and the loss of many thousands of jobs (Bain and Taylor, 2002).

The Call Centre Labour Process and Global Value Chains

Just as the call centre's digital architecture underpins its spatial flexibility, so too are its ICTs and, particularly the ACD, responsible for transforming key elements of work organization, for the measurement and monitoring of performance and output and for the structuring, standardizing and pacing of work.[2] Much has been written on work organization and managerial control in call centres (e.g. Callaghan and Thompson, 2002; Taylor et al., 2002; Russell, 2008). The labour process consists essentially of Tayloristic elements (fragmented/stylized customer interaction, repetition, standardization, structured–if not scripted–responses) imbricated with the performance of emotional labour, that is often encapsulated in the requirement to 'smile down the phone' (Taylor and Bain, 2007). For all that call centres and their constituent workflows differ according to degree of complexity of customer interaction, the value of the customer base served, product and market differentiation, depth of product knowledge, the presence of tele-mediated professional services (Prichard et al., 2014) and the inescapable tension between quantity and quality that causes variation (Taylor and Bain, 1999), it is recognized that mass production-type call centres have dominated (Batt and Moynihan, 2002; Lloyd and Payne, 2009).

Over-simplifying the labour process to a Taylorism-plus-emotional-labour formulation, though, diminishes the significance of the complex of labour indeterminacies involved in the agent-customer relationship: communicative and linguistic abilities (Forey and Lockwood, 2010); displays of empathy, sympathy and sincerity (Callaghan and Thompson, 2002); skilled emotion work (Bolton, 2004); and 'articulation skills' defined as 'a blend of emotional, cognitive, technical and time-management skills, performed often at speed' (Hampson and Junor, 2005). Central to overcoming these indeterminacies and to ensuring that agents add value in their encounters with customers[3] are control mechanisms based on agent adherence to extensive quantitative targets or qualitative standards (see e.g. Bain et al., 2002). Consequently, the call centre labour presents itself as double-sided. On the one hand, labour's communicability, linguistic capability, emotional empathy and so on are the very qualities that employers (whether in-house or third-party) seek to enlist from employees as they are recruited in particular labour markets. On the other hand, the imposition of performance metrics and quality measures are regarded by employers as indispensable as this labour is set in motion, as employers strive to ensure that agents deliver sufficient numbers of calls at a consistently, that is call after call, high standard.

This dualism, it is argued, provides the basis for an engagement with the global value chain and global production network frameworks.

GVCs have been understood as the integrative counterpart to geographically dispersed economic activities undertaken by firms with diverse suppliers and other external actors (Gibbon et al., 2008). In the GVC literature, analysis of the linkages between the chains became dominated by issues of governance, the mechanisms by which production levels and quality standards are maintained across spatially separate sites. Applying this analytical focus on the dyadic links in a value chain (Bair, 2008) to the call centre brings into sharp relief the significance of the Service Level Agreement (SLA) (Taylor, 2010a). The quantitative metrics (call volumes, handling times, fulfilment) and the customer quality standards specified in SLAs are explicable by reference to Gereffi et al.'s 'theory of value chain governance' (2005: 85), which is composed of three factors: the complexity of information and knowledge transfer, the extent to which this information can be codified and the capabilities of suppliers. The substitution of tele-mediated for face-to-face customer contact involved, to a greater or lesser extent, the standardization of hitherto variable encounters, a general simplification of the agent-customer interface[4] and, inextricably, the systemization (codification) of this interaction into calculable and assessable components. This raft of measures has aimed to reassure clients that suppliers have the capability of delivering appropriate call volumes at the requisite quality. The spatial dimension relates to fact that SLAs represent managerial attempts to exercise close control over remotely delivered services.

Call Centre Growth and Location at National and Sub-National Level

On the basis of these conceptual foundations, empirical developments are explored. Specifically, the growth of the sector in absolute numbers can be charted and its uneven spatial geography described and analysed. Figure 15.1 provides an initial reference point as it plots the expansion of employment in the UK (and within it Scotland) and for the two principal 'remote' geographies, India and the Philippines. One striking observation regards relative scale, specifically the continual dominance of onshore over offshore delivery. Such a contrast would be starker still if it were possible to include year-on-year figures for the US. However, series data do not exist beyond wildly speculative consultants' figures. Nevertheless, a reasonable approximation of the employment total for the US for 2013 is around four million (Taylor, 2014). Adding together employment for

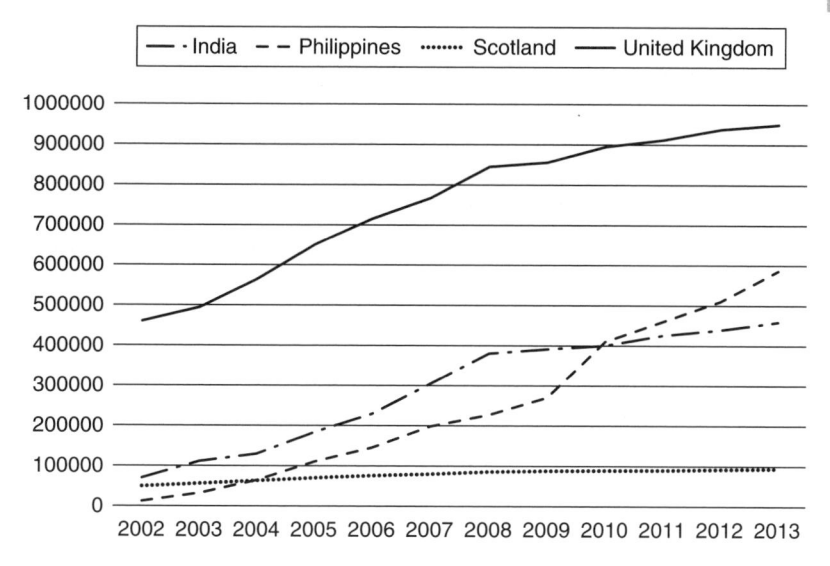

Figure 15.1 Call centre employment (2002–2013)

Source: (Authors' data: Taylor and Bain, 1997; 2000; 2003; Taylor and Anderson, 2008; 2012; IBPAP, 2014; Taylor, 2014)

the US, the UK, Canada, Australia and New Zealand – the major English-speaking onshore geographies – gives a total of around 5.5 million, which compares to slightly more than one million for the Philippines and India combined. A preliminary reflection, then, is the resilience of the call centre industry within the developed countries and, it follows, how mistaken has been the prediction made in the early 2000s that offshoring to the low-cost Global South would decimate onshore delivery.

Having indicated the general trajectories of growth, the locational dynamics can be explored for the UK and Scotland, the latter serving as an exemplar for 'peripheral' regions. Distilling a mass of evidence from the successive sector audits (Taylor and Bain, 1997; 2000; 2003; Taylor and Anderson, 2008; 2012), the importance of broader political economic factors can be seen to underpin location. Within increasingly competitive markets operating at sectoral level,[5] the first waves of call centre location were the result of firm-level decisions to locate a significant part of this model of cost-efficient customer servicing in *relatively* low-cost parts of the UK, including notably Scotland. Government-funded industry agencies, such as Scottish Development International (SDI), consistently promoted attractiveness on grounds of cost, that locating in Scotland is 25–30 per cent cheaper than London and southeast England (e.g. SDI, 2012).

Employer responses to survey questions asking organizations why they had chosen to situate their operations in Scotland (and in later surveys asking why they had decided to retain them there) confirmed that overall costs, and in particular labour costs, were significant in forming locational decisions. In the 1997 audit, almost one third of organizations stated that 'labour costs in Scotland' had been a major factor, while by 2011 it remained explicitly so for 13 per cent (Taylor and Bain, 1997: 10–11; Taylor and Anderson, 2012: 44–47). Additional cost elements are cited, including those for accommodation and telecom connectivity. A part of the wider political economy of location, and includable within the broad matrix of territorial factors perceived as salient by proponents of the GPN, are the grants and regional financial assistance made available to firms by the local state and its agencies.

Yet of all the multiple factors influencing locational decisions, what employers most strongly report as decisive relates to the availability of labour and the ensemble of qualities and skills necessary for phone-based interactive customer service work. This finding was as true in the most recent 2011 audit as it had been in the 1997 audit during the industry's formative years. Over the decades, the specific nature of skills required might have evolved (Lloyd and Payne, 2009), as an upskilling has occurred which encompasses upselling, cross-selling, on-selling, one-call resolution and the deepening complexity of customer encounters as automation 'takes out' the most standardized transactions. Particular combinations of skills have become important for firms as when, for example, generic competencies such as articulation skills are combined with bespoke product knowledge, domain expertise, particular technical skills or even multi-lingual capability.[6] In sum, then, labour process considerations are central considerations as employers seek agents whose labour power can be readily translated into concrete call centre labour.

Much could be concluded from the shifting locational map of call centre activity at the sub-national level of Scotland that confirms the salience of a GPN analysis, in which labour is accorded a leading explanatory role (Table 15.1). First, Glasgow, always the most significant city location, has continued to grow in importance relative to the rest of Scotland. By 2011 almost one in eight of the working population were employed in a call centre. The establishment of a critical mass of activity marked by high levels of service quality and cost-efficient performance encouraged further concentration that suggests path dependencies. Second is the commensurate, somewhat later, growth in the Glasgow hinterland of Lanarkshire as many organizations sought similar labour attributes and skills, albeit in a looser labour market. Third, the relatively

Table 15.1 Call centre growth in Scotland (1997–2011)

	1997	2000	2003	2008	2011
Glasgow	6,769	13,892	16,586	25,387	31,405
Edinburgh	2,275	6,762	6,853	9,218	9,419
Fife	1,485	4,048	4,340	7648	9,252
West Lothian	1,220	5,566	3,502	5,980	6,525
Lanarkshire	1,165	4,278	5,856	10,245	12,520
Tayside	691	2,576	4,695	6,868	6,160
Clydebank	345	552	920	2,015	1,188
Greenock	320	2,116	4,713	3,491	2,651
Ayrshire	220	506	1,079	1,497	1,815
Highlands/Islands	216	3,726	2,263	3,398	3,075
Stirling	165	322	767	716	601
Aberdeen	17	598	556	1,364	1,187
Falkirk	0	782	1,476	1,572	1,439
Renfrewshire	0	276	564	1,673	2,127
Dumfries/Borders	0	0	346	622	635
Scotland Total	16,000	46,000	56,000	86,000	90,000

Source: (Authors' data: Taylor and Bain, 1997; 2000; 2003; Taylor and Anderson, 2008; 2012)

expensive Edinburgh conurbation (higher accommodation and labour costs, tighter labour market) still experienced growth, but at slower rates than in those less expensive areas (e.g. Glasgow, Lanarkshire, Fife). Fourth, call centres spread from their earlier strongholds to virgin towns across the country, including remote locations in the Highlands and Islands. However, a fifth conclusion is the distinct limit to dispersion. Centrifugal tendencies have dominated to the extent that 86 per cent of employment is concentrated in the most densely populated Scottish central belt (Taylor and Anderson, 2008).

The argument here is that the GPN concepts and constructs are applicable not merely to the 'global' in the international geographical sense, when national boundaries are transcended. Grasping the 'dialectics of global-local' relations can help to understand how firm-centred service networks are deeply influenced by the concrete socio-political contexts in which they are embedded (Coe *et al.*, 2004). It provides an account, however sketchy, of the finely grained landscape at national and subnational level. Within a matrix of factors (e.g. overall costs, accommodation availability, telecom connectivity, government regional policy and financial assistance, reputation, customer feedback), those relating to labour (cost in tandem with the availability of skills and competencies) are most prominent. This longitudinal perspective uniquely enables us to map nuanced locational shifts, confirming the important point that call centre location represents not a single 'spatial fix' (Harvey, 2006) but a series of unfolding 'spatial fixes'.

While the place-based factors associated with the GPN are most influential in driving firms decisions and in shaping the topography of call centre networks, it does not render the narrower dyadic focus of the GVC on governance as insignificant. Indeed, MIS (Management Information Systems) monitor in real time employee and team performance across centres and between sites in the case of virtual centres, ensuring that the quantitative performance and customer quality criteria are attained. There is constant evaluation of the processes by which appropriate knowledge (Gereffi et al., 2005) is delivered to final customers. Where problems do emerge it may lead to the recodification of the information, it may involve the simplification of the algorithmic steps that structure the customer-agent interaction or it may prompt the recalibration of standard operating procedures and protocols. The metrics serve to control service performance and form the basis of supervisory attempts to overcome those indeterminacies of agent-customer interaction identified above (e.g. communicative ability, empathy and sincerity, articulation skills, speed, behaviours). Certain indeterminacies have greater salience in offshored locations and do not require the same attention in onshore or nearshore locations, where linguistic fluency and cultural congruence may be expected if not ever completely assumed.[7]

In extreme cases, consistent underperformance by centres overall can lead – in outsourced relationships – to a contractual change that might see lead firms replace a particular third-party supplier[8] or even to close operations. The 'capability' of suppliers (Gereffi et al., 2005) is therefore subject to continual scrutiny. Conversely, when the governance metrics of a centre show a centre consistently exceeding the requirements of an SLA, lead firms may designate such centres 'strategic sites' or 'centres of excellence'. Further investment may follow, leading to expansion in employment in the centre or proximate locations. In these polar cases, the perpetual process of benchmarking is reflective of Gereffi et al.'s (2005) three 'C's. Further, the practice of inter-firm governance has broader, political-economic and spatial implications that might not be considered if the focus were solely on dyadic links in the call centre chain. In these contrasting cases of site-wide underperformance and operational excellence, issues that arise through the mechanisms of governance may have economic and spatial consequences that more broadly shape the call centre landscape. Extending this argument, it may be suggested that the narrower domain of the GVC and more expansive territoriality of the GPN can be analytically related.

Offshoring and the Global Relocation of Call Centres

The relocation of call centres from the UK to India began in the early 2000s, prefigured by the transition of back office and software/IT services. Decisions taken by Prudential and HSBC, and then by financial services (insurance and banking) overall, were followed by firms in telecoms, utilities, transport and travel, retail and other sectors. For the most part, they involved offshoring some of the most standardized, least complex and most transactional of call centre workflows (Taylor and Bain, 2005). Just as the locational clustering of the call centres within the UK to the so-called 'peripheral' regions involved the reconfiguration of interactive work and the spatial stretching of its value chain, so too did the migration of call centres overseas necessitate a further standardization, re-engineering and codification. This transition has been described as 'Taylorism through export' (Taylor, 2010a), as the servicing chain was further elongated. From one perspective, then, the later phase of offshoring represented an extension, albeit dramatically and at a transnational scale of the same cost-saving, profit-maximizing, lean servicing, spatial dynamic that produced call centre concentrations at national and subnational scales.

Once more, location or relocation, only this time to the remote geography of India, represented a spatial fix (Harvey, 2006) explicable by reference to the macro framework of the GPN. The intersection of a lead firm's transnational customer servicing activities (whether captive, outsourced or hybrid) with the complex of socio-economic, cultural, political and territorial factors, in which they must become embedded, invokes the expansive provenance of the GPN. In the case of call centres to India it was the promise of significant cost reduction that drove firms in the Global North to offshore interactive service work. Distilling much evidence, overall cost savings of perhaps 40–50 per cent were realisable in the early phases of offshoring (NASSCOM-McKinsey, 2005; NASSCOM, 2006). Central to these perceived savings and to India's comparative national advantage was labour cost arbitrage of approximately 70–80 per cent. Such financial essentialism is often neglected in the GVC's concentration on governance and immediate links in a chain, and while GPN is more concerned with the multiple factors that embed a firm's transnational activity, the framework tends to understate the financial imperative and labour's differential costs as a driver.

Nevertheless, within the GPN's relational compass are diverse institutional, social, political, socio-economic and regulatory factors that are significant for understanding the development of India as a remote geography. Its government's de-regulatory and privatization agendas, notably in relation to the telecoms industry (1999 National Telecoms Act) and its commitment to ensuring support for Foreign Direct Investment (FDI) are self-evidently important. Proactive policies for the IT and Information Technology Enabled Services – Business Process Outsourcing (ITES-BPO) industries has produced close collaboration with industry body National Association of Software and Service Companies (NASSCOM), designed to create the business eco-system in which overseas and domestic-owned suppliers can thrive. Within the spectrum of organizations and institutions promoting India as a politically safe, risk-free and cost-effective destination are consultants, such as McKinsey, whose interests are served by assisting firms in tying down capital assets in India.

As repeatedly emphasized contra the hyperglobalists (Friedman, 2005), call centre work cannot simply be located anywhere (Taylor and Bain, 2005; 2008) as, paradoxically, 'globalization' serves to heighten the differences between place-based characteristics (Harvey, 1989). Lower (labour) costs may be a fundamental driver of offshoring, but it would be meaningless without India's other significant place-based attribute – its supplies of English-speaking labour. Thus, the particular linguistic, communicative and cultural characteristics of India's graduate workforce are central to the remotely located call centre labour process. Without minimizing the importance of technological, institutional and political-regulatory factors, it is the 'strategic coupling' of the lead firms of the US or UK servicing chains with voice agents in India that animates the call centre chain and helps shape its uneven global landscape.

If it is the qualities of labour – linguistic and cultural felicity and cheapness – that have contributed most to growing Indian employment (Figure 15.1) from 57,000 in 2002 to 459,000 by 2013, it is the difficulties experienced with these putative qualities that have constrained the scale of offshoring and limited the complexity of services to have been migrated. Overcoming labour indeterminacies has proved profoundly problematic.

Early experiences of Indian service centres by UK customers generated perceptions of poor call quality. Employers reported 'linguistic difficulties, communication problems and misunderstanding' as the most significant disadvantages of offshoring (Taylor and Bain, 2003: 56). Rather than diminishing over time, the employers' experiences were that difficulties were becoming more acute and widespread (Taylor and Anderson, 2008; 2012). At the root of the problem lies the fact that English, for all that it is spoken by the middle class in India, and despite the fact that it is the lingua franca in schools and universities, is not the mother tongue. Fifteen years of education in English does not automatically equip

Indian agents with the ability to communicate with western customers with the standards of fluency, empathy, sensitivity and cultural congruence that are deemed necessary by their service providers or, more pertinently, lead firms, given the significance of inter-firm power asymmetries in servicing chains.

The pool of labour with the requisite qualities and skills proved far shallower than anticipated. NASSCOM-McKinsey (2005: 90) infamously estimated that only 10–15 per cent of graduates possessed the skills for direct employment in an industry that then hired only 3–5 per cent of applicants. NASSCOM (2010: 178) concluded that 'while India has an ample supply of talent, it is largely trainable and not employable'. Such constraints have contributed to unwelcome outcomes for Indian management, including the perennial problem of attrition (Das *et al.*, 2013), the acute shortage of the most skilled labour (Kuruvilla and Raganathan, 2008) and the commitment of considerable resources to recruitment and training. The relatively shallow labour pool has also shaped spatial unevenness across India, for it has meant that the much vaunted move to Tier 2 and Tier 3 cities in search of untapped or looser labour markets has been circumscribed. As much as 90 per cent of IT and ITES-BPO services are delivered from the seven principal Tier 1 locations (Bangalore, Mumbai, Delhi and NCR, Hyderabad, Chennai, Pune and Kolkata (NASSCOM, 2008: 18).

From the perspective of UK employers, the second most cited disadvantage of offshoring has been the difficulty of exercising control remotely (Taylor and Bain, 2003; Taylor and Anderson, 2008; 2012). This problematic is intimately bound up with the labour process and with managerial attempts to overcome labour indeterminacy. As indicated, the SLA is the key 'governance' mechanism which seeks to ensure that the requisite number and quality of calls are delivered to customers from remote locations. Offshoring amplifies the difficulties in ensuring that consistently high standards of service delivery are deliverable. In order to overcome the anticipated linguistic, communicative and cultural shortcomings of agents, the qualitative elements of SLAs are imposed more rigorously than they would be in the UK and include distinctively Indian criteria such as speech monitoring for accent neutrality. Locutional competencies and the enactment of stylized conversations (Cowie, 2007) become more important at the Indian end of the call centre servicing chain. Indeed, there is a more pronounced use of scripting or semi-scripting in India as management seeks to achieve consistency in call quality in conditions of uncertainty over agents' syntax, forms of speech or grammar in addition to the more obvious problems with diction and accent. In short, strategic concerns exist over aspects of the call centre labour process that might be considered non-problematic in the UK.

Reflecting on Gerrefi *et al*'s. (2005) 'theory of value chain governance', it can be argued that these place-based characteristics of labour impact on the three 'C's in related ways. The degree of the complexity in the information and knowledge that can be transferred from the host geography and lead firm in the UK to the Indian supplier is beset by limitations. The constraint is not merely evident in, and caused by, linguistic incongruity. Much of the 'knowledge' is tacit and culturally familiar to those living in the UK but not in India and is therefore not amenable to codification and learning through training. Making linguistic and cultural qualities and attributes explicit and transmitting them through formal mechanisms is fraught with difficulty. Of course, acceptable standards can be achieved for many transactional services, but there will be limitations on the extent to which more complex, nuanced and empathic services can be delivered remotely, as employers have reported extensively (Taylor and Anderson, 2008; 2012).

Conclusion

The substitutability of Indian for UK call centre services has proved far more problematic than was envisaged a decade ago. This author calculates that no more than 50,000 Indian call-handlers now 'face' UK customers, as the trend to re-shore part, or all, of the voice services previously offshored by many UK companies (e.g. Aviva, Royal and Sun Alliance, Santander,[9] British Telecom) has continued. While the principal reason for this onshore drift is customer opposition, other factors including rising costs in India, efficiencies in the UK industry and the growing influence of automation have all been influential in this latest turn of the spatial wheel. Furthermore, and particularly for US clients (and certain UK-based companies), the Philippines is now the most important remote 'global' provider of voice services (IBPAP, 2014), having overtaken India in 2010 (Figure 15.1). Roughly comparable in terms of bottom line cost, the Philippines' chief attraction lies in the closer linguistic congruence of its graduate workforce with US English.

The distinctive nature of the call centre labour process means that voice services should not be conflated with either the back office or IT/software work. Voice services are 'stickier', more place-based and linguistically sensitive than non-customer facing activities, conclusions first tentatively proposed by Taylor and Bain (2005: 278–279) and now confirmed by a decade's experience. Call centres, therefore, demonstrate greater fixity and less mobility than certain other business services. The changing call centre landscape over the last two decades is characterized not by a single directional trend, but by a series of unfolding and complementary spatial fixes that have seen firms source interactive service work from multiple locations onshore, nearshore and offshore (Taylor, 2010b). Within this portfolio of servicing options, the delivery of services onshore and/or relatively close to customers has remained the dominant strategy. Thus, the 'strategic coupling' (Coe et al., 2004) of a firm's call centre 'networks with the resources of particular places and regions produces contingent outcomes.

Finally, it is suggested that the characteristics of place-based labour that are embedded in distinctive socio-economic contexts, combined with the problematic of converting labour power into concrete call centre labour, help explain patterns of call centre growth and location. The argument is that utilizing elements of the GPN and GVC frameworks can contribute to an understanding of developments at national and sub-national, as well as at the global scale. The task of researchers in the labour process tradition is to ensure that their core concerns, the conversion of abstract labour power into concrete labour, the employer's 'problem' of labour indeterminacy, the specific forms (and incompleteness) of management control strategies and so on, are integrated with the global value chain and global production network frameworks. Putting labour back in or, as is more likely, integrating labour when it has been neglected or understated, means according to labour its appropriate analytical position within the GCC, GVC or GPN frameworks.

Notes

1 Early UK research was conducted by economic geographers concerned principally with growth at regional scale (e.g. Marshall and Richardson, 1996; Richardson and Marshall, 1996; Bristow et al., 2000). This work predated knowledge of the GCC and the development of the GVC or GPN frameworks, so inevitably does not utilize their concepts, but there is an acknowledgment of labour's significance which on occasions engages implicitly with labour process concerns.
2 This is not to lapse into technological determinism, but to acknowledge the constrained strategic choice facing employers that compels them to utilize the technologies to maximize call flow, reduce costs and increase value in highly competitive markets.
3 How call centre labour creates value and contributes to the circulation of capital remain theoretical challenges beyond the scope of this chapter. Glucksmann's (2004) 'total social organisation of labour' theory

helpfully poses the interconnections between call centres, their agents and 'upstream' and 'downstream' economic activities and their workers associated, invoking comparison with Marx's concept of the collective worker and the notion of 'labour power socially combined' (Taylor and Bain, 2007: 359).

4 The most extreme manifestation is scripting, which was rapidly abandoned in the UK (except where a contractual requirement) because of customer antipathy. However, widespread semi-scripting, uniform protocols, crib sheets, algorithms and prompts for cross- or upselling evidence the extent of standardization.

5 The financial services sector was the innovator and driver, responsible for more call centres than any other sector (Bain and Taylor, 2002), and for producing the lean, cost-efficient model of customer serving and sales that was widely emulated (Taylor and Bain, 2007) in telecoms, utilities, travel, retail and the public sector.

6 Agents with the ability to speak at least one foreign language comprise 3.5 per cent of the Scottish workforce (Taylor and Anderson, 2012: 43).

7 The attractiveness (or otherwise) of agents with particular regional accents to customers prompts only occasional discussion within the UK industry. Linguistic capability is of course a central management preoccupation in multi-lingual service centres.

8 A case in point was Cable and Wireless's decision to terminate the contract of Excell in Glasgow in 2000 and install Vertex as its new subcontractor.

9 The UK head of Santander, Ana Botin, stated on 9 July 2011, 'This is what our customers have told us is the most important factor in terms of customer with the bank and we have listened to them and decided to bring all our retail call centres back from India' (The Economic Times, 2011).

REFERENCES

Bain, P. and Taylor, P. (2002) 'Ringing the changes? union recognition and organisation in call centres in the UK financial sector', *Industrial Relations Journal*, 33(3): 246–261.

Bain, P., Watson, A., Mulvey, G., Taylor, P. and Gall, G. (2002) 'Taylorism, targets and the pursuit of quantity and quality by call centre management', *New Technology, Work and Employment*, 17(3): 154–169.

Bair, J. (2008) 'Analysing global economic organisation: embedded networks and global chains compared', *Economy and Society*, 37(3): 339–364.
Bair, J. (2009) 'Global capitalism and commodity chains: looking forward, going back', *Competition and Change*, 9(2): 153–180.
Baldry, C., Bain, P., Taylor, P., Hyman, J., Scholarios, D., Marks, A., Watson, A., Gilbert, K., Gall, G. and Bunzel, D. (2007) *The Meaning of Work in the New Economy*, Basingstoke: Palgrave Macmillan.
Batt, R. and Moynihan, L. (2002) 'The viability of alternative call centre production models', *Human Resource Management Journal*, 12(4): 14–34.
Bolton, S.C. (2004) *Emotion Management in the Workplace*, Basingstoke: Palgrave Macmillan.
Boreham, P., Parker, R., Thompson, P. and Hall, R. (2008) *NewTechnology@Work*, London: Routledge.
Bristow, G., Munday, M. and Griapos, P. (2000) 'Call centre growth and location: corporate strategy and the spatial division of labour', *Environment and Planning A*, 32(3): 519–538.
Callaghan, G. and Thompson, P. (2002) '"We recruit attitude": the selection and shaping of routine call centre labour', *Journal of Management Studies*, 39(2): 223–254.
Castree, N., Coe, N. M., Ward, K. and Samers, M. (2004) *Spaces of Work: Global Capitalism and Geographies of Labour*, London: Sage.
Coe, N. and Jordhus-Lier, D. C. (2011) 'Constrained agency? Re-evaluating the geographies of labour', *Progress in Human Geography*, 8(3): 271–295.
Coe, N., Hess, M., Wai-Chung, H., Dicken, P. and Henderson, J. (2004) 'Globalising regional development', *Transactions of Institute of British Geographers*, 29: 464–484.
Cohen, L. and El-Sawadi, A. (2007) 'Lived experiences of offshoring: an examination of UK and Indian financial service employees' accounts of themselves and one another', *Human Relations*, 60(8): 1235–1260.
Cowie, C. (2007) 'The accents of outsourcing: the meanings of "neutral" in the Indian call centre industry', *World Englishes*, 26(3): 316–330.
Coyle, A. (2010) 'Are you in the country? How "local" social relations can limit the "globalisation" of customer service supply chains', *Antipode*, 42(2): 289–309.
Cumbers, A. (2015) 'Understanding labour's agency in the global economy: the unrealised potential of a GPN framing', in Newsome *et al.* (eds), this volume.
Cumbers, A., Nativel, C. and Routledge, P. (2008) 'Labour agency and union potentialities in global production networks', *Journal of Economic Geography*, 8(3): 369–387.
Das, D., Nandiliath, A. and Ramesh, M. (2013) 'Feeling unsure: quit or stay? Uncovering heterogeneity in employees' intention to leave in Indian call centres', *International Journal of Human Resource Management*, 24(1): 15–34.
D'Cruz, P. and Noronha, E. (2009) *Employee Identity in Indian Call Centres: The Notion of Professionalism*, New Delhi: Sage.
Dossani, R. and Kenney, M. (2007) 'The next wave of globalisation: relocating service provision to India', *World Development*, 35(5): 772–791.
The Economic Times (2011) 'After New Call Telecom, UK bank Santander closing its call centres in India', *The Economic Times*, http://articles.economictimes.

indiatimes.com/2011-07-09/news/29751951_1_centre-work-british-staff-uk. Accessed 21 September 2014.

Feuerstein, P. (2013) 'Patterns of work reorganization in the course of the IT industry's internationalization', *Competition and Change*, 17(1): 24–40.

Flecker, J. and Meil, P. (2010) 'Organisational restructuring and emerging service value chains – implications for work and employment', *Work, Employment and Society*, 24(1): 1–19.

Forey, G. and Lockwood, J. (eds) (2010) *Globalisation, Communication and the Workplace*, London: Continuum.

Friedman, T. (2005) *The World is Flat*, London: Allen Lane.

Gereffi, G., Humphrey, J. and Sturgeon, T. (2005) 'The governance of global value chains', *Review of International Political Economy*, 12(1): 78–104.

Gibbon, P., Bair, J. and Ponte, S. (2008) 'Governing global value chains: an Introduction', *Economy and Society*, 37(3): 315–338.

Glucksmann, M. (2004) 'Call configurations: varieties of call centre and divisions of labour', *Work, Employment and Society*, 18(4): 785–811.

Hampson, I. and Junor, A. (2005) 'Invisible work, invisible skills: interactive customer service as articulation work', *New Technology, Work and Employment*, 20(2): 161–188.

Harvey, D. (1989) *The Condition of Post Modernity*, Oxford: Blackwell.

Harvey, D. (2006) *The Limits to Capital*, London: Verso.

Henderson, J., Dicken, P., Hess, M., Coe, N. and Wai-Chung, H. (2002) 'Global production networks and the analysis of economic development', *Review of International Political Economy*, 9(3): 436–464.

Herod, A., McGrath-Champ, S. and Rainnie, A. (2007) 'Working space: why incorporating the geographical is central to theorising work and employment practices', *Work, Employment and Society*, 21(2): 47–64.

Holman, D., Batt, R. and Holtgrewe, U. (2007) *The Global Call Centre Report: International Perspectives on Management and Employment*, Ithaca: Cornell University.

Holman, D., Frenkel, S., Sorenson, S. and Wood, S. (2009) 'Work design outcomes in call centres: strategic choice and institutional explanations', *Industrial and Labour Relations Review*, 62(4): 510–532.

IBPAP (2014) *The Philippines Advantage in IT-BPM*, Manila: Information Technology and Business Process Association of the Philippines.

James, S. and Vira, B. (2010) 'Unionising the new spaces of the new economy: Alternative labour organising in India's ITES-BPO industry', *Geoforum*, 41: 364–376.

Kuruvilla, S. and Raganathan, A. (2008) 'Economic strategies and macro- and micro-level human resource policies: the case of India's outsourcing industry', *Industrial and Labour Relations Review*, 62(1): 39–72.

Lloyd, C. and Payne, J. (2009) '"Full of sound and fury, signifying nothing" – interrogating new skill concepts in service work – the view from two UK call centres', *Work, Employment and Society*, 23(4): 617–634.

Marshall, J. N. and Richardson, R. (1996) 'The impact of "telemediated" services on corporate structures: the example of "branchless" retail banking in Britain', *Environment and Planning A,* 28: 1843–1858.
Massey, D. (1984) *Spatial Divisions of Labour.* Macmillan: Basingstoke.
McDonald, H., Forey, G., Scholarios, D. and Taylor, P. (2014) *Employee Experiences of Work in Three Philippine Call Centres,* Glasgow/Hong Kong: University of Strathclyde/Hong Kong Polytechnic University.
Miozzo, M. and Soete, L. (2001) 'Internationalisation of services: a technological perspective', *Technological Forecasting and Social Change,* 67(2): 159–185.
Mirchandani, K. (2012) *Phone Clones – Authenticity Work in the Transnational Service Economy,* Ithaca: Cornell University Press.
NASSCOM (2006) *The IT-BPO Strategic Review, 2006,* New Delhi.
NASSCOM (2008) *The IT-BPO Strategic Review, 2008,* New Delhi.
NASSCOM (2010) *The IT-BPO Strategic Review, 2010,* New Delhi.
NASSCOM (2012) *Strategic Review 2012: The IT Industry in India,* New Delhi.
NASSCOM-McKinsey (2005) *Extending India's Leadership of the Global IT and BPO Industries,* New Delhi: NASSCOM-McKinsey.
Pawlicki, P. (2013) 'Control in an internationalized labour process: engineering work in global design', *Competition and Change,* 17(1): 41–56.
Peck, J. and Theodore, N. (2007) 'Variegated capitalism', *Progress in Human Geography,* 36(6): 731–772.
Poster, W. (2007) 'Who's on the line? Indian call centre agents pose as Americans for US-outsourced firms', *Industrial Relations,* 46(2): 271–304.
Prichard, J., Turnbull, J., Halford, S. and Pope, C. (2014) 'Trusting technical change in call centres', *Work, Employment and Society,* OnLine First, 3 June 2014, doi: 10: 1177/0950017013510763.
Rainnie, A., Barrett, R., Burgess, J. and Connell, J. (2008) 'Call centres, the networked economy and the value chain', *Journal of Industrial Relations,* 50(2): 195–208.
Rainnie, A., Herod, A. and McGrath, S. (2011) 'Review and positions: global production networks and labour', *Competition and Change,* 15(2), 155–168.
Richardson, R. and Belt, V. (2001) 'Saved by the bell? Call centres and economic development in less favoured regions', *Economic and Industrial Democracy,* 22(1): 67–98.
Richardson, R. and Marshall, A. N. (1996) 'The growth of telephone call centres in peripheral areas of Britain: evidence from Tyne and Wear', *Area,* 28(3): 308–317.
Russell, B. (2008) 'Call centres – a decade of research', *International Journal of Management Reviews,* 10(3): 195–219.
SDI (2012) *Scotland – A Premier BPO Location,* Glasgow: Scottish Development International.
Smith, N., Rainnie, A., Dunford, M., Hardy, J., Hudson, R. and Sadler, D. (2002) 'Networks of value, commodities and regions: reworking divisions of labour in macro-regional economies', *Progress in Human Geography,* 26(1): 41–63.

Taylor, P. (2010a) 'The globalisation of service work: analysing the transnational call centre value chain', in P. Thompson and C. Smith (eds) *Working Life: Renewing Labour Process Analysis*, Basingstoke: Palgrave Macmillan, pp. 244–268.

Taylor, P. (2010b) 'Remote work from the perspective of developed economies: a multi-country synthesis', in J.C. Messenger and N. Ghosheh (eds) *Offshoring and Working Conditions in Remote Work*, Basingstoke: Palgrave Macmillan, pp. 17–59.

Taylor, P. (2014) *Employment Relations and Decent Work in the Global Contact Centre Industry – A Report for the International Labour Organisation*, Geneva: ILO.

Taylor, P. and Anderson, P. (2008) *Contact Centres in Scotland – the 2008 Audit*, Glasgow: Scottish Development International.

Taylor, P. and Anderson, P. (2012) *Contact Centres in Scotland – the 2011 Audit* Scottish Development International/Scottish Enterprise.

Taylor, P. and Bain, P. (1997) *Call Centres in Scotland*, Glasgow: Scottish Enterprise.

Taylor, P. and Bain, P. (1999) '"An Assembly Line in the Head": work and employment in the call centre', *Industrial Relations Journal*, 30(2): 101–117.

Taylor, P. and Bain, P. (2000) *Call Centres in Scotland in 2000*, Glasgow: Rowan Tree Press.

Taylor, P. and Bain, P. (2003) *Call Centres in Scotland and Outsourced Competition from India*, Glasgow: Scottish Development International.

Taylor, P. and Bain, P. (2005) 'India calling to the far away towns: the call centre labour process and globalisation', *Work, Employment and Society*, 19(2): 261–282.

Taylor, P. and Bain, P. (2007) 'Call centre reflections: a reply to Glucksmann', *Work, Employment and Society*, 21(2): 349–362.

Taylor, P. and Bain, P. (2008) 'United by a common language? Trade union responses in the UK and India to call centre offshoring', *Antipode*, 40(1): 132–154.

Taylor, P., D'Cruz, P., Noronha, E. and Scholarios, D. (2014) 'From boom to where?: the impact of crisis on work and employment in Indian BPO', *New Technology, Work and Employment*, 29(2): 105–123.

Taylor, P., Hyman, J., Mulvey, G. and Bain, P. (2002) 'Work organisation and the experience of work in call centres', *Work, Employment and Society*, 16(1): 101–117.

Taylor. P., Newsome, K. and Rainnie, A. (2013) 'Putting labour in its place: global value chains and labour process analysis', *Competition and Change*, 17(1): 1–5.

Taylor, P., Noronha, E., D'Cruz, P. and Scholarios, D. (2009) 'Indian call centres and Business Process Outsourcing: a study in union formation', *New Technology, Work and Employment*, 24(1): 19–42.

Wright, E. O. (2000) 'Working class power, capitalist class interests and call compromise', *American Journal of Sociology*, 105(4): 957–100.

Author Index

Abernathy, F. H., 31, 156
Ackroyd, S., 69
Agarwala, R., 93, 95
Allen, J., 138
Alter Chen, M., 102
Alvarado Zepeda, C. A., 158
Amengual, M., 156
Anderson, J., 146, 147, 179
Anderson, P., 269, 273, 274, 275, 278, 279, 280, 282
Anner, M., 12, 152, 154, 156, 157, 159, 164, 165, 166
Applebaum, E., 257
Arnold, D., 181
Azmeh, S., 178

Bain, P., 11, 137, 175, 266, 269, 270, 271, 273, 274, 275, 278, 279, 280, 282
Bain, P. M., 70, 79
Bair, J., 1, 3, 5, 7, 8, 20, 47, 48, 49, 50, 51, 61, 83, 85, 86, 101, 119, 120, 121, 122, 137, 171, 198, 210, 232, 251, 252, 262, 267, 272
Baldry, C., 269
Barnes, T., 84, 92
Barnes, T. J., 106, 113
Barrett, R., 237, 240
Barrientos, S., 2, 3, 12, 64, 67, 68, 83, 89, 90, 93, 96, 100, 102, 123, 124, 126, 129, 132, 155, 171, 177, 195, 197, 198, 199, 204, 205, 208, 209, 215
Bartley, T., 199, 204–6
Basole, A., 90
Basu, D., 90
Batt, R., 67, 240, 271
Belt, V., 270
Bergene, A., 21
Bergene, A. C., 178
Bergvall-Kåreborn, B., 231

Bernstein, H., 215, 220
Bezuidenhout, A., 11, 94, 173
Bhatt, E. R., 206
Bhowmik, S. K., 201, 206
Bieler, A., 172
Billah, M., 106
Binios, D., 217, 227
Birnbaum, D., 200
Bolton, S. C., 271
Bonacich, E., 16, 31, 66, 68, 70, 74
Boreham, P., 268
Brabham, D., 235
Braverman, H., 21, 153
Breman, J., 90, 91, 93, 95, 96, 102
Breznitz, D., 78
Bridi, R. M., 186
Bristow, G., 270, 281
Brondízio, E., 200, 214, 215, 219
Brown, A., 205
Brown, S., 186
Brown, W., 86, 87
Buhlungu, S., 11, 94, 173
Bunnell, T., 108
Burawoy, M., 4, 21, 43, 90, 91, 153, 172, 176, 187, 217, 218, 225

Callaghan, G., 271
Cam, S., 85, 91
Caraway, T. L., 200, 205
Carrillo, J., 121
Carswell, G., 139, 176, 182, 217
Castree, N., 9, 10, 102, 139, 175, 180, 268
Castro, E., 215
Cattaneo, O., 22
Chan, J., 12, 145, 231
Chen, M. A., 84, 92
Cheng, L. L., 102
Chi, X., 110

287

Cho, E., 32, 33
Cleaver, H., 141, 144
Clelland, D. A., 62
Coe, N. M., 1, 2, 5, 7, 9, 10, 13, 20, 21, 31, 32, 42, 46, 51, 52, 53, 55, 65, 66, 67, 68, 83, 84, 101, 102, 135, 137, 139, 141, 142, 143, 144, 171, 172, 176, 178, 180, 221, 233, 239, 241, 242, 257, 267, 275
Cohen, L., 267
Cohn, D. V., 159
Colapinto, J., 214
Collier, D., 155
Collins, J., 119
Cowie, C., 275, 281
Cowie, J. R., 153
Cox, S., 45
Coyle, A., 266
Crang, M., 101
Cui, J., 100
Cumbers, A., 1, 2, 9, 10, 13, 21, 33, 46, 52, 53, 54, 64, 65, 67, 119, 125, 126, 135, 137, 138, 139, 143, 145, 171, 175, 178, 233, 243, 267
Cusumano, M., 234, 239

D'Cruz, P., 70, 266
Darmon, I., 64, 67, 73, 77, 78
Das, D., 279
Das, R. J., 173, 174, 175
Davis, M., 251, 253
De Neve, G., 139, 176, 182, 217
Deuze, M., 57
Dicken, P., 5, 6, 65, 139, 140, 148, 178, 198, 232
Doellgast, V., 67, 69
Dolan, C., 121
Dossani, R., 266
Dussel Peters, E., 120

Edwards, P., 53, 153
Edwards, P. K., 4, 86, 87
Edwards, R., 4, 65, 70
El-Sawadi, A., 267
Ellem, B., 173
Elson, D., 105, 131
Erne, R., 154
Esbenshade, J., 199, 205, 207
Evans, P., 172

Featherstone, D., 138, 142
Fernie, J., 30, 31
Feuerstein, P., 15, 22, 266
Fichter, M., 137, 145, 175, 179
Fine, B., 31, 34
Fine, J., 206
Fine, L. M., 173
Fitzgerald, S., 56, 58
Flecker, J., 2, 33, 46, 54, 60, 64, 66, 69, 78, 266
Forey, G., 271
Forssberg, E., 100
Frade, C., 64, 67, 73, 77, 78
Frank, T., 140
Fraxe, T., 215
Friedman, A., 4, 15, 21

Friedman, A. L., 153
Friedman, T., 278
Froud, J., 231
Fukunishi, T., 156

Gallie, D., 72
Gasper, D., 218
Gawer, A., 234
George, S., 218
Gereffi, G., 1, 6, 7, 8, 16, 20, 45, 47, 50, 56, 65, 73, 84, 86, 88, 102, 121, 122, 124, 137, 155, 197, 198, 200, 208, 209, 232, 267, 272, 276
Ghosh, J., 204
Gibbon, P., 1, 5, 7, 14, 47, 48, 49, 50, 83, 84, 122, 221, 272
Gidwani, V., 251, 252, 255, 256
Gill, R., 238, 240
Glassman, J., 143
Glucksmann, M., 14, 281
Goger, A., 187
Gooptu, N., 92, 102
Gordon, M. E., 154
Granovetter, M., 47
Grant, R., 260, 261, 262
Greer, I., 67, 69
Grimshaw, D., 85, 87, 88
Guha-Khasnobis, B., 108
Gunawardana, S., 200, 204, 205

Haidinger, B., 64, 68, 72, 73, 76
Hale, A., 119, 205
Hall, P. A., 64
Hamilton, G., 31
Hammer, A., 91, 92
Hammer, N., 2, 13, 33, 83, 126, 153, 178, 180, 182, 185
Hampson, I., 271
Harilal, K., 217
Harrison, B., 128
Harriss-White, B., 92, 102
Harvey, D., 9, 21, 34, 140, 217, 276, 277, 278
Harvey, M., 31, 32, 36, 42
Heinrich, M., 214
Helfen, M., 137, 145, 179
Henderson, J., 1, 5, 7, 8, 141, 172, 232, 237, 240, 244, 245, 267
Henderson, P., 83
Hermann, C., 66
Herod, A., 9, 16, 102, 103, 107, 153, 173, 174, 178, 220, 249, 251, 252, 255, 257, 258, 268
Hess, M., 2, 9, 21, 31, 32, 101, 119, 126, 135, 137, 140, 141, 257
Hieronymi, K., 110
Holman, D., 266, 266–7
Holmes, J., 180
Holst, H., 73, 75
Hopkins, T. K., 196
Hough, P., 119, 130
Howcroft, D., 231
Howells, J., 145
Hualde, A., 119, 121, 126, 129
Hudson, R., 153, 256, 257, 259
Hughes, A., 186
Humphrey, J., 121

Author Index

Hutchinson, J., 205
Huws, U., 66, 69
Huxley, M., 221
Huzzard, T., 237, 240
Hyman, R., 153

Ince, A., 143

Jacobides, M. G., 56
Jaffe, D., 32
James, S., 280
Jenkins, J., 91, 195, 199, 200–6
Jessop, B., 143
Johns, J., 56, 57
Johns, J. L., 57
Jonas, A. E. G., 185
Jordhus-Lier, D., 51, 52, 53, 55, 119, 126, 129, 172, 176
Jordhus-Lier, D. C., 2, 9, 20, 21, 102, 139, 172, 176
Junor, A., 271
Jürgens, U., 70

Kaplinsky, R., 121
Katz, C., 10, 174, 220
Keck, M. E., 165
Kelly, J., 11, 86, 87
Kelly, P., 119, 136, 137, 144, 217, 221
Kelly, P. F., 15
Kenney, M., 266
Kerr, A., 56, 57
Kessler, J., 122
Kidder, M., 122, 126
Kirsch, S., 259, 262
Kleeman, F., 235
Knorringa, P., 213
Korzeniewicz, M., 20
Kreibe, S., 110
Kritzinger, A., 89
Kuruvilla, S., 279

Lakhani, T., 55, 83
Larson, R., 138
Lazonick, W., 231, 244
Leopold, E., 31, 34
Lepawsky, J., 106
Levenson-Estrada, D., 153
Levy, D., 232, 233
Lichtenstein, N., 31, 43
Lier, D. C., 10
Lindberg, I., 172
Lloyd, C., 271, 274
Locke, R., 156, 157, 184, 186
Locke, R. M., 198, 199, 200, 205, 209
Lockwood, J., 271
Lukes, S., 220
Lund, F., 83
Lund, F. J., 102
Lund-Thomsen, P., 102, 180, 182, 185
Lundgren, K., 100
Lynch, C., 205

MacKinnon, D., 140, 141, 144, 146
Madhav, R., 204

Marchington, M., 67, 70, 77
Marks, A., 11, 237, 240
Marshall, A. N., 270, 281
Marshall, J. N., 269, 270, 281
Martin, C. B., 57
Martin, R., 187
Marx, K., 13, 103, 105, 106, 112, 130
Massey, D., 9, 138, 144, 270
Mayer, F. W., 12
McCallum, J. K., 154
McDonald, H., 269
McGrath, S., 139, 177
McGrath-Champ, S., 21, 173, 178, 249
McIntyre, M., 254, 255
McKay, S. C., 188
Meil, P., 2, 33, 46, 54, 66, 67, 69, 77, 266
Meiskins, P., 14
Memedovic, O., 155
Merk, J., 195, 205, 208
Milberg, W., 12, 47, 123, 156
Milkman, R., 206
Miozzo, M., 269
Mirchandani, K., 266, 268
Mitchell, D., 262
Moore, S., 21
Mosley, L., 11
Moynihan, L., 271
Munck, R., 174

Nadvi, K., 182
Naschold, F., 70
Nast, H. J., 254, 255
Nathan, D., 198, 199, 209
Neilson, B., 70
Neilson, J., 50, 51, 181, 184, 185, 217
Neo, H., 109
Newsome, K., 1, 2, 3, 29, 32, 46, 67, 79, 84, 217
Nichols, T., 85, 91
Nicholson, J., 83, 102
Nnorom, I. C., 100
Noronha, E., 70, 266

Ohmae, K., 140
Oseland, S. E., 186
Oteng-Ababio, M., 260, 261, 262

Padmanabhan, N., 175, 203
Palpacuer, F., 8, 12, 47, 49, 54, 83, 86, 198
Parker, R., 45, 56, 58, 61, 62, 243
Pawlicki, P., 15, 22, 266
Payne, J., 271, 274
Peck, J., 139, 266, 267
Pedraza Fariña, L., 163
Pegler, L., 213, 213–16, 215, 218–21, 220, 224–5, 227
Pereira, H. S., 214, 219
Petrovic, M., 31
Phillips, N., 101, 102, 103, 130, 177, 250, 263
Pickles, J., 12, 122, 178
Pickren, G., 101, 102, 249
Ponte, S., 7, 122, 182, 221
Poster, W., 266
Prichard, J., 271
Pries, L., 182, 183, 184

Pritchard, B., 181, 184, 185, 217
Pun, N., 94, 96, 97

Quan, K., 195, 208
Quinjun, W., 145

Raganathan, A., 279
Rainbird, H., 83
Rainnie, A., 1, 2, 13, 15, 16, 33, 84, 100, 101, 102, 119, 126, 130, 137, 153, 171, 176, 178, 187, 233, 238, 249, 257, 266, 267
Ramamurthy, P., 119
Ramirez, P., 83
Rasiah, R., 200
Raworth, K., 122, 126
Reddy, R. N., 251
Richardson, R., 269, 270, 281
Riisgaard, L., 2, 13, 33, 83, 126, 153, 178, 180, 182, 185
Robinson, B. H., 100
Robinson, P. K., 83
Rodrigue, J. P., 31, 32
Rogaly, B., 176
Rossi, A., 127, 128, 129
Rostow, W. W., 253
Roy, A., 103, 106, 107
Rubery, J., 67, 69, 79, 85, 87, 88
Russell, B., 271

Sakamoto, L., 177
Sandberg, Å., 240
Sankaran, K., 204
Sarkar, S., 198, 199, 209
Saxenian, A., 238
Schluep, M., 100
Schmitz, H., 121
Schrank, A., 122
Seeliger, M., 182, 183, 184
Selwyn, B., 9, 21, 33, 46, 52, 53, 54, 55, 64, 69, 70, 74, 85, 88, 100, 102, 125, 126, 128, 132, 137, 139, 178, 180, 185, 187, 213, 233
Sen, A., 218, 221
Shekdar, A. V., 111
Sheppard, E., 106, 113
Sikkink, K., 165
Silver, B., 132, 180
Silver, B. J., 153
Simonian, L., 219
Singe, I., 73, 75
Sippola, M., 204
Slade, G., 251
Smith, A., 50, 51, 100, 103, 124, 142, 143, 178, 188
Smith, C., 3, 5, 14, 15, 94, 95, 96, 97, 153
Smith, N., 1, 9, 267
Soete, L., 269
Soskice, D., 64
Srivastava, M., 204
Staritz, C., 155
Starosta, G., 143
Stopford, J. M., 140

Storper, M., 9
Strange, S., 140
Streicher-Porte, M., 110
Stringer, C., 119, 177
Sturgeon, T., 7, 122
Sturgeon, T. J., 103
Sunley, P., 139, 144
Sweeney, B., 180
Sydow, J., 175

Taylor, M., 119, 127
Taylor, P., 1, 2, 8, 11, 14, 15, 21, 33, 38, 61, 66, 69, 70, 79, 83, 85, 91, 100, 101, 102, 137, 153, 175, 182, 187, 201, 206, 217, 232, 233, 266, 267, 269, 270, 271, 272, 273, 274, 275, 277, 278, 279, 280, 281, 282
Theodore, N., 266, 267
Thompson, P., 2, 3, 4, 5, 11, 15, 45, 49, 50, 59, 66, 67, 69, 71, 73, 78, 84, 153, 187, 257, 258, 271
Thomson, D., 138
Tokatli, N., 122
Truong, T., 218
Tufts, S., 175, 176
Turner, L., 154

Vidal, M., 257
Vincent, S., 69, 71, 73, 78
Vira, B., 280
Visser, M., 3, 195, 197, 198, 199, 204, 205, 209

Wad, P., 185
Walker, R., 9
Wallace, M., 70
Wallerstein, I., 196
Wältring, F., 182
Wang, F., 259
Warouw, N., 195
Waterman, P., 174
Webster, E., 153
Weil, D., 69, 77, 78
Werner, M., 2, 8, 119, 120, 122, 171, 251, 252, 262
Whitson, R., 261
Williams, C. C., 102, 108
Wills, J., 11, 119, 138
Wilson, B., 130
Wilson, B. R., 181
Wilson, D. C., 103
Wilson, J., 31, 66, 68, 70, 74
Wilson, J. B., 16
Windebank, J., 102, 108
Winkler, D., 12, 123
Wong, A. M., 100
Wright, E. O., 9, 20, 65, 70, 136, 137, 145, 148, 267

Yates, M., 251, 254, 255, 256, 263
Yeates, N., 91

Zhu, S., 178

Subject Index

açaí berry, 214–27
Accord on Fire and Building Safety in Bangladesh, 166
Accra, e-waste scavenging in, 260
ACFTU, *see* All China Federation of Trade Unions (ACFTU)
Adidas, 167
agency
    chain environments, 225–7
    framing, 173–7
    geography, 177–81
    river dwellers, 220–5
    territorial formations, 181–8
    under globalization, 135–48
    unpacking, 9–11
    variegated landscapes of, 171–88
agents, call centers, *see* call centers
Agreement on Textiles and Clothing (ATC), 156
All China Federation of Trade Unions (ACFTU), 145–6
Anderson, J., 147
Android, 241
Animal Logic, 58
apparel industry, 152–68
app developers, 231–46
    see also Apple Inc.; mobile applications
Applebaum, E., 257–8
Apple Inc., 231
    actors and stakeholders, 240–4
    brand value, 238–9
    capturing and creating value, 237–40
    ecosystem, 245
    hardware products, 239
    in-app advertising, 238
    network embeddedness, 245–6
    outsourcing, 235
    product innovation and development, 234
    societal embeddedness, 244

App Store, 234–5
    accounts on, 245–6
    as delivery channel, 239–40
    limited showcasing, 240
ARDS, 228
Arnold, D., 181
Asian market, 245
associational power, 70, 138
asymmetric power relations, 45–60
ATC, *see* Agreement on Textiles and Clothing (ATC)
Austria, 71, 73–4, 75, 76
Automatic Call Distribution (ACD), 269–70, 272
Azmeh, S., 178

Bair, J., 5, 7, 18, 20, 49, 50, 101, 166, 251, 262
Bangalore, 200–8
    see also garment value chain, India
bargaining power, 70
    of workers, 72–6
Barnes, T. J., 106
Barrientos, S., 12, 68, 89, 93, 171, 177, 205
Bartley, T., 204
Bergene, A. C., 21
Bezuidenhout, A., 11, 94, 173–4
biopolis, 254
    see also necropolis
Birnbaum, D., 200
Blasi, J., 166
BMW, 142
Bonacich, E., 31, 66, 68, 74
Botin, A., 282
BPO, *see* Business Process Outsourcing (BPO) industry
Breman, J., 95, 96
Bridi, R. M., 186
Brown, S., 186–7

291

Subject Index

Brown, W., 86
Buhlungu, S., 11, 94, 173–4
Burawoy, M., 89–90, 91, 176, 187, 217, 218, 225
Business Process Outsourcing (BPO) industry, 268
see also call centers

Cable and Wireless, 282
call centers
 ACD, 269–70, 272
 global relocation, 277–80
 global value chain, 272
 growth and expansion, 272–6
 ICTs, 268
 labour process, 271–2
 locational clustering, 277
 overview, 266–8
 sources and methods, 269
 underperformance, 276
Cam, S., 91
Capital (Marx), 3, 256
capital, e-waste circuit of, 103–5
capitalist political economy (CPE), 46
capturing value, 38–41
 concept, 30
Carswell, G., 176, 182
cartoneros, see waste scavengers
Chains of Greed (report), 32
Chennai, 200–8
 see also electrical value chain, India
China
 labour disputes in, 145–6
 WTO, 156
Clelland, D. A., 62
Coe, N., 9, 13, 19, 20, 21, 32, 42, 52, 53, 67, 68, 126, 129, 143–4, 180, 233, 257
Cold War, 138
collective bargaining, 123
collective labour agency, 74–5
company unions, 161–2
construction sites, in India, 95
contracts
 between retailers and logistics providers, 32
 employment relationship, 91–3
Cowie, J., 153
CPE, *see* capitalist political economy (CPE)
crowdsourcing, 235
 virtual aspect, 244–5
Cumbers, A., 2, 10, 13, 19, 52–3, 125, 233, 267
Cusumano, M., 234, 239

Darmon, I., 67
Das, R. J., 173, 174, 175
Davis, M., 251, 253
debt servitude, 227
deficit, labour, 9–17
De Neve, G., 176, 182
Deuze, M., 59
Dicken, P., 139–40
digital entertainment, 45, 55–60
Distimo, 235
distribution
 classical Marxist perspective on, 29
 savings in, 32
 see also logistics
divide-and-rule strategy, 69
dock workers' unions, in Egypt, 146–7
dormitory labour, 94
drivers, 73–4

economic upgrading, 68, 195
 concept, 68, 195
 economic actors, 68
 logistics sector, 68
 modes, 68
Edwards, P. K., 4, 86
Edwards, R., 70
Egypt, dock workers' unions in, 146–7
electrical value chain, India, 200–8
El Salvador, 152–68
Elson, D., 131
embeddedness, in economic globalization, 144–7
employment
 informal, 92–3
employment relationship, contracts and, 91–3
English language communication, 278–9
Esbenshade, J., 207
e-waste, 100
 collection of, 108–10
 disassembly, dismantling and sorting, 110–12
 informal labour, 108
export processing zones, 143, 156, 163

Feuerstein, P., 15, 22
Fichter, M., 179
Fitzgerald, S., 62
Flecker, J., 18, 54, 60
Foreign Direct Investment (FDI), 278
foreign language, 282
Frade, C., 67

Gallie, D., 72
games and visual effects (VFX), 45, 55–60
gangs, 163
Gap, 167
garment industry, Cambodia, 181
garment value chain, India, 200–8
George, S., 109
Gereffi, G., 1, 6–7, 8, 20, 50, 55, 56, 61, 88, 122, 124, 197, 198, 272
Gibbon, P., 47, 48, 49, 50
Gidwani, V., 252, 255
Glasgow, Scotland, 274–5
Glassman, J., 143
global commodity chain (GCC), 5–8
global destruction networks (GDN), 251
global financial crash (GFC), 57
globalization, 278
 labour agency under, 135–48
global production networks (GPN), 5–8, 31
 labour deficit in, 33
 labour process, 33
global value chain (GVC), 5–8, 45
 frameworks, 46–7
 governance structure taxonomy, 47–9
 post-GVC framework, 49–52

Subject Index 293

Glucksmann, M., 14, 281
Goger, A., 187
goods
  immobile, 30
  movement of, 30
  see also logistics
governance, 83–96
governance structure taxonomy, 47
GPS (global positioning) system, 68
Granovetter, M., 47
Grant, R., 261, 262
Grimshaw, D., 87

Haidinger, B., 68
Helfen, M., 179
Hammer, A., 92
Hammer, N., 13, 143, 153, 178, 180, 182, 185
Harvey, M., 32, 42
Henderson, J., 1, 233, 237
Herod, A., 174, 178, 179
Hess, M., 9, 21, 31, 48, 140, 257
Hieronymi, K., 110
Holmes, J., 180
Hudson, R., 256–7, 259–60
Hughes, A., 186
Hungary, 76

IBGE, 227
ICT, *see* Information and Communication Technologies (ICTs)
immobile goods, 30
India
  construction sites, 95
  electrical value chain, 200–8
  garment value chain, 200–8
  textile industries, 95
India, call centres in, 268
  attrition, 279
  English-speaking labour, 278
  ITES-BPO industries, 278
  labour pool, 279
  labour qualities, 278
  linguistic and communication abilities, 278–9
  place-based attributes, 278
  remote geography, 277–8
  talent supply, 279
  telecoms industry, 278
informal employment, 92–3
informal sector, 100–12
Information and Communication Technologies (ICTs), 268
institutions of workers' representation, 70
International Labour Process Conference (ILPC), 3
International Transport Foundation (ITF), 146
inter-organizational contracting, 67
iOS, 242
ITES-BPO (Information Technology Enabled Services – Business Process Outsourcing), 278
iTunes, 239, 242

Jaffe, D., 32
Jenkins, J., 19

Jessop, B., 143
Jordhus-Lier, D., 52, 53, 126, 130
Jordhus-Lier, D. C., 20, 21, 176
jobbers agreements, 166

karung guni, 101, 103–13
  see also e-waste
Katz, C., 10, 21, 174
Kelly, J., 87, 89
Kelly, P. F., 15
Kirsch, S., 259, 262

labour
  as agent, 124–6
  as object, 121–4
  as productive factor, 67
  deficit, 9–17
  digital entertainment, 58–60
  embeddedness, 144–7
  informalization of, 95
  mobility of, 95–6
  power and process, 13–17
  problem(atic), 52–5
  third party contractors, 93
  wasted, *see* wasted labour
Labour and Monopoly Capital (Braverman), 3
labour geographers, 137–9
labour process theory (LPT), 1–5, 46
Lakhani, T., 55, 89
Levy, D., 232, 233
Lichtenstein, N., 43
linguistic capability, 282
living conditions, 93–5
Liz Claiborne, 167
local labour regime, 14
Locke, R., 156, 184
logistics
  cross-border transport, 67
  economic upgrading, 68
  innovations, 66–7
  inter-firm networks, 67
  political economy, 29–41
  retail, 29–41
  revolution, 66
  social upgrading, 68
  subcontracting, 67
  supply chain management, 66
  technical business developments, 66
LPT, *see* labour process theory (LPT)
Lund-Thomsen, P., 180, 182, 185

MacKinnon, D., 140
MADD, *see* mobile applications development and distribution (MADD)
Malaysia, 101, 103–13
  see also karung guni
Martin, R., 187
Marx, K, 3, 9, 14, 103, 105, 106, 112, 130, 137, 254–6
Massey, D., 138, 144
McGrath, S., 177
McGrath-Champ, S., 21
McIntyre, M., 254, 255
McKinsey, 278

Subject Index

mega slums, 254
Meil, P., 54
Meiskins, P., 14
meta theory, 143
Milberg, W., 49
mining industry, South Africa, 94
MIS (Management Information Systems), 276
Mitchell, D., 262
MNC, *see* multinational corporations (MNCs)
mobile applications
   actors and stakeholders, 240–4
   capturing and creating value, 237–40
   developers' profile, 236–7
   ecosystem, 245
   embeddedness of, 244–6
   geographical distinctions, 245
   researching, 235–6
   see also App Store; Apple Inc.
mobile applications development and distribution (MADD), 235
mobility of labour, 95–6
Multi-Fibre Agreement, 156
multinational corporations (MNCs), 140–2, 144, 146

NASSCOM (National Association of Software and Service Companies), 278, 279
Nast, H. J., 254, 255
National Union of Mineworkers (NUM), 94
necropolis, 254
   see also biopolis
Neilson, B, 70
Neilson, J., 51, 181, 184, 217
Neo, H., 109
neo-bondage, 96
neoliberalism, 15
Nichols, T., 91

offshoring, 268, 277–80
   cheap labour costs, 278
   disadvantages, 278–9
   exercising control remotely, 279
   logistics innovations, 66–7
   SLA, 279
   value chains and networks, 66
Organisation for Economic Co-operation and Development (OECD), 155–6
Oteng-Ababio, M., 260, 261, 262
outsourcing
   logistics innovations, 66–7
   value chains and networks, 66

Palpacuer, F., 49
parcel delivery sector, 71–6
   see also logistics
Parker, R., 17, 18, 243
Pawlicki, P., 15, 22
Peck, J., 139
Pegler, L., 13, 19, 227
performance management, 40–1
Philippines, 268
Phillips, N., 103, 130, 250, 263
Pickles, J., 178
piece rate system, 160–1

Planet of Slums (Davis), 253
Ponte, S., 122, 221
population surplus, *see* wasted labour
post-GVC framework, 49–52
power
   and process, 13–17
   asymmetric relations, 45–60
   governance, 85–90
preserving value, 35–8
   concept, 29–30
Pries, L., 182
Pritchard, B., 181, 184, 217
Pun, N., 94

Quan, K., 208

Rainnie, A., 13, 15, 153, 187
Reddy, R. N., 255
regional distribution centres (RDCs), 30–1
relational power, 138
resistance, by worker, 164–6
retail logistics, 29–41
   degradation of work, 38–41
   distribution, 33–4
   preserving value, 29–30, 35–8
   RDC, 30–1
   strategic transformation, 30–1
   third party providers (3PLs), 32
Review of International Political Economy, 7
RFID (radio-frequency identification) system, 68
ribeirinhos, *see* river dwellers
Riisgaard, L., 13, 143, 153, 180, 182, 185
river dwellers, 214–17
Rodrigue, J. P., 31
Rogaly, B., 176
Rossi, A., 127–9
Rostow, W. W., 253
Roy, A., 107
Rubery, J., 87

Santander, 282
Scotland
   labour costs, 274
   operation cost, 273, 274
   political economy, 274
Scottish Development International (SDI), 273
scripting, 279, 282
SDI, *see* Scottish Development International (SDI)
SEDUC, 228
Seeliger, M., 182
segmentation of workforce, 90–3
Selwyn, B., 21, 46, 53, 54, 55, 70, 125, 126, 128, 132, 182, 185, 187
semi-scripting, 279, 282
Sen, A., 218
service level agreements (SLA), 69–70, 272, 276, 279
   see also call centers
service value chains and networks, 64–80
   see also logistics; parcel delivery sector
Shekdar, A. V., 111
Sheppard, E., 106

Silicon Valley, 244
Silver, B., 132, 180
Singapore, 101, 103–13
    see also e-waste; *Karung guni*
SLA, *see* Service Level Agreement (SLA)
Smith, A., 50, 124, 178
Smith, C., 14, 90, 94, 95, 96
Smith, N., 9
social downgrading, 152–68
social networks, 244
social upgrading, 12–13, 195
    concept, 68, 123, 195
    in chain environment, 225–7
    logistics sector, 68
    operationalizing, 123
    river dwellers, 216–20
SODIPER, 71, 72, 73, 75, 80
South Africa, 94
spatial political economy, 139–44
Special Economic Zone (SEZ) of Chennai, 196
Stopford, J. M., 140
Strange, S., 140
street gangs, 163
structural power of workers, 137–8
Sturgeon, T., 122
Sturgeon, T. J., 103
subcontracting, 67
    capital-capital relations, 69
surplus population, 253–6
    see also wasted labour
Sweeney, B., 180

Taylor, P., 15, 61, 187, 280
Taylorism through export, 277
territorial formations, agency, 181–8
textile industries, in India, 95
theory of value chain governance, 280
third party labour contractors, 93
third party providers (3PL), 32
third-party supplier, 276
Thompson, P., 3, 4, 8, 9, 21, 187, 257–8
three Cs, 47
total social organisation of labour theory, 281
trade unions, 76
Tufts, S., 175, 176

uneven development, 119–32
union leaders, 164
urban labour force, 253

value capture
    between retailers and logistics providers, 32
    in distribution, 32
value chains and production networks
    capital-capital relations, 69–70
    immediate labour process, 70
value chains, labour process and, 68–71
value in motion, 29–41
    see also retail logistics
variegated landscapes, of agency, 171–88
Vidal, M., 257
violence
    against unionists, 165
    and threat, 162–4
visual effects (VFX) and games, 45, 55–60

Wad, P., 185
Wal-Mart
    domestic outsourcing strategy, 32–3
    working conditions, 32–3
waste
    in theory, 101–3
    value and, 105–8
    working lives, 259–62
    see also e-waste
waste scavengers
    in Accra, 260
    in Buenos Aires, Argentina, 261–2
wasted commodities, 249–64
wasted labour, 249–64
Werner, M., 251, 262
Whitson, R., 261
Wilson, J., 31, 66, 68, 74
women workers in Mexico, 262
work relations at workplace, 45–60
workers
    as social agents, 67–8
    bargaining power, 72–6
    living conditions, 93–5
    positional and associational power, 71–2
workforce segmentation, 90–3
workplace, work relations at, 45–60
workplace regime, 14
World Systems Theory, 49
World Trade Organization (WTO), 155–6
Wright, E. O., 9, 20, 136, 137, 148, 267
WTO, *see* World Trade Organization (WTO)

Yates, M., 254, 255, 256, 263

Zhu, S., 178